Public Administration

Public Administration

From Government to Governance

Bidyut Chakrabarty
Prakash Chand

Orient BlackSwan

PUBLIC ADMINISTRATION: FROM GOVERNMENT TO GOVERNANCE

ORIENT BLACKSWAN PRIVATE LIMITED

Registered Office
3-6-752 Himayatnagar, Hyderabad 500 029, Telangana, INDIA
e-mail: centraloffice@orientblackswan.com

Other Offices
Bengaluru, Bhopal, Chennai, Guwahati,
Hyderabad, Jaipur, Kolkata, Lucknow, Mumbai,
New Delhi, Noida, Patna, Vijayawada

First published 2017

ISBN 978-93-86689-32-0

025755

07072017

Typeset in
Adobe Garamond Pro 11.5/13.5
by Shine Graphics, Delhi 110 094

Printed in India at
Yash Printographics, Noida

Published by
Orient Blackswan Private Limited
3-6-752, Himayatnagar,
Hyderabad 500 029, Telangana, INDIA
e-mail: info@orientblackswan.com

Dedicated to our friends for having sustained our creativity despite the odds.

Contents

PREFACE

Writing a textbook in public administration is a challenging task. It is challenging because an enormous quantity of literature is already available, and a new textbook may not appeal to prospective buyers. Moreover, since the book is meant for beginners, it has to be written in a lucid language so that they are drawn to it. We have accepted the challenge precisely for these reasons. Our purpose is to put relevant (and also fundamental) ideas in a conceptual perspective which, we strongly feel, will help us explain the complex texture of public administration being located in a specific historical milieu. The idea is not novel and is thus being reiterated with reference to examples from Indian experiences. What is however distinctly different is the emphasis that the book provides in a relatively unknown terrain of public administration by dwelling on non-Western traditions. We are persuaded to believe that no study of administrative theory shall be complete without comprehending non-Western traditions. To us, Gandhi's idea of *panchayati raj*, Mao's conceptualisation of the *commune* and Nyerere's notion of *ujamaa* are powerful theoretical categories which not only introduced a new genre of thinking in governance but also exposed the inchoate limitations in the neo-Taylorist argument in support of the one-size-fits-all formula. This is the USP of the book.

Many individuals contributed to our project. Prominent among them are our students, who with their penchant for knowledge never allowed us to slip into sombre which is usually the case for most of us because research (and teaching, to a significant extent) is an individual-driven initiative. If one feels passionate about one's own intellectual creativity, one always remains on one's tenterhooks! Otherwise, there is the danger of becoming complacent, which gradually engulfs us, as is visible in most university campuses in the country. Second, we are grateful to our peers who kept our zeal high by their encouragement and also criticisms (which are sometime directed to demotivate as well). We feel privileged that we have a very alert group of peers. Our family is also a source of inspiration; besides our respective spouses who, despite not having had adequate time with us, always stand by us which also makes us believe that we are doing something worthwhile, our children have also contributed to our academic search by sharing their perspectives on various issues. We are privileged that we have multiple sources of inspiration and uncertainties which hardly give us an opportunity to stay away from our laptops!

The entire Orient BlackSwan family deserves appreciation for their faith in us. We are indebted to Roopa Sharma, who made us commit to writing the book, to Tapan Das and Vinit Mehra, who procured some books during the preparation of this manuscript, and to Antony Arul Valan, for helping us improve the text during copyediting.

Finally, our parents need a big thank-you. Without their initiation into the world of learning, we would have been lost in the maze of cut-throat competition. Their inspiration, love and blessings have given us enough food for thought to sustain our creativity. We are fortunate.

July 2017
Delhi

Bidyut Chakrabarty
Prakash Chand

INTRODUCTION*

I

How to conceptualise public administration as a discipline is a question that an author always confronts while being engaged in deciphering its nature. One of the easiest ways to address this question is to focus on what public administration is all about. As is usually understood, public administration is what government does. This is at best a layman's notion of public administration and it refers to the functions that one witnesses while seeking to define the discipline. The response is persuasive because public administration is always a function that governments or public authorities undertake. However meaningful the definition may be it will not enable us to conceptualise the discipline which undertakes various kinds of functions under various kinds of circumstances. The socio-economic context in which the functions are discharged remains critical in shaping its nature. Hence a definition can hardly be appropriate unless it takes into account the complexities of the functions that usually go with public administration. Three ideas seem important here: first, since public administration is a function, it needs to be conceptualised with reference to the context in which it evolves; second, given the fact that context is multidimensional, there cannot be a universal definition if one seeks to understand the dynamics of public administration as a functional entity; third, as public administration is also an ideational exercise, it will be conceptually erroneous to exclude the ideological foundation of public administration as an activity with a well-defined purpose. So, public administration is a specific function to accomplish a specific goal in a specific socio-economic context. A little elaboration will make the point clear: being location-specific, public administration in India needs to be conceptualised in conjunction with the prevalent socio-economic and political reality in which the concern for religious or ethnic community, for instance, figure prominently. How is this so? The reasons are to be found out in the historical evolution of India as a socio-political entity during British colonialism and later. Being embedded in a system of functioning, the root of which can easily be traced back to the colonial days, public governance in India continues with its colonial flavour to a great extent, especially the institutional foundation on which it rests. There cannot be doubt that it draws on those sets of rules, regulations and values which held colonial authority in good stead; though

* Some sections of this chapter have been developed from Bidyut Chakrabarty, *Localizing Governance in India* (London: Routledge, 2017), pp. 63–67; and Bidyut Chakrabarty, *Ethics in Governance in India* (London: Routledge, 2016), pp. 102–104. With permission from Taylor & Francis.

most of them were devised in light of the distinctive socio-cultural reality of India, they also drew on the colonialists' concern to strengthen their grip over the colonised. What is surprising is the fact that the same set of governing instruments were allowed to remain even after India became free from colonialism in 1947. There were serious debates in the Constituent Assembly that prepared the Constitution of India after an endeavour of almost three years. The members made two arguments in favour of the continuity of the governance structure that the colonial authority had bequeathed: on the one hand, they were not persuaded to discard the prevalent institutions of governance in view of the political uncertainty that engulfed the nation following the blood bath in the wake of the 1947 partition of India into two independent countries; on the other hand, they were led by the ideological faith in liberal democracy that flourished in India during colonialism. It was primarily the latter that remained critical in their preference for the system of governance that seemed organic to the Indian socio-economic reality. Hence it was prudent on their part not to disturb the available institutionalised governance format that survived presumably because of its inner ideological prowess. The idea gained ground also because the founding fathers remained unanimous in their choice for liberal democratic form of governance for independent India. Here too, three factors seem to have swayed them while being engaged in choosing an appropriate form of public administration following decolonisation: first, of the available political alternatives, it was liberalism which swayed the founding fathers to a significant extent; second, the uncertainty of Partition and its adverse consequences hardly gave them a chance to explore other possibilities, added to this is the fact that the available administrative machinery had stood the test of time; third, it was also believed that since the prevalent system of public administration was also an antidote to the archaic social values and mores, justifying the equally archaic social division around caste axis, it had instantly created a constituency of support among those in the Constituent Assembly who fought hard to purge Indian society of prejudices drawn on one's caste, religious or ethnic identity. The fear that the mere codification of liberal constitutional values was not at all adequate to change the mindset supportive of these prejudices was explicitly visible when Dr B. R. Ambedkar, the chairman of the Constituent Assembly's Drafting Committee, stated:

> On the 26th of January, 1950, we are going to enter into a life of contradictions. In politics, we will have equality and in social and economic life we will have inequality. In politics, we will be recognizing the principle of one man one vote and one vote one value. In our social and economic life, we shall, by reason of social and economic structure, continue to deny the principle of one man one value. How long shall we continue to live this life of contradictions? How long shall we continue to deny equality in our social and economic life? If we continue to deny it for long, we will do so only by putting our political democracy in peril. (Ambedkar [2003]: 979)

This is one of the most revealing statements, made by one of the major architects of India's Constitution, to understand the difficulties that the founding fathers underwent while devising a constitutional design for India. For public administration to become an instrument for justice and fair play, it was necessary to create a society which was appreciative of equality in its substantial sense. It was a gigantic task so long as caste remained an integral part of India's collective psyche. Ambedkar minced no words in his criticism of caste because he felt that 'castes are anti-national. In the first place, they bring about separation in social life. They are anti-national because they generate jealousy and antipathy between caste and caste' (ibid.: 980). According to him, caste was an impediment towards realising democratic governance given its inherently divisive character. India could hardly be a nation so long as caste remained integral to the collective psyche because, as he argued, unless there was fraternity, the idea of nation remained elusive and 'without fraternity, liberty and equality will be no deeper than coats of paint' (ibid.). By critiquing caste, Ambedkar strove to create conditions for the democratic polity to thrive which, he apprehended, was not so easy in view of the well-entrenched caste prejudices in India.

There are three fundamental points that need to be reinforced to understand how India's public administration even after Independence remained 'colonial', at least in terms of the institutions, rules and regulations of the past era. First, as was mentioned, the contingent circumstances acted as a deterrent to the search that the founding fathers were expected to make while laying out India's constitutional fabric. It was simply not possible to waste time in view of the rising tide of communalism that had already resulted in the indiscriminate killing of innocent people across the borders of India and Pakistan. Second, given their unstinted faith in liberal democracy due to complex historical circumstances in which they were nurtured in colonial India, the founding fathers seem to have been automatically drawn to the Westminster form of government. By believing that liberal democracy, as it evolved in the West, was a powerful constitutional design to fulfil their dream of creating an egalitarian India, they hardly felt the need to try-out other ideological alternatives. Liberal democracy was, it appears, a *sine qua non* for them. Finally, it was also a matter of convenience for them to adopt liberal democracy since an appropriate structure of governance was in place; what was thus required was to retune the system in accordance with what the founding fathers strove to achieve for a decolonised India. The task was much easier, given the availability of an efficient public administration that had served the British rule for almost a century since the adoption of the 1861 Councils Act which sowed the seeds of representative institutions/parliamentary system of governance in India. It was also, in other words, a politically expedient design of governance which neither required special training for the administrators nor efforts to create conditions for its success since the colonised Indians had the knowledge by being involved, in phases, in British administration.

* * *

II

As public administration is context-bound, it cannot be persuasively conceptualised in a derivative theoretical format. In other words, there cannot be a universal design in so far as public administration is concerned. Nonetheless, there are theories providing fundamental theoretical inputs which are also critical in conceptualising public administration in its historical manifestation. For instance, some of the ideas, drawn from the classical school of public administration, remain critical in comprehending the nature of governance in the Western context; they are generally futile in the case of non-Western countries, except that they help us understand the ideological roots of their public administrations that had its origin in the colonial past. Having been governed by European colonial powers, a majority of these Afro-Asian countries imbibed the fundamental ideas, liberal democratic and otherwise, while charting out an independent course of action following decolonisation. The argument relates to the distinct and also critical role that the context plays in shaping public administration. Be that as it may, there are also certain classical theoretical efforts which are definitely useful in conceptualising public administration in a historical milieu. For instance, our understanding of public administration is likely to be incomplete if we ignore the contributions that Max Weber (1864–1920) and Woodrow Wilson (1856–1924) made while seeking to theorise public administration as a field of human activity, engaged in realising the politico-ideological goals of regimes. In other words, the ideas and concepts that they developed on the basis of their comprehension of specific empirical realities are powerful theoretical aids with near-universal validity. The reasons are not difficult to seek. Instead of being instrumentalist in their theoretical inclination, they were concerned with the historical processes which contributed to the unfolding of a context-driven design of governance. Confirming the assumption that public administration is situation-specific, the argument that Weber and Wilson made reinforces the point in favour of the critical importance of the context. The following section offers an analysis of the models that they evolved in defence of their respective positions supporting the contention that, being instrumental, governance cannot be insulated from the prevalent socio-economic realities and ideological predilections of those who are responsible for its articulation. Although they were nurtured in completely different socio-economic and political milieu—Weber being raised in Germany during the heyday of Industrialisation and Wilson during the US endeavour to emerge as a well-governed society in the late-nineteenth century—their perception about public administration did not seem to be radically different since they were keen to create a system of governance in accordance with their ideological priorities.

What is distinctive about Weber is that he wrote a dedicated text on bureaucracy to argue his point about the need for an ideal form of organisation. The idea had its conceptual origin in an earlier text titled *The Protest Ethic and the Spirit of Capitalism* (1905/1930) which is a study of the relationship between the ethics of Protestantism and the emergence of the spirit of modern Capitalism. In Weber's perception, the religious groups such as the Calvinists played a critical role in creating the Capitalist spirit. Believing that profit-making did not seem to be as despicable as it was made out in public eye, the Calvinists were drawn to the processes of industrialisation since it was what God expected them to do. This was the beginning of the unfolding of the spirit of Capitalism in which profit-making was seen as an end and also virtuous. As a result, most of those values which were in vogue in the pre-Capitalist era became less viable. Once Capitalism was firmly established, the Protestant values were no longer necessary and their ethic acquired the status of being given. In other words, the Protestant values which laid the foundation for an ethic to evolve contributed to the spirit of Capitalism in course of time. According to Weber, the spirit of Capitalism gradually became the guiding force of modern economic activity in which profit-making was never a subject of criticism since it was informed, at the outset, by Protestant values. Once a system of efficient economic activity was put in place, an equally efficient system of organisation was needed to sustain the spirit of Capitalism. This was where Weber pitched-in his notion of ideal form of organisation which—by being impartial and tuned to the contemporary social, economic and political needs—was tipped to be an appropriate format with a clear ideological objective.

Besides dwelling on the characteristics of an ideal form of organisation, which is 'bureaucracy' in his lexicon, Weber devoted significant attention to the permanent character of the bureaucratic machine, which is reflective of his keenness to develop a spirit of organisation. As the spirit of Capitalism sustained a specific kind of economic activity supportive of Capitalist production, bureaucracy, in order to be ever-lasting, needed to create a spirit which was adequate to keep its viability. This was the primary concern that seems to have shaped Weber's thinking while developing his model of an ideal form of organisation. As he argued:

> Bureaucracy is the means of carrying community action over into rationally ordered societal action. Therefore, as an instrument for societalizing relations of power, bureaucracy has been and is a power instrument of the first order—for the one who controls the bureaucratic apparatus. (Weber 1996: 64–65)

So, the proposed organisation is meant to undertake activities which are societal in character and possible once the community action is linked with the societal goal. In Weber's understanding, here lies the reason as to why bureaucracy gradually becomes a social organ devoted to contribute to societal or public well-being. With its sustained engagement in such processes, Weber argued that bureaucracy not only justifies its societal role but also emerges as an instrument of power whereby it can also influence the behaviour of those who remain within its span of control.

Following his deep-rooted concern for generating 'the spirit', he furthered his argument by drawing upon those physical/technical features of the ideal form of organisation, and upheld his claim of bureaucracy being distinctly unique and unparalleled in human history. While elaborating this aspect, he mentions:

> The ruled, for their part, cannot dispense with or replace the bureaucratic apparatus of authority once it exists. For this bureaucracy rests upon expert training, a functional specialization of work and attitude set for habitual and virtuoso-like mastery of single yet methodically integrated functions. (Ibid.: 65)

This is the moot point in support of his effort towards creating the required spirit justifying bureaucracy as the only available instrument for managing 'the human chaos'. Persuaded to believe that bureaucracy was irreplaceable, Weber now drew on those distinct characteristics which bureaucracy acquired by virtue of expert training. By arguing that this was inevitable since the routine obedience to set rules and functions was certain to create a habit, Weber linked the rise of bureaucracy with the consolidation of the system, and the endorsing of a specific kind of behaviour that automatically gets transmitted from one generation to another. Here too, the objective was to contribute to the development of the spirit that would make bureaucracy indispensable for societal good.

The idea that bureaucracy is irreversible is further justified by Weber when he insisted that bureaucracy functioned in accordance with a set of rational rules and regulations. By attributing rationality, he seems to have reiterated his argument in support of the processes responsible for creating 'the spirit'. Once the spirit was imbibed, he felt bureaucracy would become organic to our societal existence:

> The objective indispensability of the once existing apparatus, with its peculiar, impersonal character, means that the mechanism—in contrast to feudal order based upon personal piety—is easily made to work for anybody who knows how to gain control over it. A rationally ordered system of officials continues to function smoothly after the enemy occupied the areas; he merely needs to change the top officials. (Weber 1996)

Here is the crux of the argument that Weber built to justify his contention for the permanent character of the bureaucratic machine. Bureaucracy is a rational organisation since it is based on written rules, an impersonal order and a clear division of labour. In other words, Weber's conceptualisation of bureaucracy consists of a hierarchically-structured, professional, rule-bound, impersonal, appointed and disciplined body of public personnel with a specific set of competencies. There is a fundamental argument in support of his concern for building 'the spirit' for societal good at two levels: at a rather mundane level, he pursues a mechanical point by insisting on the technical qualities of bureaucracy which are indispensable to make it an acceptable instrument of power and authority; at a higher level of conceptualisation, he also underlines his belief that with time bureaucracy will be organic to the system in which it requires neither artificial boost nor support—i.e. it will no longer be a structure of governance, but one that nurtures the spirit by which it becomes an integral part of society. Bureaucracy will become, in other words, an embedded social entity which is transcendental too since it survives on the spirit that makes its existence indispensable.

Woodrow Wilson too redefined the course that public administration as an area of study was expected to take with his seminal 1887 article entitled 'The Study of Administration'. Appreciative of the article, Dwight Waldo referred to the text as 'the most important document in the development of the field' (1980: 67). Despite being repetitive, we need to reiterate some of the fundamental points that Wilson made in support of his model of public administration, which was based on both German and British philosophical inputs he had derived while pursuing his PhD at Johns Hopkins University. Two German professors, Herbert B. Adams and Richard T. Elly, introduced Wilson to the complex world of public administration. Aware that the fundamental ideas of public administration were articulated in Europe, especially in Germany and France, he argued that the knowledge about the system of governance 'has been developed by French and German professors and is consequently in all parts adapted to the needs of a compact state, and made to fit highly centralized form of government' (Wilson 1887/1996: 8). In the creation of knowledge for governance, Americans sadly lagged behind, exhorted Wilson:

> No American writers have hitherto taken very important part in the advancement of this science. It has found its doctors in Europe. It is not of our making; it is a foreign science, speaking very little of the language of the English or American principle. It employs only foreign tongues; it utters, its example, its conditions are almost exclusively grounded in the histories of foreign races, in the precedents of foreign systems, in the lessons of foreign revolutions. (Ibid.)

What was the way out when the intellectual inputs did not seem to be adequate to conceptualise the distinct American system of governance? Wilson's answer was to adapt the ideas to the American socio-economic context. As he elaborated, given the diversity of the American society, the derivative ideas needed to be

> adapted not to a simple compact, but to a complex and multiform state, and made to fit highly decentralized forms of government. If we would employ it, we must Americanize it, and not formally, in language merely, but radically, in thought, principle and aim as well. It must learn our constitution by heart; must get the bureaucratic fever out of its veins; must inhale much free American air. (Ibid.)

The idea is loud and clear; it was necessary not to be blind to the ideas that had emerged elsewhere, presumably because they were not organic to the American socio-political ethos. Hence an urgent need was felt for creating a corpus of knowledge which helped understand the American public administration. Despite being influenced to a significant extent by the German philosopher J. K. Bluntschli and the English expert of constitutionalism Walter Bagehot, among others, Wilson sought to evolve a uniquely-textured model of public administration by taking into account the American socio-economic circumstances.

Persuaded to believe that public administration is context-driven, Wilson raised two important points which are critical in conceptualising public administration as a field of study. First, he saw a clear deficit in our understanding of public administration in the context of a democratic state. As he argued,

> Old as democracy is, its organization on a basis of modern ideas and conditions is still an unaccomplished task. The democratic state has yet to be equipped for carrying those enormous burdens of administration which the needs of this industrial and trading age are so fast accumulating. … Administration stands upon an essentially different basis in a democratic state from that on which it stands in a non-democratic state. (Ibid.: 14)

What are the criteria that he devised to manage administration in democratic America? Instead of preparing a definite checklist of items, Wilson made a couple of general observations, and one is the oft-quoted distinction between politics and administration which is usually referred to as 'dichotomous' in the conventional literature. However, a careful study of the point reveals that by separating the two distinct domains of human activities, he demarcated the two areas as distinctly representing two different kinds of activities which required different kinds of expertise. As he elaborated in his address, 'The field of administration is a field of business. It is removed from the hurry and strife of politics. … Administrative questions are not political questions. Although politics sets the task for administration, it should be suffered to manipulate its offices' (ibid.: 10). It is clear that there is hardly a dichotomy, as Wilson spelt-out; what he insisted upon was the two separate domains of politics and administration. This was further clarified by his characterisation of civil service which reinforced the argument. According to him, 'civil service [is] cultured and self-sufficient enough to act with sense and vigour, and yet so intimately connected with the popular thought, by means of elections and constant public counsel, as to find arbitrariness or class spirit out of question' (ibid.: 13). Wilson's primary goal was to install 'a body of responsible, ethically correct public servants who were educated to serve common will' (Sager and Rosser 2009: 1140). Two important characteristics seem to be critical here: (*a*) public servants need to be ethically responsive and (*b*) their aim is to serve the common will which also rules out arbitrariness and class-prejudices in so far as their role-discharge is concerned.

The argument supportive of the dichotomy thesis does not seem to be tenable in light of his insistence of politics being a domain in which public opinion got crystalised. By exhorting that 'administration in the US must be at all points sensitive to public opinion' (Wilson 1887/1996: 13), Wilson gave words to his ideological belief. Furthermore, the assumption that the Constitution contributed to the consolidation of the values that shaped politics also confirms that he never undermined the role of politics in administration. For him, Constitution was the repository of values which also informed the administration because it was about 'the proper distribution of constitutional authority … [and] this question of the distribution of authority when taken into the sphere of the higher, the originating function of government, is obviously a central constitutional question' (ibid.: 11). What is now clear is that Wilson's notion of administration is a creative blending of constitutional values with how they are conceptualised in the public domain and are brought back to administration through politics. However, there is a warning which needs to be taken into account to understand the so-called politics–administration dichotomy. Although Wilson was willing to concede that public opinion was important in shaping administration, he also knew that it could be a cause of delay in administrative decisions. In his words, '[w]herever regard for public opinion is a first principle of government, practical reform must be slow and all reform must be full of compromises' (ibid.: 9). As a pragmatist, he hardly wavered in making the point that public opinion could not be bypassed though it was a source of unnecessary delay in decision-making. Nurtured in the American democratic tradition, it was obvious for him not to ignore the public opinion which also provided critical inputs to the administration.

The dichotomy thesis further loses intellectual viability in light of new research showing that Wilson was heavily influenced by the writings of J. K. Bluntschli. It has been argued that 'the analysis of Wilson's reliance on German sources helps clarify his vision of the proper relationship between political and administrative aspects of government' (Rosser 2010: 50). Critical to his conceptualisation was the notion of the State that evolved over phases. This is confirmed by the fact that Wilson differentiated between the era of the Constitution and the era of administration as two distinct stages in the organic growth of the State in one of his early texts titled 'Essay on Administration', published in 1885 (cited in Rosser 2010: 550). He noted that 'the period of constitution-making is passed now. We have reached new territory in which we need new guides. … All the enlightened world has realized the fact and is preparing itself to understand administration' (ibid.). This is however not to suggest that the Constitution lost its salience in Wilson's schema of things. Contrarily, he was of the opinion that since the Constitution was not a static set of principles it needed to be reinvented in the changed historical context which by contributing to the growth of new power relationships, created new dynamics of power and authority that, if ignored, would lead to misconception. The ideas of the German philosopher Lorenz Von Stein[1] persuaded him to accept that 'if the whole living state and its organic elements were to be understood, one should no longer concentrate on the constitution making process but rather on the examination of public administration' (Rosser 2010: 550). Following this assumption, he always felt that the Constitution was at best a set of guidelines which could be reinvented if situations so demanded rather than a set of static rules. For him, public administration was simply an instrument which was allowed to function to translate the constitutional values and principles into concrete action. Hence he strongly argued for 'a body of altruistic, dutiful public servants [who] would promote the common good of society, which had primacy over the good of the individual' (ibid.: 553). Guided by the Constitution, public administrators were hardly independent; by insisting that they needed to be sensitive to public opinion, Wilson made them responsive to the prevalent power relationships which were also critical in conceptualising politics and the influences that it endangered. This was made explicit in his 1891 lecture at Johns Hopkins University where he categorically stated:

> the nature of administration … is the continuous and systematic carrying out in practice of all the tasks which devolve upon the State. … No topic in the study of the government stand by itself – least of all perhaps administration whose part it is to mirror the principles of government in operation. It is not a mere anatomy of institutions. It deals directly, indeed, and principally with the structural features and operating organs of the state life. … Administration cannot be divorced from its intimate connections with [the public opinion] without being distorted and robbed of its true significance. Its foundations are those deep and permanent principles of politics which have been quarried from history and built into constitutions. (Wilson [1969]: 114–15, cited in Stillman II 1973: 587)

The above clarification notwithstanding, Wilson's 1887 essay has elements of confusion. If one interprets sections of Wilson's essay in isolation, one gets enough fodder to defend the argument that Wilson was in favour of separating politics from administration; if, however, one understands

[1] Stein insisted that for a better understanding of how a government functions, the structure of governance (à la public administration) is a perfect index and not the Constitution, because constitutional rules and regulations remain futile unless they are applied in practice by a government.

the argument by reading the text as one statement, one is likely to get a completely different impression. Hence, there is substance when Stillman argues that 'Wilson's essay vacillates between the two poles of thought regarding the separability and inseparability of administration from politics (thereby providing generations of later scholars with ample footnote ammunition for both sides of the argument)' (1973: 586). Be that as it may, an analytical reading of the essay, as demonstrated above, suggests that the much-hyped dichotomy thesis usually attributed to Wilson does not seem to be persuasive, but exaggerated to avoid the complexities inherent in the argument he made.

The above discussion also reveals that both Weber and Wilson shared a common concern and also came up with more or less similar conclusions. What drove Weber was his concern for creating a formally-structured form of organisation to sustain the Capitalist spirit which was also supplemented by the Protestant ethic. According to him, a professionally qualified civil service was needed to realise the common will. By being impersonal and efficient, bureaucracy created an instrument of governance which was fundamentally different from its erstwhile counterpart that thrived on the spoils system. Like Weber, Wilson intended to install a scientific, professional, meritocratic, rule-based and trustworthy bureaucracy which would act as an impediment to corruption in public administration. They also converged in their condemnation of politicians who tended to rob administration of its zeal to work independently. While agreeing that administration cannot be divorced from politics, both of them held the view that politicians should not be allowed to muddle the world of administration since it required a completely different kind of expertise that the former lacked. In their perception, politicians and administrators moved around different orbits of functioning: the former represented specific ideological values which were critical to the making of policies, while the latter needed to perform their administrative tasks neutrally and follow the politicians to the point of self-denial. Here too Weber and Wilson hardly differed from each other. Wilson, for instance, did not appear to be so insistent on the dichotomous relationship between politics and administration, as his writings that followed the 1887 essay have shown. In fact, there are significant texts in his writings that show that Wilson remained 'ambivalent about the subject' (Sager and Rosser 2009: 1139). In a similar vein, Weber was not, it seems, averse to the role of politics in shaping the administrative responses because, as David Beetham argues, 'the official concerned with administrative effectiveness, and hence with power, was properly subordinate to the politician's functions of defining the ends that power was to serve and taking responsibility for them' (1985: 79). The arguments are identical: being persuaded to endorse the role of politics in administration as inevitable since they cannot be separated in watertight compartments, both Weber and Wilson put forward more or less a similar model of public administration. In view of these uncanny similarities, one is tempted to draw a parallel with Hegel's argument in defence of a formalised, professionalised, hierarchically-organised and meritocratic form of organisation of public administration—i.e. his argument for a merit-based public authority to avoid derailment in public governance. This perhaps confirms the conceptual point that both Weber and Wilson 'anchored their writings in the German tradition of a strong state with a strong executive and, consequently, with an extensive body of public servants' (Sager and Rosser 2009: 1142).

The similarities in their views were thus not accidental but contingent on being appreciative of an identical philosophical tradition insisting on regulation of human behaviour in accordance with what they defined as 'the spirit' of the system.

* * *

III

Centralisation and decentralisation are two critical ideas in conceptualising public administration as a field of activity for common wellbeing. While the Western theoretical discourse is overwhelmingly in favour of a centralised and hierarchical bureaucracy, the practitioners argued strongly for decentralisation to take root. Their ideological endeavour in support of a non-Capitalistic system of production probably explains why they were opposed to the Western approach to governance. As will be discussed, none of the major thinkers in the non-Western tradition seems to have been persuaded by the pyramidal structure of governance which owed its growth to the ideas of Hegel, Weber and Wilson, among others. In order to build a polity on the basis of their distinctive socio-political priorities, they preferred to have a system of decentralised public administration in which authority stemmed from the grassroots, in contrast to the Weberian insistence on the top-driven governance. Conceptually innovative and administratively unique, the idea of a decentralised administration is a challenging conceptualisation in which administration is a recognised space of dialogue and deliberation among the stakeholders. This is a space where, in other words, decisions are made by taking into account inputs from those at the grassroots, instead of being imposed from above (as it happens in a Weberian bureaucracy). Public administration is thus a design of governance and not merely an instrument of action which, instead of being centripetal, is centrifugal.

In the non-Western tradition, the theoretical exponents who argued strongly for civic participation are M. K. Gandhi of India, Mao Zedong of China and Julius Nyerere of Tanzania. While Gandhi largely drew on indigenous traditions to evolve his approach to civic engagement in decision-making, Nyerere and Mao preferred the socialistic way to consolidate participation in the socio-political processes of administration. What is common in these non-Western efforts is the emphasis on 'community development and decentralisation of power'. The former supports endeavours to bring villages, urban neighbourhoods or other household groupings into the process of managing development resources without being dependent on the institutionalised forms of governance, while the latter captures efforts at strengthening village and municipal governments on both the demand and supply sides: on the demand side, decentralisation bolsters citizens' participation in local government by, *inter alia*, holding regular elections, improving access to information, evolving a mechanism for sustained deliberative decision-making and involving the stakeholders as integral to the decision-making processes; on the supply side, *inter alia*, it reinforces the ability of local governments to provide services by increasing their financial resources, strengthening those associated with local governance (see Chapter 11). Public administration is thus a serious effort towards creating a space for debates and discussion whereby the stakeholders are drawn to the processes of decision-making.

Civic engagement and decentralisation remain two critical pillars of participatory discourse. These are also effective shields against political exclusion since interactive dialogues bring people closer to each other. Besides creating an environment for deliberations on issues of public importance, these are also important processes that bring power closer to the people which makes, on the one hand, the political dialogue not only more tangible and transparent but also people-centric, and on the other, deters the monopolisation of power by certain elite groups. The concern for civic engagement and democratic decentralisation of power is not new, as there is a rich theoretical tradition in both Western and non-Western approaches. Serious efforts were made from different theoretical predispositions to realise the importance of a participatory discourse for localising development. In the neo-liberal context, the effort is ideologically governed in the sense that civic participation seems to have filled a vacuum following the withdrawal of the State from social sectors which, also an obvious outcome of the processes of democratisation particularly at the grassroots, cannot be clearly grasped unless one is sensitive to the circumstances in which multiple socio-ideological forces dialectically interact.

Nonetheless, there is no doubt that indigenous knowledge and preferences are always useful in evolving appropriate methods of governance involving the stakeholders. It is easier for participatory governance to take root in India because there is a long history of 'organic participation', supported by political authorities, in different phases of her evolution as a polity. In the case of Nyerere and Mao, the execution of their civic engagement model was largely a product of 'induced participation' through sustained political campaign in its favour by well-entrenched political parties. Nyerere was supported by the Tanganyika African National Union (TANU) which he led, and it was the Communist Party of China (CPC) which helped Mao to implement, ruthlessly on occasions, the commune system of governance and the entire state machinery which was always an effective aid to the decision that the party supremo had taken. For Gandhi, the Nationalist movement was not merely to obtain political freedom from colonialism, it was also an ideological battle to evolve India as a self-reliant political entity by drawing upon her material and human resources. The motto was not mass production, but production by the masses which allowed 'every able-bodied man' to contribute to his own wellbeing. His model of village *swaraj* was an indigenous articulation of civic engagement in rural development. This was a unique model not only because it created an organically-linked forum for participation, but also for its utility as a programme for channelling human efforts towards productive purposes. Gandhi's conceptualisation of rural governance was presumably readily accepted, which was not the case with either the *ujamaa* or the commune;[2]

---

[2] The 'commune', a Maoist conceptualisation, denotes collectivisation of communities for pursuing socio-economic and political goals, benefitting those constituting the collective. On the other hand, '*ujamaa*' is Nyerere's conceptual category drawn on the traditional African familyhood; this was also an effort towards creating a collective based on the urge to be self-sufficient in terms of its demands and needs.

these two socio-politically structured forms of participatory governance in Tanzania and China heavily relied on the political parties that Nyerere and Mao respectively led to gain popularity. Nonetheless, there is one factor that seems to be identical in the case of Gandhi, Mao and Nyerere: they evolved their views on civic participation in public affairs out of their active involvement in specific politico-ideological experiments at a particular juncture of history in areas which had suffered long years of colonial exploitation; they were activist-theoreticians who had had the bent of mind to generate specific responses which were unique, presumably because of their definite contextual roots. Unlike Western thinkers who were not activists in the sense Gandhi, Mao and Nyerere were, these non-Western thinkers created a new genre of thinking by their direct involvement in socio-political movements seeking to radically alter the prevalent social texture for realising the criticality of the civic engagement for localising development in its true connotation.

The non-Western tradition is rich and theoretically innovative. Contrary to the well-established Weberian defence for hierarchical and centralised form of governance, the non-Western thinkers put forward their ideas which are context-sensitive and also reflective of their own realisation. In formulating models of analysis, they also took into account the Western wisdom that they had derived from various sources—Mao's understanding of Marxism as it evolved as a statecraft in the Soviet Union, and Nyerere's training in Edinburgh and life-long exposure to the ideas of Western Enlightenment—while evolving their distinct approaches to socio-economic issues. Interestingly, despite being inspired by completely different kinds of ideological commitment, both Mao and Nyerere were appreciative of identical values for meaningful civic engagements and participatory governance. There were two fundamental modes whereby Nyerere and Mao sought to develop models of governance: communalisation of power and decentralisation of authority under a unified command. The aim was to involve the community as a stakeholder in decision-making or governance. As already observed, the design was democratic in character and drew inspiration from indigenous traditions. For Nyerere, it was the African familyhood, while for Mao it was K'ang Yu Wei's *Ta Tung Shu*, a late nineteenth century Chinese text that attributed the rise of social harmony to the dispersal of authority. Ujamaa was therefore not an alien idea in so far as the Tanzanians were concerned; likewise, communes had Chinese roots. As the ideas were organic to the context, it was easier for them to strike an emotional chord with the people who appeared to have been persuaded, at least at the outset, once the respective models were put to test. On the one hand, by arguing that both ujamaa and communes had local roots, Nyerere and Mao respectively created an environment which prepared a base in support of their conceptualisation; they also linked these endeavours, on the other hand, to the hope of equitable development cutting across regions, clans and ethnicities. In a way, both ujamaa and communes became a source of hope, development and empowerment for those who were marginalised in socio-economic terms. In other words, these strategies worked favourably presumably due to the prevalent socio-economic circumstances in Tanzania and China where mass deprivation was hardly an aberration. Furthermore, the idea that both ujamaa and communes were endeavours towards involving the stakeholders in its organisation and functioning brought governance closer to the people. Once ujamaa and communes became integral to the mass psyche, they immediately took root in the society, which also helped build a shield of defence in case they were challenged. What is fundamental here is the idea that ujamaa and communes were context-dependent constructs, drawing on specific ideological predilections.

There is another critical dimension that cannot be underplayed while seeking to understand the importance of ujamaa and communes as instruments of socio-economic engineering in relatively backward Tanzania and China. Much of what Nyerere and Mao could achieve during their reign is attributed to the hegemonic presence of the TANU and CPC as effective aids to the implementation of what they felt appropriate for all-round socio-economic development. They led the party-driven government in an authoritarian manner. Once the decision was taken by the top leadership—which was usually Mao in China and Nyerere in Tanzania—it became mandatory to all, which also means that the hype regarding democratisation of decision-making was largely concocted to politically sway the masses and successfully combat opponents, if any. Communes were far effective as instruments of change in comparison to ujamaa. While participatory democracy ceased to be effective in communes, largely due to the hegemonic presence of party cadres, brigades and teams, ujamaa was weakened substantially from the outset since it was forced upon reluctant peasants who hardly appreciated the centralised instruction for compulsory resettlement.

Nonetheless, ujamaa and communes are meaningful conceptualisations of civic engagement and participatory governance because of two specific reasons. On the one hand they articulated alternative ways of understanding governance by drawing upon distinct ideological preferences, and on the other they provided powerful modes of explanation in which theoretical ideas both from indigenous and derived sources remain critical. Creatively construed, ujamaa and communes therefore represent a theoretical quest for conceptualising the non-European socio-economic and political formations which, despite imbibing alien values due to colonialism, nurtured ideas and thought processes which were distinctly indigenous. It is therefore not surprising that Nyerere, despite being heavily influenced by the Western philosophy of Enlightenment along with Marxist socialism and Fabianism, was drawn to the traditional African familyhood while devising his model of villagisation like Mao, who, while expanding Marxism in a non-European context, seriously took into account those ideas K'ang had laid out in *Ta Tung Shu*. There was another similarity because they had the identical aim of devising appropriate models to make their countries self-reliant. Mao sought to accomplish this by putting in place three interrelated levels of governance under the stewardship of a centralised party, while Nyerere strove to achieve his goal by forced villagisation and a supportive bureaucracy engendered by TANU. Given their contribution to reinventing the ideas of civic engagement and localising governance, the criticality of ujamaa and communes as benchmarks for theoretical parameters cannot be underplayed. And here lies the relevance of the ideas of Mao and Nyerere who, despite being projected as villains at a particular juncture of the evolution of human civilisation, will continue to inspire the search for alternative discourses of analysis and challenge the endeavour towards evolving the hegemonic 'one-size-fits-all formula'.

* * *

IV

This is an era of governance. In this avalanche, 'public administration' appears to have lost its academic viability to a significant extent. With the unfolding of neo-liberalism following the collapse of the Soviet Union, the objective has become clear. By putting a system of governance in place which is mainly process-driven, the Bretton Woods institutions—primarily the World Bank (WB) and the International Monetary Fund (IMF)—sought to devise an alternative form of governance to streamline administration in the so-called developing countries which, in their view, have already collapsed. Attributing the dwindling of governance to administrative failure, global donor agencies also joined hands with these institutions in their effort to establish an efficient system of administration in these countries as perhaps the only means to recover the loan they had extended. Governance, as a conceptualisation, is thus a practitioners' contribution that is also guided by the deep-seated fear of losing money that was sanctioned seemingly for developmental goals. This is certainly one of the major factors which explains the increasing popularity of the expression governance as opposed to public administration. In the process, there has emerged a system of governance which is sensitive to the Weberian concerns for efficiency while largely ignoring the purpose for which public administration stands out.

Governance is a conceptual construct with a clear ideological aim. It is a neo-liberal endeavour to conceptualise public administration which is no longer tenable in the context of market-driven human existence. Instead of being 'a doer', the government is reduced to being 'a facilitator' of the processes in which things move in accordance with the much-hyped market logic. Being a critical determinant of government action, the market gains precedence in circumstances where public administration is being redefined to realise certain ideological goals which are rooted in concerted attempts at homogenising by robbing the globe of its multidimensional texture. The effort produces a ripple effect. On the one hand, it is a clear signal to the non-performing administration which has allowed partisan interests to prosper at the cost of the public; it is a signal which, by making the stakeholders realise their rights and duties, has led to the consolidation of alternative perspectives and views which were never considered appropriate in the past. By exposing the limitations of a centralised administration which failed to achieve the stipulated goals, the effort created, on the other hand, a space for alternative ideas and perspectives of administration to take root; governance is therefore an outcome of a historical context in which the erstwhile State-led development strategy has given way to the market-driven neo-liberal means.

As a conceptual category, governance is not merely about government but the processes whereby public administration manifests itself as a programme of action. Governance draws our attention away from the institutionalised structure of government as monolithic and formal. As Mark Bevir points out, governance shifts our attention 'to the processes and interactions through which highly diverse social interests and actors produce the policies, practices and effects of governing' (2012: 4). It supplements a focus, Bevir further argues, 'on the formal institutions of government with recognition of more diverse activities that blur the boundary of state and society' (ibid.: 5). Governance thus refers 'to the rise of new processes of governing that are hybrid and multi-jurisdictional with plural stakeholders working together in networks' (ibid.). On the basis of governance being 'hybrid and multi-jurisdictional', one can draw-out four major features. First, in the governance era, decision-making is no longer the exclusive domain of public authority, it has to take into account inputs from the market and private agencies that have now acquired salience. Governance entails hybrid practices involving not only public institutions but also those agencies which are involved in activities relating to public wellbeing. Second, being both multi-jurisdictional and transnational, governance creates spaces for intervention by multiple actors who may not be directly connected with governing per se though they exert tremendous influence in pushing a specific kind of policy design. While donors push specific policy designs that the recipient country cannot simply ignore, there are other global agencies which also assert their authority in so far as policymaking by the nation-state is concerned. Here the growing importance of the World Trade Organization (WTO) is illustrative. By charting out a definite course of action tilting in favour of developed countries, the WTO imposes policy priorities on member countries causing socio-political imbalances not only internally but also in their relationship in the postcolonial states. Third, governance expands the range of activities by involving the plurality of stakeholders beyond what was considered integral to public governance in the past. With the involvement of multiple stakeholders, governance is conceptualised as a design to accommodate multiple socio-economic and political interests which hardly figured in the era of centralised administration. As administration is being decentred, newer practices of public-private partnerships, and collaborative governance are being encouraged. Finally, governance is also about a space in which multiple options are played out; this is a space where different levels of governance and multiple stakeholders are linked in networks. Critical here is the importance of dialogue and the need for arriving at a consensus by involving the stakeholders. Since it is multi-jurisdictional and also plural, governance provides powerful theoretical ideas to conceptually articulate the limitations of the Weberian mould of traditional public administration.[3]

Governance has gained currency at a moment in the evolution of public administration when societal problem-solving demands a multi-pronged search for the refashioning of the mode of governing. As it has eventually emerged, it is clearly a policymaking device that underlines transparency, accountability, integrity and legitimacy of the institutions, rules, practices and values on which a society functions. These characteristics are relative to the society in question

---

[3] We have also drawn on Bevir (2012: 5–7) while identifying some of the features of governance here.

because they cannot be articulated in absolute terms. But what is critical is the process whereby citizens favourably link with governance presumably because it generates trust and confidence among them. Governance is thus a mechanism involved in (*a*) 'the formation and propagation of values', (*b*) 'the creation and distribution of wealth' and (*c*) 'the emergence and consolidation of institutions' (Tarschys 2001: 28). In the governance paradigm, the traditional governance process with the State as the supreme actor is now heavily influenced by international organisations with a growing number of regulations formulated at the supra-national level. These supra-national policies '[travel across] languages and cultures, framing and positioning local discourses and being translated by the local configurations of resources and ideas' (Salskov-Iversen, Hansen and Bislev 2000: 188). As shown, the growing but critical importance of governance both as a technique and an agenda can easily be attributed to two important developments in the global order. First, the disintegration of the former Soviet Union suggesting not only the weaknesses of Marxism-Leninism as a cementing ideology in diverse societies, but also the failure of the State-directed development model in fulfilling basic human social, economic and political needs. This apparent vacuum is being filled by the consolidation of the neo-liberal discourse in which 'states should become commodified and marketized in their outlook and give way to the "market discipline" [and lead to] governance without government'. The governance without government that is market discipline can be seen as 'governmentality of neo-liberal globalization'. Drawing on Foucault, governmentality includes 'mental and practical levels of governance'. Governmentality is 'a result of mentality and the organization of conduct that composes the art of governance' (Penttinen 2000: 211). Drawing on 'the internalization of practices of governing', governmentality is a mechanism of policing the self 'according to existing conception of truth grounded in knowledge about the self' (Brass 2000: 318). The second and perhaps a more significant factor is the remarkable technological advances that shrink distance and interdependencies that arise from much wider and deeper global economic integration. In the changed circumstances, without reorienting themselves substantially, decision-makers can hardly remain appropriate in governance. As a result, public administration is bound to undergo radical changes because of historical circumstances in which the idea of 'contextual' public administration seems to have lost viability. The ecological view is replaced by the 'neo-Taylorist' philosophy of 'one best way' to organise public affairs (see Chapter 2). Neo-liberal values surged ahead predicting 'the end of history' and the natural emergence of Capitalism as 'the sole' arbiter of the fate of the world. In the contemporary socio-economic milieu, 'management' and 'market' seem to be inbuilt in public administration redefining 'public' in a radical way.

The traditional bureau model does not appear to be entirely appropriate to contemporary public administration. Two major trends—globalisation and devolution—seem to have radically altered the perspectives in which governance need to be conceptualised. They pose challenges as well as opportunities to redefine some of the major concerns of the traditional system of governance. Government must, as Donald F. Kettl emphasises, 'not only devise new strategies for managing public programmes effectively in a globalized and devolved policy world [but also] build the capacity for doing so' (2000: 11). Instead of altogether rejecting the Weberian hierarchical model of bureaucracy, Kettl argues for adaptation of the 'traditional vertical system' to the new challenges of globalisation and devolution and also for integrating new horizontal systems to the traditional vertical ones. Being aware of the 'rigidity' in which the traditional hierarchical authority works and also the fact that globalisation and devolution 'scramble its foundation', Kettl thus insists on 'enhancing the capacity of the government to govern and manage effectively in this transformed environment'. As a paradigm reflective of the new challenges, governance has thus repositioned public administration as a field of enquiry. By responding to the modern challenges 'of high fragmentation and the disarticulation of the state', the new formulation of governance enables us to redefine public administration within 'the structural and contextual dynamics of the emerging global order' (Frederickson 1999: 710), which also requires new conceptual categories. Fundamental here is the idea that public administration is being transformed radically and the Weberian model does not appear to be adequate in addressing the challenges it confronts. Governance offers an alternative conceptualisation which, by taking into account the new challenges, also creates a new genre of thinking in which government is just 'an enabler' but not 'a doer', as is usually the case in traditional public administration.

There is no denying that governance has refashioned the contemporary debate on public administration by raising certain major critical questions. However the primary goal that remains at the core of this new dispensation in the WB-sponsored model is to seek to champion universal goals within particular constraints where the role of politics is significantly minimal, if not entirely outlawed. Despite the formally apolitical stance of the WB on this question, 'there is little doubt that underlying even this limited vision of governance is a Western model, ringing with Weberian ethos, with its emphasis on free markets, individualism and a neutral but efficient public administration, subject to a legitimate government' (Leftwich 1996: 16). Without politics, democracy has a restrictive meaning. Politics is the only social process of negotiation and contestation—politics as consisting of all the processes of conflict, cooperation and negotiation involved in the use, production and situation of resources. Hence, John J. Kirlin argues that 'as long as democracy is valued the big questions of Public Administration must go beyond the big questions of Public Management' (1996: 217). In other words, the role of public administration is diminished if it is primarily understood in terms of managing public agencies. The First Minnowbrook Conference of 1968 and the Blacksburg Manifesto have both raised this issue of democratic governance in public interest. What is relevant in the context of the developing world is that public administration is being crippled in the name of structural adjustment that invokes 'the market model' of governance in utter disregard of the crucial social developmental role of the State. The interests of public administration are no longer people-related but driven by external forces. Hence, the reforms that are externally-induced do not, for obvious reasons, inspire the people for whom they are targeted. Are these reforms then self-defeating is the question that looms large in the era of governance.

* * *

V

In conceptual terms, governance seeks to reinvent public administration by formally recognising the role of multiple actors in public decision-making. Governance is, in other words, an arrangement which unfolds in networks confirming once again the idea that it is multidimensional and multi-jurisdictional. Does it mean that in its earlier avatar public administration was immune from socio-political and ideological inputs that were external to governance? It is difficult to justify such a position because the prefix 'public' entails the possible sources of inputs or influences which do not stem from within the bureaucracy. This is a claim that draws on the distinction between public and private administration: public administration is one which is meant to serve the public by being sensitive to public interests, which is not possible without being open to public inputs; in contrast, private administration is tuned exclusively to private goals and objectives and is therefore textured differently. Since their goals are radically different, the distinction is fair and analytically persuasive. In reality, however, they coalesce because it is common knowledge that, historically, private actors have provided inputs with regard to the so-called public decisions, especially in a democratic set-up. Whether in India or elsewhere, despite not always being formally recognised, private actors remain critical to decisions which are protective of public interests as well. For instance, the government policy towards labour cannot be absolutely indifferent to the views of the industrialists who instinctively pursue private goals; policymakers may have to walk a tightrope, as what they decide while devising steps to protect the workers' interests has also to take into account inputs rendered by factory-owners. This is a classic case of how private interests play a significant role in the making of policies governing a relationship in which clearly contradictory socio-economic interests are balanced. Similarly, education is another area of social concern in which private entrepreneurs continue to remain significant in policymaking. This is not a modern phenomenon. Historically speaking, there are plenty of examples from the Indian experience to show that many philanthropists, in their endeavour to provide quality education at a reasonable cost, shaped policies concerning education. Not only was their role recognised by policymakers, they were also credited for their critical contribution in building the basic infrastructure for education in India. It can thus be argued that the distinction cannot be stretched beyond a point, though it is useful to analytically separate two domains of activities primarily in terms of the goals they purportedly pursue.

Public administration is thus a creative blend of activities which are neither exactly public nor absolutely private. Although a distinction can be made through an on-the-surface reading of these activities, in reality it is overstretched. What is public administration then? By reiterating the conceptual argument that Waldo made in *The Administrative State* (1948), Camilla Stivers endeavoured to provide a persuasive definition by saying that:

> public administration is both public and administrative. It is not a unidirectional force (nor, it must be said, a dichotomy). Rather it is a flow of energy between two opposed yet joined poles: one upholding the importance of right answers, rational practice, order, results, the Truth, and the other

> standing for essentially contested questions, debate, openness, political values. One seeks finality and certainty. The other wants to keep the argument going, because when the argument stops, politics stops. (Stivers 2008: 56)

Politics is integral to administration because administrative decisions are arrived at by way of contestation and negotiation. Efficient managerial devices are certainly useful aids for administration, but they cannot be self-sustaining without being sensitive to the prevalent politico-ideological preferences. Those supportive of the governance paradigm tend to downplay the role of politics, presumably because administration for them is merely a technical exercise which can best be executed by evolving efficient techniques. Not only is this argument conceptually vacuous, it is also practically faulty because, as experience has shown, an administration which lacks organic roots in the society in which it is expected to function is likely to be an inept organ. It is true that the governance paradigm has unseated some of the fundamental assumptions of Weberian conceptualisation which tended to create a rent-seeking bureaucracy, especially in the developing world, and in that respect it has served a useful purpose by creating an alternative mode of comprehending public administration. Governance is, in that case, certainly an endeavour towards raising newer questions and newer issues though, its inherent tendency to conceptualise administration independent of socio-economic circumstances is a serious handicap. By charting out a definite administrative path for the developing countries to make them eligible for international loans, the governance paradigm justifies neo-Taylorism which, despite having mechanical viability in certain circumstances, can hardly be an effective theoretical design in unravelling the administrative dynamics across countries.

There is one last point. Public administration is also an ideational exercise which means that it is an exercise that is rooted in the battle of ideas. The classical theories of public administration owed its growth to the German philosophical traditions in support of a centralised bureaucracy, as shown above. As they were persuaded by the view that a budding Capitalism required a strong system of governance to secure its future, no exception was made by Hegel, Weber and Wilson. To them it was a situation-dictated choice. In the changed environment, the exponents of the non-Western traditions, like Gandhi, Mao and Nyerere, had reasons to challenge the Western traditions which had no organic connection to their non-Western socio-economic environment. The result was obvious: centralised governance survived so long as it had adequate coercive power which also created enough theoretical justification for arguments for decentralisation. The model that insisted on devolution of power and gained salience in the non-Western context was not fortuitous, but a dialectical outcome of an ideational war reflective of how context became decisive in shaping the form of administration and arguments in its support. Fundamental here is the point that public administration is a context-driven effort that cannot be de-linked from politics, because it is politics which is a determinant of how administration evolves out of contestation and negotiation in a specific socio-economic milieu.

* * *

VI

This book delves into the complex world of public administration as an area of activity which is also ideologically-governed and politically-designed. The basic concern is two-fold: besides elaborating the classical conceptual parameters, this exercise is also devoted to the debates and discussions that figured prominently in efforts towards rechristening public administration as governance. Written in a lucid language to reach out even to non-experts, this book conceptually defends the contention that public administration is, out and out, a context-driven effort. In order to capture its context-specific nature, care has been taken to elaborate the theme with reference to examples from within our quotidian experiences. The other objective of this book is also to draw attention to those areas of public administration which need serious attention from researchers of the future. At one stroke, this book, despite being conceptualised in a textbook format, is also a stepping stone to theoretically evolving some of the fundamental tenets of public administration, especially in the non-Western context. This is being reinforced by dwelling separately on the ideas of those non-Western thinkers-cum-practitioners who developed models of public administration in tune with the prevalent socio-economic context they experienced while seeking to sharpen their arguments against derivative wisdom in so far as public administration was concerned. By drawing attention to the multidimensional character of public administration, this book builds on the critique of governance which strives to theoretically justify neo-Taylorism in public administration.

This book has 11 chapters, grouped in three sections. Section A, with four chapters, is an introduction to the discipline. Chapter One is a detailed presentation of the journey of public administration in India as a field of enquiry. The purpose is to show how the discipline evolved over a period of several decades with reference to the difficulties it confronted in India and how it gradually surpassed the era of uncertainty to finally establish its identity in the family of Social Sciences by winning a battle for existence. Chapter Two dwells on the various classical theoretical ideas of public administration, such as scientific management theory, bureaucratic theory, human relations theory, decision-making theory and ecological theory. Chapter Three is about the conceptual journey that public administration undertook since the First Minnowbrook Conference in 1968. An analytical account of the three conferences that have taken place thus far will help us understand how the discipline changed its character in view of the changing socio-economic circumstances, which also reinforces the argument that as an area of human activity public adnministration is context-dependent. Chapter Four is dedicated to a discussion on contemporary theoretical conceptualisations in the discipline. Section B comprises of one chapter that is devoted to the three major non-Western traditions of administrative theories—that of Gandhi, Mao and Nyerere. Chapter Five seeks to grasp this new genre of thinking which is neither completely derivative nor indigenous but a creative blend of both. Section C is the crux of this volume. It contains six chapters that describe threadbare how Indian administration had undergone changes both during the era when the State-led development model was appreciated and later, following the adoption of the 1991 New Economic Policy that ushered in economic liberalisation. Not only does this section substantiate the principal argument of the book that public administration is context-directed, it also challenges the one-size-fits-all formula on the basis of a thorough study of Indian administration in two completely different socio-economic circumstances. What is striking, however, is to note that regardless of the consequences of economic liberalisation, the institutions of governance remain, more or less, unaltered. Also, Indian administration has the resilience to resist the neo-liberal avalanche to a significant extent by carving out an independent course of action in consonance with India's peculiar socio-economic priorities. This section also deals with issues that are critical to understanding public administration in the governance era. It begins by undertaking a thorough discussion of the idea of governance in Chapter Six—its historical and theoretical roots, and the various conceptualisations around the concept. Chapter Seven is a conceptual exploration into public policy, the core of public administration as an exercise. The following chapter, Chapter Eight, is aimed at understanding the nature of public policy in India with reference to some of the preeminent policies which have had a visible impact in the long-term. Chapter Nine is about the genuine concern that has gripped public attention to a significant extent—ethics in governance. Apart from dwelling on certain relevant conceptual points, the chapter elaborates how ethics became integral to Indian public administration. Following this is Chapter Ten, which is a discussion on locating citizens in governance and the role of civil society under the changed circumstances. One of the distinctive outcomes of public administration being conceptualised in the governance paradigm is the insistence of devolution of power to avoid the rise and consolidation of a rent-seeking bureaucracy. Hence the final chapter of this book, Chapter Eleven, concentrates on local governance that has a long legacy in India. Apart from providing a detailed discussion of the unique features of local governance in India, this chapter is also an elaboration of those processes towards democratising administration by involving people at the grassroots which received significant boost with the adoption of the 73rd and 74th Amendment Acts in 1992. This is also a chapter that shows how a constitutional design which was not justiciable in the immediate past in India became an instrument of empowerment as far as the peripheral sections of the population are concerned. In effect, this section reiterates that the Indian experience provides useful inputs to conceptualise changes in administration for other similar socio-economic milieu.

* * *

VII

This book is a text with a difference as visible in its structure: despite being sensitive to the conventional ideas which classical thinkers of public administration propounded, the book has couched the entire discussion around a conceptual format seeking to comprehend the discipline with reference to the prevalent socio-economic context. At one level, it provides an analytical account of the conceptual parameters that are derived from the classical texts of public administration; on another, perhaps far more critical level, this text is also a serious effort towards building conceptual models by drawing on those inputs which receive less attention, both among academics and practitioners, largely due to the hegemonic intellectual presence of Western conceptual designs. In view of the domineering Western influence, the non-Western endeavours have hardly provoked interest thus far. This book is a modest attempt at exploring public administration as a field of activity with reference to India where several kinds of experiments are being made to identify the inherent weaknesses of the classical models for being totally alien to her distinct socio-economic and political predilections. Fundamental here is the idea that, given its context-specific nature and texture, public administration can never be conceptualised in a derivative analytical format. Intrigued by futile efforts of creating universal models of public administration, Robert Dahl argued that '[i]n an attempt to make the study of public administration analogous to the natural sciences, the laws or putative laws are stripped of normative values, of the distortions cause by the incorrigible individual psyche, and of the presumably irrelevant effects of the cultural environment' (1947: 1). Unable to be persuaded by the endeavour seeking to conceptualise universal models of analysis in public administration, he further exposed the weaknesses of the argument by suggesting that there cannot be universal models since public administration has specific 'moral and political ends [and is dependent also on] the nonconformist personality of the individual and the social and cultural setting as well' (ibid.). This is the fundamental point that the book pursues by highlighting the importance of the prevalent socio-cultural milieu in conceptualising public administration as context-specific activity. Hence it can be safely conceptualised that the theoretical generalisations derived from the operation of public administration in a specific socio-economic and cultural milieu cannot be universalised and made applicable to public administration in a different context. As the book also draws on debates regarding the feasibility of derivative models devising universal principles of public administration, it has grown beyond a textbook which is usually confined to the elaboration and occasional interpretation of those major conceptual categories derived from the available treatises of public administration. *Public Administration: From Government to Governance* is, therefore, both a review of classical theories and also an attempt to provide theoretical cues to conceptualise public administration as a situation-specific exercise in contrast to those so-called axiomatic theoretical conceptualisations derived from Western experiences.

REFERENCES

Ambedkar, B. R. [2003]. 'Address in the Constituent Assembly, 25 November 1949'. *Constituent Assembly Debates*, Book 5. New Delhi: Lok Sabha Secretariat.

Beetham, David. 1985. *Max Weber and the Theory of Modern Politics*. Cambridge: Polity Press.

Bevir, Mark. 2012. *Governance: A Very Short Introduction*. New York: Oxford University Press.

Brass, Paul R. 2000. 'Foucault Steals Political Science'. *Annual Review of Political Science* 3: 305–30.

Dahl, Robert A. 1947. 'The Science of Public Administration: Three Problems'. *Public Administration Review* 7 (1): 1–11.

Frederickson, H. George. 1999. 'The Repositioning of American Public Administration: The 1999 John Gaus Lecture', *PS: Political Science and Politics* 32 (4): 701–12.

Kettl, Donald F. 2000. 'The Transformation of Governance: Globalization, Devolution and the Role of Government'. Unpublished discussion paper prepared for Spring Meeting of the National Academy of Public Administration, 1–3 June.

Kirlin, John J. 1996. 'The Big Questions of Public Administration in a Democracy'. *Public Administration Review* 56 (5): 211–19.

Leftwich, Adrian. 1996. 'On the Primacy of Politics in Development' in *Democracy and Development: Theory and Practice*, edited by Adrian Leftwich, 3–24. Cambridge: Polity Press.

Penttinen, Elina. 2000. 'Capitalism as a System of Global Power' in *Power in Contemporary Politics: Theories, Practices, Globalizations*, edited by Henri Goverde, Philip G. Cerny, Mark Haugaard and Howard Lentner, 205–20. London: Sage Publications.

Rosser, Christian. 2010. 'Woodrow Wilson's Administrative Thought and German Political Theory'. *Public Administration Review* 74 (4): 547–56.

Sager, Fritz and Christian Rosser. 2009. 'Weber, Wilson and Hegel: Theories of Modern Bureaucracy'. *Public Administration Review* 69 (6): 1136–47.

Salskov-Iversen, Dorte, Hans Krause Hansen and Sven Bislev. 2000. 'Governmentality, Globalization and Local Practice: Transformation of a Hegemonic Discourse'. *Alternatives: Social Transformation and Humane Governance* 25 (2): 183–222.

Stillman II, Richard J. 1973. 'Woodrow Wilson and the Study of Administration: A New Look at an Old Essay', *The American Political Science Review* 67 (2): 582–88

Stivers, Camilla. 2008. 'The Significance of *The Administrative State*'. *Public Administration Review* 68 (1): 53–56.

Tarschys, Daniel. 2001. 'Wealth, Values, Institutions: Trends in Government and Governance' in *Governance in the 21st Century: Future Studies*. Paris: Organisation for Economic Co-operation and Development (OECD).

Waldo, Dwight. 1980. *The Enterprise of Public Administration: A Summary View*. California: Chandler & Sharp.

Weber, Max. 1905/1930. *The Protest Ethic and the Spirit of Capitalism*. London and Boston: Unwin Hyman.

———. 1996. 'Bureaucracy' in *Public Administration: Concepts and Cases*, edited by Richard J. Stillman II, 58–66. Boston: Houghton Mifflin Company.

Wilson, Woodrow. [1969]. *The Papers of Woodrow Wilson, 1890–1892*, vol. 7, edited by Arthur S. Link. Princeton, N.J.: Princeton University Press.

———. 1887/1996. 'The Study of Public Administration'. *Political Science Quarterly* 2 (June): 197–222. Reproduced in *Public Administration*, edited by Richard J. Stillman II.

SECTION A

CHANGING DISCOURSES IN PUBLIC ADMINISTRATION

Public administration is a unique blend of an area of enquiry and a context-driven practice: the former makes no sense unless it is linked with the latter. Implicit here is the conceptual claim that public administration, as an academic discipline, needs to be re-invented. Else, it will cease to become an intellectually vibrant academic tool of analysis. Fundamental here is the assumption that since public administration is an analytical statement of lived experience it has to rearticulate its conceptual underpinning to remain viable in the family of the social sciences. The task is undoubtedly difficult, because no study of governance can be analytically persuasive if it is insulated from the contextual compulsions that human beings confront while charting a specific course of action for their wellbeing. The suffix 'public' is illustrative of the types of functions that are integral to public administration which the presently fashionable expression 'governance' may not approximate, presumably because of its inherent conceptual limitations due to its origin in a globalising world, appreciative of neo-liberal ethics. In Section C, a detailed discussion of governance as a concept seeking to redefine public administration will be undertaken. The point that is relevant here relates to conceptual weaknesses of the concept of governance largely emerging out of its concern for efficiency, effectiveness and entrepreneurial spirit. If governance is conceptualised in an ideal socio-economic condition, these aims do not appear to be problematic at all; the difficulty arises as soon as one draws attention to the fact that public administration is meant to serve the public. Can that be compromised if it is efficient, effective and entrepreneurial in spirit? Opinions vary though it is a matter of common sense that public administration cannot avoid being insensitive to the public interests only for the sake of fulfilling the mechanically-devised and also ideologically-tilted objectives. Nonetheless, the recently-constructed idea of governance is theoretically useful to capture a new perspective in the context of globalisation in which public administration is sought to be understood in a different fashion.

The aim of this section is to test the hypothesis that public administration is constantly evolving to keep pace with the context that hardly remains static. By seeking to conceptualise public administration in terms of the text–context dialectic, the section focuses on the theme with reference to the processes leading to the evolution of public administration, both as an area of activity and a discipline in India since the early part of the twentieth century. This historical trajectory is useful to understand how the discipline changes in response to the rapidly transforming socio-economic context in which public administration as an area of activity is located. Confirming that conceptual tools need to be constantly reinvented, this section will provide an analytical account of the historical trajectory of the discipline, both as an activity and a conceptual parameter in India. As will be discussed, the growth and evolution of the discipline also reveals how, over a period of time, the practitioners and analysts complement each other in the development of conceptual tools that are not only context-relevant but also ideologically appropriate. The section will then delve into a specific chapter in the history of the evolution of public administration that had begun unfolding with the First Minnowbrook Conference in 1968. So far, there have been three conferences, with the last one being held in 2008. By their distinctive contribution to the evolution of the discipline as a practice, these conferences remain significant in the history of public administration. The Minnowbrook Conferences represent a clear break with the past when public administration was just instrumental in its approach and goal; there were hardly any references to a conceptualisation of public administration as a process. The Weberian hold on governance seems to have been dominant while the competing theoretical paradigms were never considered worthwhile in efforts towards building an alternative conceptual fabric. The 1968 Minnowbrook Conference broke the ice and public administration was sought to be conceptualised differently since the Weberian formula did not seem useful to understand the rapidly changing nature of governance in the context of radical socio-economic movements. This was not exceptional to the first Minnowbrook Conference. The trend continued in the two Minnowbrook Conferences that took place in 1988 and 2008 as well.

1

TRAJECTORY OF PUBLIC ADMINISTRATION AS A DISCIPLINE IN INDIA*

HIGHLIGHTS

- Nature of the discipline
- Evolution of the discipline
- Changing stances within the discipline

Public administration is a context-driven response to problems confronting a specific society. Hence it would be conceptually misleading to argue for a universal design for public administration. The basic problem that appears to have impeded creative thinking in this area of human inquiry is linked to our uncritical dependence on models/theoretical paradigms which are rooted in the Western experience. Given the obvious limitations of such thinking, it is but inevitable that the peculiar nature of public administration in the non-Western hemisphere remains elusive or is sought to be defined in a very mechanical manner avoiding the real challenge in conceptualising the phenomenon in a specific perspective. This is a serious problem of our syllabi in public administration in most Indian universities. By choosing a relatively easy option, the academia responsible for teaching and transmission of knowledge seems to have stayed away from difficult questions concerning the unique evolutionary trajectory and nature of public administration in India. There is, however, emerging a new group in the academia which is involved in efforts at re-conceptualising public administration keeping in view its peculiar contextual nature. In such an endeavour, one cannot entirely be oblivious of the Western tradition and its theoretical value in helping us understand public administration in its most complex forms; by underlining the contextual nature of public administration, we are simply trying to argue that the one-size-fits-all approach does not appear to be a meaningful theoretical formula in so far as public administration is concerned.

* This chapter has been developed from Bidyut Chakrabarty, 'The Study of Public Administration in India: A Chequered Journey (?)', *Indian Journal of Public Administration* 60.1 (2014): 1–18. With permission from Indian Institute of Public Administration (IIPA), New Delhi.

There is a related point here that has a universal manifestation even to the extent of taking away the basic thrust of public administration by underplaying the importance of 'public' in public administration. With the acceptance of the World Bank (WB) engineered 'governance' to articulate public administration, 'public administration' has perhaps received a serious jolt since it was formally conceptualised in the seminal 1887 article by Woodrow Wilson. Public administration is not merely a goal- and process-oriented act, it has also a well-defined purpose of serving 'the public'—that cannot be captured by governance which focuses exclusively on (*a*) goal and (*b*) process, and remains completely silent about the purpose of the public authority. There is thus a clear 'disconnect' between the instrument and the target group. In contemporary studies of public administration, efforts have already been undertaken to highlight this serious lacuna in our effort at approximating to the WB guidelines; a theoretical search has already begun to unravel the theoretical limitations of the governance discourse which, by seeking to take away the publicness of public administration, is a serious source of concern. Despite the obvious discomfort that the governance discourse has caused, there is no denying the fact that it has provoked a well-informed debate among those responsible for teaching and research in public administration. Syllabi in universities have taken into account the debate that appears to have reconfirmed the viability of some of the major theoretical tools of 'traditional' public administration.

Major Arguments

1. Public administration is a contextual discipline and one should be sensitive of this to develop a meaningful theoretical design.
2. Public administrative is a purpose-oriented exercise, and the effort to delink public administration from the public is theoretically misleading and intellectually myopic.

Supplementary Arguments

1. Unlike other disciplines in the social sciences, public administration is a practice-driven endeavour in which the role of politics is also evidently significant that cannot be wished away.
2. In the context of the rise and consolidation of a 'networked society' (or global village, as some commentators prefer to argue), a scientific study of public administration is possible once this dimension of a globalising world is appropriately captured and analysed.

NATURE OF THE DISCIPLINE

Public administration is an orphan discipline in India since it has not been properly mentored by academicians who are otherwise keen to pursue their interests in other areas of social sciences. Prominent among the factors responsible for this is the lack of keenness to explore public administration as an organic discipline capable of persuasively explaining its pecularity in India. In order to understand the complex nature of India's system of governance, it is incumbent on the analyst to adequately grasp the context in which it has evolved. Besides the prevalent social, economic, political and institutional contexts, one needs to be sensitive to the colonial influences simply because they continue to remain critical to decision-making in public administration. The task is gigantic, but not insurmountable because it involves (*a*) an appropriate dissection of the context and (*b*) an anchorage in the broader social science interactional field. Once this is taken care of, one is likely to evolve meaningful theories and concepts enabling analysts to understand and explain the nature of Indian administration in a special socio-economic milieu.

The point that is made here is about the obvious methodological difficulty in comprehending an area of enquiry that one confronts while making a serious endeavour. Before we embark on what is needed to develop a meaningful methodological package, a discussion about the root causes of our failure in this respect is in order: of all the restraining factors, prominent among them is a blind imitation of the Western conceptualisation while seeking to understand our public administration. By being clearly Weberian in their perception, analysts tend to ignore the contextual influences shaping governance. Besides undermining the factors contributing to the peculiar nature of public administration, this sort of approach is intellectually limiting and hence shall not be adequate to serve our purpose of understanding the context-driven peculiarities of the system of administration. Now the scene appears to be changing, with the rise and consolidation of a group of analysts questioning the uncritical dependence on Western models through a fierce critique of the derivative wisdom from sources that are not organically linked with our reality. The intellectual discomfort over methodological bankruptcy is supplemented by efforts at building models by adequately emphasising the prevalent socio-economic circumstances. One notices such a change since the 1970s when a highly inspired group of scholars, affiliated with universities and institutes of social sciences all over the country, undertook serious research on the intricate issues of the functioning of public administration in specific contexts. In two significant ways, these endeavours were different from the past: in view of the critical importance of the context, it was strongly felt, on the one hand, that the interdisciplinary borrowing was an aid to grasp and conceptualise the unique nature of Indian public administration that was rooted in colonialism; and, on the other hand, since public administration is praxis in nature, one had to be sensitive of the contextual reality that remained a distinct influence in its actual shape. One had to, of course, guard against vulgar empiricism, and it was thus stressed that empirical research needed to be theoretically well-informed to avoid conceptual limitations linked with excessive dependence on empirical facts. This led to a remarkable change in our approach to public administration as an organic reality which, given its contextual roots, was historically-conceived and determined.

As the above discussion reveals, the search that had begun following the intellectual unease resulted in re-conceptualising some of the methodological tools that were being used to analyse the nature of public administration in India. The discipline was less analytical and was confined to mere descriptive studies of governmental institutions without paying attention to their historico-social roots. There was no dearth of research, though the outcomes were mere reproduction of easily available facts. Following the challenges in the 1970s, the weaknesses of such enterprises were exposed. In this sense, this was a watershed in the evolution of public administration as a discipline in India. Two important points came out of such an endeavour: first, public administration was not merely a part of institutionalised forms of governance, it was also integral to the processes that informed its nature of functioning; second, since public administration is enmeshed in complex social, economic and political processes, the analyst is required to have an interdisciplinary grounding, else the discussion was likely to be less persuasive and intellectually less challenging.

How was the methodological limitation sought to be grappled? A scan of the literature that came out in the 1970s confirms that analysts addressed the issues by undertaking empirical researches on the basis of the interconnectivity of the areas of concern. In other words, it had dawned on those keen to unravel the mystique of Indian public administration that to remain in the reckoning the discipline needed rigour and depth; otherwise, it would lose its academic credibility in no time. Moreover, it was also strongly felt that by focusing merely on bureaucracy, contemporary researches were highly claustrophobic in character since institution-driven studies usually lacked the depth that was expected of enquiries in the social sciences. In order to make the study of bureaucracy intellectually challenging and theoretically innovative, one has to understand bureaucracy in the wider social canvas which shape, if not determine, its actual nature in practice. Unless one is drawn to this, our understanding shall be anything but complete. What is argued here is the fact that without grasping the contextual roots of public administration no study will be worthwhile since it is devoid of those provocative questions that carry forward further research in the field.

What was the outcome of our sustained endeavour in exposing the limitations of the discipline of public administration, as it was conceptualised in the past? The challenge led to a relook at the way public administration was taught in universities. Given the obvious weaknesses of descriptive studies, serious efforts were made at various kinds of conceptualisations critiquing the uncritical applicability of what we derived from Western sources. This was evident in contemporary literature. It was a different kind of public administration which now talked about its nature as a practice-driven exercise which means that the discipline had an ideological character. One can argue here that perhaps the influence of the First Minnowbrook Conference of 1968, which clearly defended that public administration cannot be but ideological by redefining its nomenclature as New Public Administration, was visible in these endeavours. In light of the Minnowbrook tradition, Indian scholars strongly argued for public administration with a clear ideological tilt which was sought to be captured by following interdisciplinary methodologies. Less catholic in their approaches, this new breed of scholars were favourably inclined towards borrowing methodologies from other disciplines in the social sciences in order to appropriately understand public administration that was being constantly reinvented.

BEGINNING OF THE JOURNEY

As a discipline, public administration did not receive scholarly attention at the outset, presumably because it hardly had takers in the academia though students were taught some of the theories of administration as part of political science courses. So, it had a silent beginning. Since it was part of political science, the discipline was always conceptualised as integral to political science. As a result, it had the same weaknesses that Dwight Waldo had referred to in his address before the 1968 Minnowbrook Conference: 'neither the study nor the practice of public administration is responding in an appropriate measure to the mounting turbulence and critical problems of the day' (1971: 7). This is perhaps the most apt description of the discipline of public administration in Indian universities and other academic institutions where the issues of public administration usually receive serious attention. While academicians do not seem to be zealous in pursuing serious research in the discipline, the Government of India is far more enthusiastic, as evident in the growing number of reports on administration which are produced to address issues of governance and administration. There is a mismatch between the academic zeal and governmental enthusiasm in comprehending administrative malice and its possible solution. This mismatch also reveals that there exists a schism between government bureaucracy and the academicians seeking to understand its functioning. What is also striking is the absence of dialogue between these two stakeholders who do not seem to have appreciated the value of mutual borrowing of concepts, theoretical tools and descriptive details despite the obvious advantages of this dialogical interaction. Nonetheless, it can safely be argued that the governmental reports on vital issues of public administration always remain an important source of conceptualisation and theoretical enrichment. In that sense, they are useful and intellectually provocative. The story narrating the evolution and gradual consolidation of public administration as a discipline thus cannot be complete without taking into account the importance of government reports in grasping issues in Indian administration.

EVOLUTION OF THE DISCIPLINE

Till 1937, Indian universities did not appear to be welcoming public administration as a separate discipline. The ice was broken with the decision by the University of Madras to offer a diploma in public administration from within the department of political science. Within a year, in 1938, University of Allahabad also formalised a course on self-government. In the course of four years since the appearance of public administration as an independent discipline four major Indian universities—University of Lucknow, Patna University, Osmania University and Aligarh Muslim University—began offering diploma in public administration. As is evident, these initiatives represented a watershed in the study of the discipline which has now gained an independent status in the social sciences. Given its intimate linkages with political science, public administration was, at the outset, usually considered integral to political science, and, as a result, the courses in the discipline were generally structured around the institutions of governance, primarily local governance. The jinx was broken in 1949 when Nagpur University established a full-fledged department of public administration independent of the department of political science. It was a remarkable development, especially when the discipline was still embryonic in its approach and methodologies. Nonetheless, the scholars, keen to unravel the dynamics of public administration as a separate discipline, believed that training in public administration, besides imparting knowledge about the intricacies of governance, would also equip the students to stand out in the competition for jobs in the government and private sectors. In 1954, at the insistence of the American scholar Paul Appleby, the Indian Institute of Public Administration (IIPA) was founded in Delhi. This was another watershed moment in so far as the study of public administration was concerned. Now, the IIPA was charged with the responsibility of training and keeping abreast Indian civil servants of different seniorities in the art and theoretical tools of administration. Appleby was also instrumental in creating separate public administration departments in the universities of Jaipur and Chandigarh in 1956. Over time, under the influence of these major initiatives, several universities in the country began including courses in public administration at the undergraduate and postgraduate levels. Today, most major universities in India offer courses in public administration. A major boost came in 1987 when public administration was included as an integral part of the syllabus for the all-India Civil Services Examination conducted by the Union Public Service Commission (UPSC) which is responsible for recruitment to the elite Indian Administrative Service (IAS) and other allied central services. The linking of the discipline with job-related tests created an instantaneous demand of teaching in various universities. It was therefore not surprising that following the inclusion of public administration in the syllabus for competitive examinations for jobs by the UPSC and State Public Service Commissions, the discipline gained immense popularity in universities across the country.

The trajectory of public administration as a discipline, especially post-Independence, shows that it has grown in India under the patronage and academic supervision of Appleby, who was invited by India's first prime minister Jawaharlal Nehru, following the transfer of power in 1947. It was Appleby who strongly felt the need for professionalisation in governance which was possible with proper training and tutelage. His main concern was to make administration efficient. As he argued,

> [t]he general idea is that professionalization of public administration should be advanced in order to encourage more widespread and conscious study, reflection and exchange of learning and to establish certain instruments charged with special responsibility for administrative improvement in terms not adequately covered at present. (Appleby 1953: 62)

This insistence on 'efficiency' as the main goal of administration seems to have set the tempo for the study of public administration in India. Conceptualising public administration as a technical instrument for fulfilling predesigned objectives, in a typically Weberian way, Appleby sought to create an all-pervasive bureaucracy responsible for attaining goals which remained integral to socio-economic reconstruction through State intervention. From the point of view of the State, it was most efficient because the instrument was geared to the goal; whether the instrument was effective in India's specific socio-economic milieu was the question that remained unanswered in Appleby's scheme of things. Given the uncritical acceptance of Appleby's arguments, there had been a tendency to ignore the broader social science considerations in discussions on administrative problems. One of the reasons for the poverty of the study of public administration has been, Mohit Bhattacharya argues,

> its narrow practical concerns and avoidance of broader social science theorizing in allied disciplines such as Sociology, Political Science, Economics and History [and, as a result, the discipline] has busied itself with practical action intended to repair and reinvigorate administration without caring for an adequate understanding of the context and environmental conditions of such action. (1997: 67)

Public administration has thus become 'vocationalised' in which the macro-level social, economic and political concerns remain insignificant. The discipline is thus assessed on the basis of how efficient it is as a problem-solving device. It is therefore not surprising that institutes of public administration prefer technicians to those well-grounded in the discipline. This is evident from the recruitment of more and more 'technicians in public administration institutes such as computer analysts, engineers, financial and budgeting experts' (ibid.: 66).

Vocationalisation is client-oriented, which means that the discipline needs to take care of the interests of the clients irrespective of the impact it has on the core of the discipline. Given the growing importance of technicians, the discipline is sought to be designed in accordance with the needs of the client and ignoring the wider social canvas in which administration has roots. Its impact on the growth of the discipline is devastating because not only will it divert attention away from the broader socio-economic and political issues, it will also make the discipline more and more technical by taking away perhaps its kernel in the long run. The concern does not seem to be unfounded. As is evident now, several departments of public administration in various universities offer training programmes for those taking competitive examinations. This is most disheartening because public administration is reduced to a training-driven exercise in which the disciplinary concerns appear to have been undermined, if not seriously challenged, in contemporary India. Excessive emphasis on the technical aspect of administration will not only take away its core, it will also deprive public administration of its distinctive claim of being a praxis-discipline if the zeal for making it an instrument of technical efficiency in administration is not halted.

What are the problem areas in the study of public administration in India? The answer to this question is linked to the nature of the discipline which continues to remain intellectually crippled because of its failure to carve out a specific domain of query for reasons connected with its growth as a discipline in the family of the social sciences. In other words, in view of the inherent weaknesses associated with its evolution in India, public administration never became an effective aid to understand India's administrative reality since it did not pay adequate attention to the socio-economic environment in which it was located. This is a serious methodological lacuna which is usually explained as inevitable because of the efforts at conceptualising public administration in isolation. The other important area of concern is the absence of discussion of larger issues that impinge on the nature of administration. As a tool of analysis, public administration appears to have failed because of inherent weaknesses. In order to become analytically meaningful, public administration needs to be understood with reference to the nature of the State, the specific administrative history, the constitutional structure and form of government, the political processes and social structure. These are influences which are enmeshed in the context and public administration is required to take them into account to sustain its viability not merely in the domain of societal problems but also in the field of knowledge generation. As a result of the disconnect between the socio-politically distinctive reality and administration, the discipline has ceased being organic in character, which accounts for its inability to comprehend the nature of public administration in a postcolonial context. What is most disappointing is the neglect of the dialectic that always exists between text and context. In view of their uncritical acceptance of the Western paradigm in framing university syllabi, the experts appear to have pursued a line of thinking which clearly takes out the dynamism within the discipline. Attempts are now being made to address these weaknesses, though hegemonic Western influences cannot be so easily dispensed with for obvious historical reasons. Along with major theoretical constraints due to a favourable tilt towards Western ideas and concepts, there is also the debilitating factor stemming from the effort at reducing public administration to mere technical skills justifying the need to create more institutes of public administration.

Nonetheless, the study of public administration continues to flourish in India. What had begun in 1937 with the offering of a diploma appears to have become a permanent fixture in contemporary universities across the country, as is evident in a survey conducted in 2005–06.[1] On the basis of responses procured through structured questionnaires that were administered to the stakeholders, it is evident that the discipline continues to remain handicapped because of the deficiencies which were never addressed conclusively. The survey confirms that the discipline failed to create an independent space in the field of social sciences and it has become, alas, a discipline in bondage for three important reasons. First, the majority of weaknesses in public administration in India stem from the ethnocentric bias of American and European scholarship. So long as this remains, it will never be possible for the discipline to evolve as a persuasive explanatory area of enquiry. Second, the overzealous endeavour at making public administration an instrumental and goal-driven technical exercise has taken out the dynamism of the discipline as an organic search for administrative solutions for socio-economic problems in the country. The discipline is reduced to efforts at building specific skills which are required to address identified problems without recognising their socio-economic and political roots. Finally, taken together, these factors have contributed to the emergence of a comprador discipline which is neither capable of an independent response nor equipped to take a call on the issue of contemporary administrative ills. The inevitable outcome is thus a clear distortion in the evolution and nature of the discipline which fails to become a respectable area of enquiry in

[1] The reports of the survey are available Rao (2011).

the social sciences. In other words, ridden with intellectual deficiencies, public administration, despite being integral to university syllabi, remains handicapped for reasons connected with 'the intellectual bankruptcy' of the endeavours which were otherwise serious and well-meaning at evolving the discipline.

The aforementioned survey findings reinforce the assumptions that have already been made to explain the sorry state of public administration as a discipline. Are these teething problems, or are they linked with the lack of ability to pursue the queries with rigour and finesse which is usually the case in the other social science disciplines? There is no doubt that the discipline has suffered on both these counts: while it failed to attract the best minds in the country for reasons connected with its nature of being less provocative as a field of enquiry, it was also not distinct in terms of either methodological rigour or conceptual depth. What is striking is the fact that though there was a clear dearth of serious scholars in the field, some of the major areas of concern of public administration attracted scholars from other fields. For instance, historians, sociologists, political scientists and administrators have made significant contributions to unravelling the complex nature of India's public administration. These works are very useful for research, for example, in local government, the changing nature of Indian bureaucracy and the impact of political structure on governance.[2] This is not an argument to defend the urge of being boundary-conscious, which is absurd in the context of appreciation for interdisciplinary borrowing. The point that is made is about the limited appeal of what was pursued within the disciplinary focus of public administration by those being trained in the discipline. It is not difficult to locate the root cause of its declining importance given the obvious limitations that the discipline was never equipped to overcome. As a result, those with training in public administration shied away from areas other than the study of the institutions which is less challenging than studying the processes shaping the institutions in juxtaposition with their competing counterparts in extremely volatile social, economic and political circumstances. The trend towards the uncritical study of institutions seemed to have gained support and was not discouraged.

CHANGING STANCES

Since the 1980s, there have been efforts at re-conceptualising public administration, especially by those associated with universities in India. A shift to the areas of research which were no longer confined to the institutional studies of public administration was noticeable. It was strongly felt that in order to understand the institutions of governance, one needs to comprehend the prevalent socio-economic milieu; otherwise, it would be a futile exercise. Public administration is not merely institution-driven, as the argument goes, but also a process-sensitive endeavour for understanding and meaningfully addressing societal problems which are seen to have had

[2] There are plenty of books/texts that can be referred to. Prominent among them are Mishra (1977), Potter (1996), Mason (1997) and Bomball (1978).

their roots in the administration. This is a complex task for which one needs to be receptive to the tools of analysis, developed in other disciplines in the social sciences. So the effort that was undertaken in the 1980s also led to meaningful interdisciplinary borrowing which was not encouraged so zealously in the past.

A new era had dawned in the study of public administration as a discipline which, by stepping out of its orthodox/conventional mould now, sought to create an independent space in the social sciences. It is therefore surprising that new areas of research received far more critical attention than in the past. This was also reflected in the university syllabi and in the syllabi of public administration for various competitive examinations both at the national and state levels. The 1980s was a turning point in the study of public administration though one cannot designate the era as a break with the past. The studies that were undertaken then were far more analytical than mere structural descriptions of the institutions. It was felt that the study of institutions remained incomplete without judging them in the specific Indian politico-administrative and socio-economic context. This was undoubtedly a revolutionary change that radically altered the approach to the study of public administration with reference to the cobwebs of socio-economic and political processes. Administration is not merely an instrument, but a process-driven exercise which requires a thorough study of the context in which it is located and flourishes. In this sense, administration is a lived experience which can be captured by being sensitive to the existent socio-political reality shaping, if not determining, its actual manifestation. What is most critical in the entire exercise is to understand the contextual peculiarities of public administration for which the disciplinary orthodoxies of the past need to be shunted out. It is evident in the growing interest in areas of concern which were never considered pertinent in exploring the public administration either as an activity or a process. Because of constraint of space, it will be difficult to provide an exhaustive list of these issues. Hence I shall selectively identify those issues for discussion which have attracted serious scholarly attention. Furthermore, these issues are also critical because they remain significant in the making of syllabi in universities, which means that public administration as a discipline is receptive to new ideas which have already been tested by rigorous intellectual probing by academicians and researchers. Since this chapter is about the study of public administration in India, we have focused on those issues which have a clear bearing on the Indian social, economic and political contexts. This is not to suggest, however, that they are exclusively India-centric; instead, the argument hinges on issues which are reflective of the interdependent nature of the problems and their solution in a networked society. What is striking in the study of public administration in India is also the fact that while preparing the syllabi for regular courses in public administration, university departments seem to have been guided by governmental initiatives in the field of administration. It is thus not surprising that a significant part of the list of topics that are taught draws on the government reports which are always useful in conceptualising administration as organically linked with the socio-economic circumstances. Given the pedagogical limitation of the study of public administration in the confines of classrooms, several universities have made field trips to government offices and other places. Along with the focus on the issues that are raised in government reports, the other important source of inputs for university syllabi, at least in their contemporary articulation, happens to be the specific global intervention seeking to provide a university design, especially following the collapse of the former Soviet Union and the consequent rise of the hegemonic neo-liberal approach to public administration.

One of the penetrating concepts in today's discussion of public administration is governance, which is not synonymous with the mere act of governing but is an ideological ploy to universalise the neo-liberal model of government functioning. Governance as a model of public administration cannot be understood without reference to the context in which it has been conceptualised. There is no doubt that globalisation provides significant inputs to its epistemological articulation. Public administration has basically been an inward looking discipline concerned with the management of a country's domestic public affairs. It has now woken up to the need for focusing on the pulls and pressures of the on-going processes of globalisation and their impact on domestic administrative management. Since then, the search has been on how to reinvent or reposition the discipline in the context of a newly emergent world order. Public administration thus now represents 'a decisive move away from direct provision by government agencies and their employees—the standard bureau model of the past' (Lyer, Heinrich and Hill 2001: 1).

Several efforts were undertaken by the government to arrest the drift in civil service that had ceased being civil. The purpose was to transform an aloof, impersonal, paternalistic bureaucracy into one which was to be citizen-friendly and sensitive to user-needs. The government of India had appointed two Administration Reforms Commissions in 1966 and 2005, respectively. Their recommendations have had a revolutionary effect on administration. One of the important consequences of these recommendations happens to be the effort to shift our attention away from the steel frame of bureaucracy to other agencies which are equally crucial in public service, but have not been formally recognised thus far. In this sense, it has also set in motion a powerful critique of Weberian bureaucracy that is strictly hierarchical and largely status-quoist. By recognising the importance of civil society organisations in public administration, these Commissions provide a formal recognition to cooperation between the bureaucracy and these organisations. In the past such cooperation was discouraged, presumably because of the sanctity of the governmental domain in which the bureaucracy appears to be the only legitimate agency in discharging responsibilities on behalf of the State. Underlining the importance of these agencies not exactly linked with the government and its peripheral organisations, has not only redefined Indian bureaucracy but also expanded its sphere of influence.

In light of a general degradation of public administration, the importance of ethics in governance has acquired a significant place in contemporary theoretical discussion more so because of the growing decadence in governmental practices owing largely to a decline of ethical values in public administration, which is perhaps singularly responsible for the rise of 'corruption' in a virulent form. The possible reason is located in the overgrowth of the State in which bureaucracy has become 'rent-seeker', ignoring its Benthamite role of being 'a benevolent guardian'. The WB-sponsored solution is to downsize the State and allow free play of the market and civil society—consolidating the ideology of neo-liberalism. Whether this is an appropriate strategy for developing and underdeveloped nations is a challenging question that needs to be addressed keeping in view the importance of 'public' in public administration. This is a challenge that involves a thorough analysis of the circumstances and the outcome in a historical context because dwindling of ethics in governance is not an overnight phenomenon but an offshoot of a long-term process. As a sequel to the recommendation of the 1964 Santhanam Committee, which was appointed to address the issue of corruption in administration, the Government of India (GoI) introduced a series of institutional measures to arrest administrative corruption. As a result, several new institutions solely responsible for combating corruption were created: of them, the most important being the Central Bureau of Investigation (CBI), the Comptroller and Auditor General (CAG) and the Central Vigilance Commission (CVC). Besides these major institutions, the zeal to fight corruption in public life also led to the enactment of the Right to Information Act in 2005 which allows citizens access to government information. It was also reiterated in the 2005 Second Administrative Reforms Commission report: 'in our case, at times public office is perceived to be an extension of one's property. That is why sometimes, public offices are a source of huge corruption and a means of extending patronage' (GoI 2007: 6). The Commission was thus asked to suggest measures to achieve a 'proactive, responsive, accountable, sustainable and efficient administration for the country at all levels of the government' (ibid.: 11). What is striking about these Commissions is the fact that they have provoked a fierce debate on the nature of public administration, which cannot afford to be insensitive to the needs of the public in the context of the rising importance of rights-conscious citizens in India.

As in the case of the above-mentioned Commissions, the 73rd and 74th Amendment Acts of 1992 remain two revolutionary measures in local self-government that set in motion a new conceptual framework of public administration. While the former deals with local government in rural areas, the latter is a specific step to meaningfully implement the ideas of democratic decentralisation in so far as urban governance is concerned. Besides directing significant structural changes in the institutional set of governance at the respective levels of administration, the 73rd Amendment is remarkable for having recommended reservation of one-third seats for women in the panchayats, which is revolutionary for having provided a feminist perspective to public administration in India. By making the institution of local governance through direct election mandatory, these legal enactments created an environment in which local government no longer remained a personal fiefdom of the vested interests in rural and urban areas. These are efforts at meaningfully articulating devolution of power. In other words, by making the stakeholders integral to local governments, these amendments, besides translating democratic decentralisation in practice, have also contributed to refashioning the syllabi in public administration as a discipline that appears to have lost its momentum by being sterile to the rapidly changing public administration in India. What is fundamental here is the effort at re-conceptualising public administration as an outcome of the lived experience of the people in specific socio-economic and political contexts.

The above discussion is important to reinforce the argument that the study of public administration in India draws heavily upon government initiatives that have always set in motion new thinking on administration. It would not be an exaggeration to suggest that the discipline would have been handicapped without these significant government interventions. A scan of the syllabi of public administration in major universities in India confirms this: a large chunk of topics that need to be studied while pursuing courses in the discipline comes from governmental practices and reports that are prepared on the basis of thorough study of the processes of governance at various levels of administration. Is this indicative of the disciplinary weaknesses of public administration? This can be an issue of debate, but it cannot be conclusively substantiated given the well-established nature of public administration as a praxis discipline, the core of which is a creative blending of theory and practice. It is perfectly possible that these reports lack solid theoretical basis, and are largely in the problem-solving mould. So a study that is dependent on these efforts which are generally technical in nature will reduce the discipline to a mere technical exercise. This is usually the argument that is made in most syllabi-framing meetings in Indian universities, undermining the organic character of public administration as a field of social science enquiry. The major weakness of this argument stems from the fact that public administration, unlike other disciplines in the social sciences, is practice-driven. Unless students are made aware of the actual functioning of administration, much of the fun studying public administration shall be compromised to the detriment of its basic organic nature and inherent ability, largely un-utilised or under-utilised, in conceptualising governance in specific historical perspectives. In fact, such a visible disconnect with reality weakens the discipline of public administration which is not merely a theoretical exercise, but also a goal-driven design of action. Dissociation with the context in which public administration is located does not seem to be epistemologically appropriate for obvious reasons. In that sense, governmental initiatives and reports remain critical in comprehending public administration as a practical endeavour, and useful in developing a theoretical framework and conceptual tools for pedagogical purposes.

So in the development of public administration as a discipline, just as how the importance of government reports cannot be wished away, the growing interest of students studying the discipline should be considered too. Unlike other disciplines in the social sciences, public administration is perhaps the most sought-after discipline presumably because it is both interesting as an area of study which would help students understand the intricacies of public governance once they are engaged formally for jobs and also because it is a high-scoring subject that will put them ahead of others who choose other subjects in competitive examinations. It is therefore not surprising that several private institutes have sprung-up to train candidates in public administration, including some major universities in the metropolis of Delhi, Kolkata and Mumbai where the discipline is being taught even today as part of undergraduate and postgraduate degree courses in political science. Whatever be the reason, the fact remains that public administration is now an established, independent discipline in India that is no longer an appendage to other disciplines.

CONCLUDING OBSERVATIONS

This reflective text on the state of public administration in India as a discipline identifies the sources of concern and joy for those involved in the pedagogical exercise, particularly with the university system. There is no doubt that the discipline has not adequately provoked either faculty members or students to undertake sustained research in the field to develop the discipline despite its growing popularity in competitive examinations for government jobs. Even the University Grants Commission (UGC) which manages universities in India does not seem to be supportive to the extent its Bangladeshi counterpart is. Some of India's leading universities, like the University of Delhi, Jawaharlal Nehru University, Allahabad University, University of Calcutta, do not have a full-fledged department of public administration and continue to offer courses in public administration as a component of BA/MA courses in political science. This is a matter of concern since the discipline continues to be identified as an appendage of political science which perhaps inhibits its growth as an independent discipline. What is however most encouraging is the sustained endeavour that GoI has undertaken in understanding public administration and also in evolving newer mechanisms to streamline and make administration efficient. By taking into account both global and domestic inputs, various government reports have enabled us to comprehend the complex nature of government in action in India; they are undoubtedly important raw material to develop newer theoretical designs on the basis of newer conceptual categories. This does not, therefore, seem odd to find that a considerable number of topics/sub-topics in the syllabi for public administration in universities are drawn on these government reports and documents.

How to address the disciplinary weaknesses of public administration in India is a million dollar question which does not have an easy answer. Nonetheless, while laying out some of the areas of theoretical concerns which are critical in making the discipline relevant and popular among the stakeholders, one can set the ball rolling for a very engaging discussion on its nature and impact on contemporary governance. As already argued, public administration is an action-oriented, context-sensitive and practitioner-friendly field of social science enquiry. In order to sustain its disciplinary viability, the methodological catholicity has to be discarded, and the discipline needs to be appreciative of collaboration and meaningful interdisciplinary borrowing. Given the complexities of governance especially in light of the growing consolidation of the LPG (Liberalisation, Privatisation and Globalisation) regimes following the disintegration of the former Soviet Union and the consequent rise and strengthening of neo-liberalism, it would be conceptually erroneous to comprehend public administration in its traditional mould. One needs to be equipped to articulate the inevitable changes in administration which is, despite being context-specific, also subject to influences which are not exactly contextual. A strong argument is thus made for methodological diversity to capture the changed administrative reality in the context of the blurring of national boundaries following the emergence of the global village. This is surely a significant step in redefining the methodological contours of the discipline which is very persuasive. But one is required to be sensitive of the problem that stems from the endeavour at providing 'a universal design' of public administration which the WB-sponsored governance model seeks to make. By defending the 'one-size-fits-all' formula, neo-liberal thinkers have not only challenged the context-driven analysis of public administration while pursuing social Darwinism, but have also sought to universalise the governance model of administration by completely undermining the importance of public in public administration. The fundamental task is therefore to reinvent the discipline by reiterating its spirit of being public in the face of the obvious neo-liberal challenges being sponsored by those proponents willing to sacrifice the fundamental ethos of the people-centric public administration. And here the role of those involved in the pedagogical transmission of knowledge in public administration, both in the universities and institutes, cannot but be significant and critical for the future of the discipline of public administration in India.

REFERENCES

Appleby, Paul. 1953. *Public Administration in India: Report of a Survey.* New Delhi: Cabinet Secretariat, Government of India.

Bhattacharya, Mohit. 1997. 'Crisis of Public Administration as a Discipline' in *Restructuring Public Administration,* 61–74. New Delhi: Jawahar Books.

Bomball, K. R. 1978. *Indian Constitution and Administration.* Ambala Cantt: Modern Publications.

Government of India (GoI). 2007. 'Ethics in Governance', fourth report in the *Second Administrative Reforms Commission Report.* New Delhi: Government of India.

Lyer, Lawrence E., Jr., C. J. Heinrich and C. J. Hill. 2001. *Improving Governance: A New Logic of Empirical Research.* Washington DC: Georgetown University Press.

Mason, Philip. 1997. *The Men Who Ruled India.* Reprint. New Delhi: Rupa & Co.

Mishra, B. B. 1977. *The Bureaucracy: A Historical Analysis upto 1947.* Delhi: Oxford University Press.

Potter, David. 1996. *India's Political Administrators: From ICS to IAS.* Delhi: Oxford University Press.

Rao, V. Bhaskara, ed. 2011. *Movements and Public Administration.* New Delhi: Kalpaz.

Waldo, Dwight, ed. 1971. *Public Administration in a Time of Turbulence.* New York: Chandler Publishing Co.

2

CLASSICAL THEORIES OF PUBLIC ADMINISTRATION

HIGHLIGHTS

- Scientific management theory
- Bureaucratic theory
- Human relations theory
  - Hawthorne experiments
- Decision-making theory
  - Choice of Rationality
- Ecological theory
  - Prismatic–Sala model
  - Bazaar canteen model

A theory is the description, explanation and prediction of certain phenomena. Theory helps us to see and understand life in a better way. It help us to see our world more clearly. Theories also conceal or project reality. Administrative theories help us to see and understand public administration phenomena, especially organisational life. Because of this, one of the primary tasks of theory in public administration is to describe the assumptions that guide action and to develop the concepts that foster an understanding of those assumptions. The validity or usefulness of any theory depends on its capacity to describe, explain and predict the political reality. Theories are formulated and adapted to the social and cultural circumstances of the time. In this way they attempt to improve our understanding of life in public organisations or elsewhere.

This chapter discusses five administrative theories with reference to the contribution of individual thinkers—'Scientific Management Theory' is discussed with reference to the contribution of F. W. Taylor, 'Bureaucratic Theory' with reference to Max Weber, 'Human Relations Theory' with reference to Elton Mayo, 'Decision-Making Theory' with reference to Herbert Simon and 'Ecological Theory' with reference to the contribution made by Fred Riggs. We have named these theories as fundamental because they provide a foundation to the theory and practice of public administration. These theories defined the intellectual orientation of the Western world and presented some of the most articulate and influential statements on the quality of life in modern industrial society. Taken together, these theories have substantially influenced the direction of social theory over the past several decades and established an agenda which all social theorists today must address. This does not deny the significance of other administrative theories. Due to lack of time and space we will focus only on the above-mentioned theories. This chapter will discuss each theory in their socio-economic context, and present their main features, principles and contribution, and finally make a critical evaluation of their future utility.

SCIENTIFIC MANAGEMENT THEORY: ONE BEST WAY OF DOING A JOB

In the early 1900s, an organisation theory that emphasised economy, efficiency and productivity through scientific principles received great prominence. This theory, known as 'scientific management', owes its origins to Frederick Winslow Taylor (1856–1915). The origin of the scientific management theory is considered to be a major breakthrough in industrial management. With the growth and consolidation of large-scale industries in the wake of the Industrial Revolution, the Western world witnessed a resultant crisis of management. The problem was further aggravated by World War I. The growing scarcity of resources, competition and complexity in managing businesses demanded an efficient science of management. The scientific management theory was the outcome of such a need.

Taylor, the 'father of scientific management theory', was an American engineer who was interested in improving industrial efficiency. He identified the basic social problem of his day as one of efficiency. His scientific management focused on the discovery of basic principles of motion involved in the performance of physical tasks with a view to determine the one best way of performing any task most efficiently. Taylor believed that in every trade there is *one best way* of doing a job, and the objective of the manager is to explore that best way to optimally execute the job. And, to correct the existing deficiencies, Taylor charged management with the basic responsibility of developing the required scientific management principles. Taylor's own words effectively convey the essence of scientific management theory:

> … among the various methods and implements used in each element of each trade there is always one method and one implement which is quicker and better than any of the rest. And this one best method and best implement can only be discovered or developed through a scientific study and analysis of all the methods and implements in use, together with accurate, minute, motion and time study. (1911/1947: 34)

Taylor's major works on the theory include *A Piece-Rate System* (1895), *Shop Management* (1903), *The Art of Cutting Metals* (1906) and *The Principles of Management* (1911). While the theory owes to the ideas of Taylor, it has to be noted that the term 'scientific management' was first coined by Louis Brandeis in 1910 based on Taylor's ideas. Once established, scientific management theory revolutionised the science of management by ensuring maximum efficiency and the consequent economisation of time and resources. In other words, it redefined industrial relations by proposing to revamp the age-old manager–worker relationship by division of work, standardisation of work procedure and improvement in working conditions on the one hand, and making managers equally responsible for the overall productivity on the other. It suggested that the application of scientific technology would maximise overall productivity in an industry, which in effect would increase the earning of both workers and employers and minimise friction between them.

Principles of Scientific Management

While putting his arguments in favour of the principles of scientific management, Taylor argued that the greatest advantage of this style of management was the voluntary sharing of extraordinary burden and duties by managements. These duties and burdens have been divided and classified into four different groups and these four types of new duties assumed by the management have been called the 'principles of scientific management' (Taylor 1912/1987: 32). They are as follows:

1. Development of a science of work
2. Scientific selection and progressive development of the worker
3. Bringing of the science and scientifically selected and trained workers
4. Division of work and responsibility between the management and workers

The first principle of scientific management is concerned with the development of a science of work. The basic objective of this principle is to replace the 'rule of thumb' with scientific methods. The 'one best way' to perform the task can be done by observing and analysing the work assigned to a worker with respect to each element and the time involved. This procedure will decide the ideal working method or the best way of doing a job. Taylor considers this 'organised knowledge' as 'science of work'.

The second principle places emphasis on scientific selection and proper grooming of the workforce. It believes that a vibrant workforce can bring about rapid increase in productivity. Scientific selection involves selecting the right person for the right job, and a standardised selection procedure is essential to ensure this. Workers' skill and experience must be matched with the requirements of the jobs they are to perform. The workers so selected must be given training for the specific tasks they are assigned. This would help the workers to willingly and enthusiastically accept new methods, tools and conditions. Taylor holds that it is the management's responsibility to implement appropriate selection and training systems and to see to it that the workers' intellectual, psychological and physical traits match the requirements of the jobs.

The third principle advocates close coordination between the science of work and the trained workforce for smooth functioning of the organisation. According to Taylor, it is the exclusive responsibility of the management to 'bring science and workmen together', i.e. workers should be trained to work systematically on the basis of scientific principles. He believes that workers are always willing to cooperate with the management but there is more opposition from the management.

The fourth principle, a hallmark of the scientific management theory, deals with equal sharing of work between the management and workers. It puts the onus of industrial productivity equally on the management and workers. That is, industrial well-being is a joint responsibility. Taylor comments that this principle is perhaps the most difficult of all of the four principles as it consists of an almost equal division of actual work between the worker and the management: 'That is, the work which under the old type of management practically all was done by the workman, under the new is divided into two great divisions, and one of these is deliberately handed over to those on the management's side (1912/1987: 32).

The above-mentioned principles cannot be isolated and called scientific management, rather they collectively contribute to scientific management. In *The Principles of Scientific Management*, Taylor states that scientific management is 'no single element', but a combination that can be summarised as:

- Science, not rule of thumb;
- Harmony, not discord;
- Cooperation, not individualism;
- Maximum output, in place of restricted output; and
- Development of each man to his greatest efficiency and prosperity. (1911/1947: 140)

The above features constitute the philosophy of scientific management. Taylor assumed that as a result of the emphasis on maintaining a written record of work, superstition—represented by 'rule of thumb'—would be replaced by science. Sharing of work would eliminate differences between workers and the management, and lead to harmony and cooperation. The resultant new system that is based on maximum output would bring about prosperity for both workers and managers and the community as a whole.

Taylor also employed a number of techniques to facilitate the application of the principles of scientific management. These include functional foremanship, motion and time study, piece rate plan, exceptional principle and standardisation of tools. 'Functional foremanship' is a scheme of eight specialist supervisors, four of whom are responsible for planning and the rest for execution. Under 'motion and time study' technique, Taylor studied the amount of time and the particular motions required to complete a particular task and believed that once the standard methods are discovered workers can be trained towards higher productivity and efficiency. According to the 'piece rate system', payment should be made to workers on the basis of the number of pieces they make rather than their position. Under the 'exception principle', the manager should receive only condensed, summarised and comparative reports, including both the good and, especially, the bad exceptions. The last technique, 'standardisation', would ensure increase in efficiency and speed, and thereby help realise the core principle of scientific management, viz. the best way of doing the work.

For scientific management to succeed, Taylor urges a complete 'mental revolution' in the attitude of managers and workers in their duties towards their fellow workers and towards all of their problems. This new outlook would require the realisation on the part of both parties that their mutual interest is not contradictory and both can prosper only through cooperation and not conflict. Both parties should cooperate with each other and work towards increasing productivity. Increased organisational output would give better wages to workers and higher profits to the management, thereby replacing an atmosphere of conflict with one of peace and harmony. Without this mental change on both sides, according to Taylor, scientific management does not exist.

Objectives to be Realised by Scientific Principle

The attempt to evolve the 'one best way' of doing a job was to derive systematic and organised knowledge to guide the actions of practicing managers as they sought to design or modify organisational structures and their functioning. The other major objectives of scientific management theory may be summarised as follows:

- to achieve economy and efficiency in an organisational set-up;
- to assure the highest opportunity for individual capacity through scientific methods of work analysis and of selection, training, assignment, transfer and promotion of workers;
- to make possible a higher standard of living as a result of increased income of workers;
- to assure a happier home and social life to workers through removal of many of the disagreeable and worrying factors in the total situation by increase of income;
- to assure healthy as well as individually and socially agreeable conditions of work;
- to assure through training and instructional foremanship, the opportunity for workers to develop new and higher capacities, and eligibility for promotion to higher positions;
- to develop self-confidence and self-respect among workers through opportunity afforded for understanding of one's own work specifically, and of plans and methods of work generally;
- to promote justice through the elimination of discrimination in wage rates and elsewhere, and,
- to eliminate factors of the environment which are irritating and the cause of friction, and to promote common understanding, tolerance and the spirit of team work. (H. C. Person, quoted in Sapru 2013: 124–25)

Taylor was confident that if the scientific principles were properly applied, and a sufficient amount of time given to make them effective, it would produce far larger and better results for both parties.

Resistance to Scientific Management[1]

Scientific management led to a reform movement which offered the hope of minimising industrial problems. However, it was also opposed by many people. The anger of labour was so harsh that death threats were issued to Taylor and the planning room of an organisation he worked for was mysteriously burned down. Since Taylor's 'mental revolution' would resolve disputes between employers and workers, and establish an effective cooperation between them, it would make the role of the trade union redundant. Labour leaders, therefore, considered Taylorism as not only destroying trade unions but also destroying the principle of collective bargaining. They also had the fear that it would increase unemployment.

Taylorism was also attacked by managers. Their workload increased due to the application of 'equal division of work and responsibility'. Those who wanted promotion to high managerial positions opposed Taylor's stand that advocated training and assessment of managers by highly trained experts. In fact, Taylor had to resign from two of the companies he worked for—Midvale Steel Works and Bethlehem Steel Company—owning to difference of opinion. Human relations theorists criticised Taylor's principles for being impersonal and undermining the human factor. Behaviourists charged that Taylor's methods sacrificed the initiative of the worker, his individual freedom and the use of his intelligence and responsibility. March and Simon described the scientific management principle as the 'physiological organisation theory' (1958: 56). Taylor's theory was also criticised for oversimplifying human motivation in terms of economic rewards and neglecting the social and psychological aspects of motivation. Likewise, the assumption that an individual exists in isolation from the social environment is erroneous.

To conclude, Taylor was obsessed with efficiency and economy—presumably because of his professional training as an engineer. Orderliness was the hallmark of Taylor's thought. He had reacted to the disorder he found in organisations in his time. Due to his firm belief in the spirit of science, he assumed that there is always a best way of doing a job and that the manager should strive to evolve that best way through the application of scientific techniques. Instead of the rule of thumb method, he was in favour of greater autonomy for the workers who would decide the work method among themselves and select their tools accordingly. Apart from scientific management, Taylor was also known for his idea of participative management, which was implicit in his advocacy for greater autonomy of workers.

Despite a number of limitations, scientific management greatly influenced administrative thought and management practices in subsequent years. As Bertram Gross mentions: 'Even after the initial period of resistance it conquered the citadels of old fashioned industrial management in the United States and had a tremendous effect on industrial practice' (1964: 127). It even influenced administrative and managerial practices in France, Germany, England, USSR and

---

[1] This section has been developed from a few sections in Bidyut Chakrabarty and Prakash Chand, *Public Administration in a Globalizing World: Theories and Practices* (New Delhi: Sage, 2012), 58–59.

other European countries. In the inter-War period, the practices of scientific management were established in the form of Western industrial set-up across the world.

BUREAUCRATIC THEORY: THE LEGAL RATIONAL AUTHORITY

The bureaucratic form of governance is an inescapable and omnipresent phenomenon of modern organisation and it is hailed for its perceived qualities, such as merit, impartiality, neutrality, non-ambiguity, efficiency, economy, reduction of friction and of material and personal costs, unity, strict subordination and so on. Despite the centrality of bureaucracy in organisation, no serious effort was made to theorise bureaucracy before Max Weber, the 'father of bureaucratic theory'. Weber was a German sociologist and political economist who viewed bureaucracy in a positive light, believing it to be more rational and efficient than its predecessors. Weber sought to replace authority based on tradition and charisma with legal authority and to prescribe an impersonal and merit-based method of selecting, hiring and promoting employees.

Weber identifies three types of authority: traditional, charismatic and legal-rational. In traditional society, rules are derived from custom and tradition and this is therefore known as traditional authority. A tribal chief could be an example of traditional authority. Charismatic authority is where the leader derives authority from personal traits. People follow such authority because of their belief in the magical virtue, prophecy and nobility of the leader. Under legal-rational authority, people accept the obedience of the leader because the leader derives power from rules and regulations. Weber believes that such authority is most suitable for attainment of the ends of an organisation because it is based on legality and rationality.

Weber's Ideal Type of Bureaucracy

Though bureaucracy is generally identified with Weber, he neither defined bureaucracy in a clear-cut manner nor even considered it as a part of the language of social sciences. He had identified some characteristics of bureaucratic structure. His frequent use of the term within quote marks indicated that he had coined the term from everyday parlance. Moreover, Weber did not include all officials within his notion of bureaucracy. He refused to include elected or selected officials in his conceptualisation of bureaucracy. The distinctive character of Weberian bureaucracy was that he was an appointee (Albrow 1970). Despite the systematic treatment of bureaucracy in his writings, Weber's notion of bureaucracy is largely scattered. There is, therefore, an apparent inconsistency in Weber's treatment of bureaucracy. At times he uses the term in a more general sense, while at times he concentrates only on the pure and rational variety, i.e. the factual and objective values. Weber's conception of bureaucracy, thus, needs to be placed in his overall sociological perspective.

Weber's conceptualisation of bureaucracy needs to be appreciated as a purely sociological phenomenon. To be more specific, Weber's theory of an ideal type of bureaucracy as the manifestation of rational-legal authority will become more intelligible if it is placed in the backdrop of his theory of domination or '*herrschaft*' (Bhattacharaya 1996: 23). Domination, according to Weber, is not merely a structure of command that derives obedience but also that which is readily espoused. As we have already mentioned, he identified three sources of authority, i.e. traditional, charismatic and rational-legal. In traditional authority, the sources of legitimation are customs, traditions and conventions. The charismatic source of authority depends upon personal charm, which may include magnetic personality, heroic figure and other charismatic qualities of a leader. Weber believes that these two sources of legitimation are inherently fugitive and volatile. The rational-legal authority, which has legal sanction, is therefore inherently stable and permanent.

Weber considered bureaucracy as a universal, progressive and modern form of organisation that plays a crucial role in ordering and controlling modern societies. Weber heaped praises on bureaucracy in the following words:

> It is superior to any other form in precision, in stability, in the stringency of its discipline, and in its reliability. It thus makes possible a particularly high degree of calculability of results for the heads of the organization and for those acting in relation to it. It is finally superior both in intensive efficiency and in the scope of its operations, and is formally capable of application to all kinds of administrative tasks. (Weber 1927/1947: 337)

Considering the centrality of bureaucracy in the development of society, Weber came up with a heuristic-type construct of bureaucracy that is applicable to all types of societies. Weber (1927/1947) enumerated the following characteristics of bureaucracy:

1. *Hierarchy of authority*: It refers to an ordered system of superiority and subordination. Each lower office is under the control and supervision of a higher one. Every official in the administrative hierarchy is accountable to his/her superior and therefore has the right to issue directives that are relevant for official transactions.
2. *Division of labour*: It means assigning different parts of official processes or tasks to different people in order to improve efficiency.
3. *Rules-based authority*: Bureaucracy is governed by the principle of prescribed official regulations, which are generally ordered by rules.
4. *Written documents*: The management of a modern office is based on written documents in which the functions of officials are clearly specified.
5. *Specialised office management*: Bureaucratic organisations are based on specialisation. Selection and promotion of officials are based on technical qualifications, competence and performance of the candidates.
6. *Impersonality*: The bureaucratic system is governed on the basis of rational standards, and not personal considerations. The exclusion of personal considerations from official business is a prerequisite for impartiality as well as efficiency.

7. *Procedural specifications*: Clear-cut rules and regulations define the extent to which organisational members follow officially-defined techniques in dealing with the variety of situations they face.
8. *Career public servant*: Officials in the bureaucratic organisation are expected to pursue a career in the organisation. The office constitutes a full-time salaried occupation with a career structure that offers the prospect of regular promotion and advancement. (Quoted in Shafritz and Hyde 1987: 39–44)

The above-mentioned characteristics illustrate Weber's ideal type of rational and efficient bureaucracy. Within this system goals are clear and explicit. Positions are arranged in a pyramidal structure, with authority increasing as one rises in the organisational hierarchy. The authority lies in the positions rather than in the people who occupy them. The selection of members is based on merit rather than on personality. Promotions are based on merit, seniority and performance. The officials working in a bureaucracy provide continuous impartial and neutral service essential to the proper functioning of the State.

Bureaucratic Bashing

Weber's bureaucracy is viewed as an efficient method of structuring large organisations that perform routine and complex tasks. However, the word 'bureaucracy' is generally used in a pejorative sense for government employees or civil servants. In this sense, the bureaucrat is regarded as personifying the allegedly negative features of bureaucracy—being lazy, rule bound, rigid, wasteful and eager to retain power (Shafritz 2007: 128). Different people have different allegations against Weber's bureaucratic model. It has its critics in organisation theory as well as among the common people. It is said that the actual practices of bureaucracy often fall short of the ideals mentioned by Weber. In fact, bureaucracy produces a number of unintended consequences or dysfunctions. Thus, the bureaucratic model has been criticised on a number of grounds. It has been characterised as 'machine theory' and a closed system model due to excessive concern for the formal structure of the organisation and neglect of environmental factors. Critics claim that it is rigid, static and inflexible. Robert Merton (1949: 198), an early critic of Weber, argues that strict adherence to rules can become an end in itself, resulting in 'goal displacement'. This process in turn produces bureaucratic rigidity, red tapism and resistance to change. Bureaucratic procedures cause inordinate delay and frustration. By encouraging conformity to rules and regulations, bureaucracies leave little scope for original or innovative behaviour. Thus Michel Crozier describes bureaucracy as a rigid 'organization that cannot correct its behavior by learning from its errors' (1964: 56).

Weber's theory is also criticised for its anti-humanist overtones. He gives little attention to the interest, prejudices and fears of an individual as a social being. Weber's theory, therefore, is insufficient as a description of the actual functioning of organisations. Bureaucracy is also criticised as being an essentially self-seeking institution as it tends to become an interest group and places its own interest at the centre of things. Robert Presthus (1978) observes that the

Western-influenced Weberian model is not suitable for developing countries where conditions are entirely different. Developing countries require a flexible, imaginative outlook to achieve socio-economic development quickly, and the Weberian rule-bound rigid bureaucratic system is found to be incompatible with the multi-faceted complex tasks that are involved to realise that aspiration.

However, Weber was not negligent of the negative consequences of bureaucratic organisations—neither of the problem of red tape and inefficiency nor of the more enduring consequences of formalistic impersonality. Though this was a rather neglected area in his study, he has still mentioned a few defence mechanisms of sorts to withstand bureaucracy—such as collegiality, separation of powers, direct democracy and representation. Collegiality, or the relationship between colleagues who are united in a common purpose, is sought to counter bureaucratic monopoly by collective decision-making. Weber considered collegiality as the most powerful weapon of restraining bureaucracy. Separation of power has been considered as the most tried-and-tested antidote for absolutism in any form, ever since it was first propounded by Montesquieu. Weber also sought to check bureaucracy by introducing separation of power in terms of dividing responsibilities for the same functions between two or more bodies. Direct democracy was another mechanism he prescribed to contain bureaucratic authoritarianism. Weber suggested giving more power to members who elected by the people. They are free to make decisions and share the authority over those who elect them. These elected members, according to Weber, should have the power to check on bureaucracy (Albrow 1970).

To sum up, despite a number of shortcomings, Weber could be credited for starting the systematic study of bureaucratic organisations. His study has helped develop professionalism in administration by avoiding favouritism and nepotism. It has assured the rational attainment of the goals of an organisation. The permanent character of the bureaucratic model is also relevant to developing countries. While the political master may change frequently, bureaucracy continues to rule. Though, bureaucracy has become synonymous with red tapism, nepotism and corruption, no State has thus far been in a position to dispense with its bureaucracy, which in itself speaks about its utility. If Wilson is the pioneer of the discipline, Weber is its first theoretician who provided the discipline with a solid theoretical base. Weber's general account of a basic organisation has had a lasting impact on social theory in general and critical social theory in particular. His 'ideal' type of bureaucracy continues to remain fundamental in any conceptualisation of an organisation.

HUMAN RELATIONS THEORY: THE HUMAN SIDE OF ENTERPRISE

The human relations theory is a significant development in the evolution of public administration. Unlike the bureaucratic mode of organisations, this theory views an organisation in its holistic social perspective. Relationists treat workers as human beings with all humanly attributes. According to this theory, every worker carries with him/her a different culture, attitude, belief and way of life. The organisation must take cognisance of such socio-cultural aspects while engaging with an employee. The theory also identifies the presence of informal groups, which are important in achieving organisational goals. Thus, the human relations theory discovered the human side of organisations and tried to offer human solutions to human problems. This theory believes that happier workers are the secret of a successful organisation.

Unlike the traditional approach which glorifies the 'economic man', the human relations theory enthrones the 'social man'. This theory underscores four key elements of organisations, which classical theorists seem to have overlooked: (*a*) the organisation is to be viewed as a social system; (*b*) workers are human beings with all humanly attributes; (*c*) informal elements also play an important role in the overall organisational output; and (*d*) the organisation is governed by social ethics and not individual ethics.

Elton Mayo (1880–1949) is considered the 'father of human relations theory'. Mayo was a professor of industrial research at the Graduate School of Business Administration, at Harvard University. Originally trained as a graduate in medicine, Mayo subsequently switched over to psychology and philosophy. His training in medicine, psychology and philosophy helped him grasp industrial relations in a more comprehensive manner. In fact, he was instrumental in initiating the discipline of industrial sociology. His major works include *The Human Problems of an Industrial Civilization* (1933), *The Social Problems of an Industrial Civilization* (1945) and *The Political Problem of Industrial Civilization* (1947).

Hawthorne Experiments at Western Electric Company

The human relations school grew out of a set of studies carried out by Mayo and others between 1924 and 1932 at the Hawthorne plant of Western Electric Company at Chicago. The plant was a progressive firm in the US and enjoyed a unique distinction in terms of offering better wages, liberal working hours and cordial employer–employee relationships. But from the early 1920s onwards, the firm had been registering moderate productivity. Despite liberal incentives and good working environment, the firm had to be content with a modest growth rate. The management tried all possible remedies prescribed by scientific management and the classical organisation theory, to little avail. Under the circumstances, the management approached Mayo and his associates at Harvard Business School to find a solution for the problem. Thus began a series of experiments over a couple of years. The major finding of the study was the discovery of the significance of social and group actors as influences upon individuals' work behaviour. It was found that non-pecuniary factors like happier working conditions, mental attitudes and group dynamics tended to influence workers' productivity (Mayo 1933). The astonishing findings of these experiments ushered in a new vista in organisational theory. An elaborate discussion of these experiments is given below.

Illumination Experiments (1924–27): Effects of Changes in Illumination on Productivity

This experiment intended to assess the impact of the work environment on the output of industrial production. From among the workers, two groups of female workers who were engaged in assembling telephone relays were selected and placed in two different test rooms. Over a period of one-and-half years different elements of physical working conditions—such as level of illumination, room temperature, humidity, wage payments, working hours, rest periods—were deliberately altered to evaluate their impact on productivity. Quite contrary to what was expected, the groups kept a steady growth rate. This unpredictable behaviour discarded the typical incentive-driven growth hypothesis of the scientific management theory.

Relay Assembly Test Room Experiments (1927–29): Effects of Working Conditions on Productivity

As the illumination experiments could not establish the relationship between intensity of illumination and production, another set of experiments was designed to determine the effect of changes in various job conditions on group productivity. For this purpose, the researchers set up a relay assembly test room. Two girls were first chosen. These girls were asked to choose a few more girls as co-workers. The work related to the assembly of telephone relays. Each relay consisted of a number of parts which the girls assembled into finished products. The output depended on the speed and continuity with which the girls worked. The experiments started with introducing various changes in sequence with the duration of each change ranging from four to 12 weeks. An observer would supervise the girls' work. Before each change was introduced, the girls were consulted. They were given the opportunity to express their views and concerns to the supervisor.

A number of experiments were undertaken, and they produced different results. The incentive system was changed so that each girl's extra pay was based on the other girls rather than the output of the larger group. There was an observable rise in productivity as compared to before. Two five-minute breaks, one in the morning session and another in the evening session, were introduced. These were subsequently increased to 10-minute breaks, and this resulted in an increase in productivity. Then, coffee or soup was served along with sandwich in the morning and a snack was provided in the evening during the breaks. Again the productivity was found to increase. Changes in working hours and workday, such as cutting an hour off at the end of the day and stopping Saturday work, were introduced. The girls were allowed to leave at 4 PM instead of the usual 5 PM, and again productivity was found to rise. The changes brought positive results, absenteeism decreased, morale increased and less supervision was required. It was assumed that these positive changes came about because various factors were adjusted.

Now the researchers decided to revert to the original position, that is, no rest or incentives. Surprisingly, productivity increased further instead of going down. This development caused a considerable amount of redirection in thinking and the result implied that productivity increased not because of positive changes in physical factors but because of the change in the girls' attitudes towards work and their work group. Since there was more freedom of work, they had developed a sense of responsibility and self-discipline. The supervisor and the workers had become close and friendly. They had developed a positive feeling and a sense of belongingness.

Mass Interviewing Programme (1928–30): Value of Human Attitudes and Sentiments

In this experiment Mayo and his team sought to study human attitudes and sentiments. Workers were asked to freely express their likes and dislikes about their working conditions and the policies of the management. After interviewing more than 21,000 workers, the team concluded that the workers appreciated the method of collecting information on the problems of the company from them. The workers realised that they were allowed to express their views freely and thought they had valuable comments to offer. The research team also realised that the workers had acquired new skills in understanding and dealing with their fellow beings. It was felt that in the absence of proper appreciation of the feelings and sentiments of workers it was difficult to understand the real problems due to their personal history and situation at work. The study of 'human attitudes and sentiments', therefore, helped both workers and the management.

The Bank Wiring Experiment (1931–32): Discovery of Informal Organisation

This experiment involved a group of male workers who were assigned to do a wiring job, which also included the job of soldering and fixing terminals. Wages were paid on the basis of a group incentive plan and each member got his share on the basis of the total output of the group. Following Taylor's assumption of scientific management, the workers were expected to react positively to the economic incentives and show high productivity. Instead, the workers refused to act like the 'economic man' and agreed among themselves to keep production at a moderate level. Upon further investigation, the researchers discovered that the workers were members of a small, closely-knit group, governed by a code that rejected the 'rate-buster' (who did too much work), the 'chiseler' (who did too little) and the 'squealer' (who communicates detrimental information about others to the supervisor). Such behavioural pattern among the workers was directly attributed to a deep-seated distrust in the management. The workers were of the opinion that too much increase or decrease in production might cost their jobs. Workers behaved this way for a number of reasons—fear of unemployment, fear of increase in output and the desire to protect slow workers. This experiment, therefore, displayed workers' collective and informal behaviour in organisations.

The pioneering studies which resulted from the Hawthorne experiments challenged many prevailing ideas about incentives and human behaviour in the organisational set-up. The team concluded that employee-oriented supervision is more effective than production-minded, authoritarian supervision. They stressed the human aspect of administration, the need for employee recognition and satisfaction, and the importance of the social environment and group attitudes in work situations. Thus, these studies highlighted the weaknesses of the machine concept of organisation and suggested taking into account the social and psychological factors of the work situation.

Essence of Human Relations Theory

The Hawthorne experiments opened up a whole new dimension of management practices. The demonstration that a human being is a social animal led to the conclusion that there were advantages to treating the worker as a responsible being rather than as a cog in the wheel. Subsequent studies eventually emphasised the importance of social needs. As Jackson (1982) points out, the human relations approach was concerned with putting human beings back into the bloodless organisations discussed by Weber and the classical administrative theorists.

The essence of human relations theory can be summarised as follows: First, the human relation theory, unlike the machine model of organisation, views the organisation in its holistic social perspective. Second, workers are treated as human beings with all humanly attributes; instead of viewing workers as homogenous cogs in the wheel, the human relations theory puts emphasis on the uniqueness of each worker. The theory believes that each worker carries her/his culture, attitude, belief and way of life. Therefore, the organisation must take proper cognisance of such socio-cultural aspects while hiring an employee. Third, unlike the exclusive structural bias of the classical organisation theory, the human relations theory identified the impact of informal groups on motivation and productivity for the first time. Fourth, responding to the changing environment, the human relations theory insists on social ethics based on 'human collaboration and social solidarity' (Nigro 1965), unlike individual ethics, as popularised by Taylorism. And finally, the human relations theory has in effect engendered a new form of management, i.e. participative management.

Limitations of Human Relations Theory

The Hawthorne studies have received a lot of criticism as people from both academia and industry have questioned the conclusions of these experiments on various parameters. The following statement by Urwick captures the apparent disillusionment regarding the human elements of administration: 'the idea that organization should be built up around and adjusted to individual idiosyncrasies, rather than that individual should be adapted to the requirements of sound principles of organization, is as foolish as attempting to design an engine to accord the whimsies of one's maiden aunt rather than with the laws of mechanical science' (quoted in Nigro 1965: 93).

The major criticisms against the human relations theory can be crystallised under the following heads: First, critics argue that the human relations theory is based on a wrong and simplistic assumption of an organisation. Relationists often claim that any problem of an organisation can be solved by adept utilisation of human relations skills. Second, a few commentators have even gone a step further in arguing that the Hawthorne findings were conducive to many managers (Nigro 1965: 95). Based on contextual analysis, some analysts have traced the severe shortage of labour behind the emergence of the human relations movement. According to them, the human relations movement was brought into being to meet the growing demands of labour during and after World War II (Arora 1979). Third, the human relations theory is also criticised for its 'vagueness, psychological jargon, distortion of the organizational environment, and unwillingness to distinguish the administrative aspects' (Caiden 1971: 225). Finally, this theory is also criticised for overemphasising the human element of organisations at the cost of the basic structural element.

To conclude, despite a number of limitations, the bounty of the human relations theory cannot be underestimated. It revealed the fact that a positive social environment influenced the productivity of the worker. It paved the way for adequate communication systems between the lower and higher levels of organisations. It also highlighted the importance of a manager's style and therefore revolutionised management training programmes. The significance of the Hawthorne experiments in discovering the 'informal organisation' cannot be neglected. By stressing social needs and the importance of the human side of the enterprise, relationists improved on the classical theory of organisation. Thus, in spite of all the criticism, the fact that the Hawthorne experiments played a very significant role in making business organisations realise the value and need of the human factor cannot be denied. The ambience that employees get at their workplace today, which goes beyond just the financial incentive, would not have been possible if the Hawthorne experiments had not thrown light on the human side of enterprise.

DECISION-MAKING THEORY: THE ART OF RATIONAL CHOICE

The most significant dissection of principles appeared in Herbert Simon's *Administrative Behavior* (1947), a rich intellectual work which was termed 'epoch-making' when its author was awarded the Nobel Prize in Economics in 1978. Simon proposed the development of a new science of administration based on theories and the methodology of logical positivism. The focus of such a science would be decision-making. He maintained that to be scientific one must exclude value judgments and concentrate on facts, adopt precise definition of terms, apply rigorous analysis and test factual statements or postulates about administration (Corson and Harris 1967: 1). Further, he added that the logic and psychology of human choice determined administrative theory. The entire premise of Simon's work is based on the logical-rational model. The decision-making theory usually equates administration with decision-making. Decisions are made at every stage in the organisation and are considered fundamental in formulation of policy. Thus, in Simon's remarkable statement, decision-making is the 'heart of administration'.

The Complex Process of Decision-making

Decision-making is a complex process involving several steps. They can be sequenced in the following manner: identification of or locating a problem; getting related information and figuring out tentative options; weighing the tentative steps by seeking the opinion of subordinates; zeroing in on a particular option; evaluating the efficacy of the decision reached; and getting feedback and making necessary modifications if the situation so demands. Hence, decision-making is no one-shot job of the chief executive or seasoned mandarin. It requires, among others, total teamwork starting right from the chief executive down to the personnel stationed at the ground level. If we elaborate the above sequence in an actual organisational setting, the complexity of decision-making can be better understood. In a real organisational setting, identifying or locating the problem area is the first important step of decision-making.

Locating the area that requires fresh decision-making is by no means an easy task. It depends on the sagacity and administrative efficiency of the administrator or officer in-charge. However, identification of the problem is not the end in itself. The administrator now requires adequate information, viewpoints, statistics, etc. related to that problem. It is generally the staff agency in an organisation that feeds all the relevant information to the executive. And, on the basis of the information accrued from the staff agency, the administrator starts figuring out viable options to remedy the problem, and seeks the opinion of subordinate staff to weigh the tentative step. Finally, the administrator settles down on a particular option. Decision-making, however, does not end with reaching a particular decision, it also includes feedback and follow-up action, if necessary.

Simon's Rational Decision-making Theory

Herbert Simon viewed the organisation as a structure concerned solely with decision-making. According to him, decision-making is not the specific task of a particular part of the organisation; rather decisions are made at every level of the organisation. With the objective of making decision-making more effective and scientific, Simon tried to uncover the complicated inner dynamics of a decision in order to see how the multiplicity of value premises ultimately determines decision-making. In this context, Simon identifies a host of value premises that colour decision-making, viz., decision makers' preferences, social conditioning, etc. Simon breaks up the decision-making process into the following three phases:

1. *Intelligence activity*: This phase consists of searching the environment for conditions calling for decision-making.
2. *Design activity*: During this phase, inventing, developing and analysing possible courses of action take place.
3. *Choice activity*: This is the phase where the actual choice—i.e. selecting a particular course of action from among those variables—is made.

By 'intelligence', Simon refers to those activities by which one scans the environment and identifies occasions to make a decision; by 'design', he refers to finding or developing alternative options; and by 'choice', he refers to finding or developing alternative courses of action from those available options. Of course, in real life, Simon acknowledges, these phases are not distinct. However, for analytical purposes, they seem to constitute the basic elements of decision-making (Denhardt 2008: 78).

The Choice of Rationality

At the base of administrative organisation lies the concept of rationality. Organisations, according to Simon, are created in order to enhance human rationality and to structure human behaviour so that it may approximate abstract rationality. Simon argues that individual human beings are limited in their capacity to respond to the complex problems they face. As Denhardt remarks:

'The capacity of the human mind for formulating and solving complex problems is very small in comparison with the size of the problems whose solution is required for objectively rational behavior in the real world—or even for a reasonable approximation to such objective rationality' (2008: 75). Decision-making involves choice between alternative plans of action, and the choice in turn involves logical coordination between fact and value propositions. Simon views that decision-making in an organisation is based on proper coordination between fact and value proposition. Every decision involves a combination of a fair amount of fact and value proposition. The hallmark of Simon's decision-making approach, therefore, is the rationality criteria.

Bounded Rationality

However, Simon does not use the rationality criteria in the economic sense of the term. In fact, he rules out the possibility of absolute rationality in administrative decision-making. He explains rationality in terms of a means–end construct and has differentiated between different types of rationality. Simon views that total rationality in an administrative situation is almost impossible. Hence, he calls for a moderate level of rationality or 'bounded rationality' that is based on a point of 'satisfycing'. The term 'satisfycing'—a portmanteau of 'satisfactory' and 'sufficing'—was coined by Simon to explain the moderate or satisfactory state of mind of an administrator. Therefore, for Simon, a decision-maker is more a 'satisfycing man' than a 'maximising' man (Arora 2007). Nothing can capture the essence of Simon's 'satisfycing' better than his own words: 'while Economic man maximizes—selects the best alternatives from among all those available to him—his cousin, whom we shall call administrative man, satisfies—looks for a course of action that is satisfactory or good enough' (quoted in Nigro 1965: 183). Simon is pretty much alive to the problem of setting lofty targets in decision-making, which in most cases remain unattainable and romantic at best. Hence, his bounded rationality is a moderate level of rationality based on a practical level of satisfaction.

Limitations of Rational Decision-making Theory

Simon's efforts to construct a value-free science of administration have been criticised by Selznick (1957: 79–82) on the ground that it encourages the divorce of means and ends. Simon's concept of rationality has also been criticised for not recognising the role of intuition, tradition and faith in decision-making: Argyris feels that Simon's theory focuses on status quo ante; it uses satisfycing to rationalise incompetence (Argyris 1973: 255). Simon is also criticised on his idea of the 'administrative man' and 'administrative behaviour' which differ across persons and situations. Another pertinent criticism is that the decision-making theory does not take into account the emotional aspect and other such factors around decision-making.

To conclude, it can be stated that, in spite of some limitations, Simon's contribution is undoubtedly a major breakthrough in the evolution of administrative theory. His model has greatly encouraged the need for the use of various management techniques in public policy, and policy science has received the initial impulse from his formulation. The approach has immense importance in the present-day structure of administration. The State must do some work for the welfare of the people, and that requires decisions for policy formulation. The State cannot move in uncharted territory and if it tries to do so that will be a fruitless venture. Hence, for proper and effective administration, decision-making is essential because a logical and scientific method of policymaking is essential for overall wellbeing.

ECOLOGICAL THEORY: EXPLORING ADMINISTRATION–ENVIRONMENT DYNAMICS

In the post-War period, the emergence of new nations in Asia, Africa and Latin America has set a new trend in the study of public administration. Western scholars, particularly American, began to show much interest in the study of the varied administrative patterns of these newly independent nations. They recognised the importance of environmental factors and their impact on the different administrative systems, and this largely accounts for the development of a comparative and ecological administration perspective in the field of public administration (Corson and Harris 1967: 1).[2] In this regard, the contribution of F. W. Riggs (1917–2008) is significant. He is one of the few scholars who has contributed immensely to the emergence of comparative public administration and to an in-depth understanding of public administration in these postcolonial states (Haque 2010). He has tried to understand the disparity between the administrative systems of developed and developing countries. According to him, the main reason for this is the environment that nations are embedded in. Each developing nation is in a different environmental setting, which shapes the administrative system both from within and outside (Chauble n.d.). The theory which emerged out of this realisation of the significance of the environment is called the ecological approach to public administration. An ecological approach to public administration is, therefore, based on an understanding of the inter-relationship between administration and its environment.

Riggs's Ecological Approach to Public Administration

Riggs, a theorist of comparative public administration, was primarily interested in conceptualising the interactions between administrative systems and their environment. He studied the differences in social, cultural, historical or political environment and their effect on administration. In his works, Riggs emphasises that in order to become a comparative study, public administration needs to shift focus from being normative to empirical, and to include in its ambit crosscultural perspectives and approaches to administration. He was uncomfortable with the adoption of the administrative practices of developed countries by developing countries for their development without adapting them to their own socio-cultural environments. He has also studied how an administrative system affects the society of which it is a part. This interaction of the environment with administration has been termed by him as the 'ecology' of administration. His views on

[2] Extracted from http://vle.du.ac.in/file.php/688/Evolution_of_Public_Administration/Evolution_of_Public_Administration.pdf (accessed June 2017).

the ecological approach are found in his books *The Ecology of Public Administration* (1961) and *Administration in Developing Countries: The Theory of Prismatic Society* (1964). Riggs developed his first model in 1956 by classifying societies into agrarian and industrial societies. In 1957 he developed an equilibrium model named 'transitia' which represented transforming societies. Because of the limitations of that model, Riggs developed another model to analyse the administrative systems in developing countries—the Fused, Prismatic and Diffracted model. This model represents underdeveloped, developing and developed societies.

Prismatic Model: Representing the Developing Societies

Although Riggs has given three ideal typical categories, his attention is focused on the social structures of the prismatic (i.e. developing) society and their interactions with the administrative subsystem in a society. This intermediate society between the extremes—viz. fused and diffracted—has three important characteristic features: (*a*) a prismatic society is characterised by a high degree of *heterogeneity*, which refers to the simultaneous presence of quite different kinds of systems, practices and viewpoints. (*b*) In a prismatic society, although modern social structures are created, in essence the old or undifferentiated structures continue to dominate the social system. Thus, in reality, the new structures are only paid lip-service and are overlooked widely in favour of traditional structures. This is regarded as *overlapping*, i.e. the extent to which differentiated structures of a diffracted (developed) society co-exist with undifferentiated structures of a fused (underdeveloped) society. Overlapping has several important dimensions, such as nepotism and favouritism, poly-communalism (hostile interaction among diverse groups) and the existence of elects (interest groups having communal membership). In essence in a prismatic society, the modern administrative structure in urban areas co-exists with the traditional administrative set-up in rural areas. (*c*) A prismatic society is characterised by a high degree of *formalism*, which refers to the degree of difference between the formally prescribed and effectively practiced norms and realities. Because of formalism, the actual behaviour of the 'sala' officials will be at variance with the laws and regulations that are laid down. Thus formalism often results in official corruption.

Prismatic–Sala Model: Administrative Subsystem of Developing Societies

The prismatic society is characterised by various social, economic, political and administrative subsystems. Riggs calls this the 'sala model'. In a prismatic society, family welfare, nepotism and favouritism play a significant role in appointments to various administrative positions and in the performance of certain administrative functions. In a prismatic society, apart from the superimposition of new formal structures on family and kinship, the universalisation of law is disregarded. The 'sala' officer gives priority to personal increase in power and wealth rather than to social welfare.

Further, poly-communalism also creates certain administrative problems. Theoretically speaking, government officials have to implement the laws impartially. But a government official may be found to be more loyal to members of his own community than to the government. As a result, a dominant minority community may gain a high proportion of representation in, say, matters of recruitment and create dissatisfaction among the larger number of people. The elect, that is, pressure group, maintains close links with a particular group and functions primarily in their interest and pays lip-service to achievement and universalistic norms.

As a result of the overlapping of the formal and the 'effective' standard of conduct, the prismatic society's social interactions are characterised by a lack of consensus on the norms of behaviour. Sala officials may enter service by virtue of higher educational qualifications or through success in competitive exams, but in respect of their promotion and career development they depend largely on ascriptive ties and on the basis of seniority or on the influence of senior officers. The power structure consists of a highly centralised and concentrated authority structure and an overlapping control system that is highly localised and dispersed.

The prismatic society is an unbalanced polity, according to Riggs, in which bureaucrats dominate the politico-administrative system due to the weakness of the political system. As a result, the sala officials play a more dominant role in decision-making. Since the performance of the government depends on the level of output of the sala official, Riggs says, there is a close link between bureaucratic behaviour and administrative output, the more powerful a bureaucrat is the less effective s/he is as administrator. As a result, the sala is characterised by nepotism in recruitment, institutionalised corruption and inefficiency in the administration of laws on account of its being governed by the motives of gaining power for protecting its own interest.

Bazaar Canteen Model: Economic Subsystem of Prismatic Society

Riggs calls the economic subsystem of prismatic society the 'bazaar canteen model'. There is discrimination and favouritism at all levels, and prices of commodities vary from place to place, time to time and person to person. The price of any commodity or service depends on family contacts, individual relationship, bargaining power and politics. In this model, a small section of people with control over economic institutions may enjoy all the benefits and exploit a large number of people. Exploitation, poverty and social injustice, therefore, become the major features of the bazaar canteen model.

Riggs' ecological model has been criticised for being purely theoretical without having an adequate empirical basis; too static about the influence of external social forces; too indifferent towards social change; and too overgeneralised as it has been formulated on the basis of only a few case studies. However, Riggs' contribution lies not only in conceptual constructs and tools of analysis for the study of administrative problems of developing societies but also in applying the macro approach for the first time towards such studies. His prismatic sala model and value-neutral conceptualisation of development have pushed crosscultural administrative studies towards greater objectivity. His models have encouraged several empirical studies on the administrative systems of developing countries.

CONCLUDING OBSERVATIONS

A discussion of five major administrative theories reveals that each of these theories has tried to respond to their prevalent socio-economic circumstances. The classical theories, especially propounded by Taylor and Weber, came as a response to the Industrial Revolution in the West at the end of the eighteenth century. They successfully constructed certain universal principles that facilitated the smooth functioning of organisations. Taylor's scientific management theory helped avoid increasing industrial conflicts. It stressed the fusion of resources and manpower to affect predetermined goals in the most efficient manner. The goal was to find the 'one best way' to implement a predetermined policy. Taylor's influence on the early study and practice of public administration was profound. Weber's bureaucratic model provided a legal-rational base to organisational functioning. The classical theorist thus laid emphasis on the physiological and mechanical aspects of work organisations.

In the post-War period, the bases of classical theories were questioned both in theory and in practice. An effort throughout the social sciences led to considering the impact of man as a social and political animal. The classical theories were criticised for ignoring socio-cultural and environmental factors. The search for causal explanations for administrators' behaviour led researchers into psychology, sociology and politics, thereby sidetracking the more prescriptively-oriented classical theory and prefering the more descriptively flavoured modern theory. Simon argued that by assigning values to the realm of politics, the 'one best way' to administer programmes could be ascertained once the direction of substantive policy had been set. Methodologically close to Taylor, Simon suggests that social and psychological factors that affect employee attitudes should be included in the descriptive analysis of organisations. To ignore socio-psychological factors, argues Simon, could result in less, rather than more, efficiency (Morrow 1975: 47). The famous Hawthorne experiments led by Mayo lay much emphasis on non-economic incentives in motivating the workers toward higher levels of production. Similarly, Riggs' ecological approach—which criticised classical theories that treated organisations as a closed system unaffected by its environment—discovered the vital role of environmental factors in influencing the functioning of administration in developing countries.

On the basis of the above discussion two major observations can be made. First, there is a Western bias in the field of administrative theories. Second, there is a lack of formidable base of its own. In the course of its historical development, the discipline never attempted to acquire any theoretical base on which now relevant knowledge could now be developed (Manohar, Rao and Rao 1991).Thus, all these theories have emerged in the Western Capitalist system, only aimed at legitimising and maintaining the Capitalistic system intact. There has been no attempt, even at the third Minnowbrook Conference held in 2008, to develop models in administration to meet the special needs and requirements of the changing societies of the developing world. The discipline is in fact facing the challenge of restoring the 'publicness' of public administration to which we turn next.

REFERENCES

Albrow, Martin. 1970. *Bureaucracy*. London: Macmillan.

Argyris, Chris. 1973. 'Some Limits of Rational Man Organizational Theory'. *Public Administrative Review* 33 (3): 253–67.

Arora, Ramesh K. 1979. *Perspective in Administrative Theory*. New Delhi: Associated Publishing House.

———. 2007. 'Organization Theories: Concerns and Orientations' in *Administrative Theories: Approaches, Concepts, and Thinkers in Public Administration*, edited by Rakesh Hooja and Ramesh Arora, 21–38. Jaipur and New Delhi: Rawat Publications.

Bhattacharya, Mohit. 1996. *Public Administration and Planning*. Calcutta: World Press Pvt. Ltd.

Caiden, Gerald E. 1971. *The Dynamics of Public Administration: Guidelines to Current Transformations in Theory and Practice*. Illinois: Dryden Press.

Chauble, Kopal. n.d. 'Perspectives of Public Administration'. Paper prepared for Lesson 'Ecological Approach to Public Administration', Ambedkar University Delhi. Available at http://vle.du.ac.in/file.php/688/Ecological_Approach_to_Public_Administration/Ecological_Approach_to_Public_Administration.pdf (accessed June 2017).

Corson, John and Joseph Harris. 1967. *Public Administration in Modern Society*, London: Mc Graw-Hill Book Company.

Crozier, M. 1964. *The Bureaucratic Phenomenon*. London: Tavistock Publications.

Denhardt, Robert B. 2008. *Theories of Public Organization*. Fifth edition. Belmont: Thomson Higher Education.

Gross, Bertram M. 1964. *The Managing of Organization: The Administrative Struggle*, vol. 1. New York: The Free Press.

Haque, M. Shamsul. 2010. 'Rethinking Development Administration and Remembering Fred W. Riggs'. *International Review of Administrative Sciences* 76 (4): 767–73.

Jackson, P. M. 1982. *The Political Economy of Bureaucracy*. Oxford: Philip Allan Publishers Ltd.

Manohar, K., Seetha Rama Rao and B. J. Janardhan Rao. 1991. *Administrative Theory: Trends and Perspectives*. Warangal: Book Bird Publishers and Distributors.

March, J. G and H. A. Simon. 1958. *Organizations*. New York: John Wiley & Sons.

Mayo, Elton. 1933. *The Human Problems of an Industrial Civilization*. New York: Macmillan.

Merton, Robert, K. 1949. *Social Theory and Social Structure*. Glencoe, IL: Free Press.

Morrow, William L. 1975. *Public Administration: Politics and the Political System*. New York: Random House.

Nigro, F. A. 1965. *Modern Public Administration*. New York: Harper & Row Publishers.

Presthus, Robert. 1978. *The Organizational Society*. New York: St. Martin's Press.

Sapru, R. K. 2013. *Administrative Theories and Management Thought*. Third edition. New Delhi: PHI Learning Private Limited.

Selznick, Philip. 1957. *Leadership in Administration: A Sociological Interpretation*. Illinois: Row, Peterson and Co.

Shafritz, Jay M. 2007. *Defining Public Administration: Selections from the International Encyclopedia of Public Policy and Administration*. New Delhi: Rawat Publications.

Shafritz, Jay M. and Albert C. Hyde. 1987. *Classics of Public Administration*. Chicago: The Dorsey Press.

Simon, Herbert. 1947. *Administrative Behavior: A Study of Decision-making Processes in Administrative Organization.* New York: Macmillan.

Taylor, Frederick W. 1911/1947. *The Principles of Scientific Management.* Reprinted in *Scientific Management.* New York: Harper & Row Publishers.

———. 1912/1987. 'Scientific Management'. Testimony before the US House of Representatives, 25 January. Reprinted in *Classics of Public Administration*, edited by Jay M. Shafritz and Albert C. Hyde, 32–34, Chicago: The Dorsey Press.

Weber, Max. 1922/1987. 'Bureaucracy' in *Classics of Public Administration*, edited by Shafritz and Hyde.

———. 1927/1947. *Wirtschaft und Gesellschaft*, translated into English as *The Theory of Social and Economic Organization* by A. M. Henderson and Talcott Parsons and edited with an introduction by Talcott Parsons. London: Oxford University Press.

3

PUBLICNESS OF PUBLIC ADMINISTRATION

Minnowbrook Conferences

HIGHLIGHTS

- First Minnowbrook Conference, 1968
  - New Public Administration (NPA)
- Second Minnowbrook Conference, 1988
  - New Public Management (NPM)
- Third Minnowbrook Conference, 2008
  - Redesigning public administration
  - Challenges ahead

As a field of conceptual probing, public administration owes a great deal to the three Minnowbrook Conferences (I, II and III) that have been held every two decades since 1968. Distinct in their contribution in the development of theoretical tools, these conferences were also stocktaking exercises based on a thorough review of the discipline in the prevalent contexts. There were thus two aims of the Minnowbrook Conferences: (*a*) to understand the changing nature of public administration as an activity, and (*b*) to assess whether the available conceptual categories were adequate to comprehend the phenomena. The concern was to update the knowledge-base of the discipline which also represented efforts towards addressing societal problems. Confirming that public administration is grounded in praxis, these conferences always took into account the distinct texture of the discipline while devising appropriate theoretical devices.

What is striking in these conferences is the acceptance of those general theories which inform public administration as a field of enquiry and also a confirmation of transcendental character. For instance, Minnowbrook I, held in 1968, concluded that bureaucracy, despite being criticised for its inherent tendency to centralise authority, was simply irreplaceable as its role was indispensable in handling public administration. The conclusion was however tempered by certain well-defined conditions that the participants had stipulated in order to make bureaucracy accountable and also sensitive to public needs. It was thus reiterated time and again that bureaucracy was merely a goal-driven instrument which had lost its character of being 'a benevolent guardian' due to the decline of moral values. Conceptually, it was quite enlightening because the idea had its root in the text–context dialectic. A useful theoretical claim, it also resolves a dilemma that public administration had confronted when the Wilsonian politics–administration dichotomy was upheld to retain the so-called independent identity of public administration as a distinct kind of activity. A scan of the contribution of the other two Minnowbrook Conferences (II and III) that took place in 1988 and 2008 reinforces, as will be discussed, the point that public administration is dialectically connected with the prevalent socio-economic milieu. What is common in all the past Minnowbrook conferences is a concerted effort, adequately backed by relevant theoretical paradigms, to reconceptualise public administration in a constantly transforming ecosystem. In order to understand the common concern, the aim of this chapter is to comprehend the distinctive contribution that each of the Minnowbrook Conferences has made to the development of the discipline not merely as a field of study but also as a conceptual design that seeks to understand public administration differently. The Minnowbrook Conferences thus remain critical in our search for a meaningful model of public administration which is both analytically persuasive and conceptually revealing.

FIRST MINNOWBROOK CONFERENCE, 1968

Critical of the top-driven conceptualisation of public administration, Minnowbrook I sought to redefine the discipline by focusing on its contextual character. There cannot be a straitjacketed formula since public administration as a field of enquiry is contingent on the prevalent socio-economic milieu and ideological contour of the polity. The idea is easily substantiated by reference to the core focus of the participants of the conference who strongly felt that public administration, being dependent on human experiences, could not be immune to the circumstances in which they are articulated. The delegates were unanimous in their opinion that public administration, in order to remain viable, needed to be socially relevant and accountable. The idea gained ground presumably because of the specific context in the US where the conference took place. It was held soon after the adoption of the revolutionary Voting Rights Act of 1965 which abolished racial segregation in the US. Governance was thus expected to be democratic in a truly democratic country especially after the abrogation of racial discrimination. Furthermore, campus violence and the overall emotional stress that American citizens were subjected to the draft (military conscription) for the Vietnam War also created an environment in which arguments for making governance sensitive to people's needs gained easy acceptance. To this was added the deep dissatisfaction among practitioners over the state of the discipline which, by its obsession with efficiency and economy, had also endorsed the search for an alternative conceptualisation of public administration as an area of enquiry. Minnowbrook I stood by itself in two ways: on the one hand, by exposing the theoretical limitations, the conference created a space for alternative thinking; on the other, by insisting on the primacy of politics in administration, the conference reiterated some of the arguments which are usually offered to counter the Wilsonian thesis of the dichotomy of politics and administration. With a wider definition of politics entailing the processes of deliberation, negotiation and contestation in an environment supportive of different kinds of power relationships, the delegates once again upheld the axiomatic conceptualisation of public administration as the product of text–context dialectics.

New Public Administration (NPA)

The outcome of the conference were two books: Frank Marini edited a collection called *Toward a New Public Administration* (1971) and Dwight Waldo edited another volume entitled *Public Administration in a Time of Turbulence* (1971). While the latter is largely an analysis of the socio-political crises that affected the US following the Civil Rights Movement and the Vietnam War, the former is an effort at building the conceptual foundation of what is widely known as New Public Administration (NPA). Minnowbrook I remains distinct in the evolution of the discipline for bringing about arguably a new era in public administration by focusing on certain characteristics which had till then not attracted attention: it was emphasised that public administration had to be relevant and an instrument for equity, change and social justice. Couched in the old dictum that administration is meant to subserve the public (and hence called public administration), these characteristics created a space for redefining the discipline in the changed socio-political environment.

The point that public administration has to be relevant reinforces the argument that public administration is not merely a function but one which is linked with public wellbeing; it has to be socially relevant, thereby questioning the typical management-oriented public administration. In view of its well-defined goal of contributing to social wellbeing, public administration cannot afford to ignore the aspect highlighted in its prefix—the public. Along with the concern for making the discipline relevant for the public cause, the conference also raised the epistemological issue that the knowledge that public administration has disseminated thus far did not seem relevant to understanding complex human behaviour; its failure had reduced the viability of the discipline as an enquiry capable of addressing societal problems. Being unable to conceptualise complex human behaviour, public administration had hardly any takers and this would adversely affect its existence in the long run. So, the moot point was how to make the discipline relevant both as a field of enquiry and a device to meaningfully address contemporary socio-political and economic issues.

The second characteristic highlights the importance of values and is a follow-up of the first. The conference delegates were vehemently opposed to the value-neutral position of the behavioural school of the bygone era. Since its core concern is the public, public administration can never be value-neutral, for obvious reasons. Delegates argued that public administration could not be isolated from the prevalent politico-ideological social currents as they invariably contributed to what was considered to be most appropriate policy design at a particular point of time. Moreover, administration represented a creative blend of the values that politicians carried with themselves and the administrative culture perpetuated by the memory of the office. This was the principal argument that Minnowbrook I put forward to justify that public administration can never be a value-neutral exercise so long as it is an activity geared to realise public goals. The idea was most succinctly articulated by H. George Frederickson when he stated that the new public administrator is less "generic" and more "public" than his forebear, less "descriptive" and more "prescriptive", less "institution-oriented" and more "client-impact oriented", less "neutral" and more "normative" and, it is hoped, no less scientific' (1971: 310).

The third feature of social equity highlights the normative tilt that the conference had evinced in its deliberations. Since it was public administration, it had to keep in mind, the delegates felt, concern for the public; and the government needed to be directed to attain those goals which remained connected with public wellbeing. As an instrument of authority, public administration should aim at social equity and nothing else to retain its character of being a design for public good. Thus, Marini forcefully argued that 'the purpose of public administration is the reduction of economic, social and psychic suffering and the enhancement of life opportunities for those inside and outside the organization' (1971: 32). Implicit here are two ideas: (*a*) being oriented to the public, public administration needs to be instinctively connected with public wellbeing, and (*b*) being a design for public good, it has to address the sources of suffering due to social, economic and political imbalances which are largely artificially created. The concern was to make public administration sensitive to the need for social equity—i.e. to establish a society free of prejudices and discrimination. Unless this is done, public administration will also be an instrument for oppression. As Frederickson states, 'a public administration which fails to work for changes which try to redress the deprivation of minorities will likely be eventually used to repress those minorities' (1971: 311). Here too, the vibrant political context following the removal of racial segregation and radical student movements that swept university campuses in the US seem to have swayed the participants who added several new dimensions to public administration which was until then conceptualised strictly in Weberian terms, i.e. by exclusively highlighting its instrumental role.

The final characteristic of change does not require much elaboration because once public administration internalises the above features to become NPA, it has to change its character. This 'change' also entails a broader function that public administration is expected to discharge, namely it has to be an instrument for social change to remain truly tuned to the goal it seeks to realise. Once change is accepted as its primary objective, public administration also becomes a device to bring about the required changes for public wellbeing. The stumbling blocks towards realising this change happen to be the bureaucratic hegemony over governance and the illogical concern that institutions are infallible. The proponents for NPA devised a new approach whereby catholicism in public administration is not only persuasively challenged, but also discarded as an impediment towards fulfilling the primary goal of public wellbeing which public administration is meant to realise.

With the articulation of NPA, the view that gained preeminence was that public administration was not merely technical but value-based. The hiatus between value and public administration was largely explained in terms of the discipline's alienation from political science. It was argued that unless there is 'a critical interpenetration' between political science and public administration, understanding of public administration would be lopsided. This is because the study of public administration is the study of politics as well, and a separation of these two disciplines can be intellectually 'suicidal'.

Nonetheless, the conceptualisation of NPA provoked criticism for undermining the theoretical rigour that is obvious with regard to a search for a new paradigm. One of the criticisms is its approach to simplistically conceptualise the context–text interface which may not always be captured by its surface manifestation. As Dunn and Fozouni (1976) elaborated, the weaknesses of the argument supporting context-driven public administration stems from the perception that it may not always conform to the complex reality due to it being socially embedded. It is therefore not always possible to actually understand the context, as is expected, to meaningfully comprehend the text–context interlinkages. Hence, critics are not persuaded to accept the novelty of NPA as a conceptualisation. Nonetheless, the effort that the participants in Minnowbrook I made has left an indelible mark in our search for appropriate models of public administration. This was a soul-searching exercise which, by challenging the institutional catholicism, made public administration dependent on the ongoing socio-economic and political processes while seeking to create its independent existence in the family of the social sciences.

SECOND MINNOWBROOK CONFERENCE, 1988

Unlike the first conference which sought to design public administration as an instrument for public wellbeing, Minnowbrook II took place at a time when the world was witnessing events leading to the disintegration of the Soviet Union. This was not merely the physical disappearance of a nation-state but also the dwindling importance of an ideology supportive of the role of public sector in development. In its place, the Capitalist emphasis on the role of private actors for growth and development seemed to have gained preeminence. Minnowbrook II reflected on this changing nature of governance by taking into account the flash points responsible for reorienting public administration in the changed socio-economic and political milieu. With the increasing importance of the private sector, the State was no longer tenable as a major dispenser of social justice. The popular mood was against the State for its dismal performance in almost every sphere of human existence in the so-called Socialist regimes. The public sector that had gradually become a platform for consolidating partisan interests completely failed to bring about the expected changes in the economy. What was required was managerial intervention to improve human life. The aim was to make governance more 'result-oriented' and 'accountability-driven'. Hence, the following five key areas[1] were identified as needing immediate attention:

1. Government should provide high-quality services that citizens value
2. The autonomy of public managers should be respected

[1] This is drawn on Medury (2010: 51).

3. Organisations and individuals should be evaluated and rewarded on the basis of how well they meet demanding performance targets
4. Managers should be assured that human and technological resources will be available to them if they perform well
5. Public sector managers must appreciate the value of competition and not be prejudiced against the private sector if that contributes to realising their goal.

New Public Management (NPM)

The participants of Minnowbrook II were united in their concern for the dismal performance of the public sector which had become the custodian of vested interests at the cost of common wellbeing. Unlike their predecessors in Minnowbrook I, these participants were persuaded to believe that public administration was everything but an instrument for public betterment. Insisting that the root cause of the decline of public administration was the lack of managerial efficiency, Minnowbrook II preferred to overhaul the government machinery by managerial means. This was amply clear when the idea of New Public Management (NPM) was conceptualised with the following features:

- It proposed a thorough organisational revamping so that organisational structure can become conducive for organisational leadership. Organisation restructuring includes simplifying organisational procedures, flattening hierarchies, among others.
- One of the major hallmarks of NPM was the empowerment of citizens. Unlike traditional public administration, it reconceptualised citizens as active customers to be always kept in good humour.
- It called for more autonomy for public sector managers. It was in favour of greater elbowroom for managerial leadership by providing public managers with greater flexibility in personnel policy like contractual appointment, workplace bargaining, etc.
- Application of rigorous performance measurement techniques was another defining feature of NPM.
- It suggested disaggregation of public bureaucracies into agencies which would deal with one another on a user-pay basis.
- Inspired by the New Right Philosophy, the NPM endorsed crosscutting in public sector.
- It encouraged quasi-market and contracting out techniques to ensure better management of ailing cash-strapped public sector organisations.
- It believed in a decentralised form of governance. It encouraged all types of organisational and spatial decentralisation.

NPM focuses on the entrepreneurial government. It is a participatory management and community-owned governance in which citizens are considered as active consumers and not as recipients of programmes and policies. The main objective is to empower the citizens. The idea was conceptualised very clearly by David Osborne and Ted Gaebler in *Reinventing Government: How the Entrepreneurial Spirit is Transforming the Public Sector* (1992). The success of the entrepreneurial government is contingent on (*a*) improving public management through performance, measurement and evaluation, (*b*) reducing budgets, (*c*) downsizing the government, (*d*) selective privatisation of public enterprises and (*e*) contracting out in selective areas. Thus the focus is on debureaucratisation, democratisation and decentralisation of administrative processes in the interests of the citizens. The concept of entrepreneurial government has further led to the recognition of the role of multiple agencies in organising and undertaking public business. In addition to formal government, the role of non-governmental organisations (NGOs) and community-based organisations (CBOs) has also been acknowledged as supplementary agencies.

Evaluating NPM

Change was evident in public administration in the 1980s and early 1990s. The context of public administration was changed in favour of less-directly-performing government and governance, more privatisation and contracting out, more voluntarism and social-capacity building. The values of public purpose came to be steadily replaced by the emerging values of private interests. An essentially market-driven rhetoric, NPM is based on the premise that by narrowing down the scope of government activities, efficient, tranparent, effective and accountable governance would emerge. The rationale appears to be that with fewer bureaucratic structures there would be fewer problems. NPM can be distinguished from NPA by (*a*) its clear emphasis on business management practices, and (*b*) its reliance on individual rationalities and market mechanisms in the restructuring and operation of public administration. The anti-public service stand created a strong challenge for managing diversity in the public sector. Administration is something more than rational operative acton. It is full of meaning and is often mired in conflict and controversy, at the root of which lie various values which shape the cultural characteristics of any organisation (Dwivedi 2002).

As already observed, NPM is a design which is guided by global Capitalism. For Capitalism to prosper, it needs a strong State and a stable environment. It demands order and social control without which the market cannot be as efficient as is desirable for global capital. Capitalism needs a strong State and bureaucracy to flourish, as powerful business elites can then dominate the policy process and its outcomes. To protect the system from periodic collapse and provide safety nets for promoting Capitalist development, market failures demand government intervention in the economy. Thus the modern State, through public expenditure, plays a significant role in the accelerated development of Capitalism and globalisation. To be fair to these systems, it is appropriate to argue that they also spend a significant portion of their budget to support a relatively trouble-free and stable political system that is also necessary for the growth and sustenance of a socio-political order without which globalisation cannot prosper.

The rise of NPM to preeminence coincides with societal changes, which is theorised as a shift from government to governance: from coordinated, hierarchical structures and processes of societal steering to a network-based process of exchange and negotiation. The NPM is thus a paradigmatic change in public administration as the following characteristics suggest: First, the traditional output-oriented administration is replaced by the process-oriented administration with emphasis on performance indicators, evaluations and performance-related pay, and improvement in quality; second, the focus is on the flexible provision of individualised products instead of 'collective provision', hence 'customer' replaces 'citizen', and the 'production line' of public administration is broken down into individual pieces for 'contracting out' or 'privatisation'; third, structurally, 'clusters' rather than 'pyramids' are the preferred design for administration in which autonomous agencies or institutions outside the formal government are inducted in governance as 'complementary structures' of public administration; finally, there is a clear shift of general emphasis from policy to management with full cost consciousness before making any decision.

There is no doubt that NPM is a refreshing input to our search for 'an appropriate' model for public administration: first, it has brought back the old debate between government administration and business administration; second, by seeking to review the bureaucracy-centred public administration in the name of 'state-minimalism', it has raised issues which are pertinent in redefining the contours of public administration in its contemporary manifestation. The fundamental question is whether public administration can be conceptualised as NPM. The market-driven NPM is qualitatively different from public administration which is guided by the distinct purpose of supporting and developing collective life by choosing goods and services essential to the community as a whole, establishing collective efficiency and devising social and political rules in support of a particular system of order. Public administration is also a space in which citizens and government interact dialectically. Public policy is thus not merely government-driven, but an outcome of such an interaction which is conceptually understood as 'the politics of participation'.

THIRD MINNOWBROOK CONFERENCE, 2008

In the evolution of public administration as a field of enquiry, Minnowbrook III, held in 2008, was as important as the earlier Minnowbrook Conferences of 1968 and 1988. While Minnowbrook I marked the beginning of NPA, Minnowbrook II provided NPM as a theoretical discourse for the discipline in the context of globalisation. The context of Minnowbrook III is not significantly different though globalisation has manifested itself in a varied form which was inconceivable for the participants of Minnowbrook II. Unlike the first two conferences, Minnowbrook III was held in two parts: in the first pre-Conference workshop at the original Minnowbrook site on Blue Mountain Lake, junior faculty members presented their views to initiate debates on 'the problem areas' of contemporary public administration; the second workshop, held in Lake Placid, in which scholars of all ages and experience participated. This division of the conference was useful in conceptualising the difficulties that public administration was confronting in a globalising world in two different and yet complementary perspectives:

one perspective, rooted in the complex texture of globalisation, seemed to have governed the effort at building universal models; and the other related to the quest for context-specific models underlining simultaneously the possible influences from the wider global milieu. It was, therefore, an occasion to chart the future roadmap for public administration by involving both senior academics like Frederickson, Lambright and Rosemary O'Leary and their younger counterparts. By strongly arguing for a context-driven perspective, younger colleagues forcefully put their points on the table. And, there is no doubt that the critique of the new scholars seems to have set the agenda for Minnowbrook III. As it was articulated, the critique reflected the genuine concerns of those seeking to conceptualise public administration as an organic discipline that was adequately equipped to respond to the new demands of global human concerns. Primarily, the scholars focused on the specific areas of 'discomfort' that appeared to have been critical in contemporary research in public administration. Public administration has become a complex area of human endeavour simply because of equally complex socio-economic circumstances in which it is rooted as a practice. Hence the scholars highlighted the following challenges that needed to be addressed meaningfully to re-orient the discipline: (*a*) the challenge of remaining relevant, (*b*) the challenge of understanding public administration with the election of the first African-American US president, (*c*) the challenge of teaching public administration in Asia, given the clear Western bias of the discipline, (*d*) the challenge of evolving a global public administration in view of tendencies towards creating a global discourse, and (*e*) the challenge of retaining an independent identity for the discipline since public administration has reportedly been 'roofied (drugged) and rolled (mugged)' by economics (O'Leary, Van Slyke and Kim 2010: 9).

Like their younger colleagues, senior faculty members who participated in the Lake Placid deliberations identified key themes that needed a threadbare discussion to reinvent public administration given the articulation of powerful critiques of Weberian command bureaucracy. As evident in the text that emerged out of Minnowbrook III, five key themes drew the attention of the participants:

- How different is the field of public administration in 2008 from 1968 and 1988? What is public administration in 2008?
- Can there be definitive theoretical and empirical conclusions about the market-oriented NPM that had by then had a thirty-year history
- Given the influx of scholars from many disciplines into public administration, is public administration closer or farther away from developing a core theoretical base?
- How are new ideas about networked governance and collaborative public management changing the way we look at public administration, public management and public service? Are they changing the practice of public administration? Should they change what we teach in our programmes?
- How has globalisation affected our understanding of the key challenges that face the study and practice of public administration, public management and public service in the US, the developed world, and developing and transitional countries? (Ibid.: 12)

The key themes are clearly indicative of a roadmap for public administration both as a discipline and as a practice. Instead of pondering over the grand theory, the participants focused more on what works and what does not while dwelling on the changing nature of public administration. Theoretically, it is fair to suggest that Minnowbrook III represented both Simonesque and Waldonian perspectives: those upholding the former were drawn to economics, organisation theory and management, while those clinging to Waldonian methodological tools seemed to have appreciated frameworks and models from political science, sociology, philosophy and history. The prevalence of two important perspectives also confirms that as a field of study, public administration continued to be relatively diverse and 'multi-theoretical'. The advantage is obvious: as a practical science, public administration is context-driven and the participants of Minnowbrook III, by being appreciative of the philosophical concerns of Simon and Waldo, strengthened the multidisciplinary texture of the discipline. Praxis in character, public administration is another meaningful effort at comprehending human activities embedded in myriad socio-economic forces which are both contextual and also historically-articulated. By highlighting 'the organic nature' of the discipline, Minnowbrook III sought to rearticulate its 'human face' that was sadly missing in Minnowbrook II with the uncritical acceptance of the neoliberal and market-driven Structural Adjustment Programme (SAP) to address economic underdevelopment.

Minnowbrook III is undoubtedly a break with the past for two specific reasons: first, by reiterating some of the major concerns of Minnowbrook I, the participants seemed to have put in place an agenda which was based on collaboration, interaction and meaningful engagement with the stakeholders. There always existed a perceptible gap between public problems and government capacity and capability. What was thus required was goal-driven participatory governance which is surely an innovative theoretical conceptualisation in the age of shrinking governments. In this sense, Minnowbrook III reiterates the concern of the first conference which sought to redesign public administration by insisting on its 'commitment to responsiveness, social equality and participation' (Frederickson 1980: 4–12). The peculiar nature of contemporary public administration created circumstances in which agencies other than the government became important in solving public problems. The public in public administration is thus redefined because public administration is no longer understood as mere government-driven activities. Second, by reaching out to learn non-Western experiences of dealing with public problems, Minnowbrook III is a counter to ethnocentric public administration. One should adopt a global approach to public governance to understand the intricate functioning of the institutions that remain critical in public administration. Given the state of technological advancement, it is easier for scholars to interact and collaborate among themselves, it also creates opportunities for broader engagement and learning among a diverse set of communities. In the context of globalisation, despite its contextual character, public administration is well-equipped to meaningfully address human concerns of varied nature. The discipline has thus become both a scholarly enterprise and also a well-designed and goal-oriented device to offer meaningful solutions to human problems.

Redesigning Public Administration in the Changing Global Environment

In the context of globalisation, public administration ceases to become nation-centric since it is open to various kinds of influences which are rooted elsewhere in the world. In order to respond to these 'new' demands, the discipline needs to shake-off its ethnocentric character. One of the areas that clearly reflected this concern was Comparative Public Administration (CPA) which was largely oriented towards theories of governance and public management. It viewed public administration as truly interdisciplinary and appreciated crossdisciplinary borrowing unlike its earlier incarnation which heavily drew on grand theories and remained 'inflexible'. Besides its substantially-altered theoretical perspectives, the focus of CPA has also undergone radical changes. Contrary to past practices when bureaucracy remained the primary focus of attention, public administration in its present articulation is multidimensional in which bureaucracy remains one of the mechanisms for governance. This is reflected in approaches to administrative reforms that involve the role of the stakeholders in governance—an area that was never considered significant in previous conceptualisations. One of the significant outcomes of Minnowbrook III is the idea that administrative reform is not a one-time phenomenon—it is a continuous process in which the role of mechanisms other than public bureaucracy is equally significant and critical. Simultaneously, with such a conceptualisation comes another perspective critiquing the ethnocentric bias of the scholars of CPA. By highlighting the significance of crosscultural borrowing, Minnowbrook III emphasises the importance of learning from different experiences to evolve a meaningful methodology to understand the contextual peculiarities of public administration in varied socio-economic and political circumstances. Being critical of 'the top-down model', participants seem to have focused more on 'the reasons for reform diffusion' rather than attributing the failure of reforms to the inflexible, if not inept, bureaucracy in developing countries. The fundamental point that came out of Minnowbrook III is a serious endeavour to capture the changing nature of public governance in a globalising world when crossnational experiences are considered most critical in reconceptualising public administration. The most powerful voice that was articulated in Minnowbrook III was a challenge to the efforts at explaining the diverse nature of public administration with those theoretical models that have grown out of the US-specific socio-economic circumstances. So to remain meaningful in the present context, there is a need to reinvent public administration by underlining the distinctive nature of public administration in different national contexts in a global perspective.

The context in which Minnowbrook III took place needs special attention. Ours is a network society. The key driver in the emergence of network society is technology, primarily new information and communication technologies (ICTs) and its growth is dependent on the ability of actors and institutions to perform communicatively and effectively in the emerging networks by reaping the benefits of the new technology paradigm. The network society is 'new' in the sense that networks are no longer relegated to private or social life but have become key to economic production as well as public policymaking and implementation. The network society consists of networks operated by ICTs that generate, process and distribute information on the basis of the knowledge accumulated in the nodes of the network.[2] In such a context, the idea of collaborative governance seems to have taken 'organic roots', as clearly articulated by the participants in Minnowbrook III.

Minnowbrook III emphasised the importance of 'collaborative governance' as perhaps the best shield against 'government slackening' or bureaucratic delay. In an interdependent world, collaborative governance refers to ways of institutionalising coordination and by establishing decision-making processes that work in multiorganisational settings such as networks of government agencies. The key to effective decision-making is a meaningful coordination among various institutions involved in making and implementing decisions. Furthermore, there has to be compatibility between policy decisions and government capability, otherwise it will lead to policy paralysis simply because the institutional capacity of the government is inadequate to translate the decisions into deeds. This is a serious impediment to the growth of public administration as 'a solid science' as Minnowbrook III underlines. In order to address the difficulties arising out of a lack of coordination among the governmental institutions/agencies, the Conference introduced a new concept of 'interoperability'—an idea borrowed from the engineering sciences, referring to the ability of diverse systems and organisations to work together. This is a term which is often used in a technical system engineering sense, or alternatively in a broad sense; it is about a process of working together by taking into account all possible social, political and organisational factors that impact the outcome. In the wake of the ICT revolution, interoperability is a value addition in public administration through 'the creation of connected [or networked] systems that facilitate better decision making, better coordination of government programs and enhanced services to citizens and businesses' (Pardo, Gil-Garcia and Luna-Reyes 2011: 133). The key driver in the construction of interoperability is technology, primarily new ICTs. As the findings of the Conference identifies, the following list provides examples of how interoperable systems can contribute to the creation of meaningful and people-enabled governance:

- *Democracy and citizen participation*: (*a*) access to information for engaging in political activities such as advocating, debating and voting, (*b*) creation of new electronic forums for citizen engagement.
- *Transparency and trust*: access to integrated, holistic views of government resources and operations create transparency and build citizen trust in and allegiance to government.
- *Citizen and business services*: (*a*) information about benefits and services available to citizens that they would otherwise be unaware of or unable to acquire; (*b*) easy-to-use, accessible and geographically-distributed citizen and business services (multichannel access to payment services and application forms).

[2] The argument is drawn on Bang and Esmark (2009).

- *Government management and economic development*: (*a*) internal, modernised infrastructure for government operations to support the back-office processing of citizen and business services and provide information; (*b*) improved government-wide coordination for responding to crisis such as natural disasters or public health problems; (*c*) facilitating the creation of consumer–producer networks and alternative, more sustainable markets, such as fair trade.
- *Government long-term strategy and policymaking*: (*a*) consolidated databases and data warehouses providing information to support strategic planning and policymaking in government; (*b*) stimulate local, regional and national economies by attracting investments through an enhanced reputation for improved government operations and new and innovative services available to citizens and businesses (ibid.).

The primary concern of today's public governance is to make government sensitive to the public. And, interoperability creates a context for the rise and consolidation of collaborative governance that characterises the 'processes and structure of public decision making and management that enable constructive engagement within or across public agencies, levels of government, private and public interest sectors and the public at large' (Emerson and Murchie 2010: 142). Collaborative governance includes, argues Carlson, 'a variety of processes in which all sectors—public, private and civic—are convened to work together to achieve solutions to public problems that go beyond what any sector could achieve on its own' (2007: 6). This is not only a step towards serious civic engagement, but also a sure guarantee to consolidate participatory democracy that both strengthens 'public voice' and improves the responsiveness of the government by 'providing an opportunity to embed governance systems and institutions with greater levels of transparency, accountability and legitimacy' (Henton and Melville 2005: 5).

Collaborative governance is a meaningful articulation of some specific techniques (which are again situation-driven) to reemphasise 'the publicness' of public administration. This is a significant theoretical conceptualisation which is both 'enabling' and reflective of a movement towards reconfirming the public roots of governance. By laying the foundation for serious public engagement, collaborative governance is about those practices upholding some of the principles of Minnowbrook I that sought to project 'the human face' of public administration by emphasising its concern for public wellbeing. It is thus a well-defined practice that is designed to foster more effective engagement or deliberations with the whole of agencies and stakeholders, including 'creating conditions (for transparency and coordination) and capacity for people to engage constructively (by providing resources and skills)' (Emerson and Murchie 2010: 143).

The other fundamental point that attracted significant attention concerns the visible decline of democratic ethos and the relative ascendancy of bureaucratic ethos in contemporary public decision-making which is explained in terms of the failure of 'deliberative democracy' to take root in process itself. In the era of governance, public administration refers to a process-driven act in which the role of the citizen seems to be negligible and thus contrary to the idea of deliberative democracy which refers to 'infusing government decision making with the reasoned discussion and collective judgment of citizens' (Nabatchi 2011: 159). The reasons are to be located in the traditional emphasis on bureaucracy-centric public administration since the publication of Woodrow Wilson's *The Study of Public Administration* in 1887. Luther Gulick's 1937 conceptualisation of POSDCORB (an acronym for planning, organising, staffing, directing, coordinating, reporting and budgeting) and Herbert Simon's notion of bounded rationality (1947) further strengthen this perspective and public administration as a discipline remained confined, to a significant extent, to explaining various dimensions of the involvement of bureaucracy in public decision-making. The obvious result is what can be conceptualised as 'citizenship deficit', referring to the withdrawal of citizens in matters of public consequences. As a result, the discipline fails to adequately confront and grasp the issues of public administration in a democracy where the political system acts on collective choices or decides on the basis of civic engagement. Several new issues grip public attention, but so far remain peripheral in public decision-making. In the changed socio-economic circumstances of the twenty-first century, public administration is not merely a faceless function but an act that embodies 'a different set of norms and principles, such as regime values, citizenship, public interest and social equity' (Nabatchi 2011: 162). Prominent scholars—those who reconceptualised public administration within the theoretical paradigm of democratic ethos—include John Gaus, Marshall Dimock, Paul Appleby, Norton Long, Frederick Mosher and Dwight Waldo. By integrating administrative practices with democratic values, not only did these authors reinvent public administration, they also initiated a new debate in the discipline suggesting the critical importance of the context in understanding the nature of public administration—an initiative that challenged the effort at building a universal model following the Weberian theoretical dispositions. Deliberative democracy is a theoretical design for the 'rediscovery' of democratic ethos in public administration. Drawn on the basic democratic values of inclusion, equity, participation and public interest, this provides an institutionalised design for formally involving citizens in the making of public decisions because dialogue among stakeholders creates a forum for discussions and deliberations which generally lead to a consensual decision and in this sense it is a process that is more than mere aggregation of individual views. Deliberative democracy is thus an effective mechanism to relocate 'the public in the discipline of shaping public affairs [and in doing so] provides a way to help balance the tensions between the bureaucratic and democratic ethos in public administration' (ibid.).

Challenges Ahead

Similar to Minnowbrook II, Minnowbrook III is both a stocktaking exercise and also an articulation of the roadmap for public administration in the changed socio-economic environment of a globalising world. While reviewing the efforts at 'repositioning public administration' in the context of globalisation, the participants agreed that the expectations remained un-fulfilled. As a discipline, public administration does not seem to be well-equipped to manage an administrative state that is jurisdictionally, functionally and sectorally fragmented. This creates possibilities of interdisciplinary borrowings to understand the complex articulation of administration with reference to the constantly changing global scenario. There is a serious lack of meaningful theoretical yardstick. The Weberian model of bureaucracy and management is undoubtedly less relevant to public administration than it once was, yet it remains 'a sharper set of intellectual tools than the still-fuzzy concept of governance [which is] confusing because it lacks a precise definition' (Frederickson and Smith 2003: 209). Nonetheless, the idea of governance cannot be altogether ignored because it does formally recognise the role of the practitioners of public administration in re-conceptualising and repositioning the discipline in conjunction with the volatile socio-economic circumstances around the globe. Public administration has to address this concern and governance, despite its obvious theoretical limitations, seems to have provided possible tools to capture the changed reality. The growing acceptance of governance to mean public administration also confirms that the discipline no longer remains 'boundary-conscious' and the issues that had emerged in Minnowbrook III are reflective of a growing openness to new ideas, coupled with enduring issues that span the decades. Minnowbrook III is thus said to have provided a new attire to public administration by throwing away its 'orthodoxy' that appeared to have impeded its growing as a discipline with its organic link to the prevalent socio-economic circumstances.

Despite disagreements among participants over various issues, there developed a consensus on the following issues which were likely to set the basic agenda for future research in public administration. First, the most obvious and important issue that was addressed in Minnowbrook III was the impact of globalisation on the field. This is an important change since Minnowbrook II and certainly since Minnowbrook I. The globe has become a single entity. Seeking to capture such an interconnected entity within the rubric of globalisation, participants in Minnowbrook III focused more on the new dimensions of connectedness, interdependency, knowledge-sharing in governance and collaborative public management among government agencies and across international boundaries. So the challenge before analysts is not only to comprehend public administration in the changed environment, but also to identify its distinctive features which were hardly visible in the command administration of the Weberian bureaucracy-driven paradigm. The fundamental question that was raised related to reconceptualising democratic (in the liberal sense) governance as a means to transparency and accountability even in political systems which are not democratically-constituted in the conventional sense.

The second issue that attracted attention related to the effort at building and consolidating collaborative governance as perhaps a panacea to weak or inadequate administration. Critical of hierarchical governance, the governance paradigm underlines the importance of connected forms of administration through networks, contracts and a range of IT innovations in which the government is an important institutional actor, but not the only or most important one. As a result, collaboration is the principal norm in administration and power is 'diffused through a number of institutional mechanisms and policy instruments' which is manifested in the growing importance of managerial tools such as, 'facilitation, negotiations, collaborative problem solving and dispute resolution' in public administration' (Van Slyke, O'Leary and Kim 2010: 284).

Governance is not a managerial response to public administration; it is a political response underlining critical public engagement in societal issues. The concern was to ensure public participation and public engagement in policy discussion and implementation. In order to make public administration 'democratic' and 'transparent', meaningful public participation in decision-making is required, through creation of forums for effective dialogue among the stakeholders. This was a perspective in which NPA was conceptualised in the context of Minnowbrook I. What is new in the third conference is a clear shift in focus: the public always remains, at least conceptually, a critical component and hence it is assumed to be a driving force in public administration. Minnowbrook III is different from Minnowbrook I in answering when and how best to involve the public in public administration. This is a recurring problem regardless of circumstances: it is easier to conceptualise public in its reactive role; but it is difficult to make public 'pro-active' in issues of public governance unless situations change radically. Nonetheless, the basic point highlighting the importance of public participation in governance is very useful in relocating public administration in its new avatar in the field of the social sciences.

Public administration is extremely benefitted by the easy availability of new tools of communication following the IT revolution. No one can deny the growing role of IT tools in the public sector; in fact, IT has facilitated decision-making by ensuring access to a huge array of information which may not have been otherwise available. One of the most significant outcomes of IT-enabled public administration is e-governance that has become an acceptable form in contemporary governance not only because it is cost-efficient, but also because it is transparent and time-saving. A new idea of interoperability, which is a mix of policy, management and technology, has gained precedence in contemporary governance. This is an era of network governance which is based on effective coordination among stakeholders on the basis of shared information and knowledge from different sources. There are two ways in which coordination is articulated: (*a*) information sharing whereby information is transferred from one agency to another, and (*b*) information integration which involves not only the transfer of information, but also translation and transformation of information to evolve new techniques of collective problem-solving. Both these concepts converge into an integrated database of inputs that remain very useful in addressing similar problems in the future; the availability of database, once inadequate to conclusively solve problems, is likely to provoke further research in areas which need attention. So, with the access to IT-driven techniques, public administration appears to have further enriched its theoretical tools which were inconceivable in the era of command bureaucracy, but have become integral to contemporary public administration presumably because of the consolidation of a networked-global-village.

In one fundamental sense, Minnowbrook III is a continuity of the past in the sense that the principal concern of the participants since the first conference has remained the same. The common theme that ran across the Minnowbrook Conferences across four decades was the challenge of remaining relevant. There is a clear lack of connection between scholarship and practice in public administration which, the participants feared, needed to be meaningfully addressed to make public administration relevant in the era of globalisation. In other words, the focus has been on the nature of public administration. Hence the question—how to make public administration relevant—seems most pertinent. The entire discussion revolves around this question and David Rosenbloom, in his closing plenary remarks during Minnowbrook III, listed the following four proactive steps to make public administration 'a stronger and more robust field'.[3]

First, supportive of collaborative research, Rosenbloom insisted on 'the need to aggregate knowledge in the sense of making it cumulative'. In order to make public administration a meaningful tool of analysis of real human problems, the scholars need to develop a common framework on the basis of give-and-take not only from their counterparts in the discipline, but also from other disciplines. By being rigidly boundary-conscious, the scholars have done more harm than what was apprehended. Public administration needs to be interdisciplinary by shunning its orthodoxy. The second point, raised by Rosenbloom is a demand 'to maintain methodological and epistemological pluralism' in public administration. The effort here is to welcome pluralism in our choice for methodology because imposition of a single or hegemonic methodology or epistemology shall 'narrow and weaken the field'. Third, one of the sources of weakness in contemporary public administration is its failure to understand non-Western administration, presumably because of its catholicity in clinging to a single set of values—whether utilitarian, instrumental, egalitarian, libertarian or contractarian—while addressing contemporary administration-related concerns. In view of the complex nature of the prevalent system of administration which is enmeshed with equally complex socio-economic and political factors, the theoretical catholicism may certainly be an impediment to articulating a creative response. Finally, Rosenbloom is highly critical of boundary-conscious public administration. He is in favour of promoting boundary-spanning. The discipline shall never be adequately practice-driven unless the boundary-obsession of the scholars disappears, he argues. According to him, serious academic probing in public administration in comparative perspectives is a significant step towards making the discipline well-equipped to handle diverse socio-economic problems; and also, by being receptive to the developments in related fields of economics, sociology, business administration and political science, scholars of public administration will further enhance their capacity to intervene in collective problem-solving.

As the above discussion shows, while taking stock of the developments in public administration in the contemporary context, Minnowbrook III reiterated some of the concerns of those participating in Minnowbrook I. The effort was to make the discipline relevant and meaningful in addressing contemporary human concerns. With the growing ascendancy of market, public administration, in order to remain relevant, seems to have tilted in favour of private enterprises.

---

[3] The ideas in the following section, including the summary of the points, were made by David Rosenbloom in the plenary session of the Minnowbrook III. The text here draws on Van Slyke, O'Leary and Kim (2010: 290–91).

The fulcrum had, it is argued, moved to 'a position beyond the center in which government was now in a relationship not of interdependence but of dependence on private and non-profit firms to deliver government services' (Kim, et al. 2010: 14). Bureaucracy, which has become just one of the agencies in public administration, is no longer the centre of gravity in governance. So what is required is a new theoretical parameter to reconceptualise governance in the changed socio-economic environment. Minnowbrook III is certainly a meaningful step in this regard. Despite serious disagreements among the participants, however they came together by their search for acceptable theoretical designs to explain the complex administrative processes. A consensus seems to have thus arrived on the point that public administration needs to be creative to remain meaningful and relevant in rather uncertain times of our civilisation.

CONCLUDING OBSERVATIONS

The above analytical assessment of the contribution of the three Minnowbrook Conferences reinforces three important points which are indicative of the changing nature of public administration. First, the argument that public administration is situation-specific receives strong backing from the way it unfolded in these three conferences. The nature of public administration as an area of human activity has undergone a sea change since the context in which it is located is always in flux. It was therefore not surprising that the arguments that Minnowbrook I offered in favour of the public sector were hardly appreciated by those participating in the succeeding conference in 1988. Second, since the tenor of the conference radically differed from one conference to another, there was hardly any unanimity in so far as conceptual parameters were concerned. While the first and third conferences drew on a conceptual package which seems to have privileged public over private, the second conference was heavily disposed towards marketisation of public services which may not be a defensible solution across boards largely due to well-entrenched socio-economic differences separating one country from another. Third, the deliberations in these conferences also bolster the claim that for an appropriate understanding of public administration, conceptual catholicity is an impediment; what is needed is a crossdisciplinary borrowing of concepts and ideas to unravel the dynamics of the processes of governance; otherwise, the study will merely be descriptive and non-analytical. As public administration is a human endeavour it cannot be grasped mechanically; it has to be conceptualised by drawing on those relevant ideas from other disciplines which are directed to understand human activities in their actual manifestation. In a nutshell, what is distinctive about the three Minnowbrook Conferences over a period of four decades since 1968 is the insistence on the interdisciplinary exchange of ideas and concepts to unravel the dynamics of public administration in practice.

The Minnowbrook Conferences are integral to the evolution of public administration as a discipline. At one level, these are primarily stocktaking exercises at an interval of two decades; at another, they are efforts towards redesigning the discipline in response to new social needs. Fundamental here is the conceptualisation that public administration is not just instrumental which means that it is exclusively a tool, being employed by political bosses to realise public goals in accordance with their priorities; instead, it is a process-driven endeavour, directed towards fulfilling certain definite goals which are always justified as being tuned to public benefits. There are two points that need attention here: on the one hand, it is emphasised that governance is an exercise which draws on the prevalent political, economic and social compulsions; as it is a context-dependent behaviour, public administration also articulates, on the other hand, newer issues which acquire salience in the changed milieu. The campaign in India for the Right to Information Act 2005, which replaced the archaic Official Secrets Act of 1923, cannot be understood without reference to the processes of democratisation creating specific kinds of impulses among the demos. That a decision is an outcome of multiple pulls and pressures confirms that public administration is not just instrumental, but drawn on the wider ideological environment.

There is one final point. An analytical scan of the deliberations of the three Minnowbrook conferences reconfirms that public administration has hardly a static conceptual boundary; it is constantly shifting, which means that public administration is also constantly evolving in response to inputs from the ecosystem. Contrary to the Weberian conceptualisation of public administration as rigid, rule-bound and hierarchical, the delegates in the conferences argued for the importance of citizens as stakeholders in governance. The idea is a powerful input in so far as the evolution of public administration as an area of activity is concerned. There is however a point of disappointment since what runs through all the conferences is an implicit desire to build a one-size-fits-all model by ignoring the fact that public administration is also praxis. An attempt was made in Minnowbrook III by emphasising the importance of comparative studies of administrations, located in various corners of the globe. Instead of generating models of governance from within the non-Western context, delegates preferred to develop their own models on the basis of these socio-culturally distinct inputs. Implicit here is the ethnocentric attitude supportive of neo-Taylorism which is conceptually prejudice-driven and empirically misleading. To sum up, the contribution of the conferences is immensely significant if public administration is conceptualised as an exercise within the Western context; not only did the conferences lay out distinctive theoretical formulas, they also helped us understand public administration as a context-driven process. The conceptual argument, however, loses salience in the non-Western context because the designs that came out of the deliberations can hardly be of any help because they are neither connected to the unique socio-economic circumstances nor have they emerged out of the peculiar non-Western experiences. Hence it can persuasively be argued that the Minnowbrook Conferences, despite having made immense theoretical contribution to the evolution of public administration as an area of enquiry, did not appear to be free from the conceptual weaknesses of the Western approaches once they are applied to the non-Western context.

REFERENCES

Bang, Henrik and Anders Esmark. 2009. 'Good Governance in Network Society: Reconfiguring the Political from Politics to Policy'. *Administrative Theory & Praxis* 31 (1): 7–37.

Carlson, C. 2007. *A Practical Guide to Collaborative Governance*. Oregon: Policy Consensus Initiative.

Dunn, William N. and Bahman Fozouni. 1976. *Toward a Critical Administrative Theory*. London: Sage.

Dwivedi, O. P. 2002. 'The Challenge of Cultural Diversity for Good Governance'. *Indian Journal of Public Administration* 48 (1): 22–27.

Emerson, Kirk and Peter Murchie. 2010. 'Collaborative Governance and Climate Change: Opportunities for Public Administration' in *The Future of Public Administration around the World: The Minnowbrook Perspective*, edited by Rosemary O'Leary, David M. Van Slyke and Soonhee Kim, 141–54. Washington, DC: Georgetown University Press.

Frederickson, H George. 1971. 'Toward a New Public Administration' in *Toward a New Public Administration: The Minnowbrook Perspective*, edited by Frank Marini, 309–31. California: Chandler.

———. 1980. *New Public Administration*. Alabama: The University of Alabama Press.

Frederickson, H. George and Kevin B. Smith. 2003. *The Public Administration Theory Primer*. First edition. Boulder: Westview Press.

Henton, D. and J. Melville, with T. Amsler and M. Kopell. 2005. *Collaborative Governance: A Guide for Grantmakers*. Menlo Park, CA: William and Flora Hewlett Foundation.

Kim, Sonhee, Rosemary O'Leary, David M. Van Slyke, H George Frederickson and W. Henry Lambright. 2010. 'Introduction: The Legacy of Minnobrook' in *The Future of Public Administration around the World*, edited by O'Leary, Van Slyke and Kim, 1–14.

Marini, Frank. 1971. 'Introduction' in *Toward a New Public Administration*, edited by Marini, 32.

Medury, Uma. 2010. *Public Administration in the Globalisation Era: The New Public Management Perspective*. New Delhi: Orient BlackSwan.

Nabatchi, Tina. 2011. 'Why Public Administration should take Deliberative Democracy Seriously' in *The Future of Public Administration around the World*, edited by O'Leary, Van Slyke and Kim, 159–66.

O'Leary, Rosemary, David M. Van Slyke and Soonhee Kim, eds. 2011. *The Future of Public Administration around the World: The Minnowbrook Perspective*. Washington, DC: Georgetown University Press.

Pardo, Theresa A., J Ramon Gil-Garcia and Luis F. Luna-Reyes. 2011. 'Collaborative Governance and Cross-boundary Information Sharing: Envisioning a Networked and IT-enabled Public Administration' in *The Future of Public Administration around the World*, edited by O'Leary, van Slyke and Kim, 129–40.

Simon, Herbert. 1947. *Administrative Behavior: A Study of Decision-making Processes in Administrative Organization*. New York: Macmillan.

Van Slyke, David M. Rosemary O'Leary and Soonhee Kim. 2010. 'Conclusion: Challenges and Opportunities, Crosscutting Themes, and Thoughts on the Future of Public Administration' in *The Future of Public Administration around the World*, edited by O'Leary, Van Slyke and Kim, 281–94.

4

CONTEMPORARY THEORETICAL DEVELOPMENTS

HIGHLIGHTS

- New Public Administration (NPA)
- New Public Management (NPM)
- Feminist approach
- Good governance
  - Corporate governance
  - Environmental governance
  - E-governance

The previous chapter suggested the emergence of new nations in Asia, Africa and Latin America in the post-War period and how it set a new trend in the study of public administration. Western scholars, particularly American, began showing much interest in the study of the varied administrative patterns of these newly-independent nations, leading to the development of comparative, ecological and development administration perspectives in the field of public administration (Corson and Harris 1963/1967: 1). Young behaviouralists, under the direction of change-oriented academics, promoted a cross-disciplinary approach to the analysis of governmental bureaucracies. The cross-cultural and cross-national administrative studies provided the impetus necessary for the expansion of public administration. Moreover, American society was going through a turbulent time in the 1960s—the Vietnam War, domestic political scandals, etc. The government was seen as being ineffective, inefficient, irresponsive to contemporary challenges, and self-destructive to the point of alienating its own citizens. Much of the world of science and technology was under attack. Many of these developments were accompanied by significant critiques of public administration. One manifestation was the dialogue about the need for a fundamental rethinking in public administration, the need for a new public administration (Shafritz 2007: 7). In this background, this chapter discusses the contemporary theoretical developments—a period from approximately 1945 to the present. It begins with a discussion on New Public Administration (NPA), which was a response to the demands of American society of the time, and then move to

New Public Management (NPM), which was a reaction to the ineffective State-led bureaucratic development. Gender and the environment, two prominent issues in the discipline today, are also discussed in this chapter. Governance has brought a major change in the nature and scope of public administration. A discussion on good governance and its supporting associates—viz. e-governance, corporate governance and environmental governance—will get a place in the ensuing discussion. This chapter briefly describes good governance, as it will be dealt in greater detail in Chapter Six.

NEW PUBLIC ADMINISTRATION: ADDRESSING THE ISSUE OF RELEVANCE

New Public Administration, or NPA, can be defined as a new and qualitatively different phase in the growth of public administration. This new phase—infused with political values of equity, social justice, change and commitment—is often equated with the 'crisis of identity' of public administration as a separate discipline. In fact, the discipline has been wrestling with this crisis ever since it came into being. NPA can be seen as the first serious attempt on the part of practitioners of public administration to give it a stable identity by re-emphasising its core commitments to the society. The origins of NPA can be traced back to Minnowbrook I of 1968. Attended by a host of young intellectuals drawn from different branches of the social sciences, the conference was a wake-up call for theorists and practitioners to making the discipline socially relevant and accountable. A group of young American scholars advocated to make the study and practice of the discipline relevant to the demands of the post-industrial society, and this has come to be known as NPA.

What is 'New' in NPA?

The focus on relevance, equity, change and social justice gives public administration a 'new' identity in contrast to conventional administration, which is more concerned with efficiency and economy of management. Public interest formed the core of the deliberations after Minnowbrook I. Scholars chalked out the boundary of the discipline and added social equity to efficiency and economy as the rationale or justification for policy positions. They began considering equal protection of the law as important to public administrators as it is to elected representatives. Public administration was to be marked by ethics, honesty and responsibility. Bureaucrats were not merely implementers of fixed decisions, they were considered as holding the public's trust to provide the best possible service with the costs and benefits distributed fairly among everyone. A responsive government grew where new needs are clear and declined where agencies' services are no longer critical. Change—and not growth—came to be considered more critical. The standard for effectiveness shifted from just growth to managing change in the context of an active and participative citizenry. Also challenged were the rational model and the usefulness of hierarchy.

In addition to advancing these themes, participants in Minnowbrook I were influential in the field's primary professional association, the American Society for Public Administration (ASPA).

Their actions, along with those of others, facilitated making ASPA more open and democratic. It now has open elections, sections for minorities and women, and an enviable record of women and minorities in leadership positions. It has developed a code of ethics, and it now takes positions on significant public policy issues of the day, in sharp contrast to the earlier culture (Frederickson 1999: 705).

Fostering Intellectual Confusion

Dunn and Fozouni (1976) point out that, despite a few redeeming features, NPA has been subject to severe criticism. NPA is often held responsible for the propagation of an illusion of 'paradigm change, paradigm shift or paradigm revolution within the field' (ibid.: 23). The argument made is that instead of contributing to a paradigm shift, NPA has 'fostered intellectual confusion, the obfuscation of critical philosophical and methodological issues and the institutionalization of undisciplined mediocrity in the field' with the definite political intention of reinforcing the status quo. Moreover, NPA came under attack for 'philosophical dilettantism' and the absence of methodological rigor and self-criticism (ibid.).

NEW PUBLIC MANAGEMENT: ASPIRING TO REINVENT GOVERNMENT

New Public Management (NPM) was another landmark in the evolution of public administration. It is primarily an outcome of Minnowbrook II held in 1988. Its emergence reflected the changes that took place in Western countries since the late 1970s. The State was increasingly being questioned because people felt that the State's performance was dismal in the social, political and economic spheres. NPM, which responded to this in the late 1980s and early 1990s, caused a sea change in the management of the public sector in the West and soon became a standard prescription for the ailing public sector across the globe. It came with a new set of experiments that were informed by the market principles of efficiency and economy. The primary concerns were ensuring quality services to citizens and greater autonomy to public management; rewarding organisations and individuals upon fulfilling targets; and being open to suggestions from the private sector. Unlike the traditional Weberian and Wilsonian paradigm of public administration, NPM called for a radical shift in public sector management informed by three Es: efficiency, economy and effectiveness. Moreover, in order to resurrect the sagging credibility of the public sector, NPM asked for liberal borrowing of market principles in public sector management.

It would be more appropriate to see NPM as an outgrowth of the initiatives of public sector reform that has been sweeping across the Western part of the world since the late 1980s. Mark Bevir endorses this by designating NPM as the 'first wave of public sector management' (2007: 74). Christopher Hood (1991) considers NPM as 'a marriage of opposites', of which one partner is the new 'institutional economics', while the other is 'a set of successive waves of business-type managerialism'; it proposes to make inroads into the hostile domain of 'sheltered bureaucracy' and substitute it with a more flexible, market-based public administration.

Under NPM a whole set of new nomenclature—managers, service providers and customers—have been manufactured to distinguish it from its predecessor. In sum, public administration is portrayed in NPM as embodying minimum government, debureaucratisation, decentralisation, market orientation, contracting out, privatisation and performance measurement of public services (Sarker 2001).

Origins of NPM

The origins of NPM can be traced back to the administrative reform measures in the West, more specifically to the Organization for Economic Cooperation and Development (OECD) group of countries from late 1970s onwards. The societal changes that happened then are theorised as a shift from government to governance: from coordinated, hierarchical structures and processes of societal steering to a network-based process of exchange and negotiation. The NPM is thus a paradigmatic change in public administration as the following characteristics suggest: first, the traditional output-oriented administration was replaced by the process-oriented administration with emphasis on performance indicators, evaluations and performance-related pay and quality improvement; second, the focus is on the flexible provision of individualised products instead of 'collective provision'. Hence 'customer' replaces 'the citizen', and the 'production line' of public administration is broken down into individual pieces for 'contracting out' or 'privatisation'; third, 'clusters'—in which autonomous agencies or institutions outside the formal government are inducted in governance as 'complementary structures' of public administration—rather than hierarchical 'pyramids' are the preferred structural design for administration; finally, there is a clear shift of general emphasis from policy to management with full cost consciousness before making any decision.

As the above features indicate, the NPM seeks to articulate a market-based public administration by emphasising the processes and structure of governance. Public administration is redefined as 'entrepreneurial government'. The conceptual formulation of entrepreneurial government is based on two major theoretical assumptions, as David Osborne and Ted Gaebler suggest in their landmark contribution to the evolution of NPM—*Reinventing Government* (1992: 20–22): (*a*) since government is 'a dated instrument', its role in governance is not satisfactory and (*b*) what is required thus is not 'more government' or 'less government', but 'better governance' which means 'a process by which we collectively solve our problems and meet our society's needs'.

Hood (1991) has shown that the emergence of NPM coincided with four 'administrative megatrends': (*a*) attempts to slow down or reverse government growth in terms of excessive public spending and staffing; (*b*) the shift towards privatisation and quasi-privatisation and away from core government institutions, with renewed emphasis on subsidiary in-service provision; (*c*) the development of automation, particularly in IT, in the production and distribution of public services; and (*d*) the development of a more international agenda that is increasingly focused on general issues of public management, policy design, decision styles and intergovernmental cooperation, on top of the older tradition of individual country specialisms in public administration (ibid.: 3). However, there is hardly any consensus among scholars regarding the emergence of

NPM. A host of factors are responsible for this paradigm shift. For analytical convenience, we can identify these factors under the following four heads:

1. *Receding credibility of the State*: As a major dispenser of social justice, the State has been increasingly questioned across the globe since the late 1970s. The popular mood was against the State for its dismal performance in almost every sphere.
2. *Emergence of the New Right Philosophy*: The New Right Philosophy is generally used as an umbrella term that accommodates a whole range of ideas and theories pertaining to the free market and individual liberty, such as the radical right, libertarianism, monetarism, Thatcherism, Reaganomics, etc. It came into vogue in the late 1960s and early 1970s under the tutelage of Ronald Reagan and Margaret Thatcher. This philosophy sought to challenge Keynesian demand management and the egalitarian welfare package it entrusted upon the State. For proponents of this philosophy, the involvement of the State 'leads to increasing monopoly, increasing budget and suppressing of entrepreneurial behavior, limiting choice, overproduction of unwanted services and encouragement to waste and inefficiency' (Ghuman 2001). Hence, they suggest a six-point reforms agenda—deregulation, privatisation, reduction of inflation, lower taxation, increasing role of market forces in the provision of public services, and institutional and constitutional reforms (ibid.). This philosophy is considered to have been a prime mover of the spate of public sector reforms and the emergence of NPM.
3. *Emergence of post-Weberian public administration*: The changing contours of public administration, especially the transition from traditional Weberian bureaucracy to the post-Weberian type, and the pragmatic rejection of Wilsonian politics–administration dichotomy, has signalled a steady and subtle change in public sector management. The post-Weberian or post-Wilsonian avatar of public administration sought to usher in an altogether new paradigm of public administration informed by democracy, efficiency, flexibility and free flow of communication.
4. *Administrative changes in advanced Western countries*: Mohit Bhattacharya (1998) has spelt out the various ways in which said changes occurred: (*a*) structurally, from a rigid, hierarchical and bureaucratic form of public administration to flexible market-based form of public management; (*b*) substantial change in the role of government in society; and (*c*) a huge change in the citizen–government relationship.

Osborne and Gaebler (1992) argue in favour of an 'entrepreneurial government' that is certain to bring about radical changes by (*a*) improving public management through performance, measurement and evaluation, (*b*) reducing budgets, (*c*) downsizing the government, (*d*) selective privatisation of public enterprises and (*e*) contracting out in selective areas. Osborne and Gaebler intended ten principles to serve as a new conceptual framework for public administration, an analytical checklist to transform the actions of government. Based on the experience of governments around the world and on the guidelines provided by Osborne and Gaebler, and others, the US government, under Bill Clinton and at Al Gore's urging, began a massive effort to improve the performance of government at the federal level through what was termed the 'National Performance Review' (Denhardt 2008: 139). All these events provided a strong intellectual justification for the emergence of NPM.

Fundamentals of NPM

NPM is based on the principles of privatisation, performance appraisal, strategic planning and other managerial practices. Different authors give a number of key traits of NPM. Hood writes that NPM moves away from traditional modes of legitimising the public bureaucracy, such as 'safeguards on administrative discretion, in favor of trust in the market and private business methods … The ideas … (are) couched in the language of economic rationalism' (1991: 94). He mentions the following as essential doctrines of NPM:

1. *Hands-on professional management in the public sector*: NPM sought to dole out an extra ounce of the professional manager, like freedom to the public sector. It also required proactive managers having discretionary decision-making powers in public service delivery.
2. *Explicit standards and measures of performance*: NPM was in favour of laying out explicit parameters of performance; in other words, definition of goals, targets, indicators are to be clearly expressed.
3. *Greater emphasis on output controls*: NPM stressed on results rather than procedures.
4. *Shift to disaggregation of units in the public sector*: NPM proposed to break-up formerly monolithic structures in the public sector into 'manageable' units. Moreover, it also asked for 'unbundling of U-form management systems into corporatised units around products, operating on decentralised one-line budgets and dealing with one another on an arms-length basis' (ibid.: 5).
5. *Shift to greater competition in the public sector*: On principle NPM was in favour of infusing a competitive spirit among public sector enterprises. For competition brings down the cost of the product/service and ensures efficiency.
6. *Stress on private sector styles of management practice*: Since the hierarchical bureaucratic management technique has proven to be counterproductive for the public sector, NPM called for liberal borrowing of the management technique of the private sector.
7. *Stress on greater discipline and parsimony in resource use*: NPM sought to impose greater discipline and economy in resource utilisation by adopting a series of steps, viz. cutting direct costs, raising labour discipline, resisting union demands, limiting compliance costs to business, etc.

Nicholas Henry (2012) enumerates the following as the features of NPM:

1. *Efficiency and effectiveness*: Citizens and public managers alike expect their systems of governance to provide more cost-effective service to more people.

2. *Independence and accountability*: Granting public administrators greater flexibility in managing their governments would add to their productivity, but enhanced freedom cannot be attained at the expense of their accountability to the law, professional values and public interest.
3. *Competition and collaboration*: Governments compete and collaborate with other governments, companies and non-profit organisations to enhance public performance and citizen participation in governance.
4. *High performance public agencies*: The characteristics of high performance public agencies include agility, adaptability, alertness in anticipating and solving problems, and the aggressive use of information. (Ibid.: 183)

Nicholas observes that these ideas lead to a much greater emphasis on certain kinds of principles that have also been stressed in the past, notably intergovernmental administration, performance measurement and feedback, programme evaluation, decentralisation and streamlining, and innovating the procedures of budgeting and human resource management.

Patrick Dunleavy (1991) has identified three key components of NPM:

1. *Disaggregation*: The first important element is disaggregation which means refers to up the bureaucracy into smaller components with underlying emphasis on flattening hierarchies and flexibilisation in personnel, IT and decision-making power.
2. *Competition*: Competition in administration seeks to infuse competitive spirit among potential service providers. It includes quasi-market, outsourcing, intra-government contracting, public sector liberalisation, deregulation, consumer-tagged financing, user-control, etc.
3. *Incentivisation*: NPM favours performance-based incentives for augmenting productivity in the organisation. This component constitutes several elements, such as re-specifying property rights, anti rent-seeking measures, performance-related pay, private finance initiative, private-public partnership and mandatory efficiency dividends.

On the basis of the above components the following features of the NPM can be identified:

1. *Freedom of choice to citizens*: One of the major hallmarks of NPM is the empowerment of citizens. NPM asked for greater freedom of choice to citizens, such as the freedom to 'exit', 'voice' and 'loyalty'—'exit' denotes the freedom of the customer to pull back from any market transaction; 'voice' states that s/he is able to complain in a way that will lead to some changes in services or products offered; and 'loyalty' is where the customer stays with the suppliers, regardless of the standard of services provided (Hirschman 1970).

Unlike the traditional public sector, NPM reconceptualised the citizen as an 'active customer' who has to be always kept in good humour, and called for a huge perception-related change in bureaucrats.

2. *Autonomy to managers*: NPM called for more freedom and autonomy to public sector managers. Unlike in the private sector, public sector managers work within a strict regime of laws and by-laws. Hence, they have no room for innovation and contemplation. NPM was in favour of greater elbowroom for managerial leadership by providing public managers with greater flexibility in personnel policy like contractual appointment, workplace bargaining, etc. (Bhattacharyya 1998).
3. *Organisational restructuring*: NPM proposed a thorough organisational revamping so that the organisational structure will become conducive for organisational leadership. Restructuring includes simplifying organisational procedures, flattening of hierarchies and encouraging all kinds of organisational and spatial decentralisation.
4. *Strict performance measurement technique*: Application of rigorous performance measurement technique was another hallmark of NPM. The root of performance measurement as a technique of quality assurance has its first forceful advocacy in Taylor's scientific management theory. Though it has become a household name in private sector enterprises for quite some time, its acceptance in public sector management is only a recent phenomenon. Thanks to the 're-inventing government' movement in USA in the early 1990s, a host of performance measurement techniques—such as Total Quality Management, counter services, citizen's charter, etc.—have increasingly become part of bureaucratic parlance (Schiavo-Campo and Sundaram 2001).
5. *Restructuring public bureaucracy*: Public bureaucracy has an uncanny knack of expansion and extravagance. Public choice theorists have shown how bureaucracy has blown out of proportion and eaten out the vitals of society. C. N. Parkinson has unpacked the intricacies of bureaucratic expansion in *Parkinson's Law* (1957). NPM suggests overcoming this by restructuring and disaggregating public bureaucracies into agencies, which will deal with each other on a user-pay basis (Hood 1991).
6. *Managing the organisation economically*: NPM strongly advocated economy in the public sector. Inspired by the New Right philosophy, NPM was in favour of cost-cutting in the public sector through contractualisation and privatisation of public services, charging costumers for services they are provided and rolling back of the State from crucial services by encouraging open-market economy.
7. *Revamping human resource management*: Under NPM, an array of policies were undertaken to revamp human resource management. The basic objective was to draw the best talent from the market by offering an attractive salary, and accompanying it with perks, incentives and other benefits. Moreover, NPM also suggested regular periodic skill-improvement programmes to hone the competitive edge of the workforce.

Limitations of NPM

The philosophy of NPM initiated an administrative reforms movement. The most significant impact of NPM was the adoption of private sector managerial practices in public sector management. NPM moved from the bureaucratic model or Kanter model[1] of flatter (non-hierarchical) and focused structure of organisations to an entrepreneurial form of governance as Osborne and Gaebler (1992) seem to have suggested. Hence, NPM calls for greater synergy between public and private sector managements. The NPM philosophy sought management reforms in government not only through the introduction of new techniques, but also through the imposition of a new set of values, specifically a set of values largely drawn from the private sector (Denhardt 2008: 141). NPM also encouraged a customer-driven administration. Unlike the traditional bureaucratically-managed public sector management, NPM elevated the citizen to the centre of discourse. Customer satisfaction index was considered 'the' criteria of public service. Several procedural innovations like the citizen's charter, citizen's report card, etc. were introduced to reflect citizen's choice (Ghuman 2001). Another implication of NPM is it led to the reorganisation and downsizing of government. One of the direct implications of NPM for public sector management is that it made governments adopt performance as the basis of organisation. For effective implementation of policies, NPM proposed to contract-out service delivery functions to non-governmental or quasi-governmental agencies and private service providers, saving the major policymaking functions for core departments manned by seasoned public servants.

Perhaps the best example of NPM in an international context can be seen in New Zealand's administrative reforms. Seeking to achieve more effective public organisations, the government privatised substantial public functions, redeveloped its personnel system for top executives to be more performance-oriented, instituted a new process of measuring productivity and effectiveness of government agencies, and re-engineered departmental systems to reflect the government's commitment to accountability. The effectiveness of New Zealand's reform agenda—as well the success of parallel activities in Canada, Great Britain and USA—put governments around the world on notice that new standards were being sought and new roles established (Denhardt 2008: 137). The new approach was seen as a remedy to the maladies underlying red-tapism, inefficiency and despotism, and a dominant and monopolistic State.

However, NPM has come under serious challenge, especially about the way it has been packaged and marketed. Criticism against NPM ranges from questioning its claim of universality (Hood 1991) to the proclamation of its death (Dunleavy 1991). The professed claim of the universal applicability of NPM as a trusted antidote of any kind of 'management ills' irrespective of culture and contexts—the panacea—is no longer tenable. Hood (1991) has enumerated some major objections:

---

[1] The Kanter model argues that new organisations are flatter in structure and their role of directing and controlling is being replaced by the culture of facilitation, flexibility and adaptability. This organisational culture seeks to develop open, flexible and pragmatic strategies to address citizen's problems.

1. After the initial hype, NPM seems to have worked only at the superficial level, leaving most of the old problems and weaknesses intact. The only substantial change that has occurred is in the language that the public managers speak in public.
2. NPM's claim of economy or cost-cutting also sounds hollow as it has failed to bring down the cost per unit of service. Critics argue that the net result of NPM is an 'aggrandizement of management' and 'rapid middle level bureaucratization of the new reporting system', all of which in effect has hampered public service.
3. On the pretext of promoting public good, NPM actually serves the career interest of an elite group of new managerialists—the top managers, officials, management consultants, business schools.
4. NPM's claim of universal applicability is also not tenable as different administrative values call for different administrative designs.

Christopher Pollitt sees NPM as a revival of Taylor's scientific management theory, which, according to him, are contrary to the development of organisational behaviour (human relations approach).[2] The central thrust of NPM is to set clear targets, develop performance indicators to measure the achievement of those targets, and to single out those individuals who get 'results' and give them merit awards, promotion or other rewards. In this, there is far less official acceptance of the complexities of workplace norms, beliefs and aspirations or of the equally complex issues of motivational biases in decision-making and inter-institutional interdependencies. He argues that managerial reforms in the 1970s and 1980s were dominated by the values of efficiency, economy and effectiveness, while other values such as fairness, equity, justice and participation were either off the agenda or treated as constraints in the drive for higher productivity.

A number of studies have discussed the undemocratic implications of NPM (Behn 1998; Borins 2000; Box, et al. 2001; Gottfried 2001), especially its inclination to establish a 'supermarket state' model—where the wealthiest, best-informed and most assertive customers get the best quality service (Olsen 1988). While the traditional Weberian model stressed the public sector's responsibility to offer equal treatment to citizens, the NPM model is largely driven by notions of customer satisfaction (Christensen and Lægreid 2009). At the same time, numerous contradictory forces are at work within NPM doctrines. For example, calls for greater stakeholder involvement in decision-making sit very uneasily alongside planning, performance management and greater control by the central government (Coupland, Currie and Boyett 2008). Similarly, Andrews and Turner (2006) observe that it is very difficult to reconcile NPM's consumerist conception of democracy with the group rights that participative democracy demands. The *World Public Sector*

[2] Pollitt's primary work is on reforms in public management reforms. His important writings include *The Essential Public Manager* (2003) and 'Convergence or Divergence' (2007). His most popular article titled 'Justification by Works or by Faith?' (1995) explores the extent to which NPM has been subject to serious and systematic evaluation. It questions the effectiveness of the NPM and suggests better ways to evaluate NPM reforms.

Report by the United Nations (Department of Economic and Social Affairs 2001) states that one of the drawbacks of NPM is its anti-State ideology, and that it has led to a serious decline in the basic social services and the disintegration of social safety nets associated with the fundamental rights of citizens in a democratic system.

Christensen and Lægreid (2009) argue that NPM has helped broaden the options of people trying to influence public authorities and participate in public decision-making processes through market mechanisms and customer orientation, but the managerial concept of democracy that NPM espoused might weaken civic responsibility, engagement and political equality and enhance the role of administrators and managers. They believe that there is a need to strengthen the sense of trusteeship and the development of a polity with a common purpose based on trust. It is a paradox that while one goal of NPM is to open public administration to the public, it may ultimately reduce the level of democratic accountability and lead to erosion of the 'publicness' of public service (ibid.: 22). As a result of this dilemma, countries like Norway have moved to post-NPM reforms. Such reform measures are supposed to handle some of these challenges by moving the reforms away from output democracy and aggregative political processes in favour of a greater emphasis on input democracy and integrative political processes; i.e. to move the administrative system and practice more in an input-oriented direction through laying stress on traditional collective ideals and political control. NPM-related consumer orientation is supplemented and partly overshadowed by a general view of broad citizen participation directly towards the civil service and its decisions and services.

NPM-style reforms have been widely associated with neo-liberal thinking and blamed for their effect on the public service ethos, the (un)equal treatment of citizens and a corresponding decline in the cohesion of local communities. Their suitability in the public sector context have also been questioned as they are sometimes seen as undermining shared public values and the pursuit of social equality (Van de Walle and Hammerschmid 2011: 195). NPM is largely based on the New Right agenda of privatisation, deregulation, marketisation and a small State (Lane 2000). Its focus on individual rights rather than collective rights, belief in the individual rather than societal interest as a key guiding principle and strong reliance on markets as a core steering mechanism have all come under criticism in this regard. Protests against NPM-style reforms have indeed been channelled by public-sector trade unions. The introduction of reforms and the focus on performance was seen by some as a questioning of the welfare State (Lane 1997: 2) and reforms of services of general interest and former State monopolies have been criticised for their potential negative effects on social cohesion and equity (Hood 1995). Therefore, critics also debate the major premise of the superiority of the private over the public sector and its lack of concern for ethics and such other crucial issues.

Moreover, studies indicate wide disparities globally. International experience indicates that some countries even reversed the process of privatisation in certain areas. In California, the power sector, which was privatised, ran into problems and the government had to step in to correct the mess. The British Railways, which was privatised in 1984, went into liquidation and the government had to take over this sector. So too was the case with the British coal mines.

In New Zealand the government had to renationalise the airlines. Similarly, in India, the Delhi government's move to privatise distribution of water had to be put on hold due to public protest (Medury 2010: 169). More recently, the Aam Admi Party (AAP) government in Delhi has increased the subsidy on water and electricity consumption. Some studies indicate that privatisation as propagated by NPM in developing countries did not produce the desired results (Hughes 1998; Mongkol 2011; Samaratunge, Alam and Teicher 2008; Sarker 2006). In many countries, some activities have been entrusted to the public sector due to ideological reasons as well the failure or lack of trust in the market. Hence, there could not be a sudden global shift from the public to the private sector resulting in private monopoly. Intense and radical privatisation cannot be resorted to unless accompanied by appropriate conditions. In the first place, loss-making public sector enterprises do not attract private buyers. Also, there is stiff resistance from labour unions. As Medury observes, developing countries—which are already grappling with unemployment, economic inequality and the absence of a developed capital market through which funds can be mobilised—did not gain much from privatisation initiatives (2010: 167). NPM has failed to attract the attention of developing nations which have different problems and issues, and have a culture and environment quite different from the West. Thus, NPM is not just a set of managerial innovations; it is also a set of ideas about the nature of man and the role of the State in society which is inspired by the public choice theory that neglects the downtrodden and weaker sections of society.

There is no doubt that NPM is a refreshing input in our search for 'an appropriate' model for public administration in two ways: first, it has brought back the old debate between government administration and business administration; second, by seeking to review the bureaucracy-centred public administration in the name of 'state-minimalism', it has raised issues which are pertinent in redefining the contours of public administration in its contemporary manifestation. The fundamental question now is whether public administration can be conceptualised as NPM. The market-driven NPM is qualitatively different from public administration which is guided by a distinct purpose of supporting and developing collective life by choosing goods and services essential to the community as a whole, establishing collective efficiency and devising social and political rules in support of a particular system of order. Public administration is also a space in which citizens and government interact dialectically. Public policy is thus not merely government-driven, but an outcome of such an interaction which is conceptually understood as 'the politics of participation'. Although NPM underlines the importance of 'restrictive' participation, its overemphasis on the three Es clearly shows the ideological tilt in favour of 'neo-liberal' public administration by redefining public management in terms of 'process' and 'structure', and ignoring 'the purpose' completely.

FEMINIST APPROACH: STRIVING FOR PUBLIC SPACE FOR WOMEN

The feminist discourse in public administration is an inevitable outcome of heightened gender sensitivity since the 1960s. Feminists have demonstrated how patriarchy has systemically excluded women from the public space and arrested them in the private space by capturing the State and public administration. Hence, the feminist perspective seeks to access the role of public administration—especially of bureaucracy, public policy, etc.—through the gender lens. Feminist theory has shown that women have been subjugated on the pretext of biology, and that gender discrimination is so pervasive because it is socially and culturally embedded. This theory of public administration has unearthed gender biases embedded in public agencies and administrative practices. The primary attempt of the feminist approach is to make the public space, which is dominated by men, available to women.

Public Administration through the Gender Lens

The feminist perspective believes that like any other branch of the social sciences, public administration has been instrumental in systematically excluding women from the public space. Feminist thinkers argue that in patriarchal societies public institutions, bureaucracy and so on, are nothing but structures of subordination as patriarchal values are entrenched in those institutions. Therefore, to bring about gender equity, attempts should be made to dislodge patriarchy from these institutions. In her remarkable book, *Gender Images in Public Administration*, Camilla Stivers (2002) argues that images of professional expertise, management, leadership and public virtue that mark justifications of administrative power contain dilemmas of gender. Not only do they have features commonly and unthinkingly associated with masculinity, they also help to keep in place or bestow political and economic privilege on the bearers of culturally masculine qualities at the expense of those who display culturally feminine ones. Looking at public administration through this perspective, therefore, reveals that its dimensions are gendered rather than neutral.

Feminist theorists have criticised the classical liberal State for its marked individualism and for the dependence of its clear boundary between the public and private spheres on the exclusion of women and women's concerns from political life. Stivers (2002) argues this when she says that women have been expected to handle needs related to sustenance and nurturance in order that men could have the time and energy for public pursuits. This division of labour still persists despite equal opportunity and affirmative action policies, which have only enabled women to shoulder both household and paid work rather than to share them equally with men.

Women's Position in Public Organisations

While women have the right to enter into public services as equals of men, their participation is very low, especially at the top. There is still a silence, or at best only whispers, about women in the top echelons of the public sector. In this context, Shireen Lateef (2014) answers the question: 'Where are the Women Leaders in Public Administration?'

> According to UNDP's 2014 Gender Equality in Public Administration (GEPA), public sector leadership still has a long way to go before it achieves gender parity. … Although the public sector is often the largest national employer of women—anywhere between 15% and 40% of public

> administration—women occupy only 15% or less of decision-making positions, according to GEPA. … [C]ivil service remains a bastion of male privilege—patriarchal institutions, perpetuating age-old gender-biased traditions, attitudes, values and practices. … [I]n many countries today the public sector is a major employer of women especially in the "feminized" sectors or "feminine spaces" of education, health, culture, tourism, social welfare—albeit with the 'glass walls' of sectoral segregation. … Ernst & Young's Worldwide Index of Women as Public Sector Leaders across the G20 major economies shows that while women comprise about 48% of the overall public sector workforce, they represent less than 20% of public sector leadership. … In Japan, the world's third-largest economy, women make up 42% of the public sector workforce, but only 1.8% are leaders. Other Asian G-20 countries fare better, although they still hover around the bottom of the index of public sector female leaders: Indonesia 16.4%; India 14.8%; People's Republic of China 9.1%; Republic of Korea 4.8%. (Ibid.)

We can observe that women continue to struggle to rise to the top management in public organisations. Many reasons have been found for this—constraints of handling the role of wife-mother-worker, perception of women being 'unfit' for management positions, the stereotype that women are more committed to family than work. A study has suggested that marriage and family affect women's ability rather than men to pursue their career dreams. Female employees' commitment to their job is often questioned on the ground that they go on maternity and sick leave during pregnancies and also to tend to their families' needs. The traditional breadwinner–housewife division of family roles leads to the assumption that men are more committed to their work than women. All these factors contribute to the gender imbalance in public organisations.

Gender Dilemma: An Act of Balancing

According to Stivers, the most undeniable aspect of the organisational reality of women is their continued lack of access to high-ranking positions. She cites an American study which found that among 12,997 officers at the nation's 500 largest corporations, only 10 per cent were women. Among the 2500 'top earners' in these companies, only 2 per cent were women. More than 100 companies—including Exxon, Nynex and Whirlpool—had no women in top positions (Srivers 2002: 26). As far as the Indian scenario is concerned it is a fact that women have got equal right as men to enter the civil services. They also get time-bound promotions. However, they are discriminated against in the choice of postings and transfers. Even now women officers are not preferred for sensitive, crucial, important and heavy money-transacting postings. Though the number of women getting into the services has increased over the years, the stereotype of considering women as inferior to men has not changed. Swarup and Sinha (2013) write about how the most clearly defined role for women has been that of mother and wife in Indian society: 'Motherhood as distinct from fatherhood has traditionally been viewed as a fulltime job' (ibid.: 28). They cite a study which showed that women tended to remain responsible for the mothering and general housekeeping functions even when employed outside home (Davidson, Ginsburg and Kay 1974: 185–88), and another study which showed that the wife–mother syndrome pervades 'the behavior and role performance of all women in India to some extent and socializes all women to avoid success, to be unambitious and to be passive even if they have gained admittance into the administrative service cadres' (Lynn and Vaden 1979: 209; quoted in Swarup and Sinha 2013: 29). Swarup and Sinha (2013) argue that in India the barriers to the advancement of women occur primarily at the educational and socialisation levels.

> Family interference is the biggest obstacle to the career advancement of female administrators in India. ... Most female administrators in India are married and they give higher priority to home and family life than they do to their own career advancement. Weighted with duties and obligations imposed by cultural traditions and norms, many must do double duty to meet their professional demands. This phenomenon provides both an inner psychological and an explicitly overt set of constraints on women administrators. ... Women in India are passing through the twilight zone of tradition and modernity. The growth of education, the extension of vocational and professional opportunities, and to some extent, the scarcity of financial resources for a large number of people are factors which are opening the gates of change for women. However, caught between the home and the office, such women in India are engaged in a tough struggle for a viable position. Many of them have had to succumb to the pressures of family and home and try to be content with a mediocre service record. (Ibid.)

To conclude, there is still an imbalance as far as women's representation in the public services is concerned. Hence, it is the felt need today to revamp the core areas of public administration and introduce more sensitivity towards issues of gender. The following measures may be taken in this direction: spreading awareness and removing misconceptions regarding the services, providing quality education, reservations for disadvantaged women, making working conditions conducive for women, bringing changes in the mindset of men, parents and the society, doing away with the undesirable social customs on women and introducing policies for greater gender representation in public administration.

GOOD GOVERNANCE: THE ART OF MANAGING PUBLIC AFFAIRS

Human concern for good governance is as old as civilisation itself. However, the recent concern with good governance within the development paradigm received much impetus with the publication of a World Bank (WB) (1989) report on Sub-Saharan Africa that described problems of development as a 'crisis of governance' (Mander and Asif 2004: 1). 'Poor governance' was held responsible for the lack of sound development in the Sub-Saharan African nation-states. In 1992, the WB introduced 'good governance' as part of its criteria for lending to developing countries. Governance here referred to those neo-liberal reforms of the public sector—marketisation and NPM—which the WB believed led to greater efficiency (Bevir 2013: 15); i.e. the WB believed that failures in development efforts have largely been the result of 'poor governance', which has to be replaced by good governance. Good governance was seen as a panacea for 'bad governance'. Poor governance is, according to the WB, 'characterized by arbitrary policymaking, unaccountable bureaucracies, un-enforced or unjust legal systems, the abuse of executive power, a civil society unengaged in public life and widespread corruption' (1992: 27).

Since governance is 'the conscious management of regime structures, with a view to enhancing the public realm', the WB insists on 'independence for the judiciary, scrupulous respect for the law and human rights at every level of government, transparency and accountability of public monies, and independent public auditors responsible to a representative legislature, not to an executive' (1989: 192). It defines governance as 'the manner in which power is exercised in the management of a country's economic and social resources for development' (WB 1992). The bank underlined that good governance was necessary for sound economic, human and institutional development and emphasised four key elements of governance: (*a*) public sector management; (*b*) accountability; (*c*) legal framework for development and (*d*) information and transparency. To improve governance, an assessment of the institutional environment—i.e. accountability, rule of law, openness and transparency—should be initiated.

The UNDP has characterised governance as being participatory, consensus-oriented, accountable, transparent, responsive, effective and efficient, equitable and inclusive and follows the rule of law (1997: 19). It goes on to state that good governance assures that corruption is minimised, the views of minorities are taken into account and that the voices of the most vulnerable in society are heard in decision-making. It is also responsive to the present and a future need of society. Therefore, according to UNDP, governance is a checklist of criteria of managing public affairs.

Governance is thus another mode of conceptualising public administration in the changed global scenario. As the neo-liberal view began downplaying the State and overvaluing the market, and the trend was set to decentre the State from its monopoly status in social control, the idea of 'governance'—that connoted to a plurality of rules replacing the State's monopoly—gained in prominence.

The growing respectability of governance as a paradigm coincides with those societal changes sometimes theorised as a shift from government to governance in the context of globalisation: from coordinated hierarchical structures and processes of societal steering to a network-based process of exchange and negotiation. The society is seen as a network of negotiating units, whose compositions vary, as do their positions in the power structure, over time and across subjects. Broadly speaking, good governance refers to an administration that is sensitive and responsive to people's needs and is effective in coping with emerging challenges.

> [It includes] strict rules of accountability. It could be centered on community groups and individuals, and based on a notion of rights as inherently comprising duties. Rules must be strictly bound by generally accepted norms and controlled by institutions to enforce those. (Mander and Asif 2004: 14)

It can be safely said that governance is integral to the WB rhetoric and lending policies toward the developing nations, addressing 'not only issues of political legitimacy and democracy, but also the need for administrative efficiency by means of marketization and competition' (Salskov-Iversen, Hansen and Bislev 2000: 194). Thus, 'good governance' demands more dynamic, result-oriented, transparent and accountable government on the one hand and a networking of formal institutions of government, the market and the private sector, and the civil society on the other.

Corporate Governance: Ensuring Private Sector's Accountability

Corporate governance is another variant of governance. It is an endeavour to make the private business transparent and accountable. The issue of corporate governance came into the limelight from relative obscurity after a string of collapses of high profile companies in the 1990s. News of the unethical and illegal operations of Enron and Worldcom shocked the business world. It was clear that something was amiss in the area of corporate governance (Sharma and Kumar 2011: 645). Since then corporate governance has become a new buzzword of corporate boardrooms across the globe. It is considered to be a necessary precondition for a free and fair market economy. Simply put, corporate governance presupposes a code of conduct for the corporate sector. Keeping the house in order is perhaps at the heart of corporate governance. It can be defined as the sum total of processes and structures involved in the process of governing a corporation with the underlying objective of ensuring transparency, accountability, innovation and social responsibility.

Corporate governance is not something new, it has always been a necessary mechanism of managing business. The onset of globalisation and the resultant opening up of the economy has only accentuated the need for corporate governance. The need for a self-imposed disciplinary regime exists because, by nature, humans are insatiable and prone to frailties like corruption, misuse of power and position for personal benefit, nepotism and so on. A corporation, therefore, is bound to be fraught with the danger of human frailties. The absence of any regulatory mechanism at the onset of free market economy has further accentuated the necessity of a self-conscious moratorium on the part of companies for better functioning of the market. Also, the immediate reason behind the frenetic need for corporate governance can be attributed to the unprecedented global crises of receding credibility of corporations. Owing to the series of corporate failures in the US and the domino effect that followed all across the world has justified the urgency of having the framework of accountability for the corporate world. Thus, to salvage global business, traditional ethics and obligations of running a corporation have been brought back under the new garb of corporate governance.

Salient Features of Corporate Governance

In this interconnected world of global business, no one is absolutely immune to the influence of others. In fact, any irregularity of business in one corner of the world will have a definite and debilitating impact in the rest of the world. Hence, good governance is imperative for business corporations across the globe. Christine Mallin (2004/2008) lists some of the important features of good corporate governance:

1. It helps to ensure that an adequate and appropriate system of controls operates within a company and hence assets may be safeguarded;
2. It prevents any single individual from having too powerful an influence;
3. It is concerned with the relationship between a company's management, the board of directors, shareholders and other stakeholders;
4. It aims to ensure that the company is managed in the best interests of the shareholders and other stakeholders.
5. It tries to encourage both transparency and accountability, which investors are increasingly looking for in both corporate management and corporate performance.

Conceptualising Corporate Governance

The formal beginning of corporate governance can be traced back to the famous report of the Committee on the Financial Aspects of Corporate Governance (1992) set up by Cadbury in the UK. Established in 1991 under the chairmanship of Adrian Cadbury, the committee aimed at streamlining corporate governing amidst a series of corruption charges and corporate malpractices. The report of the committee is deemed as the first serious effort at trying to encapsulate the diversified world of corporations and companies into a disciplinary framework of sorts. Though prepared in the context of the UK, it had a universal applicability as the entire world was reeling under a chain of corporate debacles. It virtually opened the floodgates of research for good corporate practices throughout the world. The report put forth a voluntary code of best practices, which if followed properly would substantially restore creditors' confidence and thereby ensure good corporate governance.

The committee defined corporate governance as 'the system by which companies are directed and controlled' (ibid.). Internalising the essence of the report, the Organization for Economic Cooperation and Development (OECD) has defined the term in a more exhaustive manner:

> Corporate governance is the system by which business corporations are directed and controlled. The corporate governance structure specifies the distribution of rights and responsibilities among different participants in corporation, such as, the board, managers, shareholders, and other stakeholders and spells out the rules and procedures for making decisions in corporate affairs. By doing this it also provides the structure through which the company objectives are set and the means of attaining those objectives and monitoring performance. (Quoted in Arjoon 2005: 346–47)

Corporate governance can thus be conceptualised as 'inclusive of the structures, process, cultures, and systems through which the company sets out its objectives and defines the means of attaining those objectives and monitoring its performance' (Ghosh 2012: 134). It demands that some kind of disciplinary or accountability regime is necessary to counter dubious corporate practices. However, corporate governance puts a lot of emphasis on the ethical dimension of compliance for at least two reasons: (*a*) by nature the corporation is a semi-autonomous body, governed by its own constitution or statute; so, forcing a company to comply even on certain accountability parameters is nothing but making hostile inroads into its autonomy; (*b*) any legal framework that is binding is impossible to be implemented because of the sheer number of big multinational or transnational corporations. Hence, corporate governance does not rely on a legal framework alone.

Basic Elements of Corporate Governance

Corporate governance cannot be reduced to any single ingredient or criterion. In fact, it includes a host of principles. The basic elements of corporate governance can be enumerated as follows:

1. *Leadership*: Leadership is the most important component of corporate governance. It is said that adept governance is largely contingent upon the quality of leadership. Good leadership in a company includes providing proper direction to the enterprise, designing strategies of innovation, organisation restructuring, strategic management, stakeholders management, evaluation and monitoring performance.
2. *Accountability*: Accountability is considered the bedrock of corporate governance. Effective accountability has two components—answerability and consequences. First, answerability is the requirement for officials to respond periodically to questions concerning how they used their authority, where resources have been spent and what was achieved with them. Second, there is a need for predictable and meaningful consequences (Schiavo-Campo and Sundaram 2001).
3. *Transparency*: In corporate governance, transparency includes proper financial reporting, disclosure of executive remuneration package, etc.
4. *Internal controls*: Internal controls refer to attempts to ensure that risks—i.e. those factors which stop the achievement of company objectives—are minimised. As a primary tool used to manage a company's risks, internal controls protect the investments made by stakeholders and safeguard the company's assets. It also aims to promote business operations and ensure the effectiveness of external and internal reporting. In addition, an internal control mechanism is designed to detect and investigate fraud in complying with rules and regulations.
5. *Development of the board*: Formation of a competent board is an equally significant part of corporate governance. Usually, a perfect combination of executive and non-executive directors is prescribed for adept governance of an enterprise.
6. *Boardroom composition and structure*: This element incorporates the allocation of rights and responsibilities among different participants in the corporation (such as the board of directors, managers, shareholders, creditors, auditors, regulators, customers and other stakeholders) and specifies the rules and procedures of engagement in corporate affairs. The structure is the frame through which corporations define and pursue their

corporate goals, while taking into account the impact of its social, regulatory and market environment (Tricker 2009: 26). The boardroom structure is also a means of supervising the conduct, policies and decisions of the corporation so that it promotes the interests of the stakeholders. The boardroom composition and structure, therefore, determines the effectiveness of overall governance and performance of the organisation.

7. *Boardroom appraisal*: Boardroom appraisal is another crucial element of corporate governance. Periodic appraisal of the functioning of the corporation, especially evaluations of the performance of the board, the CEO, etc., is key to good corporate governance. It enables the board as a whole and the directors individually to reflect upon their actions. Boardroom appraisal facilitates learning from the past to be able to do better in the future.
8. *Code of ethics*: This is perhaps the kernel of corporate governance. In fact, corporate governance presupposes an ethical code of conduct on the part of all the stakeholders of the company.
9. *Performance-based executive pay*: A disproportionate pay structure of the executive is a major challenge in implementing good corporate governance. A report that has come to be known as the Greenbury Report (Study Group 1995) may be mentioned in this regard. The report acknowledged the importance of remuneration package in the overall performance of directors. However, it was equally vigilant on the astronomical increase of executive salary, unfounded by their contribution. Hence, it was argued in the report that remuneration packages should link rewards to performance, by both company and individual; and align the interest of the directors and shareholders in promoting the company's progress.

India's Endeavour to Regulate Private Enterprises

Corporate governance gained prominence in India when companies started raising funds in foreign markets in the 1990s. Corporate governance rules were first introduced by a series of committees set up by the Securities and Exchange Board of India (SEBI), Central Bank of India (CBI) and Ministry of Finance (MoF) with the objective of making corporate governance rules mandatory. In tandem with global efforts of corporate governance, the Confederation of Indian Industry (CII) came up with India's version of a corporate governance code in 1997—'Code of Desirable Corporate Governance'. The economic reforms of the early 1990s created the regulatory body SEBI in 1998 and gave it statutory status in 1992. The SEBI was created to replace a fragmented regulatory framework and provide for investor protection through disclosure requirements, accounting standards and arbitration procedure. The SEBI has three umbrella functions—draft regulations in its legislative capacity; conducting investigation and enforcement action in its executive capacity; and passing rulings and orders in its judicial capacity. The SEBI has introduced a rigorous regulatory regime to ensure fairness, transparency and good practice.

Another important contribution in the direction of corporate governance was made by the Kumar Mangalam Birla Committee (2000). In 1999, the SEBI set up a committee under the chairmanship of Kumar Mangalam Birla, who was member of the SEBI Board, to promote and raise the standards of good corporate governance in Indian companies. The committee, for the first time, recommended specifying the responsibilities and obligations of company boards and managements while instituting systems for good corporate governance and emphasised the rights of shareholders in demanding corporate governance. The Chandra Committee report on the role of external auditors recommended that annual accounts be certified by Chief Executive Officers (CEOs) and Chief Financial Officers (CFOs) (Committee on Regulations of Private Companies and Partnerships 2003). The Irani Committee report of 2003 suggested major amendments to the Companies Act, 1956 (Sharma and Kumar 2011: 653). The Irani committee report also defined an independent director as a non-executive director of the company who does not have any material, financial or transactional relationship with the company, its promoters, management, holding company or any associate company.

In other words, the recent epidemic of corporate scandals and subsequent interest in corporate governance has resulted in the constitution of a number of regulatory norms and standards around the globe and India is no exception to the rule. Several committees and groups have looked into this issue. On paper, the Indian legal system provides one of the highest levels of investor protection in the world, but the reality is different—marked by slow proceedings, overburdened courts and significant corruption. The shareholdings of larger companies remain relatively concentrated with promoters, and family business groups continue to dominate the corporate sector. Moreover the enforcement of security laws has been very poor. Despite these shortcomings, the Indian economy and its financial markets have shown impressive growth in recent years. The reason for this positive trend is that India is now clearly and strongly committed to sustaining and furthering the major economic reforms initiated in the early 1990s.

Environmental Governance: Caring for Mother Earth

Today governance of the natural environment has emerged as one of the most complex challenges ever faced by humanity. The environmental changes caused by human activities—from the local to the global—are not new. However, the magnitude of the changes and the resulting impact on the functioning of the natural ecosystem has grown rapidly over the past two centuries, more so in the second half of the last century. Due to this rising ecological crisis there has been a corresponding increase in the awareness and concern about environmental protection and conservation all over the world. There has been a growing recognition that many environmental problems, in particular those of a trans-boundary nature, cannot be successfully tackled solely at the national level. Nation-states can no longer act alone to solve many of the environmental problems that they face. States, along with other international actors, have responded by creating international 'regimes' in an attempt to tackle problems ranging from ozone depletion and climate change to loss of biodiversity and export of toxic waste (Connelly, et al. 2012: 50). This is how the concept of environmental governance has today become significant.

Environmental Challenges

Rapid econonomic expansion in the twentieth century has had two major consequences for the natural environment: high demand for the earth's natural resources and pollution. A combination of these two has given rise to the threats we now face globally. There are complex linkages among varied environmental problems. It is impossible to isolate one environmental issue from another; they are all intertwined. For example, deforestation contributes to loss of biodiversity, climate change and desertification. In turn acid rain, depletion of the ozone layer, untreated effluents and reduction in the water table adversely affect the forests.

Global Efforts at Environmental Governance

Clapp and Dauvergne note that '[c]oncern with the environmental abuses of rapid industrialization gained momentum in the First World in the 1960s. There were protests against nuclear weapons and chemical pollution. The World Wildlife Fund (WWF) was founded in 1961 to preserve global bio-diversity' (2008: 48). The most significant event that happened during this period was the publication of Rachel Carson's *Silent Spring* (1962) which argued that the increasing use of chemicals, particularly pesticides, was killing nature and wildlife, and apprehended a spring in the future without the songs of birds. The book drew people's attention to the impact of indiscriminate development on the environment. The strength of her message endured with the general public, and forced the US government to ban DDT (dichlorodiphenyltrichloroethane) and other synthetic chemicals.

Connelly, et al. (2012) argue that the year 1972 was significant in the history of green governance: '*The Limits to Growth*, published that year, argued that the post-War rate of economic expansion and population growth cannot be sustained without exhaustion of global natural resources, irreparable environmental damage and an increase in poverty and malnutrition' (ibid.: 236). These ideas not only attracted the attention of the common people but also proved influential at the level of national and international policymakers, ultimately leading to demands for global solutions.

Connelly, et al. (ibid.) point out that the first major international opportunity for the developing world to highlight the link between environmental degradation, international economic system and poverty was at the United Nations Conference on Human Environment held in Stockholm in 1972. The result of this conference was the Stockholm Declaration which included 26 guiding principles that focused on reducing the human impact on the environment and a related Plan of Action. The conference is also credited with the creation of the United Nations Environment Programme (UNEP). Through the conference the international community recognised that the world is in danger and collective efforts are required to tackle the same.

The internationalisation of green governance gradually increased in the post-Stockholm period. Several UN-sponsored environmental regimes emerged—such as treaties on preventing dumping of waste in the sea, pollution by ships, trading in endangered species and degradation of the marine environment. Concerns over growing marine pollution led the United Nations to initiate the Regional Seas Programme in 1974. This became the precursor to the signing of many related global legal treaties suggesting that, as neo-liberal institutionalism would contend, states are able to reach cooperative agreements where institutions are perceived as stable and mutually enforceable. Thus, it was a good beginning for collective international efforts to address environmental challenges.

Sustainable Approach to Environmental Governance

By the 1980s, there was a realisation in the international community that the economic model of development was primarily responsible for environmental degradation. But the dilemma was that nations, especially developing nations, needed economic growth to remove poverty and attain a level of prosperity. In an effort to get around the economy–environment paradox, the UN General Assembly authorised the establishment of a World Commission on Environment and Development (WCED) chaired by the Norwegian Prime Minister Gro Harlem Brundtland in 1987. WCED produced 'Our Common Future', a report that identified sustainable development as the solution. Sustainable development reconciled environmental and economic interests by framing them as interdependent (Hough 2014: 12).

Also known as the Brundtland report, 'Our Common Future' noted that '[s]ustainable development is the development that meets the needs of the present without compromising the ability of the future generations to meet their own needs' (WCED 1987: 41). This definition emphasised the mutual reinforcing of economic growth, social development and environmental protection, and forcefully argued for a higher level of multilateral cooperation and the need to reform economic practices such as trade, finance and aid. The report assumed that we can continue on the path of economic development and yet leave enough resources behind for the future generations. Thus, sustainable development focuses on promoting social justice, equity, cultural diversity and protecting ecology. Its objective is to harmonise the economic, social, cultural and environmental factors. It treats the social, economic, cultural and ecological factors as interdependent and therefore inseparable.

> The Brundtland Report changed the discourse of global environmentalism. It tried to chart a middle ground between the North and the South and between market-liberal and institutionalist views on growth on the other hand and social green and bio-environmentalist views on the other. It proposed a global development and environment strategy designed to be palatable to all. It did not see further economic growth and industrialization as necessarily harmful to the environment, and thus did not foresee any necessary "limits" to growth. At the same time, it argued, very much in line with Third World sentiments at Stockholm, that poverty harmed the environment as much as industrialization. This poverty was in large part due to the place of developing economies within the global structure. The best way to move forward, the report contended, was to promote economic growth – not the kind of growth seen in the 1960s and 1970s, but environmentally sustainable growth. (Clapp and Dauvergne 2008: 60–61)

The Brundtland report reflected the developmental concerns of the developing world. It supported the transfer of environmental technologies and economic assistance so developing nations could afford to pursue sustainable development and economic growth. The other significant recommendations of the report were: controlling population growth, promotion of education, ensuring food security, conserving energy, fostering urban sustainability and developing cleaner industrial technologies. Since the report stressed that effective environmental protection rested on continued economic growth, the recommendations found widespread support among many states and multilateral economic institutions. The concept of sustainable development is now part of mainstream national and international policies and developmental planning. There have been many other conferences, protocols and conventions since then and four of these have been discussed briefly here.

1. *The Earth Summit*: A follow-up conference to 1972 Stockholm to flesh out the concept of sustainable development was proposed to be held after 20 years. The 1992 Earth Summit (formally, UN Conference on Environment and Development [UNCED]) at Rio de Janeiro had a much larger and more diverse gathering than in 1972 (Hough 2014: 13). It recognised the need to couple the two issues of environment and development, and brought out five major commitments to conserve the environment.
2. *Kyoto Protocol on global warming*: The most well-known of the treaties negotiated in the years following the Earth Summit was the Kyoto Protocol (1997) to the UN Framework Convention on Climate Change (UNFCCC). The Protocol called for individual commitments by industrial nations to reduce emissions of six greenhouse gases by 2008–12. This was expected to lead to an overall reduction of greenhouse gas emissions to 5 per cent below 1990 levels by 2008–12, the so-called first commitment period (Speth and Haas 2006: 74–75). There was a dispute on the cut in the level of emissions between developed and developing nations. Developing nations were of the opinion that their economic conditions do not allow them to follow the Protocol. They also stressed that their level of emissions were much lower in comparison to developed nations.
3. *Johannesburg Conference*: The United Nations called for a new summit to review the commitments of Rio and rekindle fresh political and financial commitments for sustainable development. As a result, the World Summit on Sustainable Development was held in Johannesburg in 2002, exactly 10 years after the Earth Summit. The conference was the biggest UN meeting ever. Over 180 nations and 100 heads of states attended the conference. The major outcome document, the 'Plan of Implementation', contains targets and timetables to spur action on a wide range of issues, including access to clean water, proper sanitation, preserving biodiversity, phasing out of toxic chemicals, increasing the use of renewable energy. However, the conference failed to embrace new verifiable goals or significantly advance efforts for the protection of the global environment.
4. *United Nations' Climate Change Conference*: It was held in Paris in 2015. This was the 21st yearly session of the Conference of the Parties (CoP) to the UNFCCC and the

11th session of the Meeting of the Parties to the 1997 Kyoto Protocol. The conference negotiated the Paris Agreement, a global agreement aimed at mitigating climate change, the text of which represented a consensus of the representatives of the 196 signatories (Wikipedia Contributors n.d.). The agreement will become legally binding if joined by at least 55 countries which together represent at least 55 per cent of global greenhouse emissions. Such parties had to sign the agreement in New York between 22 April 2016 (Earth Day) and 21 April 2017, and also adopt it within their own legal systems (through ratification, acceptance, approval or accession). Members agreed to reduce their carbon output as soon as possible and to confine the rise of global temperature to under 2°C. The agreement established a 'global stock take' which would revisit the national goals to update and enhance them every five years beginning 2023. But, unlike the Kyoto Protocol, the Paris Agreement[3] does not contain a timetable or country-specific goals for emissions.

Thus, the journey of green governance has travelled from Stockholm (1972) to Paris (2015) in the hope of collectively addressing environmental challenges. However, the international community has not been able to achieve the desired goals. There are two barriers in the way: first, there is a conflict of interest between developed and developing countries; second, global policy stands in stark contrast to domestic environmental laws, which results in the non-implementation of international commitments. As Hough observes, 'Governments are still prone to take blinkered decisions informed by short-term economic interest in the face of epistemic consensus and longer-term utilitarian calculations of "national interest", as has most clearly been seen in the US's stance on climate change' (Hough 2014: 16). Despite these constraints it can be concluded that governance of the natural environment has emerged as arguably one of the most complex challenges ever faced by humanity. The Stockholm conference in 1972 turned out to be a watershed event in the recognition of the challenges in environmental governance by the global community. And, since then, the environment has increasingly become part of the governance agenda at all spatial levels.

E-governance: Seamless Service via Technology

E-governance (electronic governance) or e-government involves the provision of public services and information sharing through electronic media. It harnesses IT and ICTs (such as the internet and mobile communication) to increase the efficiency and economy of public administration. It involves both redesigning the public services system and the much wider transformation of the relationship between public and private actors—thereby effecting a renewal of the democratic decision-making process.

---

[3] For details, see http://unfccc.int/files/essential_background/convention/application/pdf/english_paris_agreement.pdf (accessed 1 June 2017).

Defining E-governance

In the words of Douglas Holmes (2001/2007), e-government is

> the use of information technology, in particular the Internet, to deliver public services in a much more convenient, customer oriented, cost effective and altogether different and better way. It affects an agency's dealing with citizens, business and other public agencies as well as its internal business processes and employees.

Baum and Di Maio (2000) define e-government as the continuous optimisation of service delivery, constituency participation and governance by transforming internal and external relationships through technology, the internet and new media. The principal aim is to use digital network technologies to open the State to citizen involvement. It opens up government processes and enables greater public access to information. E-governance can include publication of information about government services on a website, and make available application forms for these services that citizens can download. It can also deliver services, such as filling of a tax form, renewal of license and processing online payments. The purpose of digital government is to create 'super counters in [the government departments] and eliminate the endless maze citizens have to negotiate in going from door to door, floor to floor, to obtain service' (Kapoor 2000: 394). The use of various ICT techniques has ushered in a new era in public administration that is more transparent and accessible.

E-governance involves new styles of leadership, new ways of debating and deciding policy and investment, new ways of accessing education, new ways of listening to citizens and new ways of organising and delivering information and services. The purpose is to enhance good governance which is generally characterised by participation, transparency and accountability. Recent advances in IT and ICT provide opportunities to transform the relationship between governments and citizens in a new way, thus contributing to the achievement of good governance goals. The use of IT can increase the broad involvement of citizens in the process of governance at all levels by providing the possibility of online discussion groups and by enhancing the rapid development and effectiveness of pressure groups. Also, while it is concerned with the ability of citizens to choose the manner in which they wish to interact with their government, e-governance is also concerned with the choices governments make about how ICT will be deployed to support citizen choices.

Genesis of E-governance

The use of IT and ICT in governance was first emphasised in the scientific model of administration of the 1950s and 1960s. However, e-governance, as it is commonly understood today, emerged during the early 1990s. The US administration under President Bill Clinton led the way for an agenda of public sector reform with the setting up of a National Performance Review of the federal bureaucracy in 1993. And with the explosion of internet use the idea gained impetus and other liberal democratic political systems, such as the UK, Canada, Australia and New Zealand, soon followed suit. For instance, in the UK the Labour government, which was elected to power in 1997, placed electronic service delivery as the focus of its modernising programme.

The *E-government Survey* of the United Nations (Department of Economic and Social Affairs 2016) mentions that more countries are making the effort to ensure that public institutions are more inclusive, effective, accountable and transparent through e-governance. They are opening up their data for public information and scrutiny. According to the survey, 128 countries now provide datasets on government spending in machine-readable formats.

Bata Dey notes that through technological innovation e-governance 'has changed the basic character of governance – its operational methodology, functional style, ideological orientation, even the spirit, heart and soul' (2000: 306). In developed countries, e-governance is a well-established mode in which governmental services are made available to citizens. In India, digital governance has been legally endorsed by the Information Technology Act of 2000. The Act provides

> legal recognition for transaction carried out by means of electronic data interchange and other means of electronic communication, commonly referred to as "electronic commerce" which involve use of alternatives to paper-based methods of communication and storage of information, to facilitate electronic filling of documents with the government agencies. (GoI 2000: 417)

Advantages of E-governance

Abhijeet Joshi (2008) lists the following as the main advantages of e-governance:

1. *Speed*: Technology makes communication speedier. The internet, phones and mobiles have reduced the time taken in normal communication.
2. *Cost reduction*: Much of government expenditure is appropriated towards the cost of stationary. Paper-based communication needs a lot of stationary, printers, computers, etc. which calls for continuous heavy expenditure. The internet and phones makes communication cheaper saving valuable money for the government.
3. *Transparency*: Use of ICT makes governing transparent. All the information of the government would be made available on the internet. Citizens can see the information whenever they want to see. Current governing processes leave many ways to conceal information from the people. ICT can help eliminate all possibilities of concealing information.
4. *Accountability*: Once the governing process is made transparent, the government is automatically made accountable—i.e. it is answerable about its deeds to the people.

E-governance thus helps in reducing the cost of government, increases citizens' input to the government, improves public decision-making, and ensures accountability and transparency in government transactions. In this way e-governance is also a very meaningful step in combating corruption. Not only does it not take any discretion, thereby curbing opportunities for arbitrary action, e-governance also empowers citizens by making their intervention in the transactions of governmental business regular through ICT (Bhatnagar 2003: 8–9).

Limitations of E-governance

Though e-governance articulates public administration in a refreshingly new way, its application is considerably limited. The public sector cannot realise the full potential of e-governance for two reasons: access to internet and loss of jobs. Access to internet is still limited, even in developed countries. Thus, while transactions through ICT cost less than when done by conventional devices, the government has to maintain both the old and new systems to sustain its 'public' character. Else, a large portion of the people will remain outside governmental transactions. E-governance threatens mass retrenchment of workers involved in the government. Since downsizing and reducing public sector employment results in economic hardship of those losing jobs, it has severe political repercussions in many countries. For the leadership, therefore, it is not a desirable option unless no other option is available (Kamarack 2004: 36). In other words, given the obvious adverse consequences of e-governance, both in developed and developing countries, its applicability is both uncertain and limited.

Despite these limitations, e-governance provides an opportunity to bring about a change in the traditional bureaucratic nature of functioning, characterised by red-tapism, secrecy and inaccessibility of information. It improves governmental functioning by making it more transparent and accessible, and facilitates seamless delivery of services. If implemented well, it will radically change the way public services are organised and delivered, and has the potential to transform a government into one that is centred around its citizens.

CONCLUDING OBSERVATIONS

A discussion of contemporary theoretical developments makes it clear that the traditional administrative model, drawn heavily on the bureaucratic theory of organisation, appears to have lost its significance because of the growing importance of non-State actors in administration and the 'pluralisation of state'. Given the increasing role of transnational forces in domestic administration, the State-centred theories of bureaucracy seem to be inadequate in addressing the radical metamorphosis in public governance both in developed and developing countries. In his address at a book release function in 2006, the then Speaker of the Lok Sabha noted: 'One can thus safely argue that while the twentieth century was the age of organization where bureaucracy symbolized the core values of governance, the twenty-first century has ushered in an era of "network-based" organization, drawn on neo-liberal values' (Office of the Speaker of the Lok Sabha 2006). As evident, the complex socio-economic and political circumstances have raised issues that cannot be grasped within the traditional boundary-conscious social sciences. A holistic and interdisciplinary knowledge is required to understand and address the new societal issues.

Globalisation—the movement toward greater interaction, integration and interdependence among people and organisations across national borders—is a catalyst in radically altering the texture of public administration. Corporate discipline and entrepreneurial spirit have merged with government which has shed its traditional image of 'a doer'. It is now 'an enabler' that seeks to accommodate 'the market impulse'. Governmental functions are being redefined within neo-conservative theoretical parameters. The national government is restricted because of its limited policy options. The shrinking of the role of the State has resulted in the corporate state becoming a reality. Citizens have become clients and administrators have become functionaries seeking to approximate to the corporate culture. Public administration is now 'governance', a checklist of certain activities designed both to stabilise and also to consolidate market-driven neo-liberal ethics. This rapid translation of business values into the public sector raises substantial and troubling questions that public administration as a discipline has to handle with great care and alertness.

REFERENCES

Andrews, R. and D. Turner. 2006. 'Modelling the Impact of Community Engagement on Local Democracy'. *Local Economy* 21 (4): 378–90.

Arjoon, Surendra. 2005. 'Corporate Governance: An Ethical Perspective'. *Journal of Business Ethics* 61 (4): 343–52.

Baum, C. and A. Di Maio. 2000. 'Gartners Four Phases of E-government Model'. Available at https://www.gartner.com/doc/317292/gartners-phases-egovernment-model (accessed 1 June 2017).

Behn, Robert D. 1998. 'The New Public-Management Paradigm and the Search for Democratic Accountability'. *International Public Management Journal* 1 (2): 131–64.

Bevir, Mark. 2007. *Public Governance*. Berkeley: University of California Press.

———. 2013. *A Theory of Governance*. Berkeley: University of California Press.

Bhatnagar, Subhash. 2003. 'E-government and Access to information' in *Global Corruption Report 2003: Access to Information*, 24–32. New York: Transparency International.

Bhattacharya, Mohit. 1998. 'Conceptualizing Good Governance'. *Indian Journal of Public Administration* 44 (3): 289–96.

Borins, S. 2000. 'Public Service Awards Programs: An Exploratory Analysis'. *Canadian Public Administration* 43 (3): 321–42.

Box, Richard C., Gary S. Marshall, B. J. Reed and Christine M. Reed. 2001. 'New Public Management and Substantive Democracy'. *Public Administration Review* 61 (5): 608–19.

Christensen, Tom and Per Lægreid. 2009. 'Democracy and Administrative Policy: Contrasting Elements of NPM and post-NPM'. Paper prepared for the EGPA Annual Conference 'The Public Service: Public Service Delivery in the Information Age', Study Group VI: Governance of Public Sector Organizations, Malta, 2–5 September. Available at http://soc.kuleuven.be/io/egpa/org/2009Malta/papers/EGPA%202009%20Tom%20christensenPer%20laegreid.pdf (accessed 1 June 2017).

Clapp, Jennifer and Peter Dauvergne. 2008. *Paths to a Green World: The Political Economy of the Global Environment*. New Delhi: Academic Foundation.

Committee on the Financial Aspects of Corporate Governance, Cadbury. 1992. *Financial Aspects of Corporate Governance*. Report. London: Gee and Co. Ltd. Available at http://www.ecgi.org/codes/documents/cadbury.pdf (accessed 31 December 2011).

Committee on Regulations of Private Companies and Partnerships. 2003. 'Report of the Committee on Regulations of Private Companies and Partnerships', submitted to the Department of Company Affairs, Ministry of Finance, New Delhi.

Connelly, James, Graham Smith, David Benson and Clare Saunders. 2012. *Politics and the Environment: From Theory to Practice*. London: Routledge.

Corson, John and Joseph Harris. 1963/1967. *Public Administration in Modern Society*. London: McGraw-Hill.

Coupland, C., G. Currie and I. Boyett. 2008. 'New Public Management and a Modernization Agenda: Implications for School Leadership'. *International Journal of Public Administration* 31 (9): 1079–94.

Davidson, K. M., R. B. Ginsburg and H. H. Kay. 1974. 'Marriage and Family Life' in *Sex based Discrimination: Text, Cases and Materials*, 753–85. St. Paul, Minnesota: West Publishing.

Denhardt, B. Robert. 2008. *Theories of Public Organization*. Belmont, CA: Thomson Wadsworth.

Department of Economic and Social Affairs, United Nations. 2001. *World Public Sector Report: Globalization and the State 2001*. New York: United Nations.

———. 2016. *United Nations E-government Survey 2016: e-Government in Support of Sustainable Development*. New York: UN.

Dey, Bata K. 2000. 'E-Governance in India: Problems, Challenges and Opportunities, A Future Vision'. *Indian Journal of Public Administration* 46 (3): 300–10.

Dunleavy, Patrick. 1991. *Democracy, Bureaucracy and Public Choice: Economic Explanations in Political Science*. Hemel Hempstead, UK: Harvester Wheatsheaf.

Dunn, William N. and Bahman Fozouni. 1976. *Toward a Critical Administrative Theory*. London: Sage Publications.

Dwivedi, O. P. 2002. 'The Challenge of Cultural Diversity for Good Governance'. *Indian Journal of Public Administration* 48 (1): 14–28.

Frederickson, George H. 1999. 'The Repositioning of American Public Administration'. KSG Working Paper No. RWP04-010, 26 February.

Ghosh, B. N. 2012. *Business Ethics and Corporate Governance*. New Delhi: Tata McGraw-Hill Education.

Ghuman, B. S. 2001. 'New Public Management: Theory and Practice'. *The Indian Journal of Public Administration* 47 (4): 769–79.

Gottfried, P. E. 2001. *After Liberalism: Mass Democracy in the Managerial State*. Princeton: Princeton University Press.

Government of India (GoI). 2000. *The Information Technology Act, 2000*. New Delhi: Government of India. Reproduced in *Indian Journal of Public Administration* 46 (3): 417–55.

Henry, Nicholas. 2012. *Public Administration and Public Affairs*, twelfth edition. New Delhi: PHI Learning Private Limited.

Hirschman, Albert O. 1970. *Exit, Voice, and Loyalty: Responses to Decline in Firms, Organizations, and States*. Cambridge: Harvard University Press.

Holmes, Douglas. 2001/2007. *e-Gov: E-Business Strategies for Government*. Reprint. London: Nicholas Brealey Publishing.

Hood, Cristopher. 1991. 'A Public Management for all Seasons?' *Public Administration* 69 (1): 3–19.

Hood, Cristopher. 1995. 'The "New Public Management" in the 1980s: Variations on a Theme'. *Accounting, Organizations and Society* 20 (2): 93–109.

Hough, Peter. 2014. *Environmental Security: An Introduction.* New York: Routledge.

Hughes, O. 1998. *Public Management and Administration: An Introduction.* Second edition. Basingstoke: Macmillan.

Joshi, Abhijeet. 2008. 'Advantages of E-Governance'. *E-Governance in India.* Available at http://indiaegovernance.blogspot.in/2008/03/advantages-of-e-governance.html (accessed 19 February 2017).

Kamarck, Elaine. 2004. 'Government Innovations around the World'. Faculty Research Working Paper, John F. Kennedy School of Government, Harvard University.

Kapoor, Jagdish C. 2000. 'IT and Good Governance'. *Indian Journal of Public Administration* 46 (3): 386–95.

Kumar Mangalam Birla Committee. 2000. 'Report of the Committee Appointed by the SEBI on Corporate Governance under the Chairmanship of Shri Kumar Mangalam Birla'. Submitted to the Securities and Exchange Board of India (SEBI), Mumbai.

Lane, Jan-Erik. 1997. 'Introduction: Public Sector Reform: Only Deregulation, Privatization and Marketization?' in *Public Sector Reform: Rationale, Trends, and Problems,* edited by Jan-Erik Lane, 1–16. London: Sage.

———. 2000. *New Public Management: An Introduction.* London: Routledge.

Lateef, Shireen. 2014. 'Where are the Women Leaders in Public Administration?' *Asian Development blog,* 13 November. Available at https://blogs.adb.org/blog/where-are-women-leaders-public-administration (accessed 1 December 2016).

Lynn, N. and R. E. Vaden. 1979. 'Towards a Non-sexist Personnel Opportunity Structure: The Federal Executive Bureaucracy'. *Public Personnel Management* 8 (4): 209–17.

Mallin, Christine A. 2004/2007. *Corporate Governance,* second edition. New Delhi: Oxford University Press.

Mander, Harsh and Mohammed Asif. 2004. *Good Governance: Resource Book.* Bangalore: Books for Change.

Medury, Uma. 2010. *Public Administration in the Globalisation Era: The New Public Management Perspective.* Hyderabad: Orient BlackSwan.

Mongkol, K. 2011. 'The Critical Review of New Public Management Model and its Criticisms'. *Research Journal of Business Management* 5 (1): 35–43.

Olsen, J. P. 1988. 'Administrative Reform and Theories of Organization' in *Organizing Governance: Governing Organizations,* edited by C. Campbell and B. G. Peters, 233–54. Pittsburgh: University of Pittsburgh Press.

Office of the Speaker of the Lok Sabha. 2006. 'Address at the release of the Book *Indian Administration: Politics, Policies and Prospects*'. Speech delivered in New Delhi, 29 May. Available at http://speakerloksabha.nic.in/speech/SpeechDetails.asp?SpeechId=153 (accessed 1 June 2017).

Osborne, David and Ted Gaebler. 1992. *Reinventing Government: How the Entrepreneurial Spirit is Transforming the Public Sector.* New Delhi: PHI Learning Private Limited.

Parkinson, Cyril Northcote. 1957 *Parkinson's Law, Or The Pursuit of Progress,* seventh reprint. Cambridge: The Riverside Press.

Pollitt, Christopher. 1995. 'Justification by Works or by Faith? Evaluating the New Public Management'. *Evaluation* 1 (2): 133–54.

Pollitt, Christopher. 2003. *The Essential Public Manager*. Buckingham and Philadelphia: Open University Press and McGraw-Hill.

———. 2007. 'Convergence or Divergence: What has been Happening in Europe?' in *New Public Management in Europe: Adaptation and Alternatives* edited by C. Pollitt, S. van Thiel and V. Homburg, 10–25. Basingstoke: Palgrave/Macmillan.

Salskov-Iversen, Dorte, Hans Krause Hansen and Sven Bislev. 2000. 'Governmentality, Globalization and Local Practice: Transformations of a Hegemonic Discourse'. *Alternatives: Social Transformation and Human Governance* 25 (2): 183–222.

Samaratunge, R., Q. Alam and J. Teicher. 2008. 'The New Public Management Reforms in Asia: A Comparison of South and Southeast Asian Countries'. *International Review of Administrative Sciences* 74 (1): 25–46.

Sarker, A. E. 2001. 'New Public Management in Bangladesh: Chasing a Mirage'. *Indian Journal of Public Administration* 47 (2): 154–69.

———. 2006. 'New Public Management in Developing Countries: An Analysis of Success and Failure with Particular Reference to Singapore and Bangladesh. *International Journal of Public Sector Management* 19 (2): 180–203.

Schiavo-Campo, S. and P. S. A. Sundaram. 2001. *To Serve and To Preserve: Improving Public Administration in a Competitive World*. Manila: Asian Development Bank. Available at http://www.adb.org/documents/manuals/serve_and_preserve/default.asp (accessed 31 May 2017).

Shafritz, Jay M. 2007. *Defining Public Administration: Selections from the International Encyclopedia of Public Policy and Administration*. Jaipur: Rawat publications.

Sharma, Vijay Kumar and Anuj Kumar. 2011. 'Corporate Governance in India: Some Thoughts' in *Challenges in Governance*, edited by Mamta Mokta, S. S. Chauhan, Sanjeev Mahajan and Simmi Agnihotri, 534–56. New Delhi: Anamika Publishers.

Speth, James Gustave and Peter M. Haas. 2006. *Global Environmental Governance*. New Delhi: Pearson.

Stivers, Camilla. 2002. *Gender Images in Public Administration: Legitimacy and the Administrative State*, second edition. California: Sage publications.

Study Group. 1995. 'Directors' Remuneration'. Report by a study group chaired by Sir Richard Greenbury, 17 July. Available at http://www.ecgi.org/codes/documents/greenbury.pdf (accessed 2 January 2012).

Swarup, Hemlata and Niroj Sinha. 2013. 'Women in Public Administration in India' in *Women and Public Administration: International Perspectives*, edited by Jane H. Bayes, 13–30. London: Routledge.

Tricker, Bob. 2009. *Essentials for Board Directors: An A–Z Guide*. New York: Bloomberg Press.

United Nations Development Programme (UNDP). 1997. 'Reconceptualising Governance'. Discussion Paper 2, Management Development and Governance Division, Bureau for Policy and Programme Support, UNDP, New York.

———. 2014. *Gender Equality in Public Administration*. New York: UNDP.

Van de Walle, Steven and Gerhard Hammerschmid. 2011. 'The Impact of the New Public Management: Challenges for Coordination and Cohesion in European Public Sectors'. *Halduskultuur – Administrative Culture* 12 (2): 190–209.

Wikipedia Contributors. n.d. '2015 United Nations Climate Change Conference'. *Wikipedia*. Available at https://en.wikipedia.org/wiki/2015_United_Nations_Climate_Change_Conference (accessed 1 February 2016).

World Commission on Environment and Development (WCED). 1987. 'Our Common Future'. Report. Available at https://sustainabledevelopment.un.org/content/documents/5987our-common-future.pdf (accessed May 2017.)

World Bank (WB). 1989. *From Crisis to Sustainable Growth, Sub-Saharan Africa: A Long-term Perspective Study.* Washington, DC: The WB.

———. 1992. *Governance and Development.* Washington, DC: The WB.

Websites

https://www.britannica.com/place/Canada (accessed 14 December 2016)

http://www.egov4dev.org/success/definitions.shtml (accessed 14 December 2016)

SECTION B

NON-WESTERN TRADITIONS OF ADMINISTRATIVE THEORIES

A conventional study of public administration begins with the elaboration of Western administrative theories, usually starting with Weber's classical conceptualisation of the ideal form of organisation and forms of authority. This is certainly persuasive with immense theoretical value. Born out of his concern for protecting and consolidating Capitalist production, Weber's theory of bureaucracy is an unavoidable segment of the course curriculum in universities across the globe. Similarly, Wilson's distinctive approach to public administration remains another basic reference point for efforts towards grasping public administration as a contextual experience. Despite powerful theoretical critiques, the ideas that Weber and Wilson evolved are usually accepted by later analysts as axiomatic in some respects. A scan of the Western theories, both classical and contemporary, reveals that the foundational ideas that Weber and Wilson had put forth are immensely important to our understanding of public administration as an area of activity. While Chapter Two dealt with the classical theories in the Western tradition, Chapter Four focused on contemporary theories which are more interdisciplinary in character. There is however a common bridge between them in the sense that they seem to appreciate, to a great extent, the instrumental conceptualisation of public administration; the idea that public administration is purely an institution-driven exercise, directed to achieve certain well-defined goals. One of the major weaknesses of such a conceptualisation stems from the fact that since public administration is scarcely static, conceptualising public administration in its instrumental sense may not always be theoretically useful. Nonetheless, it cannot be denied that with their concern for a functional public administration, Weber and Wilson built a model which, despite not being universal, provokes further debate in the field.

Section B focuses on the contribution of non-Western thinkers in the field of public administration. Given the hegemonic grip of Western theories of administration, the non-Western counterpart hardly receives any importance, which is why a full chapter is devoted to this aspect. In view of space constraints, it has not been possible to provide an exhaustive account of the non-Western tradition. What has thus been attempted is to identify major thinkers and elaborate their distinctive ideas in the socio-economic milieu in which they articulated their responses. By concentrating on the theoretical ideas of Mahatma Gandhi, Mao Zedong and Julius Nyerere in the context of India, China and Tanzania, Chapter Five is devoted to analysing their distinctive nature. It is true that unlike Weber who devoted his attention to creating an appropriate structure of organisation for capitalism, Gandhi, Mao and Nyerere evolved their models while being engaged in campaigns for political liberation. While Mao and Nyerere had the opportunity to execute their ideas once they captured political power in China and Tanzania, respectively, Gandhi had not had the occasion to see how his ideas of localising governance implemented in independent India, though it became a reality in 1992 when the Indian government implemented democratic decentralisation. The issue will be discussed in Chapter Eleven of this volume.

The Western and non-Western traditions in public administration represent two conceptual yardsticks: on the one hand, the Western tradition draws on the Weberian conceptualisation of centralised-hierarchical form of governance as perhaps the only effective design; on the other, the non-Western thinkers devised options for democratic decentralisation of power and authority which, they were persuaded to believe, was the most appropriate means of administration because it allowed the *demos* to participate. Whether it is a foolproof mechanism is difficult to predict though there are reasons to believe that democratisation of administration provides a persuasive alternative in contemporary governance. With the collapse of the former Soviet Union due to it being, inter alia, highly centralised, the idea of involving the stakeholders in public administration appears to have gained ascendancy. Also, in view of powerful critiques for shedding-off of the overloaded state, the theoretical parameters that the non-Western thinkers championed remain critical in conceptually devising an alternative mode of public administration which is unique in texture and spirit.

5

NON-WESTERN TRADITIONS
Gandhi, Mao and Nyerere*

HIGHLIGHTS

- Village swaraj
- Commune
- Ujamaa

As an area of academic enquiry, public administration is Western since Western thinkers have contributed to its conceptualisation in a scientific manner. Beginning with Weber, public administration has provoked interest among a large number of thinkers who have also sharpened the available theoretical tools by reference to their contextual experiences. What runs through their efforts is their common concern for Capitalism which, according to them, was preferable to the declining feudalism as a mode for inclusive socio-economic development. They also insisted on a centralised and hierarchical bureaucracy and discarded the inherently weak paternalistic form of leadership which was prejudiced against the larger social interest. This is one part of the narrative. The other part, rather a neglected one, relates to a completely different kind of conceptualisation which, by challenging the pyramidal structure of governance, led to an alternative discourse in public administration. Being opposed to the centralised-hierarchical and impersonal system of governance, the thinkers belonging to this genre of thought championed a well-thought-out model of decentralised administration borne out of their distinct individual experiences. According to them, a centralised administration is contrary to the fundamental ethos of democracy and in an open society, instead of being supportive, it is an impediment towards fulfilling the system's ideological mission. Public administration needs to be dispersed and power devolved for creating a space for meaningful involvement of the *demos* (common people) in decision-making. Critical of the Western mode of thinking, these thinkers were also guided by their concern for evolving an

* Some sections of this chapter have been developed from Chakrabarty, *Localizing Governance in India*, pp. 80–144. With permission from Taylor & Francis.

appropriate model of governance which was organic to the indigenous experiences. Their ideas do not seem to be entirely novel because of their derivative roots. Nonetheless, the arguments for decentralised governance, while exposing the obvious limitations of an exported model of governance, also provide powerful theoretical inputs to conceptualise public administration in the non-Western milieu. In the following pages, an attempt will be made to comprehend the model with reference to the ideas of M. K. Gandhi, Mao Zedong and Julius Nyerere. Despite the fact that they were located in different socio-economic circumstances, they held compatible views as they were persuaded to believe that decentralised governance was an appropriate mode for inclusive administration.

GANDHI (1869–1948): THE IDEA OF VILLAGE SWARAJ

As a critic of positivist rationalism, Gandhi was opposed to the 'one-size-fits-all' syndrome because each society had its exclusive track record. The purpose of Gandhi's work was two-fold: (*a*) to mobilise new segments of Indian society, and (*b*) to make such participation meaningful as well as to lend a perspective to the freedom movement. He therefore launched a variety of social and economic programmes which were designed for instantaneous appeal to peasants, artisans, craftsmen and Harijans—in short, for every underprivileged group of society. According to him, 'true democracy cannot be worked by twenty men sitting at the centre; it has to be worked from below, by the people of every village' (1962/2007: 41). What was unique in Gandhi's conceptualisation of civic engagement in public affairs was his notion of 'oceanic circle' that he developed while defending village swaraj:

> Life will not be a pyramid with the apex sustained by the bottom. But it will be an oceanic circle whose centre will be the individuals always ready for the village, the latter ready to perish for the circle of villages, till at last the whole becomes one life composed of individuals, never aggressive in their arrogance but even humble, sharing the majesty of the oceanic circle of which they are integral units. (Gandhi 1946; reproduced in Gandhi 1947/2006: 100)

Two of his ideas are pre-eminent here: first, a circle of interdependent villages is perhaps the most viable unit for sustained and equitable economic growth for any society; second, and more importantly, systematic economic well-being would certainly make individuals within the circle self-reliant and thus confident. Hence, Gandhi was very critical of the doctrine of 'the greatest good of the greatest number'; he called it 'a heartless doctrine' that 'has done harm to the humanity'. To him, '[The only] real and dignified human doctrine is the greatest good of all, and this can only be achieved by uttermost self-sacrifice' (Desai 1953: 149). In his view, this could be as it happens in the oceans where creatures of varying sizes and strengths survive presumably because of certain natural laws governing their behaviour.

It is evident that Gandhi was deeply uneasy with the modern state. For him, a society based on *swaraj* (self-rule), 'true democracy' or non-violence was the only morally acceptable alternative to the modern State. According to him, the swaraj-based polity would be composed of small, cultured, well-organised, thoroughly regenerated and self-governing village communities; elected by these communities, a small body of people would administer justice, maintain order and take important economic decisions out of interactive dialogues with the community as a whole. These units would not merely be administrative but also powerful economic and political units fulfilling their role by seeking to articulate swaraj in its true form. As such they would have a strong sense of solidarity, provide a genuine sense of community and act as nurseries of civic virtues. In conceptualising the village swaraj which would finally lead to *sarvadaya* (welfare for all), Gandhi was drawn to *dharma* which, in his view, consisted of sensitivity and responsiveness. After having theoretically justified swaraj as an efficient form of civic engagement emphasising the importance of both individuals and communities, the Mahatma evolved his model of village swaraj which would be an authentic form of participatory democracy.

The conceptualisation of the oceanic circle is an innovative design to view governance in a participatory mould. This model is neither discriminatory nor appreciative of division in terms of class, creed and power; in other words, an egalitarian mode of organising governance. This was to be a system in which, as Gandhi argued, 'the last is equal to the first, or in other words, no one is to be the first and none the last' (1947/2006: 100). The oceanic circle represents a system where 'the outermost circumference will not wield power to crush the inner circle but give strength to all within and derive its own from the centre' (ibid.). So, at one level, Gandhi prepared a mental map to appreciate the values of equality as an antidote to the exploitation of human beings by human beings; on another level, he laid out the broad outlines of a structure of governance which is constituted by interdependent units pursuing common aims. This may appear to be utopian, as Gandhi himself admitted and countered saying, 'if Euclid's point, though incapable of being drawn by human agency, has an imperishable value, my picture has its own for mankind to live' (ibid.). The idea has obvious limitations unless it is complemented by a comparable mindset among the people, which may not be feasible in the real world where human greed for more at others' cost cannot be completely ruled out. Nonetheless, the Gandhian oceanic circle is a powerful conceptual innovation for two complementary reasons: (*a*) since it is integrally connected with the well-entrenched global intellectual tradition in favour of creating an egalitarian socio-economic order, the Gandhian intervention articulates its manifestation in the non-Western context where colonialism had created a divided society for consolidating processes in its favour; (*b*) not only is the idea of the oceanic circle inventive, it is also a useful intellectual tool to conceptualise the notion of peaceful coexistence by addressing the sources of irritation and discomfort in the spirit of togetherness and commonality for an identical purpose of common well-being.

What is Village Swaraj?

Having been raised in colonial India, Gandhi naturally imbibed specific ideas which weren't exactly anti-British but surely against the prevalent British government that he fought tooth and nail. His critique of racism in South Africa and British colonialism in India was based on his appreciation of the philosophy of Enlightenment. He was simply not agreeable to a regime that, despite being based on liberalism, had an explicit discriminatory character. He felt that this was a contradiction that had to be meaningfully addressed to avoid further distortions in governance in South Africa and India. Simultaneously, Gandhi also sharpened his counterattack on the regime for its failure to uphold the basic values of liberalism while governing the citizens of the Empire. His insistence on Indians being treated equally as citizens of the Empire followed from the liberal tenets that he held so dearly. Gandhi's approach to racism and colonialism was therefore marked by his emphatic faith in liberalism as an empowering ideology because of its egalitarian nature and its desire to create sameness in humanity. Nonetheless, despite being appreciative of Western liberalism, he also held views which ran counter to the 'liberal-democratic reification, objectification and technocratization of the political and the alienation of the people's political rights' (Pantham 1983: 173) because he firmly believed that 'swaraj will be an absurdity if individuals have to surrender their judgment to a majority' (Gandhi 1961: 45). Unlike its conventional mould, liberalism was conceptualised differently by Gandhi who drew on the distinctly-textured village republic which allowed localising of governance in its true connotation. Instead of blindly conforming to the fundamental ethos and principles of liberalism which were not politically relevant but to which he was deeply committed, Gandhi devised village swaraj in which power was dispersed and authority decentralised. His aim was to make governance genuinely participatory by insisting on exercising power by the villagers themselves rather than by their representatives.

Gandhi's entire project was to build a system of governance on the basis of his understanding of liberalism as the guiding principle. As is argued above, being vehemently opposed to State hegemony, he preferred a village-based national polity which drew upon his fascination for village swaraj. So emphatic was his belief about the village being the focal point India's socio-economic rejuvenation that he exhorted that 'if village perishes, India will perish too' (Gandhi 1936; reproduced in Gandhi 1962/2007: 30). True to his own conceptualisation of the British State, he evolved the idea of village swaraj as the only means to combat the omnipresent colonial state which also prevented individuals from realising their full potential. While elaborating his notion of village swaraj, he says:

> My idea of village swaraj is that it is a complete republic, independent of its neighbours for its own vital wants, and interdependent for many others in which dependence is a necessity. Thus every village's first concern will be to grow its own food crops and cotton for its cloth. It should have a reserve for its cattle, recreation and playground for adults and children. (Gandhi 1942; reproduced in Gandhi 1962/2007: 31)

Two important features of being a republic and independent of its neighbours for basic needs are critical to village swaraj. In order to ascertain the republican character of village swaraj, Gandhi prescribed the familiar system of panchayat governance—i.e., to be elected by the adult villagers regardless of caste, class, gender or ethnicity. These little village republics needed to be self-sufficient as well, as Gandhi insisted. Such an argument is likely to be misleading if Gandhi's notion of self-sufficiency is narrowly conceptualised. According to him, 'to be self-sufficient is not be altogether self-contained [because] in no circumstances would we be able to produce all the things that we need [and hence] … we shall have to get from outside the village what we cannot produce in the village' (Gandhi 1935b; reproduced in Gandhi 1962/2007: 63). Further, in his scheme of things, villages were also interdependent on one another for their survival. In order to address this aspect of village swaraj, Gandhi suggested that 'we shall have to produce more of what we can in order thereby to obtain in exchange what we are unable to produce' (ibid.). The fundamental point here is how to make village swaraj a workable scheme. The formula is easy to understand: along with his insistence on self-sufficiency with regard to food, cloth and other basic necessities, he also suggested a scheme for mutual exchange of goods which villagers could part with after having satisfied their requirements. Unless this was done, Gandhi warned, village swaraj would be a utopian construct which could be conceptually thought-provoking but impractical.

One of the fundamental pillars of village swaraj happened to be individuals who, unless adequately empowered, were just numbers with no consequence whatsoever. Based on his concern for individual freedom, he argued that the 'individual, [being] guided by nonviolence … is the architect of his own government … and will suffer death in the defence of his and his village's honour' (Gandhi 1942; reproduced in Gandhi 1962/2007: 32). Here Gandhi was talking the typical liberal language. That he was a true liberal is further evident in his conceptualisation of 'an ideal state' where the importance of individuals is established beyond doubt. With the setting of individual as indispensable in village swaraj, Gandhi now talked about its actual functioning. In order to make villages an ideal liveable place, he suggested

> There will be no castes such as we have today with their graded untouchability. Nonviolence with its technique of Satyagraha and non-cooperation will be the sanction of the village community. As far as possible, every activity will be conducted on the cooperative basis. [Furthermore,] the village will maintain a village theatre, school and public hall. It will have its own waterworks ensuring clean water supply. This can be done through controlled wells or tanks. Education will be compulsory up to the final basic course. (Ibid.: 31)

This is a well-defined structure which is both indicative and elaborate. As a step towards creating 'a communal self' that is appreciative of one another, village swaraj drew its sustenance from stable social relations which were possible by creating a caste-free society. Here, in tune with his basic social view, Gandhi laid out a structure of governance that had no place for caste discrimination, especially untouchability which was, he always felt, a sin in humanity. By creating village theatre and public hall, he put forward a structure for regular social interactions among members of village swaraj which would act in creating and cementing a bond among villagers and also helping remove the source of irritation by addressing them collectively. As one who always endorsed the idea that human efforts could do miracles, Gandhi laid out a structure of human collectivity based on his belief that 'human beings are capable of building a community [drawing] on cooperation and sharing, on altruism, and on the denial of greed. It is the world of sarvodaya' (Ronald deSouza 2008: 85). A unique conceptualisation, the village swaraj was thus meant to articulate an aspired world which was free from want, greed and prejudices. He firmly believed that the idea could easily be translated into reality with sincere human endeavour. According to him:

> [Village swaraj] will contain intelligent human beings; they will not live in dirt and darkness as animals. Men and women will be free and able to hold their own against anyone in the world. There will be neither plague, nor cholera nor smallpox; no one will be idle, no one will wallow in luxury. Everyone will have to contribute his quota of manual labour.[1]

Village swaraj provides a model of localising governance with reference to Gandhi's own understanding of multiple intellectual resources, drawn from both Western and indigenous inputs. A surface reading of the construct reveals that it has utopian characteristics because, as Gandhi himself admitted, it hardly corresponded with what existed as village life in the then India.[2] An idealistic formation undoubtedly, it was also an intellectual device to generate support for village-centric governance in a context when there were opponents, as we will see later. Nonetheless, the idea of village swaraj was a refreshing idea of self-belief in a structure of governance that also had conceptual roots in Western thinking besides visible indigenous sources of inspiration. What was unique in Gandhi was his ability to put forward a persuasive scheme of things which was also realistic enough to gain acceptance. It was not surprising that his idea of 'ashram' led to several experiments all over India. What he devised in the context first of Phoenix and Tolstoy Farms in South Africa, and later Sabarmati Ashram created a realistic alternative which was not only feasible but also conceptually thought-provoking. A Gandhian alternative, village swaraj thus represented a powerful design of localising governance during the British rule when a hegemonic state reigned supreme, for all practical purposes.

Basic Principles of Village Swaraj

As an activist-theoretician, Gandhi always preferred to articulate his views as clearly as possible. That is the beauty of his writings. As is evident, besides theoretically defending the notion of village swaraj by drawing on major intellectual tracts of the era, he elaborated the idea with reference to the features that, he considered, were appropriate for realising the goal. For Gandhi, an idea remained exclusively in the realm of thought unless it has the potential of being realistic. It is thus fair to argue that his political philosophy is that of praxis which means that conceptual ideas are both explanatory and contribute to their articulation. By being sensitive to the prevalent socio-economic context, Gandhi was perhaps one of those rare activist-theoreticians who always searched for alternatives that were both self-fulfilling and transcendental.

---

[1] 'Gandhi to Jawaharlal Nehru, 5 October 1945', reproduced in Gandhi (1997: 150–51).

[2] In his letter to Jawaharlal Nehru, he made it very clear by saying that 'you must not imagine that I am envisaging our village life as it is today' (ibid.: 150).

Since village swaraj was a format of participatory governance, it can be said to have emerged from Gandhi's critique of the limited democracy adopted by the colonial government in India. For him, it was not at all democracy in its actual connotation because the majority of the population remained peripheral. What was therefore required was to instil the democratic spirit by inculcating complementary values. This was easier said than done because the prevalent socio-economic processes did not seem to have been favourable in a colonial context. It was a daunting task—though the Mahatma, in his familiar style, elaborated some basic principles which were easy to internalise not because they were articulated in a lucid language but because they emerged out of the prevalent socio-economic circumstances. For the majority of Indians, these principles were persuasive since they were organically connected with their aspired universe which was free from exploitation due to socio-economic and political reasons.

In his defence of the self-governing village swaraj, Gandhi endorsed the Pluralist approach to State sovereignty, of which Henry S. Maine (1822–88) was an exponent.[3] According to Maine, State sovereignty stood in the way of realising the idea of popular government in its substantial form since the latter could be a threat to the former. What is basic to the Pluralist approach is the notion that a host of voluntary associations—from church to trade unions—holds sovereignty which cannot be abdicated under any circumstances in a democracy. The State cannot therefore be allowed to appropriate the space these self-administered organisations independently retain. In opposition to the contractualists—Hobbes, Locke and Rousseau—Pluralists further argued in favour of the pluralisation of State or a process of decentralisation of authority to legitimately accommodate these self-governed structures of authorities. For Maine, the village community was a mode of governance challenging and also supplementing State sovereignty by way of endorsing decentralisation as an empowering device. In tune with this argument, Gandhi insisted on village swaraj as the only device to inculcate the spirit of self-governance. He was anti-statist in his theoretical leaning, as was manifest in his arguments for village swaraj. As little republics, villages were vested with political authority which they acquired by being directly elected by the people. These republics were the 'oceanic circle' comprising village panchayats which held, for all practical purposes, substantial authority to pursue common objectives. Critical of the pyramidal structure of the State because it represented institutionalised hierarchy, Gandhi evolved village swaraj as a decentralised structure of governance which, by creating 'the forms of self-rule, would work to eventually displace the State, a state understood to be inherently violent' (Mantena 2012: 558–59). He thus looked upon 'an increase in the power of the state with the greatest fear because although while apparently doing good by minimizing exploitation, it does the greatest harm to mankind by destroying individuality which lies at the root of all progress' (Gandhi 1935a; reproduced in Gandhi 1947/2006: 79–80). Gandhi's choice was very clear: a nonviolent village republic in which the individual would be 'the architect of his own government' by transforming the village into 'a perfect democracy based upon individual freedom'.[4]

---

[3] We have drawn this argument on Mantena (2012).

[4] Gandhi's statement, no date (quoted in Mantena 2012: 563).

The story will however be incomplete unless one refers to the tension in Gandhi's idea of village swaraj: despite being critical of the modern industrial state, he did not completely reject the notion of an organised authority which an anarchist would have done. Instead, Gandhi gave an alternative form of authority by drawing on his philosophical preferences for pluralisation of State. It was a State of a completely different kind because it was neither exploitative nor insensitive to the importance of individuals. Village swaraj was thus a creative blend of what he derived from Maine and those from the classical liberal thinkers. At one level, it was thus a derived but uniquely-textured concept, at another, village swaraj also represented a typical Gandhian model of organisation of authority that was conceptually compatible with what the Pluralists stood for. The Gandhian arguments in favour of village swaraj are, in other words, both derivative and novel at the same time: derivative because the imprint of the ideas of the Pluralists, including Maine, is visible; creative since the Mahatma left his own stamp while elaborating village swaraj by emphasising its distinct character of being nonviolent and individualistic.

MAO ZEDONG (1893–1976): THE IDEA OF COMMUNE

Besides Marx's own text and the Soviet experiment of commune, Mao appeared to have drawn his inspiration from the Chinese *ta-tung* (great unity) tradition, which refers to a society based on public ownership and free from class exploitation and oppression. While restoring cultural identity, the ta-tung ideal 'sees man as the most important factor in economic production and once his contribution is justified as part of his social being, he will automatically be drawn to it' (Diamond 1976: 383). The ta-tung tradition creates an environment in which engagement in work for common well-being seems to be motivating. For the Chinese, the ta-tung ideal is instinctively acquired. Historically, the idea was nurtured during the Ming (1468–1644) and Qing (1644–1911) dynasties when the imperial bureaucracy extended only to the *xian* (county) level, leaving control of the countryside largely in hands of the local people (Mansuri and Rao 2013: 35–36). It was therefore easier for the Communist leadership to work on this while seeking to organise collective life in China around the communes. There are important texts that drew on this tradition. In fact, Mao had referred to one of the most thoroughly researched monographs on this theme while elaborating his views on 'people's democratic dictatorship'—*Ta Tung Shu*, or the *Book of Great Harmony* (which was written earlier, but published in 1935), in which the author K'ang Yu Wei provided a blueprint for peace by advocating human beings to live together. By dividing human history into the three ages of disorder, order and peace, K'ang reiterated some of the fundamental ideas that the Chinese saint Confucius had articulated for global peace:

> The sage-king, Confucius, who was of godlike perception, in early times took thought of this problem, i.e, the problem of the way of attaining happiness and doing away with suffering, and grieved over it. Therefore, he set up the law of the Three Governments and Three Ages: following the Age of disorder, the world will change to the Ages, first of increasing peace and equality and finally of complete peace and equality. (K'ang 1958: 47)

After distinguishing the three ages of history, K'ang commented on how one stage of history led to another till the final stage was realised. What is striking is his insistence on the dialectics of movements of history as a driving force for significant socio-economic transformations. He says:

> A principle more important than the three systems is the three stages: in the first phase of disorderly stage, primitive civilization is just arising from chaos, and the social mind is still very rude; in the second, the advancing peace state, there is a distinction only between all the civilized countries and barbarians. ... In the third, the extreme peace stage, there is no distinction at all [and] the whole world is one unit and the character of mankind is on the highest plane. (Ibid.: 48)

There are two important points that seem to have critically influenced Mao when he conceptualised the commune as a forum for collective existence. First, K'ang's futuristic assumption highlighting that there would be no distinction among human beings in the final stage of human civilisation remained the first reference point for Mao presumably because it was indigenous and also corresponded with what Marx conceptualised as the highest stage of human development with the disappearance of classes. That Mao was heavily influenced by K'ang's optimism is evident in his text on 'people's democratic dictatorship' where he underlined the contribution of K'ang to his conceptualisation. Second, extant research shows that *Ta Tung Shu* provided the foundational ideas of the commune and decisively influenced the Maoist articulation of the notion. It has thus been argued that '*Ta Tung Shu* supplies a detailed blueprint for an ideal society for Mao which was not available in Marxist writings, [which] means that the ideals of a perfect society embodied in the people's communes are borrowed by Mao from *Ta Tung Shu*, and were not entirely of his creation' (Wen-shun 1967: 76).

What is a Commune?

Etymologically, a commune provides a forum where a group of people live together, sharing resources and responsibilities, which means that it is both a device of coming together and a means of instilling the value of being together by sharing resources and responsibilities. For the Chinese Communists, communes did not emerge all of a sudden; they were the outcome of specific objective conditions in which the need for coming together arose. It was thus emphasised that 'the people's communes are the result of the march of events. ... The basis for the development of the people's communes is mainly the all-round, Great Leap Forward in China's agricultural production and ever-increasing political consciousness of the 500 million peasants'.[5] As shown in literature, the transformation from private ownership to collective ownership began in China in the early 1950s when the peasants were organised into 'mutual aid teams'. In order to address the common hardships and uncertainties which the villagers regularly confronted due to drought,

[5] 'Resolution of the Central Committee of the Chinese Communist Party on the establishment of People's Commune in rural areas, 29 August 1959', quoted in Wen-shun (1967: 65).

flood or epidemic, they pooled their labour, draught animals and farm equipment. From mutual aid teams, the peasants came together to form small cooperatives by pooling in individual plots of land, animals and heavy farm equipment. This was the beginning of the processes that finally culminated in the conceptualisation of communes.[6] So, small cooperatives were precursors of communes in China. The massive agricultural production that was achieved due to communes exposed the limitations of small cooperatives in handling large projects that hardly took off because of the boundary-conscious mindset of those involved in small cooperatives. And the failure to handle such massive production created objective economic conditions for the consolidation of a mindset challenging the prevalent small cooperatives. According to Mao, this was at the root of a new political awareness in support of communes which were considered to be appropriate for sustaining the growth that China had achieved with the establishment of a socialist regime following the 1949 socialist revolution. For the communes to take root, political awareness remained a critical factor; otherwise, it would be difficult to successfully counter the old system of thought endorsing small cooperatives that had roots in the old bourgeois society. The aim was therefore to replace 'the right-wing bourgeois ideology and also to overcome the conservative ideas in agricultural production [by] socialist values and leap forwardism' (Wen-shun 1967: 65), which helped build a mindset supportive of specific ideological preferences. Hence, it has been argued that 'the rapid growth of the people's communes definitely does not stem solely from economic causes; instead, the keenness shown by the mass of peasants towards the people's communes speak first of all of their greatly increased socialist and communist consciousness' (ibid.). Communes can be said to have emerged out of a socio-economic context which encouraged a specific level of political consciousness to replace the archaic mindset linked with the bourgeois social order. In this sense, communes also represent a definite politico-ideological course to radically alter the level of consciousness.

The idea of the commune was unveiled by Chen Po-ta, the spokesman for Mao, in two articles published in the *Red Flag* on 1 and 16 July of 1958. The idea had, as mentioned above, its origin in the small cooperatives that became 'a basic-level organization of both agricultural and industrial cooperation [which laid the foundation of] a people's commune in which agriculture and industry are combined' (CIA 1959: 1). Here Mao seems to have drawn on the classical Marxist formulation that Engels put forward: 'The citizen's commune will engage in both industrial production and agricultural production as a matter of course and will combine the advantages of urban and rural ways of life while avoiding the one-sided tendencies and shortcomings of each'.[7] Characterising the commune as 'the latest in a series of creative developments of Marxist-Leninist theory by Mao Tse-tung', Chen quoted Mao's conceptualisation by saying that 'the aim of comrade Mao is to gradually and systematically organize industry, agriculture, commerce,

[6] Lucy Jen Huang graphically illustrates the progression from small cooperatives to communes in 'The Communes in People's Republic China' (1976: 190–92).

[7] Engel's introduction to Marx's *The Civil War in France*, reproduced in Tucker (1978: 625).

education and the militia into a big commune, thereby to form the basic units of our society' (CIA 1959: 3). Marxist in its tone and spirit, the formulation underlines the concern of coming together on the basis of certain common causes which will otherwise remain distant. Hence, it was categorically mentioned that 'in the commune, industry, agriculture and commerce are the material life of the people; culture and education are the spiritual life reflecting the material life of the people; and the militia will protect such material and spiritual life' (ibid.: 5). Justifying that the militia was 'absolutely necessary pending the complete elimination of exploitation of man by man in the world' (ibid.), communes thus became, as Chen argues further, integral to the transition to a class-less Communist society.

Once the idea of the commune was shown to have had its root in Mao's own ideological preferences, half the battle was won. In a revealing statement, the prominent ideologue Li Shao-chi came out strongly in favour of the idea as an indispensable step towards realising the communist goal of class-less society, in a publication in the *People's Daily* on 30 July 1958:

> a commune … must not engage in a single occupation, but must develop in an over-all manner in various ways: 1) [one] can operate industry, and run more small factories of a local nature; 2) in operating agriculture, [one] must attend to water conservancy, preparation of fertilizer, undertake activities for tool-reforms and also seed-selection; 3) [one] can operate commerce—socialist commerce and combine credit cooperatives and supply and marketing cooperatives with the agricultural cooperatives; 4) [one] can also take-up education, rid yourselves of illiteracy and let all children attend school; and 5) [one] can also take-up the responsibility of being a part of militia. (Ibid. 6)

Being clearly an ideological construct, the commune was linked to the transition to Communism. While explaining how communes would become an aid to the transition, Mao was persuaded to believe that

> the People's commune is a product of economic development in 1958 and the Great Leap Forward of 1958. It is the product of two transitions. At present, we are making a transition from socialism to communism—i.e., from socialist collective ownership to ownership by the whole people. We would make a transition from socialist ownership by the whole people to communist ownership by the whole people. Communes are [therefore] the best grass roots unit for a communist social structure.[8]

As well as being part of the ideological transformation, communes were basically a structure of production, governance and sustenance of what the Chinese Communist Party deemed appropriate while translating Marxism into practice. Communes were organised around three complementary structures: (*a*) the commune at the top, followed by (*b*) the production brigade and (*c*) the production team—households were organised into teams, which then formed brigades and the brigades constituted the commune. Each level of organisation was responsible for organising

[8] Mao's public statement, cited in Zhihua and Xia (2011: 867–68).

farm labour: the brigade for establishing small workshops and elementary schools; the commune for large-scale land reclamation projects, a hospital, a high school, small factories and other-side-line industries as well as a welfare fund to aid the poor communities within the commune (Jones and Poleman 1962: 10–11). The main purpose of communes was to make people self-reliant by being together. To reinforce cooperative lives, therefore, it advocated 'community dining rooms, kindergartens, nurseries, sewing groups, barber shops, public baths, happy homes for the aged, agricultural schools, red and expert schools' (Liu 1972: 155). Besides organising production, farm cooperatives therefore also played the critical role as 'organizers of the way of life' (ibid.). In actual practice, communes were independent and self-sufficient units 'where there is all-round management of agriculture, forestry, animal husbandry, home enterprise, fishery, where industry (the worker), agriculture (peasant), exchange (trader), culture and education (student) and military affairs (militia man) merge into one'.[9] As a very complex compact combining multiple functions, the communes had four distinct features.[10] The first and most significant feature happens to be its scale and ownership. Communes were enormous in size and ownership was collective and by the entire population. Such large-scale social and organisational restructuring was required to release productive forces which had remained stifled under the old system of individual-centric production. Once communes were in put in action the State took over the economic function. Everybody worked for the nation, for the people and for the common good. By taking care of the basic needs of the members,[11] the communes gradually evolved systems that also addressed the special needs of those who were challenged physically or otherwise. By being together in the communes, peasants developed affinity with one another despite not being related by blood or marriage. This was not unusual in China because in rural areas people tended to become emotionally close in view of being together for generations in one location under situations of both stress and enjoyment. The second characteristic feature of the commune was its design for structural and functional intermingling. Communes were endeavours at uniting the available agricultural producers, cooperatives with the political authority at the township level which was also a significant step at erasing the distinction between the urban and rural domains. In terms of functions, the communes were meant to combine the five tasks of industry, agriculture, commerce, culture and education and military to accomplish inclusive development. With their involvement in these various kinds of roles, the members of the communes would thus become 'red and expert thereby politically committed to revolution and professionally competent in

---

[9] 'Resolution of the Central Committee of the Chinese Communist Party on the establishment of People's Commune in rural areas, 29 August 1959', quoted in Wen-shun (1967: 65).

[10] The discussion of the functions of communes is drawn on Byong-Joon (1978: 632–33), unless otherwise stated.

[11] Communes fulfilled sixteen basic needs of members: food; clothing; housing; maternity benefits with 45 days leave; sick leave and free medical aid; free old age care; free funeral; free burial; free upbringing of children; free recreation; a small marriage grant on the eve of one's wedding; twelve free haircuts per year; twenty free bath tickets per year (hot water); free tailoring; and free lighting (electricity or oil). Reproduced from Jen Huang (1976: 191–92).

development' (Byong-Joon 1978: 632). The third important feature of the commune was linked with the endeavour that it undertook to promote mass mobilisation and self-reliance. The purpose of being self-supporting was sought to be attained by the slogan of 'four transformations' which entailed (*a*) organisational militarisation, (*b*) militarisation of action, (*c*) collectivisation of life and (*d*) democratisation of management. In short, this strategy involved the creation of an environment where individuals remained intertwined with the goal that communes stood for. It was also an attempt to pursue the idea that individuals remained mere entities without being connected with the collective that communes conceptually represented. This final feature underlines the importance of politics in shaping how the commune unfolds. Communes were an offshoot of specific kinds of power-relationships that are politically-contrived. That is, communes were also vital in pushing the specific agenda that drew its sustenance from the prevalent power-equations. In concrete terms, as communes were governed by the party dictum, it had its roots in the party directives following the fundamental Maoist ideological formulation of 'uninterrupted revolution and simultaneous development'. What is relevant here is the assumption that since communes were hardly independent of the ideological preferences that the party ideologues had upheld, their role in community development and the articulation of communalisation need to be viewed accordingly.

As functional units, communes were independent in the sense that they were always coordinated by those who mattered in the decision-making at the three levels of commune, brigade and team. They remained interconnected because there was a unity of command in the Weberian sense and each level was accountable to its immediate superior level of authority in the hierarchy—communes were accountable to the State; as the coordinating units, brigades had to account for their work to both the communes and teams; and as production units, teams were responsible to the peasants. On top of these grassroots structures of governance was the party which usually acted as the hegemon. Given the domineering presence of the party in society, it was possible for the top Communist leadership to maintain a firm grip, even in remote areas, through their cadres who exercised control over the communes, brigades and teams. Acting as a bridge between the top leadership and their counterparts at the grassroots, these party cadres also provided useful inputs to the decision-makers at the top echelon of administration on the basis of their understanding of the local situation (ibid.: 640). Ideally, it was a perfect arrangement which also created a symbiotic network between the cadres and those who were involved in the activities of the communes, brigades and teams. In course of time, a vicious nexus had developed between the party cadres and those who gradually rose to become powerful at these three levels, and this was an impediment to the realisation of the Maoist twin goal of revolution and development. The party, instead of being a facilitator, was reduced to an instrument of self-gratification which ran counter to the kind of mass campaign—educational, ideological and mobilisational—that Mao had in mind. In order to contain the evil design of those holding authority, which was attributed to the inherent bourgeois prejudices, Mao gave a call for a Cultural Revolution as perhaps the only means to rid human society of bourgeois vices.

Communes were purposive units serving to make people self-dependent on the basis of their appreciation for dignity of labour and concern for others. The basic aim was to create an agency that augmented agricultural production to the optimal level unlike the earlier small cooperatives. Hence it is argued that people's communes in China arose 'not as an experiment in egalitarianism, but as a merger of agricultural cooperatives to create a larger unit for better control of rural environment, and especially, but not exclusively for water control and irrigation' (Strong 1964: 218, cited in Milton, Milton and Schurmann 1977: 29–31). Communes thus became the only form of organisation in rural areas to which all peasants belonged. The other distinctive function of the communes is linked with wider functions because they are meant to handle not only agriculture, but also local industry, commerce, education and home-defence on a township scale. As an all-purpose unit, communes thus represent a combination of functions to make life both self-fulfilling and innovative. The final important feature that distinguishes communes from all other forms of farm collectivisation elsewhere is the integration of production with governance. Based on the basic Marxist concern for integrative human life, communes were made as nurseries for creating conducive socio-cultural values. Communes were given the responsibility of managing production as well as conducting the administration at the grassroots. In other words, simultaneously with its involvement in agricultural production, communes were also meant to serve the peasants as instruments of governance. Communes were therefore not only an organisation of peasants as a collective farm as in the Soviet Union (Ganguly 1959: 257), but, based on the deployment of local resources and initiatives, also represented a definite way of life towards community development.

In order to guide the communes in accordance with Mao's teaching, the education cells were endowed with the responsibility of creating an appropriate mindset by pursuing specific learning methods and packages beginning with training in primary schools. Also, revolutionary committees were set up to help communes fulfil their mission according to the direction of the central authority. In Maoist description, these revolutionary committees were 'three-in-one' because they are revolutionaries, representatives and custodians of proletarian authority. In Mao's words:

> The basic experience of revolutionary committees is this—they are threefold: they have representatives of revolutionary cadres, representatives of the armed forces and representatives of the revolutionary masses. This forms a revolutionary three-in-one combination. The revolutionary committee should exercise unified leadership, do away with redundant or overlapping administrative structures, have better troops and simpler administration and organize a revolutionized leading group which is linked with the masses.[12]

Given the presence of the revolutionary committees, it was easier for the communes to fulfil their mission. Not only were the committees complementary to the communes, they were also

[12] *Peking Review* 14 (5 April 1968), cited in Milton, Milton and Schurmann (1977: 101).

hailed as a critical instrument to lead 'the proletariat and the revolutionary masses in establishing proletarian authority and in playing a vital revolutionary role in the momentous struggle to win all-round victory in the great proletarian cultural revolution'.[13] Another aspect is the nature of their interaction with the communes. Here Mao uses the metaphor of a piano to explain how these committees should behave while discharging their responsibilities.

> [To produce good music] the ten fingers should move rhythmically and in coordination, ... [Similarly, revolutionary committees] should keep a firm grasp on its central task and at the same time, around the central task, they should unfold the work in other fields [because] ... at present we have to take care of many fields [and] wherever there is a problem, we must put our finger on it and this is a method we must muster.[14]

This was a unique formation which, despite not being exactly a constituent of the communes, played a domineering role in executing the ideological agenda that the party leadership had set in motion. Implicit here is the fundamental Maoist idea of forcing people to educate themselves in accordance to certain preconceived and ideologically-justified views. Opposition to this was quelled by drawing on the importance of coercion in the transitional phase pending the complete liquidation of the exploiting classes. So the presence of hegemonic revolutionary committees was justified by reference to their contextual role in a class-divided society; which means that communes, however strong and well-organised they were, remained incapable of pursuing their ideological mission independent of these revolutionary committees.

The aim of the commune is to expedite the processes of democratic revolution to establish a proletariat dictatorship in China with Mao as its leader. Critical of Western democracy which is 'usually monopolized by the bourgeoisie' (Mao 1949b: 8), the people's democratic dictatorship refers to a system of governance in which 'the system is shared by all the common people and not privately owned by the few' (ibid.). Communes are an aid to the final transition to Communism. Since they are responsible in evolving a mindset favourably disposed towards common well-being, communes become integral to the Maoist approach to the radical socio-economic transformation that Communism represented. Like the people's democratic dictatorship, communes are to be led by an alliance of the working class and the peasantry since they constitute the majority of the population. Although peasantry form the majority of the population, the commune's democratic governance 'needs the leadership of the working class [for] it is only the working class that is most farsighted, most selfless and most thoroughly revolutionary. ... In the epoch of imperialism, in no country [can] any other class lead any genuine revolution to victory except the working class' (ibid.: 9). By being the core of radical socio-economic transformation, communes remained the primary ideological institution at the grassroots to guide the perception of the masses in accordance with what was considered appropriate during the transitional phase; they thus became nurseries

---

[13] Ibid., p. 105.

[14] Mao's (1949a: 2) concluding speech at the Second Plenary Session of the Seventh Central Committee of the Communist Party of China.

of those civic and politico-ideological virtues which helped create an environment where concern for others was instinctively acquired. The method that commune leadership would resort to was democratic, which basically meant the method employed was one of persuasion and not compulsion. Even deviants were to be punished by being given an opportunity to plead innocence if that was the case. Thus, democratically-constituted and ideologically-governed communes truly became a centre of people's democratic dictatorship. The ultimate aim was to create a democratic state qualitatively different from its Western counterparts primarily because it was based on people's will. Communes thus contributed to the consolidation of people's democratic dictatorship that would facilitate the final transition. Once the hegemony of the proletariat was established, other processes would take their natural course.

JULIUS NYERERE (1922–99): THE IDEA OF UJAMAA

The specific steps to realise *ujamaa* as a scheme for radical socio-economic transformation were devised and adopted by the Tanzanian government through the Arusha Declaration of 1967. The Declaration had its roots in various discussions that Tanganyika African National Union (TANU) had undertaken since 1965. The Nyerere-led government accepted the Declaration that was clearly a party document. In other words, what TANU devised as its Declaration was appropriated by the government in power. Nonetheless, it can be argued that the Declaration was based on what Nyerere articulated in his 1962 essay, 'Ujamaa: The Basis of African Socialism', which remained its reference point. Given the continuity, at least in terms of ideas and pledges, both these documents can be said to have constituted the foundation of ujamaa socialism that Nyerere developed.

Divided into four parts, the Arusha Declaration dwells on the context, and the distinct socio-economic problems that impeded the growth of socialism and their solutions within the prevalent system of governance. The first part of the Declaration refers to the TANU ideological creed that draws on the fundamental principles of socialism and reiterates ideas which had also figured in its Constitution. Supportive of State-centric socialism, the Declaration insists that

> it is the responsibility of the state to intervene actively in the economic life of the nation so as to ensure the well-being of all citizens, and so as to prevent exploitation of one person by another or one group by another, so as to prevent accumulation of wealth to an extent which is inconsistent with the existence of a classless society. (Nyerere 1967: 2)

As the Declaration proceeds, the distinction between the State and the government disappears and, while elaborating the aims and objects of TANU, the government becomes the only instrument to bring about ujamaa socialism. The Declaration thus forcefully argues that, given the critical role that the government was expected to play, there was no alternative but to insist that 'government exercises control over the principal means of production and pursues policies which facilitate the way to collective ownership of the resources of this country' (ibid.). The intention is very clear: to guide Tanzania along the lines of a preset ideological agenda, the ruling authority was given a free hand to implement policies which complemented the task in hand. It may be laudable at one level, but it also raises concerns of single party governance generating authoritarian tendencies that eventually consolidate under the hegemonic control of the government over dissenting voices.

The second part of the Declaration elaborates the policy of socialism crafted by TANU to bring about socialism in Tanzania under its care and leadership. Accordingly, socialism means (*a*) absence exploitation, (*b*) control of the means of production and exchange by the peasants and workers, (*c*) existence of democracy and (*d*) appreciation of values for inclusive society. The Declaration also acknowledges the fact that 'Tanzania is not yet a socialist society [since] it still contains elements of feudalism and capitalism—with their temptations [which] could spread and entrench themselves to the detriment of the processes leading to socialism' (ibid.: 3). It is categorical in attempting to address this problem. In typical socialist language, it says that the most effective shield happens to be the control of the means of production and exchange by the peasants. In tune with this, it announces that 'to build socialism, it is essential that all major means of production and exchange in the nation are controlled and owned by the peasants through the machinery of their government and cooperatives' (ibid.). Here too the role of the government happens to be crucial, confirming that the Declaration upheld the spirit of government-centric endeavour in bringing about socio-economic change in accordance with Nyerere's design in his essay.

The third and fourth parts are complementary to each other: while the former underlines the importance of the democratic ways of electing rulers, the latter endorses the idea that the leader has to lead by practice and not precept. Democracy is conceived here in its very limited meaning because the Declaration talks only about political democracy, which simply ensures participation in the processes for electing the government—this idea, clearly liberal in tone, may not assure economic democracy. By emphasising that the leader is responsible for spreading socialist values by practice, the Declaration seems to have emphasised specific qualities that a leader needed to imbibe. A genuine TANU leader, the Declaration underlines, 'will not live off the sweat of another man, nor commit any feudalistic or capitalistic actions … because socialism is also a belief in a particular system of living, and it is difficult for leaders to promote its growth if they do not themselves accept it' (ibid.: 4). What is emphasised here is character-building which remains at the core of nation-building. It was expected that leaders could influence followers through their deeds, and thereby help build a socialist system where exploitation was to disappear.

The most critical part of the Declaration from the point of view of ujamaa socialism is the third part which is about the policy of self-reliance. The aim here is to do away with poverty and oppression, and initiate a revolution with the ujamaa as an effective instrument to accomplish the goal. In order to be self-reliant, the country needed to generate resources, which was not an easy task since extra taxation was not feasible given the stark poverty in Tanzania. To address this lacuna, one could think of raising funds from external sources in the form of gifts, loans and private investment. Despite being attractive, this option did not seem to have gained acceptance because of an inherent flaw. As the Declaration rightly observes, 'there is no country in the world which is prepared to give us gifts, loans or establish industries to the extent that [Tanzania] would be able to achieve all [her] development targets [because] the prosperous countries have not accepted the moral responsibility to fight world poverty' (ibid.: 8). Also, no foreign assistance was likely to come without conditionalities since, as per an English proverb, 'he who pays the piper calls the tune'. So, dependence on others was not an option for achieving the goals that ujamaa set-out.

Since Tanzania was an agriculture-based economy, where the largest chunk of the population depended on agriculture, it was important to make agriculture an effective and profitable source of engagement. While industry was needed, it was not an essential device for development. Hence the Declaration underlines that certain prerequisites for development had to be linked with what majority of the people aspired for—people, land, good policies and good leadership. First, the Declaration begins with the need for people who are known for their capability to work hard in the field. Once people knew the advantage of being self-sufficient, they would transmit their feelings to the next generation, and this would have a snowballing effect in the days to come. This realisation would make people a continuous source of resources. Second, the land had to continuously be a source of benefit for the country—once it was utilised for a purpose, it had to be sustainably used to endow other benefits to the country. Since the land belonged to the nation, the government had to see to it that it never became a source of personal gratification for one individual or just a few. Instead, it should serve the entire nation. Third and fourth, TANU believed that even if resources were in place, development could not be taken for granted; to ensure development, good leadership should be engaged in devising good policies. In other words, the complementarity of good leadership and good policies always results in development. Hence, the Declaration emphatically makes the point that unless the leadership is committed to the ideological thrust of the polity even the very talk of good policies would be pious. Good policies are needed to ensure self-reliance which would remain distant unless it was appreciated by the leadership. The idea of being self-reliant needed to be nurtured to fulfil the goal of the ujamaa. The Declaration states 'in order to maintain our independence and our people's freedom we ought to be self-reliant in every possible way and avoid depending upon other countries for assistance' (ibid.: 16). Once this was ingrained, it would have spiralling effect on the entire nation:

> If every individual is self-reliant, ten-house cell will be reliant; if all the cells are self-reliant, the whole ward will be self-reliant; and if the wards are self-reliant, the district will be self-reliant. If the districts are self-reliant, then the region is self-reliant, and if the regions are self-reliant, then the whole nation is self-reliant and this [is] our aim. (Ibid.)

Ujamaa may not have been a panacea for the ills affecting Tanzania; nonetheless, it 'offered the oppressed, the exploited, the disregarded and the humiliated, a new life of freedom, equality, and respect, a life of enjoying the fruits of one's labour without exploiting or being exploited'

(Cornelli 2012: 219). It was therefore not an exaggeration when Nyerere hailed the Arusha Declaration for giving shape to ujamaa by saying that 'the Arusha Declaration offered a hope. A promise of justice, hope to the many. … [Ujamaa] did not do away with poverty, but it has given you, the capitalists and socialists alike, an opportunity to build a country which holds out a future hope to the many'.[15] By kindling hope for appropriate socio-economic changes, ujamaa no longer remained a mere scheme, but a pragmatic design seeking to fulfil specific ideological aims. This was not a mean achievement especially in the context of despair and hopelessness. The Arusha Declaration can thus be said to have generated a space for ujamaa which gave voice to the voiceless in a context when the government also became an active partner in the mission for change.

Despite its propagandistic character, the Arusha Declaration is useful to understand the distinctive TANU approach to ujamaa socialism that consisted of 'a societal project [combining] nation-building policies with a social and economic development strategy' (Fouéré 2014: 3). The discussion of the Declaration above makes two basic points critical to conceptualising ujamaa as a form of governance at the grassroots. First, by describing ujamaa as a context-driven phenomenon, the Declaration enables us to identify its conceptual/theoretical roots in the prevalent socio-economic milieu. Based on familyhood, ujamaa is also a testimony to a search for an alternative model of development drawing on indigenous resources. As an institutionalised system of collectivity, ujamaa also articulates local aspirations that TANU upheld presumably because of obvious politico-ideological gains. Second, the Declaration reaffirms the hegemonic importance of the State in shaping the development discourse in which people's voice does not seem significant. As the conceptualisation is clearly State-centric, the role of the government becomes pivotal, which also creates tendencies towards authoritarianism especially in a single-party rule—as history has shown, Tanzania was no exception, and Nyerere who was hailed as *baba wa taifa* (Father of the Nation) did not escape being charged as a dictator. So, it is fair to argue that the Declaration was a sugar-coated pill of authority that clearly had a partisan goal which helped the incumbent political authority to flourish in the absence of countervailing ideological forces.

The ujamaa model of local self-government is basically an indigenous model of participatory governance, based on distinct African inputs which did not receive serious attention because of the hegemonic grip of the Western mode of governance in Tanganyika (which later became Tanzania after its merger with Zanzibar in 1965) both during colonialism and after. Drawing on his concern for 'freedom, equality and unity', Nyerere's philosophy of ujamaa was rooted in traditional African values and had as its core the emphasis on familyhood and communalism of traditional African societies: 'freedom' because the individual does not get drawn to society unless s/he enjoys freedom in its substantial sense, which means 'independence of the compulsory will of another'; 'equality' in the sense of being treated equally and thereby instilling a sense of

---

[15] Julius K. Nyerere's speech, no date, quoted in Cornelli (2012: 219–20).

belongingness; 'unity' because only when the society is free from divisions shall its members live in peace and harmony and work with a zeal to contribute to the society as a whole.[16]

While articulating ujamaa, Nyerere heavily drew upon the indigenous sources as well, as is evident in the Arusha Declaration. Ujamaa did not appear to be an alien arrangement presumably because of its pronounced indigenous character as evident in the following features: first, the idea of the extended family in which 'a group of people who live together for the good of all' remained most critical. The extended family was a perfect shield against all kinds of uncertainties of life. Its purpose was 'to create a social unit which was strong enough to withstand all but the worst disasters, and which accepted the necessity for social stability, so that the struggle for food and shelter could go on under conditions tolerable to human beings' (Nyerere 1968: 12, cited in Cornelli 2012: 115). The extended family was said to have been 'nationalised' and 'universalised': it looked so in the sense that every person in the country was considered as a brother or sister, a process, which in Nyerere's thought, was intended to make the entire population of Tanzania to be one big extended family. The idea is basically 'ideological' to motivate and encourage unity by building certain types of social relationships amongst the Tanzanians. The task was not difficult, as Nyerere believed that 'the idea of togetherness' was not alien to the Africans and democracy that upheld the idea remained ingrained in them. By referring to the common belief that 'they talk till they agree' (Nyerere 1966, cited in Stoger-Eising 2000: 136), Nyerere defended the claim that democracy was always a part and parcel of African psyche. Since it was not easy to inculcate the complementary social values, the State needed to be firm in its resolve. Nyerere did not seem to be averse to the use of force, if necessary, as he argued:

> If these principles are to be preserved and adopted to serve larger societies which have not grown up, the whole of the modern educational system must be directed towards inculcating them. They must underlie all the things taught in the schools and all the things broadcast on the radio, all the things written in the press. And if they form the basis on which society operates, then no advocacy of opposition to these principles can be allowed. (Nyerere 1966: 14, cited in Cornelli 2012: 114)

Second, the idea of participation—as a means for inclusion—was an instrument to create 'togetherness' among the members; through their participation, individuals became part of the extended family which ensured their 'growth' and gave them 'security and dignity'. Participation was thus 'the element of connection' with the rest of the humanity in a particular area of locality. Third, participation through assigned work was a device for general well-being. Nyerere thus argued that 'an individual who can work—and is provided by the society the means to work—but does not do so, is equally wrong. He has no right to expect anything from society because he contributes nothing to society'. This resonates the Marxist principle of 'each according to his

---

[16] Bonny Ibhawoh and J. I. Dibua develop this argument in detail in 'Deconstructing Ujamaa' (2003: 62–63).

ability, to each according to his needs'. Finally, in regard to property ownership, Nyerere seems to have held a classical Marxist position. He thus built his argument by saying that 'individual owns property, but this along with other sources of wealth is to be shared if a member of the extended family is in need'. This is also reflective of the Marxist idea of collective ownership of communal resources where individual needs are decided not on the basis of absolute needs, but on the basis of relative needs of those in the collectivity. Nyerere confirmed this when he emphatically argued that 'unconditional or free hold ownership of land must be abolished [and] land should be communally-owned', and that an individual is entitled to a piece of land 'on condition that he uses it for the extended family to which he belongs' (Cornelly 2012: 126–47). The purpose here is to conceptually defend the idea of togetherness by drawing on each other.

As explained above, indigenous influences remained critical in the construction of ujamaa, which was an endeavour to bring about an egalitarian society. It is also fair to argue that Nyerere's concern for common well-being had its roots in his upbringing in a non-hierarchical Zanaki society that was known for its egalitarian and non-authoritarian features, as he has himself stated. The available description confirms that Zanaki society stood for nurturing an acephalous complex socio-political order without 'a hierarchical, centralised power structure'. In order not to allow vested interests to prosper, a uniquely-textured 'generation class system' was instituted for 'horizontal integration' cutting across lineage and class affiliations and which created 'far-reaching solidarity that [went] beyond the bounds of descent (lineage, clan), locality and even beyond the border of one's own ethnic group'. By stressing the importance of 'political discussion as the means to reach accord', Zanaki society contributed to the formation of 'a solid community … free from discord and disharmony' where individuals and community remained inclusive to one another; and hence 'the pursuit of private advantage at the expense of the community was frowned upon'. With the sharing of authority among the various classes, a concerted attempt was also made 'to prevent the accumulation of power in the hands of a few' (Stoger-Eising 2000: 124, 127). In light of this ethnographic description of Zanaki society to which Nyerere belonged, there is a sense when he claimed that 'I grew up in a perfectly democratic and egalitarian society'.[17] While elaborating ujamaa, it was obvious that he would draw upon those inputs which he gathered during his growing-up years. The result was evident because one of the recurrent themes in Nyerere's arguments defending ujamaa was the importance of 'traditional African values' and the centrality of 'the traditional African family'. It is now possible to argue that the socialist ideas that ujamaa sought to articulate were neither alien nor exactly derivative, but stemmed from the African socio-cultural milieu that was appreciative of familyhood. It was Nyerere's brilliance that he tapped the indigenous sources to devise a socialistic design of governance to bring about radical socio-economic transformation in Tanzania. However, what is puzzling was the effort that Nyerere undertook to evolve a

[17] Drawn on a personal interview of Julius K. Nyerere by Viktoria Stoger-Eising (2000: 127).

pan-African model of governance on the basis of his individual experience of Zanaki society, since Africa's cultural diversity resists such a sweeping generalisation. This is 'a romanticised portrait' that hardly corresponds with 'the multiplicity of African traditions' in general and Tanzania in particular (Stoger-Eising 2000: 131). It is also difficult to conceive that Nyerere was ignorant of Africa's immanent diversity. What explains the romanticised portrait of 'the African familyhood' as the basis of ujamaa was his ideological concern to bring people together in his resolve to make Tanzania self-reliant. In this sense, the idea of familyhood which may have obvious conceptual weaknesses is a perfectly valid ideological category with enormous capacity to draw people to the cause.

CONCLUDING OBSERVATIONS

There are thus enough theoretical inputs to argue that the non-Western traditions in public administration are as rich as their Western counterpart. This chapter has shown how activist-theoreticians Gandhi, Mao and Nyerere evolved their models of localising governance on the basis of what they deemed appropriate for India, China and Tanzania, respectively. Persuaded by their concern to democratise administration, and besides having drawn on indigenous intellectual sources, these leaders paid adequate attention to Western ideas as well in support of decentralised administration. It was therefore obvious for Gandhi to derive his theoretical cues from Maine while Mao drew on classical Marxism and Nyerere built his argument on the basis of what he received from the ideas of Kant. That they were also indebted to Western conceptualisation of democratic decentralisation confirms that there existed a parallel endeavour in the Western tradition in contrast to the well-established centralised-hierarchical mode of public governance.

Gandhi's village republic represented a site of contestation of two contrasting models of governance: one that came in the wake of the British rule and the other which Gandhi had articulated as little village republics. They are conceptually at variance with each other, since the former drew on centralisation of power and authority while the latter represented just the opposite. For Gandhi, however, the success of village republic as a mode of self-generating governance was contingent on meaningful decentralisation of authority and power. The urge for localisation of power remained vacuous unless authority was decentralised in the real sense of the term. What is fundamental in regard to Gandhi's village republic is the fact that it is linked with his overall concern for involving individuals in an effort which allows them to realise their full potential through participation.

Despite its derivative and indigenous roots, the Maoist conceptualisation of the commune has certain parallels with the way both Nyerere and Gandhi had articulated participatory governance with reference to their respective theoretical leanings. As is evident in our analysis of the non-Western tradition, in order to achieve an identical goal—localising governance—they devised different schemes which became popular so long as they were on their respective positions despite criticisms on occasions. There is also a strange coincidence—all three models were discarded as soon as they appeared on the scene. What is striking, however, is their reappearance at a later stage as alternatives to the prevalent schemes of socio-economic transformations. Communes were vehemently criticised for having established the party hegemony, though their role in radical socio-economic transformation was always hailed as revolutionary; ujamaa, which ruffled many feathers for forcible villagisation, was appreciated later as perhaps an effective alternative to bring about inclusive growth; similarly, Gandhi's village swaraj, despite being questioned as a moralist design with hardly any objective basis, was brought back in a different form in the early 1990s, possibly as a persuasive antidote to the unifying tendencies towards globalisation. Given their critical importance in conceptualising what we prefer to characterise as 'non-Western tradition in participatory governance', village swaraj, commune and ujamaa thus remain important landmarks in our search for a meaningful alternative on the basis of a creative blending of indigenous sources with derivative wisdom.

REFERENCES

Byong-Joon, Ahn. 1978. 'The Political Economy of the People's Commune in China: Changes and Continuities'. *Journal of Asian Studies* 34 (3): 631–58.

Central Intelligence Agency (CIA). 1959. 'The Commune: Revelation and Initial Organization, Summer 1958'. OCI No. 4354/59, 4 September. Available at https://www.cia.gov/library/readingroom/docs/esau-05.pdf (accessed 1 June 2017).

Cornelli, Evaristi Magoti. 2012. 'A Critical Analysis of Nyerere's Ujamaa: An Investigation of its Foundations and Values'. Unpublished PhD dissertation, University of Birmingham, UK.

Desai, Mahadev. 1953. *The Diary of Mahadev Desai*, vol. 1, translated by V. G. Desai. Ahmedabad: Navajivan Publishing House.

Diamond, Stanley. 1976. 'The Paris Commune in Communist China: An Anthropological Perspective'. *Dialectical Anthropology* 1 (4): 383–86.

Fouéré, Marie-Aude. 2014. 'Julius Nyerere, Ujamaa and Political Morality in Contemporary Tanzania'. *African Studies Review* 57 (1): 1–24.

Gandhi, M. K. 1935a. 'The Sarvodaya State'. *The Modern Review*.

———. 1935b. 'Self-sufficiency and Cooperation'. *Harijan*, 30 November.

———. 1936. 'The Place of Village'. *Harijan*, 29 August.

———. 1942. 'The Village Swaraj'. *Harijan*, 26 July.

———. 1946. 'Panchayat Raj'. *Harijan*, 28 July.

———. 1947/2006. *India of my Dreams*, compiled by R. K. Prabhu. Reprint. Ahmedabad: Navajivan Publishing House.

———. 1961. *Democracy: Real and Deceptive*. Ahmedabad: Navajivan Publishing House.

———. 1962/2007. *Village Swaraj*, compiled by H. M. Vyas. Reprint. Ahmedabad: Navajivan Publishing House.

Gandhi, M. K. 1997. *Gandhi: 'Hind Swaraj' and Other Writings*, edited by Anthony J. Parel. Cambridge Texts in Modern Politics. Cambridge: Cambridge University Press.

Ganguly, B. N. 1959. 'People's Commune in China: A Study in Theory and Technique'. *The Economic Weekly* 11 (7): 253–60.

Ibhawoh, Bonny and J. I. Dibua. 2003. 'Deconstructing Ujamaa: The Legacy of Julius Nyerere in the Quest for Social and Economic Development in Africa'. *African Journal of Political Science* 8 (1): 59–83.

Jen Huang, Lucy. 1976. 'The Communes in People's Republic China: Retrospect and Prospect'. *International Review of Modern Sociology* 6 (1): 189–200.

Jones, Philip P. and Thomas T. Poleman. 1962. 'Communes and the Agricultural Crisis in Communist China'. *Food Research Institute Studies* 1. Available at www.ageconsearch.umn.edu/bitstream/136607/2/fris-1962-03-426.pdf (accessed 16 April 2016).

K'ang, Yu Wei. 1958. *Ta Tung Shu: The One-World Philosophy*, translated by Laurence G. Thompson. London: George Allen & Unwin Ltd. Available at https://archive.org/stream/ServingThePeopleWithDialectics/TaTungShuTheOne-worldPhilosophy_djvu.txt (accessed 20 April 2016).

Liu, Joseph. 1972. 'The People's Communes and the Paris Commune'. *Studies in Soviet Thought* 12 (2): 146–65.

Mansuri, Ghazala and Vijayendra Rao. 2013. *Localizing Development: Does Participation Work?* Washington, DC: The WB.

Mantena, Karuna. 2012. 'On Gandhi's Critique of the State: Sources, Contexts, Conjunctures'. *Modern Intellectual History* 9 (3): 535–63.

Mao, Zedong. 1949a. 'Methods of Work of Party Committees, March 13, 1949'. *Selected Works of Mao Tse-tung*, vol. 4. Peking: Foreign Languages Press. Available at https://www.marxists.org/reference/archive/mao/selected-works/volume-4/mswv4_59.htm (accessed May 2017).

———. 1949b. 'On the People's Democratic Dictatorship: In Commemoration of the Twenty-eighth Anniversary of the Communist Party of China, June 30, 1949'. *Selected Works of Mao Tse-tung*, vol. 4. Peking: Foreign Languages Press. Available at http://www.marxists.org/reference/archive/mao/selected-works/volume-4/mswv4_65.htm (accessed 2 May 2016).

Milton, David, Nancy Milton and Franz Schurmann, eds. 1977. *People's China: Social Experimentation, Politics, Entry onto the World Scene, 1966–72*. Harmondsworth: Penguin.

Nyerere, Julius K. 1966. *Freedom and Unity—Uhuru na umoja: A Selection from Writings and Speeches, 1952–65*. Dar-es-Salaam: Oxford University Press.

———. 1967. 'The Arusha Declaration', 5 February. Available at https://www.marxists.org/subject/africa/nyerere/1967/arusha-declaration.htm (accessed May 2017).

———. 1968. *Ujamaa: Essays on Socialism*. Dar-es-Salaam: Oxford University Press.

Pantham, Thomas. 1983. 'Thinking with Mahatma Gandhi: Beyond Liberal Democracy'. *Political Theory* 11 (2): 165–88.

Ronald deSouza, Peter. 2008. 'Institutional Vision and Sociological Imaginations: The Debate on Panchayati Raj' in *Politics and Ethics of the Indian Constitution*, edited by Rajeev Bhargava, 79–91. New Delhi: Oxford University Press.

Stoger-Eising, Viktoria. 2000. '"Ujamaa" Revisited: Indigenous and European Influences in Nyerere's Social and Political Thought'. *Africa: Journal of the International African Institute* 70 (1): 118–43.

Strong, Anna Louise. 1964. *The Rise of the Chinese People's Communes: And Six Years After*. Peking: New World Press.

Tucker, Robert C., ed. 1978. *The Marx-Engels Reader*, second edition. London and New York: WW Norton & Co.

Wen-shun, Chi. 1967. 'The Ideological Source of the People's Commune in Communist China'. *Pacific Coast Philology* 2 (April): 62–78.

Zhihua, Shen and Yafeng Xia. 2011. 'The Great Leap Forward: The People's Commune and the Sino-Soviet Split'. *Journal of Contemporary China* 20 (72): 861–80.

SECTION C

GOVERNMENT TO GOVERNANCE

Democracy as Collaborative Exercise

There are two sources of theorisation in the discipline of public administration: on the one hand, it has drawn on the fundamental contributions of a large group of thinkers, including those who do not belong to the discipline; on the other hand, as it is also a practice, a large contingent of practitioners also provide useful theoretical cues to grasp the conceptual peculiarities of public administration. The contributions from these two sources are not mutually exclusive but complementary to each other. As is commonly known, the idea of government is an important component of public administration and theorists have provided several theoretical schemes to explain as persuasively as possible the functioning of government in different socio-economic contexts. Also, one cannot ignore the role of the Bretton Woods institutions—the World Bank (WB) and International Monetary Fund (IMF)—and other international donor agencies which have given enough theoretical inputs to conceptualise public administration. Since the focus has moved to the processes and rather than the institutions of governance, this can be called an era of journey from government to governance. The change is usually explained by the steady decline of the State-centric developmental paradigm that the former Soviet Union had championed; in its place, the neoliberal emphasis on market-driven governance appears to have gained salience.

This section has six chapters: Chapter Six is about governance that has its roots primarily in donor agencies who are worried about recovering loans from developing countries; the failure to repay is attributed to the decline of governance; hence the insistence on streamlining the processes of governance. Governance is the product of specific socio-economic circumstances and the processes of governance are, the chapter argues, linked with the context in which it was privileged over public administration. Chapter Seven deals with public policy, which is an emerging field of study in the discipline. Chapter Eight is a continuation of the previous chapter in that it discusses in detail four specific policy domains. Chapter Nine is on ethics in governance. In view of the contextual peculiarities of the Indian polity, it is difficult to formulate a general theory either in understanding the nature of ethics in governance or its decline. So, there is a need for a contextual understanding of the phenomenon. Besides dealing with the relevant conceptual issues, the chapter elaborates some of the theoretical issues with reference to the specific case of India to argue the point that since governance is influenced by the country's ideological predilections, ethics is also part of processes. Chapter Ten is on situating citizens in administration. The final chapter, Chapter Eleven, delves into the intricacies of governance at the grassroots. The chapter draws on the distinct Indian experiences and shows how the demand for democratic decentralisation finally paved the way for localising governance in the form of the *panchayati raj* in India. A sustained struggle for devolution of power and authority led to the reconceptualisation of governance at the localities in various parts of the world. This is also complemented by a distinct global trend in favour of democratic decentralisation which, at one level, articulates a powerful critique of State-led development paradigm, and, at another, provides an institutional platform for stakeholders to establish the legitimacy of their claims.

On the whole, this Section C identifies governance as a theoretical device by focusing on how it is conceptualised while emphasising the importance of ethics in public administration and localising governance. These concerns are interwoven because they argue for the criticality of the processes in which governance is articulated. Unless public administration is ethics-sensitive, it can by anything but public administration; similarly, unless the stakeholders are involved in decision-making, it can be anything but democratic. On the basis of these two points, one can now make the general argument that dispersal of authority and democratic decentralisation are mutually inclusive. A mere deconcentration of authority is not what governance aims at; a meaningful devolution of power and authority to make participants in the governance as stakeholders is the goal that governance seeks to achieve. Governance thus provides enough theoretical inputs to reconceptualise public administration which is being rearticulated in a completely different fashion—characterised by being critical to the Weberian preference for a centralised and hierarchical form.

Governance is an offshoot of an ideological inclination in favour of the neo-liberal understanding of public life. The orientation is also towards structuring governance in such a way as to inculcate the entrepreneurial spirit along with ensuring efficiency. In reality, however, governance is a design to pursue the ideological goal supportive of individualising collective existence. The neo-liberal ideological inclination cannot be a universal model since the needs of the countries differ in view of the disparities in their levels of development. Nonetheless, governance is a fresh input in the conceptualisation of public administration that has created a space for an extensive review of public administration as an area of enquiry. In that sense, it is—besides being an alternative conceptual category—a reasonably persuasive theoretical design to understand public administration in a different light.

6

DEFINING GOVERNANCE*

HIGHLIGHTS

- Historical roots of governance
- Theoretical roots of governance
  - Initiatives of the World Bank
- Good-enough governance
- Privileging the private over the public
- Deconstructing governance
- New governmental designs

In a neo-liberal globalising world, the expression 'public administration' appears to have lost its validity, presumably because of its evident ideological limitations in conceptualising public governance under the changed environment. Nurtured in the Weberian conceptual mould, the idea of public administration does not seem tenable with the unfolding of a world which is far more global than in the past. Public administration, if monocentric, is simply inappropriate in a situation where multiple actors intervene in public decision-making. Governance is thus a product of specific kinds of circumstances in which it has acquired a distinctive ideological flavour. It is not an innocent construct denoting just ruling or processes of ruling because of the implicit ideological tilt in its conceptualisation in the neo-liberal global environment. In simple terms, governance is not merely administration, but also the manner in which it is structured to attain certain pre-determined socio-economic and political objectives. By linking the guarantee of financial assistance to the acceptance of the governance package, the donor agencies created an environment where the idea gained prominence. Besides the obvious socio-political tenor, there is no doubt that the model also contributed to the establishment of a functioning public administration in many countries by replacing undemocratic and also highly prejudiced patrimonial authority. In that respect governance, notwithstanding its clear neo-liberal tilt, seems to be a refreshing endeavour since it has set in motion processes which are likely to initiate efforts towards

* Some sections of this chapter have been developed from Chakrabarty, *Localizing Governance in India*, pp. 102–03, 196–97; and Chakrabarty, *Ethics in Governance in India*, pp. 97–102. With permission from Taylor & Francis.

democratising public administration. Governance is not a magic wand, though it has elements seeking to refashion public administration in such a way as to make it accountable, responsible and also efficient. The aim here is to provide a structure of governance which is also acceptable to all since it is transparent, functional and sensitive to the prevalent needs. Conceptually, this is fantastic. However, there are certain fundamental limitations, in view of its ideological texture, which also needs to be addressed while analysing governance as a meaningful tool of analysis. Central to the argument is the view that governance, despite being an instrument of efficiency, tends to ignore the importance of politics in shaping the exact nature of public administration, which also confirms that the effort towards conceptualising governance as a universal model of analysis does not seem to be tenable given the diverse socio-cultural milieu in which it unfolds in different countries. One is therefore required to take into account the text–context dialectic to persuasively grasp the complexities of governance as a theoretical parameter. In a nutshell, since governance carries with it a clear ideological message, it cannot be immune to the obvious criticism that usually accompanies any ideologically-charged conceptual category. Nonetheless, it has its own value in the study of public administration for two important reasons: first, by providing a counter-conceptualisation to the Weberian centralised and hierarchical authority, governance articulates a powerful critique of what has so far been considered axiomatic; second, the governance challenge is also useful to understand the functioning of public administration—especially in developing countries which, by encouraging the growth and consolidation of a rent-seeking bureaucracy, have created an environment where governance has been reduced to an instrument for realising partisan goals. Public administration was anything but a means to realise private ends! It was therefore not surprising that despite having a clear ideological tone, governance was accepted in many countries as a design because it facilitated loan from the donor agencies and also simultaneously generated the hope of an impersonal government that is committed to development for all. What is argued here is the point that governance is also adequately equipped to lay out a system of administration in countries that are suffering from a perennial governance-deficit. This is perhaps one of the stronger reasons explaining the growing acceptance of the model of governance in place of the traditional State-controlled system of public administration.

Notwithstanding various persuasive critiques, there is no doubt that the idea of governance has upset the applecart. The idea is being serious dealt with by both practitioners and scholars of public administration. Drawing on the extant literature on governance, this chapter seeks to provide an analytical account of the concept with reference to its conceptualisation at a historical juncture of human civilisation and its consolidation in course of time, presumably because of its success in creating a system of public administration in circumstances where there was none in view of the well-entrenched patrimonial authority.

HISTORICAL ROOTS OF GOVERNANCE

Historical circumstances appeared to have favoured the articulation of governance as a mode of public administration. To be precise, governance is conceptualised in a historical context supporting the decline, if not the end, of authority. As an OECD (Organization for Economic Co-operation and Development) publication formulates, four sets of historical developments seem to have influenced the profound shifts in governance: first, the impact of struggles for 'greater democracy and competitive markets'; second, the ways in which 'changes in economic productivity and material wealth alter both the aims and methods of governance'; third, demands for reforming the well-entrenched and excessively rule-bound system of administration; fourth, managerial innovations and their application to transform the institutional design and organisational structure of administrative operations (quoted in Michalski, Miller and Stevens 2001: 9). The search for a new conceptualisation had an antecedent also in the collapse of the Soviet Union where 'alternative management practices', grounded in Marxism-Leninism were articulated and successfully executed. Within the developed Capitalist countries, almost contemporaneously, there was the rise of strong anti-bureaucratic and anti-State criticism directed against what came to be called 'government overload' as a consequence of 'welfare backlash'. The State, it was alleged, has over the years taken upon itself a large array of activities that have inflated its budgetary and financial commitments, and led to the 'overgrowth' of bureaucracy. The battle cry was to 'downsize' government and allow more free play to the market and civil society—giving rise to the new ideology of neo-liberalism.

With the onset of globalisation, the traditional bureaucratic model appears to have lost significance, presumably because of the growing importance of the non-State actors in administration. The instrumental view of administration does not therefore appear to be tenable for reasons connected with 'the pluralisation of state'. Given the increasing role of transnational forces, even in domestic administration, the State-centred theories of bureaucracy seem inadequate in addressing the radical metamorphosis of public administration, both in developed and developing countries.

THEORETICAL ROOTS OF GOVERNANCE

The theoretical roots of governance are located especially in the New Right ideology of neo-liberal economic theories. In this new dispensation, governance is an interface between State, market and civil society. The 'governance' discourse has its origin in (*a*) the new thrust toward neo-liberalist restraint on the State along with the positing of the market as a competing social authority, and bringing in the civil society as a provider of local-level social services, (*b*) the concern of international funding authorities (particularly, the World Bank [WB]) for more accountable, transparent, open and participative rule, and (*c*) the newly emergent 'globalisation' trend—a socio-economic integration of the world propelled by economic, technological and political considerations.

The New Right ideology seeks to redefine public administration by championing the cause of the free market and calls for a significant reduction in the size and role of government in society. In this respect, Mohit Bhattacharya observes:

> Although the advocacy has generally been in favour of a greater role for the market and a lesser role for the state, the new right had within it a neo-liberal wing and neo-conservative wing. The former has been primarily concerned with the promotion of individual liberty and the latter with the restoration of traditional values. (Bhattacharya 2003: 71)

Government is being reinvented not only structurally but also ideologically in an environment where neo-liberal values seem to have triumphed. The State and the government withdraw from areas that were traditionally their domain. As observed in Chapter Four, globalisation has led to a marriage between corporate discipline and entrepreneurial spirit, governments have discarded their traditional image of 'a doer' and are seeking to accommodate the market impulse to become 'an enabler'. Globalisation thus restricts the national governments and limits its policy options. The governmental functions are redefined with the neo-conservative theoretical parameters. The corporate state has become a reality. Public administration is now governance which is, as shown earlier, nothing but a checklist of certain activities designed both to stabilise and consolidate neo-liberalism. Accountability in public bureaucracy is ascertained, for instance, not only internally but also through various external agencies, including the civil society.

Introducing the Idea

The argument in favour of more governance and less government appears to have gained ground in the early 1970s. It was Harlan Cleveland who first drew attention to actual governance which was a casualty due to bureaucratic hegemony. Insisting on more governance and less government, Cleveland argued:

> The organization that gets things done will no longer be hierarchical pyramids with most of the real control at the top. They will be systems interlaced webs of tension in which control is loose, power diffused and centres of decisions plural. Decision making will become an increasingly intricate process of multilateral brokerage both inside and outside the organization which thinks [that] it has the responsibility for making, or at least announcing, decision. Because organizations will be horizontal, the way they are governed is likely to be more collegial, consensual and consultative. The bigger the problem to be tackled, the more real power is diffused and larger the number of persons who can exercise it—if they work at it. (1972: 13)[1]

Critical of the Weberian hierarchical and top-directed form of governance, Cleveland put forward an alternative highlighting some of the ideas that are vital in conceptualising public administration in the globalising world of today. There are three important features: first, to make government provide more governance, decisions need to be pluralised, i.e. there should be multiple centres of decision-making. Cleveland argued for the diffusion of power in support of a system of decision-making in which multiple stakeholders are considered integral to the entire processes. Second, once the role of the stakeholders was recognised as legitimate, it created a

---

[1] Reproduced by permission of Seeley G. Mudd Manuscript Library at Princeton University.

space for discussion and deliberation on issues critical to governance. And, Cleveland argues that the decision arrived at out of consensus and meaningful consultation was best, because once an individual became a stakeholder s/he was likely to develop an emotional attachment with the decision that involved her/him. With an expansive diffusion of power, a far more democratic system of decision-making would be in place since it would give a larger group of people the opportunity to participate. There was no best decision till then because, as Cleveland mentions, decisions were always an offshoot of multilevel brokerage. Conforming to the argument that Lindblom and Braybrooke made in *A Strategy of Decision* (1963)—that decisions are generally an outcome of 'a mutual partisan adjustment'—Cleveland characterised governance as a process of constant dialogues just like a brokerage firm that is engaged in negotiations till the final decision is made. Third, the future organisation was to be horizontal and not hierarchical. A hierarchical organisation tends to be inherently centralised since it favours top-centric governance; in its place, the author preferred a horizontal organisation in which power is diffused and decentred. Conceptually contrary to the well-established Weberian ideas of organisation, Cleveland strove to refashion public administration by insisting on what it provides while governing. In so doing, not only did he challenge the conventional approaches to public governance, but also gave enough theoretical inputs for its reconceptualisation by drawing our attention to the complex processes that usually go with governance in the context of growing democratisation, as in the case of the sustained civil rights movement in the US in the 1960s. His arguments for governance thus remain critical in reconceptualising public administration as an important instrument for translating governance into action in an environment in which strictly Weberian ideas seem to be untenable.

INITIATIVES BY THE WB AND ITS OTHER ASSOCIATES

Cleveland's suggestion appears to have been endorsed first by the WB and later by the other global donor agencies. The idea struck an emotional chord with the WB when it failed to recover the financial loan it had extended to many countries in Sub-Saharan Africa. According to the WB, the recipient nations were unable to honour the commitment largely due to the political instability caused due to rapid regime changes. On the basis of its probing into the circumstances leading to political instability, the WB attributed the phenomenon to widespread political and institutional decay. Besides the large-scale dwindling of institutions of authority, including the Judiciary, equally worrying was the breakdown of governance. In a report titled *From Crisis to Sustainable Growth*, the WB states:

> breakdown of the system of governance [leading] to widespread corruption, oppression and nepotism [which] are not unique to Africa, … may have been exacerbated by development strategies that concentrated power and resources in government bureaucracies, without countervailing measures to ensure public accountability or political consensus. As a result, in several countries, the neglect of due process has, on the one hand, robbed institutions of their legitimacy and credibility; and, on

> the other hand, the proliferation of administrative regulations, such as licensing, controls and quotas has encouraged corruption and set the individual against the system. (WB 1989: 22)[2]

The consequences of the scenario described above were disastrous. Since they were clearly privatised or tuned exclusively to partisan interests, public administration had become woefully 'weak'; due to the resulting vitiated public life, it completely lost its public character and became a form of authority which was meant to subserve the interests of those who appropriated authority for private gains. Therefore, the WB argued that 'underlying the litany of Africa's development problem is a crisis of governance [which simply] means the exercise of political power to manage a nation's affairs' (ibid.: 60). There was hardly a system of governance, adequately backed by the rule of law and its concomitant values and conventions. Due to the absence of a countervailing power, 'state officials … have served their own interests without fear of being called to account'. In order to survive and also to expand their benefits, individuals tended to build-up 'personal networks of influence' which made politics 'highly personalised' and patronage 'essential to maintain power'. The leadership 'assumes broad discretionary authority and loses its legitimacy; information is controlled and voluntary associations are co-opted and disbanded' (ibid.: 60–61). As an instrument of governance, the civil service was also too weak to discharge its responsibility with confidence. Because not only did the managers 'lack competencies [since] they are recruited for being loyal to those holding authority, they also face difficulties in motivating and disciplining their staff owing to the social and political context in which they operate' (ibid.: 55). In order to get out of the mess, the WB devised some measures that insisted on

> (a) staff testing to help select the best qualified candidates and the release of redundant staff with compensation and assistance to enter the private sector, and (b) better personnel management, with competitive entrance examinations, regular staff appraisals as the basis of promotion based on merit rather than patronage and longevity. (Ibid.: 56)

The WB was aware that it cannot substantially revamp the civil service, unless the socio-economic context in which it has its organic roots is radically transformed. Hence, attempting to address the structural ills of civil service, it suggested that 'a systematic effort to build a pluralistic institutional structure, a determination to respect the rule of law, and vigorous protection of the freedom of the press and human rights' (ibid.: 61) was required. This is primarily a checklist of items which are universally applicable. What it confirms is the assumption that governance is a set of technical requirements which, if fulfilled, will create conditions for efficient governance, regardless of the socio-economic and political circumstances. The argument may have validity in a controlled environment, since its success is attributed to certain well-defined terms and conditions without reference to the fact that they are also contingent on the type of society in which governance is to be articulated as a function.

The 1992 WB Documents

While the 1989 WB report introduced the technique of governance to Sub-Saharan Africa, two documents in 1992 universalised the model by arguing that it was appropriate for revitalising public administration across the globe. The recommendation was made in a context when, with the disintegration of the Soviet Union, the neo-liberal mode of thinking appears to have gained credibility. It was also a period when the paradigm of State-led development had lost its appeal. Structuring the discussion around a specific mode of institutionalised administration, one of the documents states that governance is a design that seeks to combat 'corruption [that] has affected development and … pervasive patronage [that] has led to public investment choices being used to finance white elephants, usually by contracting excessive foreign debt' (WB 1992a: 4). Besides highlighting the importance of agencies other than the government, governance is primarily a checklist of items to ensure efficiency in administration. Governance is thus sought to be universalised as a condition of development. This also implies that failures in development efforts have largely been the result of 'poor governance', explained in politics-specific terms and democratic processes that induce 'inefficiency'.

Governance generally means 'the act or process of governing, specifically authoritative direction and control'.[3] To be precise, governance can be further defined as 'the political direction and control exercised over the actions of the members, citizens or inhabitants of communities, societies and states'.[4] While conceptualising good governance in the context of debt-ridden Sub-Saharan Africa, the WB was guided by the understanding that

> efforts to create an enabling environment and to build capacities will be wasted if the political context is not favourable. Ultimately, better governance requires political renewal. This means a concerted attack on corruption from the highest to lowest level. This can be done by setting good example, by strengthening accountability, by encouraging public debate, and by maturing a free press. It also means … fostering grassroots and non-governmental organizations such as farmers' associations, cooperatives and women's groups. (1989: 18)

Underlining the above goal, the WB defined good governance in the following manner: 'Good governance is epitomized by predictable, open and enlightened policymaking, a bureaucracy imbued with a professional ethos acting in furtherance of the public good, the rule of law, transparent processes and a strong civil society participating in public affairs' (WB 1992b: 29). Four key elements are evident in the above conceptualisation: (*a*) public sector management; (*b*) accountability (*c*) legal framework for development and (*d*) information and transparency. Improving governance would begin with an assessment of the institutional environment (accountability, rule of law, openness and transparency) which determines the patrimonial profile of the country.

---

3 *Webster's New Universal Unabridged Dictionary* (London: Dorset & Baber, 1979).

4 *Random House College Dictionary*, revised edition (New York: Random House, 1984), p. 571.

Good governance is also contrasted with 'poor governance' that is held responsible for the lack of sound development in these sub-Saharan African nation-states. Poor governance is, according to the WB formulation, 'characterized by arbitrary policymaking, unaccountable bureaucracies, un-enforced or unjust legal systems, the abuse of executive power, a civil society unengaged in public life and widespread corruption' (WB 1994: 27). According to the WB (1992a: 9), some of the main symptoms of poor governance are as follows:

1. Failure to make a clear separation between what is public and what is private, hence, a tendency to divert public resources for private gain
2. Failure to establish a predictable framework of law and government behaviour conducive to development, or arbitrariness in the application of rules and laws
3. Excessive rules, regulations, licensing requirements, and so forth, which impede the functioning of markets and encourage rent-seeking
4. Priorities inconsistent with development, resulting in a misallocation of resources
5. Excessively-narrowly based or nontransparent decision-making

As mentioned above, underlying the litany of Africa's development problems is 'a crisis of governance'. The WB expressed concern for 'the lack of official accountability, the control of information and a failure to respect the rule of law'. Since governance is 'the conscious management of regime structures, with a view to enhancing the public realm', the Bank insists on 'independence for the judiciary, scrupulous respect for the law and human rights at every level of government, transparent accountability of public monies, and independent public auditors responsible to a representative legislature, not to an executive' (WB 1989: 60–61). Such a distortion in public institutions appears to be unavoidable because they

> superimposed on political and economic systems in which they had no roots, continued to lack accountability, ... but were captured by clan pressures, politicized by booty [resembling largely] the kinds of patrimonial states common in early Europe ... The tragedy of mismanagement and corruption seems to have its root in this colonial imposition of states and bureaucratic institutions, rather than their natural evolution through a process of citizen demands for accountability and ruler adjustments. (Brautigam 1991: 8–9)

The WB also defines governance in the following words 'the manner in which power is exercised in the management of a country's economic and social resources for development' (1992a: 3). This definition denotes (*a*) the form of political regime (parliamentary or presidential, military or civilian and authoritarian or democratic); (*b*) the process in which the power is exercised; and (*c*) the capacity of the government to design, formulate and implement policies to discharge its functions. While the first aspect of governance falls outside its ambit, the second and third aspects are critical to the Bank (ibid.: 58, fn1). However, on a closer look at the subsequent elaboration of the concept by other international agencies that endorse the WB agenda, it is clear that these three aspects remain integral to governance. The UNDP, for instance, elaborates the concept by underlining that governance is 'the essence of economic, political and administrative authority to manage a country's affairs at all levels. It comprises mechanisms, processes and institutions through which citizens and groups articulate their interests, exercise their legal rights, meet their local obligations and mediate their differences' (UNDP 1997a: 9). The nature of governance is thus contingent on the historical circumstances in which it is articulated simply because the relations between the ruler and ruled differs across countries. As mentioned in a working paper of the WB:

> History, custom, law, society and political economy affect the way in which the ruled in a country hold rulers to account for their performance, the relative openness of a socio-political system or an economy, and the degree of predictability in government decision-making and interaction with the public. (Brautigam 1991: 6)

Governance assures that corruption is minimised, the views of minorities are taken into account and that the voices of the most vulnerable in society are heard in decision-making. In other words, governance can also be articulated in terms of eight major characteristics as listed by the UNDP (1997a: 19):

1. *Participation*: Participation by both men and women is a cornerstone of good governance. Participation could be either direct or through legitimate intermediate institutions or representatives. It is important to point out that representative democracy does not necessarily mean that the concerns of the most vulnerable in society would be taken into consideration in decision-making. Participation needs to be informed and organised. This means freedom of association and expression on the one hand and an organised civil society on the other.
2. *Rule of law*: Good governance requires fair legal frameworks that are impartially enforced. It also requires full protection of human rights, particularly those of minorities. Impartial enforcement of laws requires an independent Judiciary and an impartial and incorruptible police force.
3. *Transparency*: Transparency means that decisions are taken and enforced in a manner that follows rules and regulations. It also means that information is freely available and directly accessible to those who will be affected by such decisions and their enforcement. It also means that enough information is provided and that it is provided in easily understandable forms and media.
4. *Responsiveness*: Good governance requires that institutions and processes try to serve all stakeholders within a reasonable timeframe. By being responsive, governmental institutions gain 'legitimacy' in the public realm which will automatically ensure their wider acceptance and thus effectiveness in governance. Apart from well-designed structural devices, responsiveness of public institutions can be meaningfully ascertained only if there is a serious engagement of civil society in public affairs.

5. *Consensus-oriented*: There are several actors and as many viewpoints in a given society. Good governance requires mediation of the different interests in society to reach a broad consensus on what is in the best interest of the whole community and how this can be achieved. It also requires a broad and long-term perspective on what is needed for sustainable human development and how to achieve the goals of such development. This can only result from an understanding of the historical, cultural and social contexts of a given society or community.
6. *Equity and inclusiveness*: A society's well-being depends on ensuring that all its members feel that they have a stake in it and do not feel excluded from the mainstream of society. This requires all groups, but particularly the most vulnerable, to have opportunities to improve or maintain what they need to survive as human beings.
7. *Effectiveness and efficiency*: Good governance means that processes and institutions produce results that meet the needs of society while making the best use of resources at their disposal. In this context, efficiency also covers the sustainable use of natural resources and the protection of the environment.
8. *Accountability*: Accountability is a key requirement of good governance. Besides governmental institutions, private sector and civil society organisations must also be accountable to the public and to their institutional stakeholders. Who is accountable to who varies depending on whether decisions or actions taken are internal or external to an organisation or institution. In general an organisation or an institution is accountable to those who will be affected by its decisions or actions. Accountability cannot be enforced without transparency and the rule of law.[5]

Strategic Vision

Another characteristic of good governance is for leaders and the public to have a broad and long-term perspective on human development. They should have a sense of what is needed for such development. Good governance is therefore grounded on an understanding of the historical, cultural and social complexities of the society (UNDP 1997b).

Thus, governance appears to be a checklist of criteria of managing public affairs. As Lewis Preston, then WB President, categorically states in his foreword to *Governance and Development*:

> Good governance is an essential complement to sound economic policies. Efficient and accountable management by the public sector and a predictable and transparent policy framework are critical to the efficiency of markets and governments, and hence to economic development. (Preston 1992)

Broadly speaking, good governance is conceptually three-dimensional. First, it refers to certain espoused principles of public administration, namely, accountability, transparency and participation.

[5] Unless otherwise stated, this section largely draws on UNESCAP (n.d.).

Second, it dwells on the processes in which political power is articulated and exercised. The process involves a complex interplay among the prevalent values, policies and institutions which are critical to making and implementing decisions for the society in question. Third, successful application of governance, both as principles and processes, is contingent on the regulatory capacity of the State. While control without good governance is oppressive, good governance without the capacity to apply them is an empty slogan. These features suggest that governance is not a magical formula. Instead, it seeks to articulate a device to improve governmental functioning in areas where the government is apparently minimal and is largely appropriated by 'partisan' interests. In the words of a WB document:

> Governance is a continuum, and not necessarily unidirectional, it does not automatically improve over time. It is a plant that needs constant tending. Citizens need to demand good governance. Their ability to do so is enhanced by literacy, education and employment opportunities. Government needs to prove responsive to those demands. … Change occurs sometimes in response to external or internal threats. It also occurs through pressures from different interest groups, some of which may be in the form of populist demands. Although lenders and aid agencies and other outsiders can contribute resources and ideas to improve governance, for change to be effective it must be rooted firmly in the societies concerned and cannot be imposed from outside. (WB 1992a: 11–12)[6]

Upon a careful reading of the WB formula, Keraudran and Mierlo (1998) suggest the following checklist of requirements for the new governance paradigm:

1. A recommended shift to general emphasis from policy to management, with administrators becoming fully cost-conscious in every action they take and before making decisions;
2. Clusters rather than pyramids as the preferred model for the design of administrative systems (for example, autonomous agencies liaise with the major ministries as equal partners in various governmental projects);
3. In place of planning and hierarchical execution of decisions, a dichotomy between core policy activities and adaptive operational services;
4. A process-oriented administration gives way to an output-oriented administration (hence the insistence on performance indicators, evaluations and performance-related pay and quality improvement);
5. Flexible provision of individualised products instead of collective provision (the customer replaces the citizen, and 'the production line' of public administration is broken down into individual pieces for contracting out or privatisation);
6. An emphasis on cost-cutting rather than spending (the modern administrator's motto is value for money, that is to do more and better with less or the same);

---

7. The purpose of ownership is seen as efficient management rather than possession (budgeting in terms of simple input/output quantities is replaced by 'accrual' accounting, and all public services are considered for privatisation, if their commercial viability may be sustained at less cost in the private sector). (Ibid.: 40)[7]

Evidently, there is no standard recipe for good governance except (*a*) respect for rule of law—it's the duty of civil society to ensure that the rule of law is maintained and protected; (*b*) special care for the disadvantaged and weak; (*c*) tolerance and broad-mindedness to embrace unity and diversity—values of multiculturalism; and (*d*) respect for the institutions upholding the spirit of democracy, primarily procedural democracy.

To sum-up the discussion on the definition of good governance, one can safely make the following points: governance is a conceptual approach (*a*) concerning 'big questions' of a 'constitutional' nature that establish the rules of political conduct; (*b*) involving creative intervention by political actors to change structures that inhibit the expression of human potential; (*c*) emphasising the nature of interactions between the State and social actors and among social actors themselves; and (*d*) referring to particular types of relationships among political actors which are socially sanctioned rather than arbitrary.[8] Taking all these features together, governance refers to 'the traditions, institutions and processes that determine how power is exercised, how citizens are given a voice and how decisions are made on issues of public concern'.[9] Governance is thus inherently 'political' since it involves 'bargaining and compromise, winners and losers, among actors with different interests and resources' (Lynn, Heinrich and Hill 2001: 10). Thus, governance is also a platform for interactions between stakeholders and the government, and that which is always frictional due largely to the obvious incompatibility of interests between them. Informed by this concern, governance is also defined as 'engaged governance' whereby engagement between government and civil society is formally recognised. The primary focus is on the policy cycle of the government within a value-driven governance system. Drawing on the UNDP description of governance as 'processes' involving civil society institutions, the engaged governance can be seen as a serious theoretical formulation underlining how authority is exercised and what mechanisms and processes are seen to be legitimate from the point of view of the stakeholders. What is striking in this conceptualisation is the endeavour to respond to some of the major normative questions that relate to questions around the distribution and the exercise of power and the empowerment of citizens, broadly defined as 'participants' in governance lexicon.[10] Governance is thus integral to the WB rhetoric and its lending policies to the developing world, addressing

---

[7] Reproduced with permission of Edward Elgar Publishing. http://www.e-elgar.com/shop/innovations-in-public-management

[8] These points are drawn on National Party of South Africa (n.d.).

[9] This is how 'governance' is defined by The Institute on Governance, Canada at www.log.ca/about.html (accessed 18 February 2017).

[10] The discussion on 'engaged governance' is drawn on Gurthrie (2003).

'not only issues of political legitimacy and democracy, but also the need for administrative efficiency by means of marketization and competition' (Salskov-Iversen, Hansen and Bislev 2000: 194). Drawing on the WB concern, the Development Assistance Committee (DAC) of OECD thus underlines,

> The concept of "governance" is complex. The term is used … in accordance with a WB definition, to denote the use of political authority and exercise of control in society in relation to management of its resources for social and economic development. The broad definition encompasses the role of public authority in establishing the environment in which economic operators function and in determining the distribution of benefits as well as the nature of relationship between the ruler and the ruled. (OECD 1995: 14)

Governance is institutionalised structure of authority, being driven to realise goals which are also drawn on the neo-liberal concern for private interests. It also entails efforts towards universalising the model irrespective of the socio-economic milieu, though the WB had emphasised that 'it is important to be aware of [the non-Western cultural settings] when pursuing policy reforms and institution building' (1992a: 8). As a result, the model is reduced to a design which is technically persuasive, but culturally inadequate to address the genuine problem of misgovernance affecting a large number of states across continents.

Nonetheless, governance is a useful theoretical construct that has injected new thrust in our search for an appropriate model of governance. Governance entails 'all processes of governing, whether undertaken by a government, market, or network, whether over a family, tribe, formal or informal organization, or territory, and whether through laws, norms, power or language' (Bevir 2012: 1). Unlike government, which focuses on the State and its institutions, governance refers to 'processes of rule wherever they occur' (ibid.: 3). It is more than government because it opens up the governing arena to multiple actors, including the private sector, civil society and the undifferentiated public, as each of these actors play important roles in regulating aspects of society and in shaping societal responses to developmental needs. As a conceptual category, governance includes multiple actors and processes of ruling, and is appreciative of social norms and prevalent power-relationships. This was clearly recognised by the Commission of Global Governance which stated in its report titled *Our Global Neighbourhood*:

> Governance is the sum of many ways individuals and institutions, public and private, manage their common affairs. It is a continuing process through which conflicting or diverse interests may be accommodated and cooperative action may be taken. It includes formal institutions and regimes empowered to enforce compliance, as well as informal arrangements that people and institutions either have agreed to or perceive to be in their interest. (1995: 2)

Governance is thus a mode of functioning involving multiple actors and institutions. It is an ongoing process seeking to build a system on the basis of a neo-liberal understanding of public administration. It also insists on the creation of appropriate institutions to take care of the needs of the public. On the whole, the governance paradigm is about a laboratory model that can be easily conceptualised, but not deployed in real circumstances since it involves a radical transformation of the prevalent mindset that needs to appreciate institutional reforms as perhaps the only meaningful way of addressing the concern for development. This gigantic task cannot be accomplished simply by replacing the available public institutions or by devising mechanical means for revitalising them.

GOOD-ENOUGH GOVERNANCE

In light of the obvious inability to bring about good governance, the new conceptualisation of 'good-enough governance' has emerged. In contrast to the generic notion of governance, good-enough governance insists on the dialectical interconnection between the form of governance and the socio-economic and political milieu. The aim is to determine a minimum acceptable level of good governance within the historical, institutional and cultural context of each country, thereby challenging the argument in support of universalising governance as a model of public administration. Instead of arguing for a perfect design of governance, this conceptualisation seeks to provide a contextual interpretation of public administration which is far more realistic. Proponents of this model argue that good governance is 'deeply problematic as a guide to development [because] … getting good governance calls for improvements that touch virtually all aspects of public sector which is simply impossible to achieve' (Grindle 2004: 525). The situation gets further complicated in view of the well-entrenched vested interests that are opposed to reforms of any kind. Practitioners are required to assess what is possible under the circumstances and devise strategies accordingly. Hence, the imperative of good governance might be recast as 'good enough governance [which refers to] a condition of minimally acceptable government performance and civil society engagement that does not significantly hinder economic and political development and that permits poverty reduction initiatives to go forward' (ibid.: 526). There are, however, no technical or easy fixes to what is inevitably 'a long, slow, reversible and frustrating path toward better-performing governments' (ibid.: 527). For policymakers to effectively implement the governance model, a nuanced understanding of the processes of governance in a specific context, allowing them to meaningfully address developmental issues, is required. By making a realistic assessment of the circumstances in which governance is appropriated for private benefits, the idea of good-enough governance creates a space for local actors to intervene with their knowledge of the system that has survived so long.

Two ideas seem to be critical in conceptualising good-enough governance: on the one hand, it exposes the limitations of the one-size-fits-all formula, since the socio-economic contexts of countries for which governance was conceptualised radically differ; on the other hand, it also exposes the futility of viewing the development issues mechanically since they evolve in circumstances which rarely remain static. What is emphasised here is the conceptual argument that the task of defining governance deficits is 'inherently political' (ibid.: 537–38) and depends on the priorities that the constituents of the public sector set as their own. While donors insist on an efficient functioning of the system, politicians favour reforms provided they do not disturb the existing political balance; similarly, economic elites support changes in the system only if those changes do not pose a serious threat to their inherent profit-making desire; in the case of the poor, they will encourage reforms as long as it creates avenues for them to earn a livelihood. So, contrasting needs are nurtured by different segments of society, making it doubly difficult to devise a universally acceptable design of governance. In such a situation, the conceptualisation of good-enough governance gains credibility since it allows us to capture governance not as a neo-Taylorist design but as a realistic mode of public administration in terms of 'what needs to be done, how it needs to be done and when it needs to be done' (ibid.: 530). Each country is unique and the problems they confront are also peculiar. It would therefore be simply imprudent to devise a common solution to problems which are distinctly country-specific. This is a foundational limitation of the governance agenda and, by accepting a more nuanced understanding of the evolution of institutions and government capabilities, the idea of good-enough governance provides a realistic formula that suggests that whole-scale reforms cannot be pursued at once because it is contingent on what works best in specific circumstances.

PRIVILEGING PRIVATE OVER PUBLIC

As observed earlier, governance is not an innocent construct. It does not simply mean the mode of governmental functioning. Rather, governance has been charged with ideological attributes, i.e. a government articulates its responses in accordance with well-defined ideological priorities considered appropriate and pertinent at a particular juncture of history. Implicit here is also the idea that governance is contextual, which confirms that there is hardly a universal format of governance or, in other words, governance cannot be conceptualised in a derivative theoretical format. The idea that is being addressed here is the persuasive critique of the 'neo-Taylorist' endeavour insisting on the transplantation of a model of governance regardless of social, economic and political circumstances. Two co-related arguments are being made now: first, governance cannot be conceptualised independent of the global context, especially in view of the evolution of the globe as 'a village' emphasising that the countries, being occupants of the same global space, cannot be aloof from the global influences when domestic policies are being framed and implemented. For instance, cases of human rights violation, terrorism or the concern for environment have global implications and no State can evolve a policy without taking note of its global responsibility. In fact, for those countries which are largely dependent on the financial support of donors, both individual countries and international financial institutions, another dimension has become very critical: the freedom to choose policy designs that appropriately suited for them seems to be highly restricted. This important aspect cannot be ignored if one seeks to understand the policy profile of these countries. The second argument underlines the importance of indigenous movements which are ideologically inspired by similar kinds of movements elsewhere or similar kinds of thought championing issues that are global in character. For instance, the Arab Spring that had begun in Tunisia in 2010 spread to large areas in West Asia, presumably because of the re-kindling of the fire by civil society activists around certain common human grievances against torturous domestic authorities. The target of attack was the nature of governance which was claimed to have been vitiated by ignorance of genuine human concerns. While there is no denying that the domestic preparedness of the civil society created and sustained the momentum for the campaign despite adverse consequences, we should also note that the campaign was supplemented by inspiration from across the borders.

The above elaborate exposition of the events in West Asia has two definite purposes: on the one hand, we see that governance is a complex outcome of multiple influences, from the prevalent domestic and global contexts, and that the government response needs to be understood by taking into account these influences. On the other hand, we also see the importance of external players (the large number of foreign donors) who tend to provide conditional grants on the basis of astute commercial and political calculations. That is, donor countries or agencies are governed by 'the market strategy' of calculating cost-benefits before they commit to a specific kind of help. The idea is very clear: a country's governance needs to be conceptualised not merely as an outcome of institutional activities that are conducted within an established format of rules and regulations, but also as an offshoot of calculations in which both market and civil society remain active players. What this means is that governance is a consequence of multiple kinds of activities involving not only the politico-ideological institutions, but also important players who may not have been formally (or institutionally) involved in designing specific policy preferences. In view of the critical role that civil society and the market discharge in the making of specific public policies or policy designs, it will be conceptually debilitating to ignore them since they are not formally recognised units in governance. So, to understand governance as a conceptual entity in the domain of public administration, one needs to be sensitive to the environment in which policy preferences are made and justified. This does not seem to be entirely new because the argument that public administration is a context-driven exercise, and not at all Weberian in its articulation, appears to have captured the crux of the contention that was made by those being persuaded by the Marxist notion that public administration is 'a praxis'. In that sense, the revival of the theoretical concern of governance as being 'multidimensional' does not seem entirely new. What is new is the effort to impose the idea of one-size-fits-all and ignoring the distinct socio-economic and political texture of the country in which the model of governance is sought to be transplanted.

Nonetheless, our primary goal is to understand the governance paradigm as a mode of governance which draws sustenance from both the market and civil society. Whether that is conceptually empowering or useful is not our concern; but the objective is simply to understand the phenomenon in light of the neo-liberal endeavour that appears to have gripped global thinking. The idea has certain inherent theoretical (and empirical) limitations, though it has provoked debates among practitioners and theoreticians, presumably because governance is being conceptualised in a wider perspective keeping in view the importance of multiple players who appear to have been peripheral in governance in the past. The contemporary conceptualisation of governance has shifted our attention away from the institutionalised system of governance to the activity and also processes of governance; i.e. a proper understanding involves taking into account the role of the institutions which are not formally connected with the State. So, governance, therefore, refers

> to all processes of governing, whether undertaken by a government, market, or network, whether over family, tribe, formal or informal organization, or territory and whether through laws, norms, power or language. Governance differs from government in that it focuses less on the state and its institutions and more on social practices and activities. (Bevir 2012: 1)

The above definition is explicit in the sense that it has identified the broad features of governance as a conceptual category. Besides emphasising the importance of market and networks, by shifting our attention away from hierarchy this definition is also a critique of the Weberian approach to public governance. The growing salience of the market needs to be understood with reference to the rising importance of the neo-liberal justification of the role of market. The neo-liberal view is critical of State-led planned development in which the decision is taken by planners, and whose decision has to be accepted because of their State-assigned role. Proponents of the governance view vehemently criticised these planners who made plans for all stating that it was humanly impossible to capture the subjective preferences of those people for whom allocations needed to be made. The obvious consequence of such planning was that, in the name of allocating funds for the people, they actually discharged their responsibilities in accordance with their subjective preferences and predilections. Instead of contributing to the development for all, these skewed designs of governance created an environment which bred corruption, nepotism and, in fact, bad governance. So, the neo-liberals champion free markets as an alternative to planning and do not allow for the State to intervene; for them, the State is required to uphold the rule of law and enable the market to articulate its priorities freely. They do not shut their eyes to the role of the people, and the new domain of civil society is conceptualised as integral to governance. This is a space where demands are articulated, voices are given concrete shape and guided to bring about changes in the nature of specific polices and also the perspectives in which policy priorities are designed.

The distinction between public and private governance is no longer critical in conceptualising public authority. Citizens are customers, and those involved in public governance are functionaries striving to approximate to the corporate culture. One of the most powerful and persuasive presentations of this argument was made by James Buchanan and Gordon Tullock in *The Calculus of Consent* (1965). They provide a design of an ideal Constitution which could establish a satisfactory trade-off between the rational individual requirements for public goods and the injury to her/his interests from State coercion. 'The collectivization of an activity', they argue, 'will be supported by the utility-maximizing individual when he expects the interdependence costs of this collectively organized activity … to lie below (to lie above) those involved in the private voluntary organization of the activity' (ibid.: 62). According to this formulation, self-seeking individuals willingly agree to incur 'decision-making costs' in exchange for what s/he derives while participating in the decision-making process. However, 'the relative cost of collective organization of activity can be expected to be much greater in a community lacking some basic consensus among its members on fundamental values' (ibid.: 116). Two important points emerge out of this calculus of consent: (*a*) decision-making costs are proportionate to individuals' satisfaction and (*b*) the cost is less if there is a consensus among them on some basic values of democratic governance. Instead of interpreting the calculus of consent in pure technical terms, Buchanan and Tullock seem to have underlined the importance of 'consensus' which is linked to the prevalent social, economic milieu and political awareness of the participants in the decision-making process. The importance of the individual, despite being part of the collective, is fundamental to public choice analysis. 'Individuals are,' Buchanan and Tullock thus argued, 'the relevant philosophical entities … and that all individuals are to be considered equally capable of choosing' (ibid.: 312). Simultaneously, by accepting that individuals are capable of making choice, they further state that the 'individual … is motivated by self-interest [and] his fellows in the constitutional decisions are similarly motivated, and that, within the chosen set of rules for collective choice, individual participants are likewise directed' (ibid.). The idea is very clear: the 'load-shedding' of the government strengthens democracy by empowering individuals who, while being directed by their self-interests, participate in governance to chart-out the best course of action in accordance with their priority. They are now proactive entities in governance in contrast to the past when they lost their authority once the election was over except under exceptional circumstances such as mass upsurges or strong oppositional campaigns/movements. The government is hardly now an arbiter because it is governed by the collective action which is 'viewed as the action of individuals when they choose to accomplish purposes collectively rather than individually, and the government is seen as nothing more than the set of purposes, the machine, which allows such collective action to take place' (ibid.: 13). A public choice perspective thus reinforces, as argued above, the importance of participation in governance as perhaps an effective mechanism for democratising decision-making because (*a*) it allows citizens to remain proactive entities to choose what is best for them and (*b*) it also gives space to multiple agencies involved in pursuing public causes. Governance is not thus government-centric, but represents processes whereby public causes are best served even by soliciting the support of those agencies, institutions and individuals who seem to be equally concerned for public well-being.

Bhattacharya (2003: 76–77) observes that the focus of this model is on limiting the government, i.e. to ensure there are checks against over-government such as constitutional reforms limiting government growth or reducing the influence of interest groups on policy or decentralisation of political power. He notes that 'individuals would then have the option to "exit" by moving to another jurisdiction when dissatisfied with the mix of taxation and services provided in their area' (ibid.). He presents Niskanen's (1971) suggestions to mitigate the 'evils of bureaucratic monopoly': (*a*) stricter control on bureaucrats through the Executive or the Legislative; (*b*) increased competition in public services delivery; (*c*) privatisation or contracting-out to reduce wastage; and (*d*) dissemination of more information about the availability of alternatives to public services—alternatives that are offered on a competitive basis and at competitive costs. Bhattacharya notes that the public choice school has been successful in pointing out these alternatives:

> The role of 'market' as a competing paradigm has challenged the hegemonic position of the State. Also the power of bureaucracy has been similarly slashed opening-up possibilities of non-bureaucratic citizen-friendly organisational options. It is not however a state versus market debate, as it is often made out to be. The real issue is how to make the state more democratic and citizen-friendly and not to relegate it to the background altogether and install the "new god" of market in its place. (Bhattacharya 2003: 77)

The assumptions of the public choice school are not above board, nor are the arguments in favour market always justified, though there is no denying the fact that the public choice perspective recreates a space for debate over the role of government in the changed socio-economic milieu in the aftermath of the ideological decline of the State-led development paradigm. Governance is being conceptualised differently in its new avatar. The theories and practices of governance now stand in contrast to older ideas of government as monolithic and formal. It is argued that governance 'opens up the black box of the state [by drawing] attention to the processes and interactions through which highly diverse social interests and actors produce policies, practices and effects of governing' (Bevir 2012: 4). Since governance refers to 'the rise of new processes of governing that are hybrid and multi-jurisdictional with plural stakeholders working together in networks' (ibid.: 5), it has radically altered the State–society interface. New practices of governance find the political actors 'increasingly constrained by mobilized and organized elements in society' (ibid.: 4). Since social life is inherently messy and constantly in flux, governance as theory and practice 'prompts people to pay less attention to allegedly fixed institutions and more to shifting processes [by highlighting the fact that] institutions are made of individuals who act on their personal and perhaps conflicting beliefs and desires' (ibid.: 114). Two important ideas are preeminent here: first, the much-hyped claim of sanctity for institutions of governance appears to be over-stretched since they are made-up of and governed by individuals who work towards what they deem appropriate under specific circumstances; hence they cannot be sacrosanct as their rise is contingent on specific individual desires, if not whims. Second, the governance perspective also conceptualises a surreal space in which the engagement of individuals with one another is viewed as essential for participatory governance; the participants remain critical to decision-making and its execution; primarily a facilitator, the government is just an actor in the network of actors. Democratic governance is thus conceptualised as nothing but the sum total of 'ongoing experiments in which the members collaboratively solve their collective problems and manage their collective affairs not in accord with the ideal type of modernist social science but by engaging with one another' (ibid.: 119). The idea, despite being conducive to citizens' empowerment in democratic governance, has its pitfalls which may escape one's attention if viewed uncritically. Governance creates a mindset which is justified by certain rules and regulations in consonance with what is considered as 'rational'. For Foucault, for instance, the mindset which he prefers to call governmentality sustains a system of domination in the name of stability and security. As he argues,

> By governmentality I understand the ensemble formed by institutions, procedures, analysis and reflections, calculations and tactics that allow the exercise of this very specific albeit very complex,

> power that has the population as its target, political economy as its major form of knowledge, and apparatuses of security as its essential technical instrument. (Foucault 2009: 108)

There are two critical ideas that Foucault tried to articulate while seeking to conceptualise democratic governance in his own perspective. First, he was persuaded to believe that governance can never be a neutral exercise as it evolves in specific power relationships that leave imprints; so it cannot be immune from the prevalent power-equations which are usually tilted, if not completely lopsided, in favour of the dominant classes. Second, he was also aware that governance in a liberal democratic framework cannot be democratic in its undiluted form since the institutions that it creates are hardly independent of class interests on which they rest; governance is a political machine committed to articulate its responses in a specific fashion that is not contrary to what is conceptualised as the fundamental ethos of liberal democracy.[11] Foucault's idea of governmentality is a powerful critique of governance that has acquired prominence in the wake of the consolidation of the globalising world.

DECONSTRUCTING GOVERNANCE

In the context of 'de-administered development', the top-down bureaucracy-led development model appears to have lost its viability since it has been ill-equipped to bring about development in the real sense of the term. Poverty has shown no signs of abatement and the benefits of development are appropriated by the elite. The inadequate State-directed development paradigm has given rise to an approach involving local people and local resources in a decentralised, people-centric self-development mode. Development is not the brainchild of experts, but rather the outcome drawn upon the inputs from the grassroots. What is critical in this conceptualisation of development is civil society that has emerged as the third sector along with the State and the market. This is a new venture of societal problem-solving in which public administration is far from bureaucratic. A significant departure from the conventional conceptualisation of public administration, civil–society centred governance creates spaces for voluntary action in areas where the State has already retreated. In such a conceptual mould, governance is articulated as 'a collaborative venture' in which actors from civil society who are interested in designing policies play 'an active role in the policy process from initial discussion over the agenda to completion' (Bevir 2012: 109). Core to policymaking are thus civil society actors who, by collaborating with the government machinery, contribute to policies which are tuned to the local needs. A good example is the people's campaign for decentralised planning in Kerala that has been in practice since 1996. By allowing people to be partners in the process of planning, the campaign for decentralised planning has created a useful resource-base for effective governance. This model involves a sequence of participatory meetings in which citizens become the core of decision-making. With the withdrawal of the State from the delivery of provisions and services in the neo-liberal

[11] A very refreshing interpretative account is available in Walters (2012).

context, the growing ascendancy of citizens thus creates a space for democratic innovations leading to their meaningful participation in decision-making processes. So, collaborative governance is a useful conceptual construct in articulating as well as capturing a unique experiment.

The growing importance of civil society in governance can be traced back to three sources: first, civil society is critical in reducing 'the governmental overload' especially in the developed countries where governments were downsized to achieve the goal; second, the role of civil society is justified as pertinent to governance in the WB 'Good Governance' policy of aid-conditionality as it focuses on transparency, human rights and accountability; third, civil society gains salience in the developing countries presumably because the State-directed development paradigm fails to a large extent to eradicate poverty and also to contain the emergence of 'an insensitive' and mechanical bureaucracy. Civil society contributes to the consolidation of decentralised bottom-up people-centric grassroots governance. It works in two complementary ways: on the one hand, there seems to be a growing realisation that wider social space is available outside governmental institutions for autonomous social action; as a result, the dependency syndrome (or dependence on government) seems to have, on the other hand, evaporated and people are drawn in the processes of development no longer as 'mere target groups', but as active participants shaping the course of development. In the changed environment, civil society organisations, commonly defined as non-governmental or voluntary organisations, are crucial aids to governance, especially in areas like environment, human rights, gender and transparency in public administration.

In its new avatar of governance, public administration articulates a trilogy of State, market and civil society. Governance is not merely governmental, but a design which is both market-driven and civil-society-induced. The market redefines citizens as clients or consumers while civil society expands the public sphere by including a whole range of civic actions that hardly figured in the bureaucratic model of public administration. Civil society is also the arena in which social movements become organised. Representing diverse and even contradictory social interests, the civil society is an arena that generally articulates responses that invariably reflect the social base, constituencies and thematic orientations of the concerned group.[12] The civil society can thus be most effective in governance by mediating between citizens and the State, by articulating the interests of citizens to the government, by inculcating participatory norms and by enhancing the involvement of citizens in the day-to-day functioning of the government. Drawn on shared accountability of stakeholders, the new governance paradigm secures accountability by reducing discretion or delegation in public bureaucracy through collaborative governance. This also makes participation meaningful and effective in the sense that the involvement of the stakeholders in decision-making brings about changes in the organisational structure from a hierarchical, and centralised form to a more decentralised and flexible form for enhancing self-management.

Two important points emerge out of the above discussion: first, while the market seems to provide an effective alternative to the inefficiencies of State planning, the civil society is an

---

[12] For details of this argument, see Cohen and Arato (1992).

arena where governance is both contested and defended. Second, the failure of the West-induced Structural Adjustment Programme (SAP) confirms the inherent weaknesses of a programme that lacks indigenous roots. SAP had not only miserably failed to stimulate economic growth in developing countries but also aggravated inequalities and diminished access for the poor to basic needs such as education and health. And then attention was drawn to the 'inefficiency' of indigenous governments. Rather than redesigning the SAP, international donors stressed the importance of good governance, and underlined the need for democratisation, accountability and participation. Here lies the theoretical justification for civil society which is being projected as 'a critical stalwart' against governmental excesses and also as a site for people's participation in the development process. Civil society makes participation in governance people-centric and development-oriented.

So there is no doubt that civil society is integral to governance. That it is a contested terrain adds a new twist to its relationship with governance. Civil society, just like the State, is a site of power relations. So the tendency to treat civil society as benign is theoretically misleading and empirically wrong. Civil society cannot be depoliticised simply because one cannot wish away the contradictory relations along class, caste or gender axes, for instance, in which it is articulated. Furthermore, civil society can never be a universal category since it is specific to historical circumstances. Hence the assumed shared meaning seems to be futile for two reasons: first, since civil society is specific to the cultural context of the country in question, it cannot be translated so comfortably into other languages and social milieu; second, in many State-directed economies the civil society may not be an accepted partner simply because it has no antecedent in the sense that organisations outside the State were always suspect. In a nutshell, what it suggests is the difficulty in conceptualising civil society as a universal category, presumably because the history of State–society relations differs profoundly from one society to another.

NEW GOVERNMENTAL DESIGNS

One of the striking features of the governance paradigm is the importance of citizens who are not merely recipients of change but also its instigators. Central to governance are citizens, and the government–citizenship relationship is governed by what is conceptualised as the Citizen's Charter. Democracy demands that the citizen's voice be heard and taken note of in the delivery of services to her/him, particularly if those services are rendered by government agencies. In fact, the parameters of services are needed to be defined by the requirement of the citizens. It is at this interface between the citizen and the service provider that trust is demanded and it is at this point that, very frequently, trust breaks down. Problems relating to transparency, accountability and responsiveness of the public administration arise. The Citizen's Charter was perceived as an instrument that could be used to chisel out the possibilities of a healthier relationship between the service provider and its user. In India, it was also seen as a vehicle for building greater awareness of their mutual responsibilities among both, the government and citizen.

Under the Charter, citizens have been brought to the centre of all government activities, upsetting the prevalent concept of treating citizens as passive recipients of government service. The idea behind the Charter is tapping citizens' responses to the actual working of government organisations. Normally, the Charter would cover all public services and aim at demanding from the government and service organisations (e.g., post office, railways) accountability, transparency, quality and choice of services, provided by them to the people.

The Citizens' Charter was first introduced in Britain in 1991 to streamline the administration and also make it citizen-friendly.[13] The Citizen's Charter was described in the 1992 Conservative Party election manifesto as 'the most far-reaching document ever devised to improve quality in public services. It addresses the needs of those who use public services, extends people's rights, requires services to set clear standards—and to tell the public how far those standards are met'. Tuned to this perception, the first report of the Charter clearly underlines the importance of the citizens as consumers[14] of public services by suggesting:

> The Citizen's Charter sees public services through the eyes of those who use them. For too long the provider has dominated and now it is the turn of the user. ... The principles of the Citizen's Charter, simple but tough, are increasingly accepted. They give the citizen published standards, results; choice and competition as a spur to quality improvement; responsiveness and value for money to get the best possible service with the resources the nation can afford. They give more power to the citizen and more freedom to choose.[15]

Many government departments and service organisations have been brought under its purview since its formulation. As citizens are at the centre of public administration, the Charter insists on the following key elements to fulfil its aim:

1. *Standards*: Setting, monitoring and publication of standards of the services that individual users can reasonably expect
2. *Information and openness*: Full and accurate information, readily available in a plain language about the performance of those involved in delivery
3. *Choice and consultation*: The public sector should provide choice wherever practicable, and there also should be regular and systematic consultations with those for whom the service is slotted
4. *Courtesy and helpfulness*: Courtesy and helpful service from the those involved in public administration

---

[13] For a detailed discussion of the Charter and its evolution in Britain, see Lewis (1993) and Falconer and Ross (1999).

[14] For a theoretical and persuasive discussion of citizens as consumers in the context of the new economic order, see Gyford (1991).

[15] *The Citizen Charter, First Report*, Cm 2101, Cabinet Office, HMSO, London, 1992, p. 2–3.

5. *Putting things right*: In case there is delay in delivery of services, the Charter stipulates for a full explanation with an apology
6. *Value for money*: Efficient and economical delivery of public services within the resources the nation can afford[16]

As evident, the Charter is not at all a list of new principles of governance. Rather, it has merely reiterated those norms which should ideally constitute the foundation of public administration. It is, therefore, an attempt to bring back the basic of values of public administration that are eroded due to various socio-political reasons, connected with the evolution of the British political system.

The Citizens' Charter and Administrative Change

As a strategy, the Charter is revolutionary especially when public institutions are declining. What is remarkable in this effort is the emphasis on disseminating information to the public and laying down some of the basic principles that organisations involved in the delivery of public service should adhere to. Apart from the listed steps which public administration should take into account to attain 'good governance', the Charter is equally important in conceptualising some of the changes in governance as a process. First, the governance agenda, as set by the WB, subsume a set of State–society regulating disciplinary procedures. There is the underlying belief that accountability of government through checks and balances, available under a liberal democratic system, would ensure that State activity meets the needs and expectations of the society. So, the right kind of State and the right kind of society are both posited as the ultimate objectives of the overarching neo-liberal agenda. Second, as suggested earlier, the WB's 'good governance' has been linked to the problem of sound development management in developing nations. And very explicitly, the Bank dictates terms and conditionalities for being eligible for its assistance though '[t]here is little clear guidance as to how well or badly a government must perform before it is granted or disqualified from funding' (Currie 1996: 803). In this context, governance stands for establishment and operation of social institutions complementing the activities that are undertaken by the public administration. Concretely, it manifests itself in formal rules and regulations, decision-making procedures and programmatic activities that serve to define social practices, and guide and regulate the interactions of participants in such practices. In real life, there are many forms of community organisations or voluntary, collective self-approaches through which a group of people organise themselves to achieve common purposes, such as irrigation, water distribution, resolution of local disputes and community defence. Governance, as conceptualised by the WB, is also a way of crafting social institutions as a matter of public concern. So, governance has reintroduced the debate on the relative importance of formally-constituted government or the existing communitarian life, embedded with mechanisms for collective problem-solving. Finally, by striving to go beyond the institutionalised administration, governance, as a practice, has

---

[16] Drawn from *Raising the Standards* by the Citizens' Charter Unit of Her Majesty's Government, London, 1992, p. 6, quoted in Jain (1998: 367).

created conditions under which 'governance without government' can prosper. It is, therefore, a theoretical device to relocate the significance of various community organisations in many parts of the world through which local communities have sought to solve collective problems in their own way. This had led to two specific kinds of responses with immense theoretical significance for the discipline of public administration: (*a*) it has shifted our attention away from the formal organisations which have failed due to various socio-political reasons; and (*b*) it has also resurrected interest in community organisations as forms of collective problem-solving mechanisms in civil society. So, governance, conceptualised as a device to revitalise collective institutions which are 'non-governmental' provides a theoretical cue challenging privatisation as the only solution of the whole range of problems affecting the growth of non-Western societies. So the primary issue is to restore the 'publicness' of public administration. The Charter, also implemented by GoI, is a significant influence in the latest efforts by governments across the world to make administration citizen-friendly, open, transparent, sensitive and accountable.

CONCLUDING OBSERVATIONS

Governance is a policymaking device that underlines transparency, accountability, integrity and legitimacy of the institutions, rules, practices and values on which a society functions. These characteristics are relative to the society in question because they cannot be articulated in absolute terms. But what is critical is the process whereby citizens favourably link with governance presumably because it generates trust and confidence among them. Governance is thus a mechanism that is involved in (*a*) 'the formation and propagation of values', (*b*) 'the creation and distribution of wealth' and (*c*) 'the emergence and consolidation of institutions' (Tarschys 2001: 28). In the governance paradigm, the traditional governance process with the State as the supreme actor is now heavily influenced by international organisations and a growing number of regulations formulated at the supra-national level. These supra-national policies travel across 'languages and cultures, framing and positioning local discourses and [are] being translated by the local configurations of resources and ideas' (Salskov-Iversen, Hansen and Bislev 2000: 188). As is shown, the growing but critical importance of governance both as a technique and an agenda can easily be attributed to two important developments in global order in recent times: first, the disintegration of the former Soviet Union suggesting not only the weaknesses of Marxism-Leninism as a cementing ideology in diverse societies, but also the failure of the State-directed development model in mitigating the basic human social, economic and political needs. This apparent vacuum is being filled by the consolidation of the neo-liberal discourse in which 'states should become commodified and marketized in their outlook and give way to the "market discipline" [paving the way for] governance without government'. The governance without government that is market discipline can be seen as 'governmentality of neo-liberal globalization'. Drawn on Foucault, governmentality includes 'mental and practical levels of governance'. Governmentality is 'a result of mentality and the organization of conduct that composes the art of governance' (Penttinen 2000: 211). Drawn on 'the internalization of practices of governing', governmentality is a mechanism of policing the self 'according to [the] existing conception of truth grounded in knowledge about the self' (Brass 2000: 318). The second and perhaps a more significant factor is the remarkable technological advances that shrink distance and interdependencies that arise from much wider and deeper global economic integration. In the changed circumstances, without reorienting themselves substantially, decision-makers can hardly remain appropriate in governance. As a result, public administration is bound to undergo radical changes because of historical circumstances in which the idea of 'contextual' public administration seems to have lost its viability. The ecological view is replaced by the neo-Taylorist philosophy of 'one best way' to organise public affairs. Neo-liberal values surged ahead predicting 'the end of history' and the natural emergence of capitalism as 'the sole' arbiter of the fate of the world. In the contemporary socio-economic milieu, 'management' and 'market' seem to be inbuilt in public administration redefining 'public' in a radical way.

Public administration as management thus misses altogether the overarching perspective of a democratic polity. Sustained capacity of the political system for collective action, effective citizenship and developing and nurturing the civic infrastructure for protecting citizens' rights and promoting collective life are of vital significance for any public administration in democracy. Governance is particularly ominous for public administration in developing nations, as it tends to strengthen bureaucracy further impending the development of alternative people's institutions necessary for both generating social capacity to govern and creating more democratic spaces independent of bureaucratic administration. Characterised as 'neo-Taylorism', good governance seems thus a rehash of 'the one-best-way-principle' of the classical administrative theory which is a complete mismatch with the contemporary global context that demands more 'open-endedness' in governance than rigidity of any kind. While critiquing the model of governance, Frederickson argued that a serious impediment stems from the fact that

> governance theorists persist in looking for an all-pervasive pattern of organizational and administrative behaviour, a general theory that will provide an explanation for the past and a means to predict the future. Despite the accumulated evidence based on decades of work on theory and the empirical testing of theory, no such pattern has been found. Does the governance concept beguile a generation of scholars to set off in the vain search for a meta-theoretical design? (2008: 144)

Governance is thus not a magic wand, but a construct with a clear ideological goal. Conforming to the neo-liberal global ethos, it represents a concerted effort to organise public administration in a particular format. The idea may have theoretical validity because it seeks to understand governance as an interactional activity; but what is conceptually restricting is its claim to have evolved a universal administrative design. By insisting on the one-size-fits-all formula, governance is thus reduced to a mere mechanical option to organise administration which is empirically faulty and conceptually tilted in favour of a partisan aim.

REFERENCES

Bevir, Mark. 2012. *Governance: A Very Short Introduction.* New York: Oxford University Press.

Bhattacharya, Mohit. 2003. 'Public Choice Theory: Government in the New Right Perspective' in *Contemporary Debates in Public Administration*, edited by Alka Dhameja, 71–78. New Delhi: PHI Learning Private Ltd.

Brass, Paul R. 2000. 'Foucault Steals Political Science'. *American Reviews of Political Science* 3:305–50.

Brautigam, Deborah. 1991. 'Governance and Economy: A Review'. WPS 815, Policy and Review Department Working Paper, The WB, December.

Buchanan, James M. and Gordon Tullock. 1965. *The Calculus of Consent: Logical Foundation of Constitutional Democracy*. Paperback edition. Ann Arbor: The University of Michigan Press.

Cleveland, Harlan. 1972. *The Future Executive: A Guide for Tomorrow's Managers*. New York: Harper & Row.

Cohen, J. L. and A. Arato. 1992. *Civil Society and Political Theory*. Cambridge, MA: The MIT Press.

Commission on Global Governance. 1995. *Our Global Neighbourhood*. Oxford: Oxford University Press. Available at http://www.gdrc.org/u-gov/global-neighbourhood/chap1.htm (accessed 20 June 2017).

Currie, Bob. 1996. 'Governance, Democracy and Economic Adjustment in India: Conceptual and Empirical Problems'. *Third World Quarterly* 17 (4): 787–808.

Falconer, Peter K. and Kathleen Ross. 1999. 'Citizen's Charters and Public Service Provision: Lessons from the UK Experience'. *International Review of Administrative Sciences* 65:339–51.

Foucault, M. 2009. *Security, Territory, Population: Lectures at the College de France, 1977–78*, translated by G. Burchell. New York: Palgrave Macmillan.

Frederickson, H. George. 2008. 'What Happened to Public Administration? Governance, Governance Everywhere' in *The Governance Discourse: A Reader*, edited by Bidyut Chakrabarty and Mohit Bhattacharya, 122–33. New Delhi: Oxford University Press.

Grindle, Merilee S. 2004. 'Good Enough Governance: Poverty Reduction and Reform in Developing Countries'. *Governance: An International Journal of Policy, Administration, and Institutions* 17 (4): 525–48.

Gurthrie, Diane M. 2003. 'Engaged Governance: An Institutional Approach to Government-Civil Society Engagement'. Background paper for Interregional workshop on 'Engaged Governance' organised by United Nations Department of Economic and Social Affairs at Colombo, Sri Lanka, 9–11 December.

Gyford, J. 1991. *Citizens, Consumers and Councils*. London: Macmillan.

Walsh, K. 1995. *Public Services and Market Mechanism*. London: Macmillan.

Jain, R. B. 1998. 'Citizen's Charter: An Instrument of Public Accountability'. *Indian Journal of Public Administration* 44 (3): 362–73.

Keraudran, Philippe and Hans Mierlo. 1998. 'Theories of Public Management Reform and their Practical Implications' in *Innovations in Public Management: Perspectives from East and West Europe*, edited by Tony Verheijen and David Coombes, 209–22. Cheltenham: Edward Elgar.

Lewis, Norman. 1993. 'The Citizen's Charter and Next Steps: A New Way of Governing?' *The Political Quarterly* 64 (3): 316–26.

Lynn, Laurence E., Jr., Carolyn J. Heinrich and Carolyn J. Hill. 2001. *Improving Governance: A New Logic for Empirical Research*. Washington, DC: Georgetown University Press.

Michalski, Wolfgang, Riel Miller and Barrie Stevens. 2001. 'Governance in the 21st Century: Power in the Global Knowledge Economy and Society' in *Governance in the 21st Century: Future Studies* by OECD, 7–26.

National Party of South Africa. n.d. 'Governance Barometer: Policy Guidelines for Good Governance'. Available at www.gdrc.org/u-gov/governance-understand.html (accessed 18 February 2017).

Niskanen, William A. 1971. *Bureaucracy and Representative Government*. Chicago: Aldine-Atherton.

Organization for Economic Cooperation and Development (OECD). 1995. *Participatory Development and Good Governance*. Paris: OECD.

Penttinen, Elina. 2000. 'Capitalism as a System of Global Power' in *Power in Contemporary Politics: Theories, Practices, Globalizations*, edited by Henri Goverde, Philip G. Cerny, Mark Haugaard and Howard Lentner, 205–20. London: Sage.

Preston, Lewis T. 1992. 'Foreword' in *Governance and Development, v*. Washington, DC: The WB.

Salskov-Iversen, Dorte, Hans Krause Hansen and Sven Bislev. 2000. 'Governmentality, Globalization and Local Practice: Transformation of a Hegemonic Discourse'. *Alternatives: Journal of Social Transformation and Human Governance* 25 (2): 183–222.

Tarschys, Daniel. 2001. 'Wealth, Values, Institutions: Trends in Government and Governance' in *Governance in the 21st Century: Future Studies*, OECD, 11–18.

United Nations Development Programme (UNDP). 1997a. 'Reconceptualizing Governance'. Discussion paper 2, New York, January.

———. 1997b. *Governance for Sustainable Human Development: A UNDP Policy Document*. New York: UNDP.

United Nations Economic and Social Commission for Asia and the Pacific (UN-ESCAP). n.d. *Human Settlements*. Available at www.unescap.org/huset/gg/governance.html (accessed 18 February 2017).

Walters, William. 2012. *Governmentality: Critical Encounters*. Oxford: Routledge.

World Bank (WB). 1989. *From Crisis to Sustainable Growth, Sub-Saharan Africa: A Long-Term Perspective Study*. Washington, DC: The WB.

———. 1992a. *Governance and Development*. Washington, DC: The WB.

———. 1992b. *World Development Report*. New York: Oxford University Press.

———. 1994. *The WB in Governance: The WB Experience*. Washington, DC: The WB.

7

PUBLIC POLICY
Conceptual Exploration

HIGHLIGHTS

- Public policy as an emerging field of study
- Defining public policy
- Public problems as reasons for public policy
- Texture and dimensions of public policies
- Classification of public policies
- Models to understand public policy dynamics
- Public policy cycle
- Emerging dimensions in policy science

Public policy is a combination of decisions, commitments and actions taken by those in power to address public demands. It is a device employed to meaningfully address societal problems. It helps explain the causes and consequences of government activity. In recent years, public policy has assumed substantial importance in response to the increasing complexities of society as they not only help us understand social maladies, but also offer the remedy. Needless to say, successful policies make for successful government and administration. Hence the saying, 'When policy fails, the government fails'.

Public policymaking is a complex and dynamic process that decides major guidelines for action directed at the future, mainly by governmental organs. Given its critical importance, several theoretical attempts have been made to conceptualise the idea of public policy. This chapter concentrates on the nature, scope, significance, distinct models and approaches to comprehend the intricate nature of public policy. The aim is to provide preliminary inputs on the notion of public policy by exploring its major conceptual features, and also various other emerging dimensions.

Governments frequently make broad statements about the future direction of development in different sectors, also generally called 'policy'. The proposed New Education Policy of 2016 or the

Telecom Policy of 1994 are examples of 'policy' in this sense. Through a number of such public policies, the State seeks to intervene positively to relax societal complexities by ensuring development as well as distributive justice. The entire thrust remains on improving the quality of life of all the citizens. As Jéquier states, 'policy might be viewed as a means of creating a new future, and the absence of policy is an acceptance of the status quo' (1972: 344).A public policy is a goal-oriented course of action that is adopted and implemented by government bodies and officials in pursuit of certain objectives or goals of public interest. In other words, public policy includes all of the schemes, programmes, rules, regulations and laws formulated by various tiers of government, and judicial decisions. These policies have come to assume vital importance in modern times as a result of increasing complexities and this chapter seeks to examine important developmental policies in the larger policy perspective and socio-economic framework.

Good Public Policies

The making of public policy for a country as large, populous and diverse as India is a complex task. This makes a study of the institutions which make policy all the more important. Measured by economic growth or attainment of human development objectives, India remains not only an underdeveloped country but one which is usually regarded as an under-performer, and one that can do better. A good policymaking process according to Agarwal and Somanathan (2005: 10) would meet the following criteria:

1. Experts consult on (or study) the problems and issues confronting a sector;
2. Information on overlaps and trade-offs with other sectors is systematically gathered and made available to policymakers;
3. Opposing points of view within and between sectors, are properly articulated, analysed and considered and those likely to be benefited or harmed are identified and their reactions anticipated;
4. Decisions are made with due legal authority, after consultation of those likely to be affected, and with the involvement of knowledgeable persons in the sector(s) concerned;
5. Those responsible for implementation are systematically involved in the process, but are not allowed to take control of it;
6. Policymakers and/or their advisers have the honesty, independence, intellectual breadth and depth to properly consider and integrate multiple perspectives and help arrive at optimal policy choices within a reasonable period of time.

PUBLIC POLICY AS AN EMERGING FIELD OF STUDY

Indian democracy is full of aspirations and anxieties. Issues like, environmental pollution, generating employment, healthcare, skill-oriented education, rural backwardness and urban developmental chaos are mounting pressures before the Indian policymakers. The knowledge revolution has also catalysed new demands. Democracy is no more a passive exercise of citizenship limited to vote exercise in the periodic elections. Today, democracy is more proactive. The citizens know more and demand more. They sense that their active role is required to sustain a society. The public sphere today is more dynamic and contested (Visvanathan 2015). The recent debates around growth, development and the emerging environmental challenges have also raised issues that public policy must answer. A subject like public policy is an invitation to construct a feasible future.

The focus on public policy as a field of study has developed with the emergence of modern society and Industrialisation. During the nineteenth century, representative government began to evolve in some parts of the world. With increased political participation by larger portions of the public, government decisions assumed greater importance and legitimacy. Clashing values with respect to social, economic and political questions began having profound implications on politics and government. With these changes, governments began to focus on the problems of their citizens (Gerston 1974: 4). And in doing so, public policy was looked upon as a problem-solving discipline. Edward S. Quade credits a number of such converging factors—war, poverty, crime, race relations and pollution—for having caused the rise of interest in policy sciences (1970: 1).

Contemporary public policy and policy analysis have a particular American and 20th-century flavour. It was in America where initiatives towards a more unified approach to the study of public problems and policy really began, with the work of Harold Lasswell: *Psychopathology and Politics* (1930), *The Analysis of Political Behavior* (1948) and the essay 'The Policy Orientation' in *The Policy Sciences* (1951), which he co-edited with Daniel Lerner (Sapru 2010: 20). According to him, the policy sciences study the process of deciding or choosing and evaluate the relevance of available knowledge for the resolution of particular problems. In Lasswell's initial vision, the policy sciences were explicitly problem-oriented and utilised broad contextual approaches. This came in part from his realisation that most social problems could not be extracted from their political, economic, social and cultural environments. His focus was primarily on enhancing democratic values in the policy sciences. Lasswell is therefore regarded as the founding father of the policy sciences.

The discipline of public policy analysis is considered today a revolution in the social sciences and has developed into an engaging discipline—in fact, it has evolved into a new branch of social science. Many universities across the globe offer separate degree courses in public policy. There are now extensive offerings in public health, social welfare, environmental policy, and transport and urban affairs studies. Often there are separate degree programmes for each of these issues (Shafritz and Hyde 2012: 489). A vast literature within public policy supports the full development of what can only be described as a separate discipline within the fold of social sciences.

DEFINING PUBLIC POLICY

Public administration is an instrument to serve the 'public'. People and their problems are, therefore, the central concern of public administration. Public policies are those programmes of action formulated by policymakers to address people's problems. Thus, public policy is a device that is relevant to the public or people at large. Different experts have endeavoured to theorise the concept of 'public policy'. Yehezkel Dror describes public policymaking a 'dynamic process which decides major guidelines for action directed at the future, mainly by Governmental organs. These guidelines (policies) formally aim at achieving what is in the public interest by the best possible means' (1974: 12). According to him, policy science is a discipline that seeks general policy-issue knowledge and policymaking knowledge, and integrates them into a distinct study. Thomas Dye states that 'public policy is whatever governments choose to do or not to do' (quoted in Birkland 2011: 8). This definition views all actions, and inactions, of the government as public policy. Extending this linkage, Guy Peters adds that public policy is the 'sum of government activities, whether acting directly or through agents, as it has an influence on the lives of citizens' (1996: 4). James Anderson defines public policy as 'a purposive course of action followed by an actor or set of actors in dealing with a problem or matter of concern' (1975: 3). Larry Gerston seeks a definition that responds to the actions and exchanges of both people and governments in a dynamic public policy as 'the combination of basic decisions, commitments, and actions made by those who hold or affect government positions of authority' (1974: 7). Thomas Birkland defines public policy as a 'statement by government—at whatever level—of what it intends to do about a public problem' (2011: 9).

David Easton calls the public 'authorities', 'elders, chiefs, executives, legislators, judges, administrators, counselors, monarchs, and the like' and adds that people who 'engage in the daily affairs of a political system' are recognised by most of the public as having the 'responsibility for these matters', and that they take actions that are 'accepted as binding by most of the members so long as they act within the limits of their roles' (Easton 1965a: 212; quoted in Anderson 2003).

On the basis of these definitions it can be summarised that public policy is a course of action adopted and pursued by the government to serve the public interest. The role of the public is significant since public policies are the articulations of priorities that emerge from social values and their affirmation in the public domain. Public policy is an instrument to attain specific politico-ideological goals that have emerged out of a dialectical interconnection between governments and the governed. That public policy is the authoritative decision by the government not only highlights public policy as mandatory but also emphasises that the making of public policy is the exclusive domain of the government. Public policy is binding because it is approved by the public authority, i.e., the government. There are authorised functionaries who are allowed to design and implement public policies. Though, non-governmental actors and factors may, of course, influence policy development, they are primarily formulated by the government.

Overall, public policy is a problem-solving device that has authoritative sanction and is aimed at redressing public grievances.

PUBLIC PROBLEMS AS REASONS FOR PUBLIC POLICY

Public policy differs from the private one because of the public nature of the former—i.e. it reflects public will and desire. Due to its problem-solving capability public policies are significant in any political system. They play a vital role in shaping the society for its betterment. While narrating the role of public policy, W. Parsons states that 'the wider purposes of public policy involve enlightenment, the fuller development of individuals in society and the development of consensus, social awareness and legitimacy, rather than simply the delivery of goods and services' (1995: 613–14). Public policies, therefore, involve improving the democratic and political capacities of the people, and not simply the efficiency and effectiveness of the delivery of services.

Public policies also play an important role in the socio-economic development of a nation. The case of India is a good example in this regard. Post-independent India forged a number of policies aimed at socio-economic transformation. The planning commission was set up. Five-year Plans were formulated. Policies regarding agricultural development, industrial growth, poverty eradication, rural development, etc. were framed. And today we see the positive results of these policies. Sound policies helped India in its nation-building. India could defend itself not only from external aggression but also succeed in keeping divergent groups, castes, linguistic and religious sects united. Thus, besides helping achieve socio-economic development, public policies have also strengthened the national unity and integrity.

Public policies have also a futuristic perspective. By extrapolating the present trends the future momentum can be visualised. The idea of projecting some key social trends into the future may be of great help for the progress of a society. The data for these purposes may include changes in the rate of population growth, education, environment, public health and the like. We can carry the process further by forecasting what these projections might look like after a decade, since people cannot avoid being concerned with the consequences of public policies (Sapru 2010: 38–39). Therefore, the study of public policy helps shape the future by projecting new policies and choices.

The study of public policy helps in describing, analysing and explaining the causes and consequences of a particular governmental activity. It is eloquent in understanding the real politics underlying the framing of policies. In other words, three reasons may be cited for studying public policy: scientific understanding, professional advice and policy recommendations. First, public policy should be studied in order to gain greater knowledge about the origins of various policy measures, the processes by which they have developed and their consequences in society. This, in turn, will increase our understanding of the political system and society in general. Second, an understanding of the causes and consequences of public policy permits us to find solutions to practical problems. Third, people with political goals study public policy to learn how to promote their preferred policy options. A careful study of policy ensures that the nation adopts the right policies to achieve the right goals. Thus, policy studies can be undertaken not only for scientific and professional purposes but also to inform political discussion, advance the level of political awareness and improve the quality of public policies.

TEXTURE AND DIMENSIONS OF PUBLIC POLICIES

The above discussion makes it clear that one of the most important reasons to study public policy is that it is about problem-solving. As noted earlier, policy science involves studying the content of public policy, an analysis of the impact of social, economic and political forces on the content of public policy, an inquiry into the effect of various institutional arrangements and political processes on public policy, and an evaluation of the consequences of public policies on the society as a whole. In this sense, the nature and culture of public policy may be narrow or wide. Sometimes a policy may be devised keeping in mind the interest of a particular section or group of society. It may serve the interest of women, children, peasants and workers. For example, a policy on women's reservation in Parliament would facilitate the empowerment of women. A policy may also serve the interest of all sections of society. For example, a policy on air pollution in Delhi would protect every citizen of the state from pollution. Thus, policies may be sectional as well as comprehensive in nature.

In a democracy, politics is the chief vehicle for citizens to influence the decisions through decision-makers who frame public policy at many levels. People expect their governments to address most of their issues. It could be basic problems like water, electricity, housing, security, employment, or new challenges like environmental pollution or terrorism. In a democratic nation like India, over the years, more and more people have turned to the government to resolve the society's problems. As a result, the government has grown in size and public policy has expanded in scope to encompass just about every sector of Indian life. Even during the period of open-market economy, the public expects their government to stand up for them. The government is expected to formulate policies that regulate market forces and protect the interest of the common public. There is hardly any personal or societal problem for which some group or the other will not demand governmental solution. As a result of increasing public trust in government the jurisdictional dimension of public policy has expanded to almost every aspect of life. Public policy process responds to the community needs from local to the national one because policy decisions are taken at the local government level, the state level and at the level of the Centre. This speaks for the expanding scope and dimensions of public policies.

CLASSIFICATION OF PUBLIC POLICIES

In a political system the government performs a number of activities. It regulates conflicts within society, it organises society to carry on conflict with other societies, distributes a great variety of symbolic rewards and material services to the members of the society, and collects money from the society in the form of taxes. Thus, on the basis of these activities, there may be different categorisation of public policies. Theodore Lowi was the first who highlighted the policy dynamics in his scheme of classic policy types in 1964. Lowi (1972) suggested three types of policies; each associated with a particular political process and behaviour: regulatory, distributive and redistributive. Regulatory policies are concerned with regulation and control of individual conduct by coercive techniques. These policies deal with the regulation of trade, quality of education, safety measures, etc. Securities and Exchange Board of India (SEBI), Telecom Regulatory Authority of India (TRAI), Bureau of Indian Standards (BIS) and Reserve Bank of India (RBI) are examples of regulatory agencies. Distributive policies grant goods and services to specific interest groups of the population. All public welfare programmes are distributive; for example, agricultural subsidies to the farmers, subsidised food to the poor and government health services. Redistributive policies are aiming at redistributing resources from one group to another. The main objective of such policies is to set up an equitable society through redistribution of social and economic rewards. Income tax policies are often cited as examples of redistributive policies. Redistributive policy is intended to manipulate the allocation of wealth, property, personal or civil rights, or some other valued items among social classes.

The above classification of public policies explains the various activities accomplished by the government. They show that the pattern of action is either to resolve conflicting claims or provide incentives for cooperation. Thus, different types of policies are useful in understanding why and how certain kinds of policies are made the way they are. They help us understand why some groups do better than others in the process of public policymaking. They also help us by revealing the politics underlying the policy process.

MODELS TO UNDERSTAND PUBLIC POLICY DYNAMICS

A model is a simplified representation of some aspect of the real world. It helps in identifying problems and to understand the content and consequences of the corresponding policy better. It assists policymakers in comprehending the actual world. It also enables the common man to get acquainted with the dynamics of policy formulation which usually happens behind closed doors. Over the years, political scientists have tried to develop some models and approaches to help us understand political life. The purpose of such exercise according to Dye (1975: 17) is to simplify and clarify our thinking about the government and politics, to identify important political forces in society, to communicate relevant knowledge about political life, to direct inquiry into politics and to suggest explanation for political events and outcomes. These models represent different ways of looking at public policy. These are of course not mutually exclusive. Each has a distinct focus and each suggests specific things about political life and policy. They try to simplify political life so that we can think about it more clearly and understand the relationships we find in the real world. Drawing on Dye's classification, let us look at a brief description of each model, with particular attention to the varied ways in which public policy can be explored.

Each of these models focuses on separate elements of politics and helps us understand different things about political life.

Institutional Model: Public Policy as Institutional Output

This model is based on the premise that there are certain competent institutions in society that determine the public policy objectives and outcomes. The Legislative, Executive and the Judiciary are examples of such institutions. A policy becomes a public policy only when it is authoritatively determined by the government institutions. Public policy is authoritatively determined, implemented and enforced by government institutions. These institutions are involved in the policymaking process because they are authorised by law or the Constitution, and therefore have the power to make and enforce policies.

According to this model, therefore, institutional structures and procedures have important consequences for the adoption and content of public policies. They provide part of the context for policymaking, which, according to Anderson (2003), must be considered along with the more dynamic aspects of politics, such as political parties, groups and public opinion, in policy studies. By itself, however, institutional theory can provide only partial explanations of policy. It has little to say about what drives the policy process. The approach has been criticised for ignoring the living linkages between institutions and the public policy. It is not backed by any systematic enquiry into the impact of these institutional characteristics on policy decisions. The study of linkage between government structures and policy outcomes, therefore, remain largely unanalysed and neglected. With the onset of the behavioural revolution in political science, institutional studies of the policy process were swept aside in favour of studies that relied more on the group, the system and the elite and mass model. Subsequently, political scientists have turned their teaching and research attention to the political processes within governmental or political institutions, concentrating on the behaviour of participants in the process and on political realities rather than formal institutions (Anderson 2003: 5). Political parties, pressure groups and public opinion have become part of the study of the institutional approach. Thus, there has been a shift from institution to process and from static to dynamic aspects in the nature and study of institutional approach to public policy.

Process Model: Public Policy as Political Activity

The process model is useful in helping us understand the various activities involved in policymaking. In this framework, public policy is a sequential pattern of actions and the model attempts to capture the flow of actions in the policy process. Accordingly, there are four main steps in the public-policy process: identifying a problem, formulating a policy, implementing the policy and evaluating the result. First, outlining the problem. This step involves recognising that an issue exists, and studying in detail the problem and its causes. Second, a new public policy may be formulated or developed after discussion and debate between government officials, interest groups and individual citizens. At this stage the aim is to identify potential obstacles, to explore solutions, and to set clear goals and list steps required to achieve them. Third, the policy must be put into effect by determining the organisations or agencies that will be responsible for carrying it out. This step involves the conscious conversion of policy plans into reality. Upon implementation, the strengths and weaknesses of the decision-making process come to the fore. And the final step in public policy involves studying the effectiveness of the new policy in addressing the original problem. Often, this step leads to additional policy changes and reviewing the resources that are available to ensure that the policy can be maintained. In the words of Dye (2004), 'Sophisticated versions of the model portray a "feedback" linkage – evaluations of current policy identify new problems and set in motion the policymaking process once again'. Though most policy evaluations are unsystemic and impressionistic, they often succeed in stimulating reforms, i.e. policy changes designed to remedy perceived mistakes, inadequacies, wasteful expenditures and other flaws in existing policy (Henry 2007: 290).

System Model: Public Policy as System Output

This model, put forward by David Easton (1965a), views the policy process in terms of conversion from inputs into policy outputs and then to outcomes. The policymaking process is regarded as a 'black box' which converts demands of the society into policies. In his analysis of political system, Easton argues that the political system is that part of society engaged in the 'authoritative allocation of values' (ibid.: 384). Forces generated in the environment which affect the political system are viewed as inputs. Inputs are received into the political system in the form of both demands and support. Demands occur when individual or groups act to affect public policies in response to environmental conditions. Outputs are the authoritative value allocations of the political system, and these allocations constitute public policies. System theory portrays public policy as an output, that may have a modifying effect on the environment and the demands generated therein, and may also have an effect upon the character of political system. In this model, feedback plays a vital role in generating the suitable environment for future policies. Policy outcomes may produce new demands, which lead to further policy outputs, and so on in a continuing, never-ending flow of public policy. This continuous process attempts to fulfil the aspirations of the people in a society.

This model makes a significant contribution to the enrichment of policy approaches. Despite its usefulness, however, it suffers from some limitations. It has been criticised for being too simplistic in nature. In many cases, policies do not appear to follow such a logical sequence. This model also ignores how decisions are made and policy is developed within the 'black box' called the political system. Another shortcoming of this model is that it neglects an important element of the policy process, namely, that the policymakers—including institutions—have a considerable potential in influencing the environment within which they operate. Nonetheless, system theory is a useful aid in organising our inquiry into policy information. It enlightens us about the role of environmental inputs to affect the content of public policy, gives answer to some significant aspects of the political process such as: what factors in the environment act to generate demands upon the political system and how is the political system able to convert demands into public policy and preserve itself over time? Thus, system model is highly acknowledged as a useful tool to look into the dynamics of the policy process.

Group Model: Public Policy as Group Equilibrium

Group theory holds that public policy is the product of group struggle. Group interest and attitude are influential factors in determining public policies. As Earl Latham states: 'what may be called public policy is the equilibrium reached in this (group) struggling at any given moment, and it represents a balance which the contending factions or groups constantly strive to weight in their favour' (quoted in Bhattacharya 2013: 84–85). As different interest groups struggle among themselves to influence public policy, actual policymaking in government tends to tilt toward the groups that are gaining in influence. By contrast, public policy moves away from the demands of the losing groups. Therefore, at any given time, public policy will reflect the interests of dominant groups. For example, in a liberal market economy, the big businessmen are prominently successful in getting more concessions and freedom of trade from the government.

Group theory rests on the contention that interaction and struggle among groups are the central facets of political life. Dye (2004) observes that individuals are important in politics only when they act as part of, or on behalf of, group interests. The group becomes the essential bridge between the individual and the government. Politics is really the struggle among groups to influence public policy. The influence of groups is determined by their numbers, wealth, organisational strength, leadership, access to decision-makers and internal cohesion (ibid.: 21). From this narration it is evident that public policy at any given time is the equilibrium reached in the group struggle. The relative influence of interest groups determines this equilibrium. Any change can be expected in a public policy due to the change in the relative influence of these interest groups. A policy will move in the direction desired by the influential groups, and away from the desires of groups having weak influence. A central concept in group theory is that of access to policymakers. To have influence and to be able to shape governmental decisions, a group must have access or the opportunity to express its viewpoints to decision-makers. Surely, if a group is unable to communicate with decision-makers, i.e. if no one in the government is listening to its appeals, chances of affecting policymaking are slim. Access depends on the group's organisational strength, leadership and economic power.

Group theory is denunciated for overstating the importance of groups and undermining the constructive role played by public officials in the policymaking process. It is also misleading and inefficient in explaining politics or policy formulation without giving attention to other factors like ideas and institutions, which independently affect the policymaking process. Another shortcoming of this theory is that many people, especially the underprivileged and disadvantaged, are either not represented or only poorly represented in the group struggle. Thus, group theory is criticised for neglecting the interest of the underprivileged sections of society.

Elite Model: Public Policy as Elite Preference

The credit for the elite model primarily goes to Vilfredo Pareto, Gaetano Mosca and Robert Michels (Delican 2000: 324–27). This model is based on the assumption that a small elite group is solely responsible for policy decisions. Thus, public policies are viewed as the values and preferences of the governing elite. It believes that common people are passive, apathetic and ill-informed about public policy. Initiative for public policy does not come from the masses. The elite actually shape mass opinion into a policy question. Thus, public policy really turns out to be the preferences of elites. Public officials and administrators merely carry out the policies decided by the elite. In this model, policies flow 'downward' from elites to masses, they do not arise from mass demands. It is evident that elites dominate the masses as they are organised and effective. Force, punishment and financial fear are the main instruments which the elites use to retain power. The masses are seen as passive, inactive and ill-informed. Mass opinion is shaped and determined by the elites. Even the electoral process does not enable the masses to govern. The policy issues are determined and carried forward only by the elite. In this model democratic institutions, elections and parties are important only for their symbolic value. The masses are connected to the political system only through the process of elections. The masses have an indirect influence over the decision-making process of elites whereas the stability of the system, even its survival, depends on elite consensus on the basic rule of the game.

The elite theory seems to be close to the group theory, as both refer to policy generation through pressures from specific interests in the society. Group theory, however, is basically pluralistic, whereas the elite theory is essentially monistic. But both of them reveal the real politics behind the policymaking process and contribute to better understanding of the social and political life of societies.

Rational Model: Public Policy as Maximum Social Gain

The rational model implies that the policymakers rely on comprehensive rational decision-making and have a full range of policy options to choose from. It believes in achieving the maximum social gains, i.e. the government should choose policies resulting in gains to the society that far exceed the costs. Maximisation of net value achievement is, therefore, the central point of a rational policy.

> As an intellectual endeavour, rationalism tries to know all the preferences existing in a society, assign each value a relative weight, discover all policy alternatives available, know all consequences of each alternative, calculate how the selection of any policy will affect the remaining alternatives in terms of opportunity costs, and ultimately select that policy alternative which is the most efficient in terms of the costs and benefits of social values. (Mandal 1997: 346)

Policymaking is a choice among policy alternatives on rational grounds. Herbert Simon is a leading contributor to the rational model of policymaking. His work *Administrative Behavior* (1968) is primarily concerned with rationality in decision-making. In a rational model, policy has to be logical and factual. Thus, Simon's decision-making model separates 'facts' and 'values' and introduces new scientific techniques like mathematical modelling. According to him, rationality is concerned with the selection of preferred behaviour alternatives in terms of some system of values whereby the consequences of behaviour can be evaluated. Three kinds of activities are involved in a rational policymaking process: intelligence activity, design activity and choice activity. Simon recognises efficiency as the primary objective of administration, and the limits of individuals and the organisation to behave rationally. Simon observes, 'It is impossible for the behavior of a single, isolated individual to reach any high degree of rationality' (ibid.: 39). The concept he develops to describe a rationality which is limited but not 'irrational' is 'bounded rationality'. Thus, his decision-making man is a 'satisfying man', who accepts alternatives which are satisfactory or sufficient enough because of the limited cognitive and analytical abilities.

Simon's rational–decision making model is attacked on a number of grounds. Argyris observes that Simon, by insisting on rationality, has not recognised the role of institution, tradition and faith in decision-making. He argues that Simon's theory uses 'satisfycing' to rationalise incompetence, and that his theory has not taken into account the material conditions, historical and cultural factors which largely govern human behaviour. The human relations factors which largely determine value judgment and choice of behaviour have been neglected in his approach. Besides this, the rational model is also confronted with a number of barriers. It is said that due to these barriers, it rarely takes place at all in government. Also, there are no uniform societal values. We only have the values of specific groups and individuals which are conflicting. The environment of policymakers renders it impossible to see many societal values. To have an understanding of all possible policy alternatives and the consequences of each alternative, huge costs and time are involved. These costs are—prohibitive and therefore there is a lack of information. Policymakers have personal needs, inhibitions and inadequacies which prevent them from performing in a highly rational manner. That is why even a rational policy scientist such as Dror wants a policy analyst to broaden their use of extra-rational information including intuition and exceptional leadership with acute perception of social reality. Thus, the applicability of the rational policymaking model is limited by the uncertainty of its consequences, time involved, the focus on individualistic goals and the bureaucratic work culture. Despite these limitations, this model remains significant for analytical purposes as it helps in the identifying barriers to rationality.

Incremental Model: Public Policy as Variations on the Past

Under this model, public policy is a continuation of the previous policy with minimum changes. Charles Lindblom first presented the incremental model in the course of a critique of the traditional rational model of decision-making. According to Lindblom (1959), decision-makers do not annually review the whole range of existing and proposed policies because of the constraints of time, intelligence and the cost involved. Policymakers accept the legitimacy of previous policies because of the uncertainty about the consequences of completely new or different policies. There are also heavy investments in existing programmes which preclude any radical change.

Incrementalism is also politically expedient because it is easier to achieve consensus among various groups when the issue is only modification of existing programmes; that is, new policy issues of greater magnitude lend an 'all or nothing' scenario. This model presumes that people are essentially pragmatic, and do not always seek the single way to deal with a problem, but to work modestly, 'something that will work'. In most cases modification of existing programmes will satisfy particular demands, and the major policy shifts required to maximise values are overlooked. Also, in the absence of any agreed-upon societal goals or values, it is easier for the government to continue existing programmes rather than engage in overall policy planning toward specific societal goals. In short, incrementalism yields practicable and acceptable decisions, helps reduce conflicts, and maintain stability of the political system.

However, this model is also not free from impugnment. It is regarded as conservative in nature as the policymakers generally accept the legitimacy of established programmes and tacitly agree to continue previous policies. So, there is little space for change and innovation through this model. Within the framework of this model, a completely rational policy may turn out to be inefficient if the time and cost of developing the policy are excessive. There is also uncertainty about the implications of a new or different policy. Due to such uncertainty, policymakers prefer to continue the previous policies irrespective of their effectiveness. Despite these weaknesses, the incremental model has much educational value, because it emphasises the limits of human knowledge and so helps policy reformers and policy scientists avoid the cardinal sins of hubris and intellectual arrogance. It is especially significant for policymakers in developing countries as it draws their attention to the dangers of radically new policies and thus to the need to guard against uncertainty and risks as much as possible while introducing necessary innovations.

Normative-Optimal Model: Balancing the Rational and Extra-Rational Factors

Yehezkel Dror (1968) rejects the incremental model and proposes the optimal model as an alternative. According to him, the incremental approach is unsatisfactory as it creates a gap between those who have more power and who have little power. The oppressed find it difficult to bring about change. The gap between the actual and optimal qualities of public policymaking according to Dror is due to conservative ideologies, vested interests and the general inertia of men and society. In this background Dror proposes to construct the 'optimal model' of policymaking which tries to avoid both extremes, by rejecting pure rationality on the one hand and by providing an optimal goal that is more than an incrementally-improved extrapolation of the present. He intends the optimal model to be both an analytical tool for understanding policymaking and a goal that actual public policymaking can approximate if policymakers are willing to try. It should be judged not as an end in itself, but only as an operational tool, that is, by its usefulness for analysing, evaluating and improving public policy-making. Dror identifies the following as major characteristics of the optimal model:

- It is qualitative, not quantitative
- It has both rational and extra-rational components

- Its basic rationale is to be economically rational
- It deals with meta-policymaking (policymaking on how to make policy)
- It has much built-in feedback. (Ibid.: 154)

Through the 'optimal model' Dror aims to increase the rational content of the government and build into his model the extra-rational dimensions of decision-making. He calls it 'normative optimalism', which combines core elements of the 'rational' model with extra-rational factors that are excluded from the 'pure rationality' model. Dror's model has three major stages: meta-policymaking, policymaking and post-policymaking. Within these three stages there are eighteen sub-stages, one of which involves a continuous communication and feedback channels that interconnects all the stages. As Bogason observes:

> *Meta-policymaking* involves seven stages of processing values, processing reality, processing problems, developing resources, designing the policymaking system, allocating problems, values and resources, and finally determining the policymaking strategy. *Policymaking* involves another seven stages of sub-allocating resources, making and prioritizing operational goals, ditto for other significant values, preparing a set of major alternative policies (including some "good" ones), predicting benefits and costs of those policies, identifying the best policies in that light, and then deciding whether the best alternatives are "good" policies. *Post-policymaking* involves motivating the execution of the policy, executing it, and evaluating the results. (2006: 99)

Dror's normative-optimal model is like a cycle which has its rational as well as extra-rational components. Normative optimalism combines both the descriptive and prescriptive approaches. According to Dror, there is a need to bring about changes in the personnel, and in the structure, process, and in the general environment of policymaking. His model therefore, aims at analysing the real world which involves values and different perceptions of reality. That is a strength of this model.

Game Theory: Public Policy as Rational Choice in Competitive Situations

This model is a study of the rational decision in situations where two or more participants have to make choices which influence the outcome. It is the study of rational decisions in a situation of conflict. The idea of a 'game' is that decision-makers are involved in choices that are interdependent. Each player has their own goals or objectives. Each must consider how to achieve as much as possible, and yet each has to take into account that there are others whose goals differ from their own and whose actions have an effect on all others involved in the situation. All have to make their independent choice, but the outcome would be conditioned by the choices made by each actor. This model is applicable to policymaking where there is no independently 'best' choice that one can make—where the 'best' depends upon what others do. Game theory can be applied in situations of war and peace, in the use of nuclear weapons, international diplomacy, bargaining in the United Nations and in a variety of other important political situations. Game theory is useful in understanding collective human activity as the outcome of interactive decisions.

In other words, game theory presumes that decisions are not randomly derived but rather arrived at through a process where each player seeks to maximise positive rewards relative to costs in situations when there are competing perspectives. The conditions of game theory are seldom approximated in real life. However, game theory provides an interesting way of thinking clearly about policy choices in conflict situations. The best example of a game theory is 'The Prisoners' Dilemma': Two prisoners who conspired to commit a crime are caught. They are put in separate cells and each told that if they confess they will receive a mild punishment. The dilemma for each is the fear that if the other confesses and they do not it will result in a severe punishment for themselves. The optimum for both is if both do not confess (they can possibly avoid punishment). However, can they trust each other to stay silent in the face of the temptation to avoid a severe punishment? This is the dilemma before the prisoners.

Table 7.1: The Prisoners' Dilemma

	Prisoner A confesses	*Prisoner A does not confess*
Prisoner B confesses	1. Mild punishment for both	2. Severe punishment for A, light one for B
Prisoner B does not confess	3. Severe punishment for B, light one for A	4. Possible avoidance of punishment for both

Source: Hill and Varone (2014: 101). Reproduced by permission of Taylor & Francis.

Though the prisoners' dilemma seems to present an artificial situation, it can be argued that its equivalent arises in the policy process in situations such as when conflicting actors, particularly actors that may not communicate well with each other—such as the nation-states of today—are clear about what they have to do in their own interest and do not trust each other. Game theory is, therefore, helpful to explore to what extent in a real situation will actors be likely to move from conflicting to collaborative strategies. It is fruitful in understanding collective human activity as the outcome of interactive decisions.

Public Choice Model: Decision-Making by Self-Interested Individuals

This model holds that individuals are rational and therefore pursue their self-interest. All political actors seek to maximise their personal benefits in politics just as they do as in the marketplace. It believes that individuals come together in politics for their own mutual benefit and can enhance their own well-being in the same way as trade happens in the marketplace. In simple terms, people pursue their self-interest in both politics and the marketplace, but even with selfish motives they can mutually benefit through collective decision-making (Dye 1992: 59–63). One of the basic axioms of this model is that political actors—like economic actors—act rationally in pursuing their own self-interest. This led economist James Buchanan to contend that politicians are guided by their self-interest rather than an altruistic commitment to such goals as statesmanship or the national interest. Buchanan states that this is a very common thing because governments are made up of individuals and individuals operate from self-interest when they are engaged in a system of exchange. Anderson observes:

> Individuals who are engaged in decision-making exchanges or transactions, such as voting, also have preferences that vary from person to person. Being rational, individuals are able to comprehend and rank their preferences from most to least desired. In making decisions (whether economic or political), they are guided by these preferences and will seek to maximize the benefits they gain. In short, people are self-interested utility maximizers, not the uninformed, confused, or irrational choice-makers often depicted in analyses of political behavior. A second basic axiom of rational-choice theory involves methodological individualism. The individual decision-maker is the primary unit of analysis and theory. The individual's preferences or values are assumed to be more important than other values—collective, organizational, or social. Conversely, rational-choice theorists argue that the actions of organizations and groups can be satisfactorily explained in terms of the behaviour of a model individual. (Anderson 2003: 15)

Bhattacharya (2003) states the following about the model:

> The public choice model is useful in pointing out that there are alternatives available for the delivery of services to the citizens. The role of the market as a competing paradigm has challenged the hegemonic position of the State. Also the power of bureaucracy has been similarly slashed by opening-up possibilities of non-bureaucratic citizen-friendly organisational options. It is not, however, a State vs market debate, as is often made out to be. The real issue is how to make the State more democratic and citizen-friendly and not to relegate it to the background altogether and install the 'new god' of market in its place. The assumptions of public choice school are not above board, nor are the arguments supportive of market always justified. (Ibid.: 77)

Again, the situations differ from one country to another and their prescription to check governmental overgrowth may not be of universal relevance. For instance, State-led development activities may not be entirely discarded because of the prevalent socio-economic conditions which allow politicians to become hegemonic in some parts of the globe. This condition is clearly circumstantial and likely to change as social forces challenging shackles-free politicians gain momentum. Public choice theory, therefore, may not have universal application. Nonetheless, it has raised pertinent questions which are relevant to conceptualise individual/collective choice in a context where the State seems to have considerably lost its predominant role to the market in a neo-liberal globalising world.

Garbage Can Model: Multiple Stream Theory

The garbage can model of organisational theory was developed by Michael Cohen, James March and Johan Olsen (1972) and further developed by John W. Kingdon. This model emerged as part of a critique of the rational model of decision-making.

> Rather than portray decision-making in public administration as a matter of rational choice, John Kingdon and other theorists in this school have described it as a process characterized

> by organizational anarchy. Organizations do not function like computers solving optimization problems. Rather they function like garbage cans into which a mix of problems and possible solutions are poured, with the precise mix determining decision outcomes. The mix reflects how many decision areas are handled by the organization, how people have access to the organization, the decision load of the organization, and the organization's level or resources, time, energy, and attention. (Faculty of Law and Political Science n.d.)

As Richard Daft argues:

> The theoretical breakthrough of the Garbage Can Model is that it disconnects problems, solutions and decision makers from each other, unlike traditional decision theory. Specific decisions do not follow an orderly process from problem to solution, but are outcomes of several relatively independent streams of events within the organization. (2010: 139)

Paul Cairney (2013) writes:

> Kingdon draws on Cohen et al's [Cohen, March and Olsen (1972)] 'garbage can' model of policymaking in organizations. It contrasts with 'comprehensively rational' policymaking in which—in this order—policymakers identify problems (or their aims), bureaucracies perform a comprehensive analysis to produce various solutions (or ways to meet those aims), and policymakers select the best solution. Instead, policymaker aims and policy problems are ambiguous and bureaucrats struggle to research issues and produce viable solutions quickly. Sometimes people wait for the right time to present their ready-made solutions. Sometimes aimless policymakers just want to look busy and decisive. So, Cohen et al suggest that the problem identification, solution production, and choice are 'relatively independent streams' (W.L.). The garbage can is where a mix of problems, solutions and choices are dumped.

It was suggested that organisations tend to produce many 'solutions' which are discarded due to a lack of appropriate problems. However problems may eventually arise for which a search of the garbage might yield fitting solutions. The garbage can model is relevant to describe the problem-solving or policymaking process in everyday organisational situations. It can also be utilised to describe government actions and policymaking activities in complex situations.

The preceding section delves into various models and approaches to get a better understanding of the public policy process. Each model provides a separate focus on political life, and each can help us to understand different things about public policy and it is not possible to say which is the 'best' or 'most satisfactory'. It would be better to use them as organising concepts that seem most useful for the satisfactory analysis and explanation of a particular public policy or political action, because each of these approaches can contribute to our understanding of public policy.

PUBLIC POLICY CYCLE

Policymaking is a many step process. Scholars have identified various interfaces to map the stages of the policy process, thereby helping structure its analysis. In this framework public policy is a sequential pattern of action. The advantage of this framework is that it helps to capture the flow of action in the policy process. In reality, policymaking often does not chronologically follow the sequence of activities. However, in order to simplify our discussion we will discuss the policy-making cycle in three broad categories: formulation, implementation and evaluation.

POLICY FORMULATION

Public policymaking takes place when people with authority make decisions or commitments on important public questions. It responds to the demands pressed by the people. In this process, a number of events, actors and political institutions take part. Prior to the exercise of formal authority by a legislative body, an executive or a court, several phases or types of activities by public and private individuals shape the emergence and development of policy decisions. As mentioned earlier, James Anderson describes four stages in the policy formulation process: identification of public problems, setting the policy agenda, formulation of policy proposals to deal with the problem and making policy decisions.

Identification of problems of the public is the starting point for public policy questions. Larry Gerston (2008/2015) identifies four triggering factors which play a vital role in identifying and clarifying emerging issues for public policy: scope, intensity, time and resources. Regarding the first factor, he says:

> The first test of a public policy question centres on the scope of the issue, which refers to the number of individuals who are connected with the topic. *Scope* tells us much about the universality of a problem, it is a quantitative variable. If a large percentage of the potentially affected population is influenced by a dilemma or matter of concern, then the problem has widespread scope. More often than not, people in decision-making positions are very sensitive to scope. Without this critical mass, the issue remains a private 'problem' for a few concerned individuals. (Ibid.: 33)

The second triggering component centres on *intensity*, or the extent to which people feel psychologically affected by the issue. Sometimes, an issue may attract strong reactions from people. In a world where all kinds of problems arise each day, intensity helps to separate public policy issues from nonissues. If sizable numbers are not engaged or worked-up about a particular situation, then the likelihood is that the concern will not emerge as a policy issue. The third element, *duration*, centres on the length of time that an issue has bothered people. The longer that an issue attracts the interest of the affected population, the more likely that sizable numbers of that group will demand change from policymakers. If an issue becomes a long-standing part of the public agenda, policymakers feel growing pressure to deal with it. Wise policymakers pay attention to matters that stay on the public agenda for long periods of time. If an issue comes and goes, then it fails to capture enough momentum to resonate as part of the public agenda. The fourth triggering mechanism is *resource*, which centres on what and how much is at stake with the emergence of a potential public policy issue. For example, as expensive it may be to build a public transport system, citizens and policymakers sometimes conclude that the benefits will outweigh the costs, and on other occasions they may decide that the costs exceed the benefits (Gerston 1974).

Setting a policy agenda is the second stage in the policy formulation process. Of the thousands of demands that are made upon the government, only a small portion receive serious attention from policymakers. Those demands that policymakers either choose or feel compelled to act upon constitute the policy agenda. Some matters are seen as public problems requiring action while others are not based on the triggers mentioned above. David Truman, in *The Government Process* (1952), states that groups seek to maintain themselves in a state of reasonable equilibrium and if anything threatens this condition they react accordingly, triggering policy change. Whether motivated by considerations of political advantage, concern for the public interest (or both), political leaders may seize upon particular problems, publicise them and propose solutions. Protests, including violence, is another means by which problems may be brought to the attention of policymakers and put on the policy agenda. The media has also a long-standing reputation for placing issues on the public agenda. News reports raise the awareness of both policy-makers and the public. By transforming a once-private question into a public issue, media agents expand the size of the audience and thus alter the dynamics of the policymaking process.

Formulation of policy proposals is the third stage in the journey of policy formulation. It comes when a problem becomes a part of the public agenda. Policy formation involves the development of pertinent and acceptable proposals for a course of action that deals with the identified public problem. The government is the major source of initiative in the development of policy proposals. Many policy proposals are developed by the bureaucracy. Special study groups or advisory commissions are also created by the government to examine particular policy areas and develop policy proposals.

Taking policy decisions is the culmination of the policy formulation process. However, typically in practice, policy formulation is blended with the policy decision stage. Formulation is directed toward winning the approval of a preferred policy alternative. An affirmative decision is the pay-off of the entire process. A policy decision involves action by some official person or body to approve, modify or reject a preferred policy alternative. It then proceeds to become a legislation that is enacted or an Executive order that is issued. In democracies, the task of making policy decisions is most closely identified with the Legislative, which is designed to represent the interests of the populace. Policy decisions made by the Legislative are usually accepted as legitimate, as being made in the proper way and hence binding on all concerned. The policy formulation procedure is completed only after the appropriate authority has adopted the policy.

Actors Involved in Policy Formulation

Policymaking involves actors in the government and those outside the government. Anderson (1979) categorised these crucial actors into official and unofficial policymakers. The following section will discuss some of the official and unofficial participants in the policy formation process.

Official Actors

Official policymakers possess the legal authority to participate in policy formulation. Each has their own responsibility by virtue of their formal public positions and political offices.

1. *Legislators*: Legislators are concerned with the central political tasks of policy formation and law-making in a political system. In the course of approving, the various legislatures perform other important functions like deliberating, scrutinising, criticising and publicising government policies and their consequences on the floor of the house. Usually, it lays down the broad objectives that the administration wishes to pursue and, in more important cases, the machinery and the procedure through which they are to be pursued. From the perspective of public policy, the Legislative is an important centre of policymaking, and it is the institution we most often study when trying to assess what issues are gaining and losing prominence and which alternative policies are being weighed. In India, for example, Parliament, state legislative assemblies and local bodies provide an ideal political platform for raising issues that are important to the people.
2. *The Executive*: In democracies the Executive is crucial to policymaking. In most cases the Executive comprises the President, Prime Minister and her/his council of ministers, advisers, administrators and assistants. The Executive initiates policies and supervises, coordinates and manages ministries, departments and agencies that implement those policies. So modern governments depend on the leadership in the Executive for policy formulation and execution. In a parliamentary form of government all policies must have the approval of the cabinet and the ministers introduce the bill in the house. In developing countries, the Executive probably has even more influence in policymaking than in developed countries, due to the lack of a strong bureaucratic base and little influence of pressure groups—both of which facilitate greater concentration of power. In the Indian political system, the primary policymakers are members of the cabinet, which is a relatively small body comprising only of a few ministers and the Prime Minister (Sapru 2014: 113).
3. *Administrators*: Administrators are also involved in the policy formulation process in more than one way. In complex industrial societies, the technicality and complexity of many policy matters, the need for continuing control, and lack of time and information have led to the delegation of much discretionary authority to administrative agencies formally, and this is recognised as 'the rule-making power'. Government officials are associated with policy formulation in three important ways. First, they supply facts, data and analysis (regarding the workability of a policy) to the ministers or to the Legislative concerned and impart content to a policy. Second, they are constantly in touch with the public, so they have a better understanding of their problems and the solution required in the form

of policies. Third, on account of lack of time and knowledge, the Legislative passes 'skeletal' acts and leaves the 'body' to be filled by the administration. It is here that administrators have the maximum scope for 'policymaking'. Thus, in the post-War period, the classical doctrine of politics–administration dichotomy has proven to be an exploding fallacy as a greater role is being played by bureaucrats in the policymaking process.

4. *The Judiciary*: Besides adjudicating conflicts between individuals, groups, and the various levels and institutions of the government, the Judiciary is also tasked with interpreting the Constitution and the laws of the land. Though the Judiciary is not constitutionally empowered to initiate, formulate or implement policies it contributes significantly to the policymaking process, through its crucial responsibility of interpretating the Constitution and laws (Popoola 2016: 47). The Judiciary primarily employs four important instruments to influence public policies: (*a*) judicial review, (*b*) statutory interpretation of cases brought before the judges, (*c*) cases on economic matters and (*d*) judicial activism (Egomwan 1991). Through these instruments, the Judiciary brings about judicial intervention which can not only modify policies but policy and action as well as moderate implementation. Through the power of judicial review vested in the Judiciary in certain countries, it may take it upon itself to determine the constitutionality of the actions of the legislature and the Executive concerned and also declare them null and void if such actions are found to be in conflict with the constitutional provisions. The Judiciary is also an instrument of socio-economic change. For example, in delivering a number of judgments on important issues like land reforms, child labour, environmental pollution, and women's empowerment, it has given direction to social, economic and political policies of national importance. In a nutshell, the Judiciary is that official actor that ensures fairness, respectability, constitutionality, justice and moderation in the policymaking process.

Unofficial Participants

Besides official policymakers, many other unofficial players may participate in the policymaking process, and they may considerably influence policy formation without possessing the legal authority to participate or take binding policy decisions. However, it does not mean that they are less important than the official ones. Indeed, these actors are involved because they have the right to be, because they have important interests to protect and promote, and because our system of government would simply not work well without them. Thus, unofficial actors are involved in the policy process not because they are sanctioned by law but because they are an effective way for many people to collectively express their opinion. A brief discussion of the role played by some of the unofficial policymakers is given below.

1. *Political parties*: In modern societies, political parties generally perform the function of 'interest aggregation', i.e. they seek to convert the particular demands of interest groups into general policy alternatives. Every political party has its own programmes or policies.

These programmes, policies or values are presented to the people in the form of manifestos before the elections in order to gain their support. The professional purpose of the manifesto is that it lends a promise—if the party comes to power, it will implement the policies promised therein. Since the government is formed by leaders of the political party that wins the majority of seats in the legislature concerned, party cadres get involved in the formulation of policies to which they have already committed.

2. *Interest groups*: These are associations of individuals who share common interests, beliefs and aspirations regarding their demands. Unlike the parties mentioned earlier, they strive to influence the policies of the government without occupying political office. The main function of these groups is to express demands and present alternatives for policy action. They constantly try to protect the interest of their members either by pressurising the government or the bureaucracy to take decisions that are likely to be in consonance with their interest. They employ various methods such as publicity campaigns, lobbying, personal meetings with the officials or legislators, writing letters or memoranda for this purpose.
3. *Individual citizens*: The interests and desires of common citizens are substantial for public policies. Today, it is not possible for a government to impose policies that don't reflect the will of citizens for a sustained period of time. Public policies have to be consistent with the interest of the citizens. A democratic government cannot adopt policies to which a large body of citizens is opposed. Thus, the citizens exercise indirect influence on policy-making. The exercise of the right to vote enables citizens to make a choice of public policies. Elections are opportunities for citizens to select between the alternative policies thrown up by the political parties.

The above discussion makes it clear that in the policy formulation process a number of official and non-official actors play an important role. An official actor, the Executive, plays a critical role in the policymaking function of the government. The bureaucracy is crucial in supplying data and necessary information to the government. Legislative bodies enact policies into laws. The Judiciary keeps a check on the Executive and determines the legality of the laws passed by the legislative body. As un-official actors, political parties, media, pressure groups and enlightened citizens contribute in the policymaking process in an indirect way.

Constraints in Policy Formulation

Policymakers face a number of challenges in policy formulation, and these can be categorised as political, technical and institutional challenges. As far as political challenges are concerned, policymakers do not always find the political environment conducive to a systematic policy formulation. Often government officials at the top do not know exactly what is required and will only form ideas in a general manner. As Xun, et al. (2010) observe:

> Even when the political masters know which problems they want to address and express their views transparently, the public may not be supportive of the possible solutions. For example, people

> dislike traffic congestion in urban areas, but they dislike many solutions like, expansion of public transport, because it is inconvenient, pricing of road use (such as additional charges for licensing, fuel, peak hour road use, or parking), because it is both expensive and inconvenient. To complicate the situation, local residents want to continue to use personal cars, while wanting controls against non-resident traffic. This potential public opposition to possible measures to ease traffic congestion is distinct from the opposition of business departments of the government itself. The government agency in-charge of business development, for example, may actually want more cars coming in order to enhance patronage of local business by well-heeled suburban consumers. In contrast, an environmental agency concerned about the pollution caused by vehicular traffic would be likely to advocate just the opposite. All these contradictory demands and expectations make the task of policy formulation a challenging task. (Ibid.: 35–36)

They go on to note that technical aspects of issues can also become barriers in policy formulation—starting from even as basic as understanding the cause of the problem. In the absence of a consensus or clarity about the source of the problem, policymakers cannot identify the objectives, alternatives or the criteria used to shift or sort policy options. In this regard, Xun et al. (2010) give the following example: 'The problem of global warming cannot be solved in the near future because there is no known solution to carbon and other greenhouse gas emissions that can be deployed without causing large-scale economic and social disruption in the short term.'

Policy formulation is also disrupted by institutional constraints. Citizens' rights as per the provisions of the Constitution form a significant constraint that can limit the options available to policymakers. The existence of two or more levels of government in a federal nation like India imposes such constraints, because many national policies require intergovernmental agreements, which sometimes becomes impossible due to conflict of interest. The bureaucratic rules and procedures also pose challenges to policy formulation. While procedures are important for ensuring uniformity and accountability, they also become barriers to smooth and innovative policymaking.

Policymakers need to adopt some strategies in order to overcome the above mentioned constraints. These could include proper understanding of the source of the problem, clarity of policy objectives, anticipating changes and building political support, formulating policies with implementation in mind, exploring innovative policy solutions, promoting research and engaging trained and experienced policy analysts.

POLICY IMPLEMENTATION

Implementation is the task of putting formulated policies to practice. It represents the conscious conversion of policy plans into reality. It is the 'follow-through' component of the policymaking process. Policy implementation reveals the strengths and weaknesses of the decision-making process. Very little work had been done in this field since when Presman and Wildavsky (1973) christened this infant area of study as 'Implementation'. Implement actually a continuation of the political process that originally authored the policy. For implementation to occur, the political authority has to assign an agency with sufficient resources to carry out the tasks listed. The agency will then translate the policies into action under the operational framework designed and deliver on its assignment, and be accountable for its actions during this process (Ripley and Franklin 1986: 10–11). In other words, the implementation process has the following characteristics:

- Implementation translates policies into collective action. It brings beneficiaries and passive people together so that the implementation could be effectively channelised
- Implementation deals with the problem of control and accountability in administration
- Implementation largely depends on street-level discretion. Luther Gullick has found that the actual discretion in administration is used at the very bottom of the hierarchy where public servants touch the public
- While the implementation of the first part of the policy begins this stage, the process in its entirety has no clear-cut end point. It is an ongoing process which ends only when the policy is withdrawn or funding is stopped
- Every policy involves the concerted and cooperative effort of several agencies. Since mutual understanding, cooperation and coordination is important, it can be said that policy implementation involves intergovernmental bargaining
- Allocation of grants plays a decisive role in getting the policy implemented

It is apparent that successful achievement of the goals of a policy depends on its proper implementation. The implementing actors have to establish an appropriate set of activities that will bring about the result intended in the policy. As mentioned earlier, implementation demands smooth coordination among a wide range of actors. It affects and is affected by a multitude of actors who define problems and solutions under the given policy framework. Therefore, this process is also seen as a form of network governance.

Actors Involved in Policy Implementation

Bureaucracy and Administrative Agencies

In the modern political system, public policy is implemented by a complex system of administrative agencies. These agencies perform most of the day-to-day work of the government and thus directly impact citizens. They operate under broad and ambiguous statutory mandates that leave them with much discretion to decide what should or should not be done. Lack of time, interest, information and expertise on the part of politicians may also contribute to the delegation of authority to these agencies. Without cooperation of top administrators—i.e. bureaucrats—in these agencies, little can be achieved in terms of implementation. The bureaucracy is the most significant player in the scene because implementation is its primary task.

With their skills, experience and abilities, bureaucrats are better placed to implement public policy in the most effective manner. For effective implementation to occur, Gerston (1974) suggests that bureaucracies and their workforce must operate with four important elements at their disposal: translation ability, resources, limited number of players and accountability. Sapru (2010) lists the following as necessary characteristics of the administrative agencies and bureaucrats:

- While they are responsible for advising during the formulation phase, they are crucial to mobilising, organising and managing the resources required to carry through these policies. Therefore, bureaucrats must have a clear understanding of the nature and significance of policies the political masters have set.
- They should be able to assist policymakers to avoid ambiguities and advise them on the importance of adopting policies that can be implemented.
- Implementation involves converting the objectives of the said policies into operational targets. Bureaucrats should be able to adopt a rational approach and use management techniques in this process.
- At a particular point in time various policies may be in action. Bureaucrats should, therefore, analyse the new policy in relation to other policies to see for any inconsistencies or contradictions, and see if it complements or supplements other policies. The ability to pay special attention to the question of coordination of policies and policy instruments would lead to better results in implementation.

The Legislative Bodies

Though the administrative machinery is the primary implementing body, the Legislative bodies are is also involved in policy implementation. As Sapru (2014: 155) notes, they play an indirect role by affecting the administrative organisations in the following ways:

- They may examine and criticise administrative action and clearly state limits to administrative discretion and delegation while formulating the policy.
- The various committees of the Legislative bodies—such as the Public Accounts committee, the committee on Public Undertakings, the Estimates committee and other standing committees of Parliament in the case of India—often attempt to influence the actions of administrative agencies that fall within their purview.
- The Legislative body may specify limits over the use of budgetary funds—in terms of setting taxation and expenditure, for example. The Legislative is also empowered to hold the Executive to account for its financial decisions.
- Parliamentary approval is required for top-level administrative appointments, and this may be used to influence the implementation process.

The Judiciary

Besides legislative bodies, the Judiciary also plays an important role in policy implementation. The courts affect implementation through their interpretation of statutes and administrative rules and regulations, and their review of administrative decisions in cases brought before them. If a policy proves contrary to the provisions of the Constitution, thereby violating the fundamental rights of the citizens, the Judiciary can intervene on behalf of the victims and redress their grievances. So, courts can facilitate, hinder or largely nullify the implementation of particular policies through their decisions. Also, some laws are enforced primarily through judicial action. In this way, the Judiciary sets things right and participates in the process of policy implementation.

Other Institutions and Groups

A variety of other institutions, both governmental and non-governmental, also influence implementation. A few of them are political parties, civil society groups, non-governmental organisations (NGOs) and panchayats. Political parties are the principal agents for engaging, arguing and deciding the priorities and public resources to be allocated to each issue. Political parties affect the policy implementation process by influencing the Executive and the bureaucracy to implement policies in a manner that serves their purpose. At times, they even prevent the implementation of a policy that goes contrary to their ideology. Civil society groups and NGOs play a catalytic role in policy implementation. Though these groups and NGOs cannot substitute government agencies in implementing public policies, they play a major role in spreading awareness about policies among the people—enabling them to become beneficiaries and enabling efficient implementation of the policy among the target population. After the enactment of the 73rd Amendment Act, panchayats have emerged an integrating device for grassroots agencies. The involvement of these agencies, primarily in the grassroots level, enables effective translation of policy from being an idea to becoming a reality.

Approaches to Policy Implementation

Early theories and models of decision-making and policy formulation were straightforward and top-down, i.e., bureaucrats were expected to carry out the policies formulated by their political bosses. However, this view changed as it became clear that implementation can and does lead to reformulation of policies, outcomes other than those expected or even policy failure. This implementation gap was attributed to different causes, for example to a lack of conditions necessary for successful implementation such as control and monitoring (Pressman and Wildavsky 1973). These critiques showed that the earlier, rational models of policymaking and public management were neither effective in practice nor convincing in theory. New bottom-up models that emphasised the dynamics and complexities of putting policy into practice were developed. Let us look at these approaches in some detail.

Top-down Approach

Top-down theorists see policymakers as the central actors and concentrate their attention on factors that can be manipulated at that level (Matland 1995: 145). They claim that one can understand policy implementation by looking at the goals and strategies adopted in the statute or the policy document, as structured by the formulators. They focus on the gaps between the goals set by the drafted policy and the actual implementation and outcomes. This approach involves the development of a programme of control which minimises conflict between the various levels or any type of deviations from the main goal. It believes in getting the actors involved in implementation do what they are asked to do and keeping control over the sequence of stages in the system. As per this model, there is an implementation chain that begins with the policy message at the top. This is followed by commitment of the implementers to carry out the policy message. A high level of commitment can only be achieved if the lower-level implementers—such as teachers, police officers, social workers—share the values and goals of the policy designers (Birkland 2011: 265). This approach, therefore, stresses on control and compliance. However, this approach has been criticised for ignoring bottom-level realities, for being authoritarian and over-structured, and for neglecting to account the interactions of various factors and levels.

Bottom-up Approach

This approach is a response to the flaws of the top-down model, in particular to the dissatisfaction with that method's inability to explain unsuccessful outcomes. Bottom-up theorists emphasise target groups and service deliverers, and argue that policy is made at the local level—i.e. implementation from the perspective of 'street-level bureaucrats'. Richard Elmore (1979) calls this 'backward mapping', in which the implementation process and the relevant relationships are mapped backward, from the ultimate implementer to the topmost policy designers. The bottom-up approach recognises that goals are ambiguous rather than explicit and may conflict not only with other goals in the same policy area, but also with the norms and motivations of the street-level bureaucrats. It also refutes that there is a single defined policy in the form of a statute or other form. Rather, it believes that policy can be thought of as a set of laws, rules, practices and norms—such as energy policy—that shape the ways in which the government and interest groups address problems. Thus, implementation can be viewed as a continuation of the conflicts and compromises that occur throughout the policy process, not just before it begins and at the point of enactment. Although this makes for a more realistic depiction of the implementation process, the approach has been criticised for overemphasising the ability of the street-level bureaucrats to frustrate the goals of the top policymakers.

Policy–Action Approach

Besides the top-down and bottom-up approach, policy–action is another attempt to understand the policy implementation process. It is a behavioural approach that views the process of implementation as a policy–action continuum in which an interactive bargaining process takes place between those who are enacting the public policy and those who have control over the resources. This approach was developed by Lewis and Flynn (1979). In this approach, emphasis is laid on issues of power and dependence, interests, motivations and behaviour (Dey 2012: 125). It believes that a policy evolves over a period of time and is the outcome of an evolutionary process.

Managerial Approach

The managerial approach is another significant endeavour to address policy implementation issues. It is based on the concept of reinventing government to be more business-like—downsizing, transparency, debureaucratisation, etc. In this approach, changes involve a more market-driven decentralisation process. The focus of implementation shifts from hierarchy to participation and teamwork in order to properly facilitate the management of a complex society. It expects the government to serve the people in an efficient and economical manner. Citizens are treated as customers and they are given a variety of service delivery options.

Overall, implementation is characterised by complexity, which can create both benefits and risks. That is why Wanna, Butcher and Freyen (2010) argue that it is not possible to come up with any single or simple model for meeting the challenges of implementation. There is no universal approach to understand the policy implementation process; each approach offers some advantages and also disadvantages. They provide an insight into some dimension of the implementation process. Moreover, policy implementation is done within a particular environment, in the presence of certain values, beliefs and dimensions of power. The context of the problems have to be mapped to understand the various dimensions of the policy process. Therefore, the various implementation frameworks should be carefully considered and combined according to specific needs and policy requirements.

Impediments to Policy Implementation

Policy failure is one of the most frustrating parts of the job of the policymaker. The success of any government and administration depends largely upon successful implementation of the policies. Implementation requires strong determination, will and action. Moreover, formulation of policy also directly impacts implementation—the ground has to be systematically prepared for implementation. Policies must be proposed, structured, funded and directed in such a way that the implementing bureaucracy has a clear framework for application. Clear lines of transmission and jurisdiction must be drawn. Policymakers have to be precise, constraining the discretionary authority of the bureaucracy. Poorly designed policies may fail even if they are implemented as intended.

Another hurdle involves the lack of adequate bureaucratic and political support for implementation. Implementation requires the willing cooperation of relevant actors and institutions. Support for policies can often stop at the rhetorical level, or at the agencies or levels of government that initiated them. Lower levels of government and grassroots actors, on whom the actual success of implementation depends, may discover that they have little understanding of, or stake in, the policies they are asked to execute. Besides, operational capacity is the bedrock of implementation—a range of capacity-related difficulties in the lower levels will impact implementation. Many ambitious attempts at integrated planning stop at the level of paper plans because the multiple types of capacity necessary to implement these plans were ignored during planning (Xun, et al. 2010: 83). In short, the high degree of interdependence among stakeholders involved in policymaking increases the complexity and vulnerability while implementing the policy.

POLICY MONITORING AND EVALUATION

Policy monitoring and evaluation are indispensable elements of the policy cycle. These processes are applied to public policies for reasons of effectiveness, efficiency, service orientation, accountability, democracy and trust (Regional School of Public Administration 2015). Monitoring and evaluation of the results of public policies are a necessary precondition in assuring adequate government responsibility and accountability in the allocation and spending of public funds. Moreover, they are also prerequisites to frame well-elaborated and implementable public policies. Monitoring and evaluation enable and facilitate improvement of public policies throughout their natural cycle, so as to reflect the situation on the ground and respond to challenges that have been noted. They are crucial in elaborating the desired outcomes and set the objectives of new policies, because they enable the policymaker to draw on the experiences gained from the successes and failures of what has already been, or is being, implemented in the same policy area. Therefore, building an effective policy monitoring and evaluation system strengthens governance principles, improves responsiveness of policies, helps generate public trust and formulate better policies.

Monitoring comprises a range of activities describing and analysing the development and implementation of policies, identifying potential gaps in the process, outlining areas for improvement, and holding policy implementers accountable for their activities. It can be defined as 'systematic data collection towards gaining insight of the specific policy at a given time in relation to targets and results'. It should be distinguished from evaluation which bases itself in the previously acquired data and analyses the impact of a particular policy upon its implementation. Policy evaluation is, therefore, the final stage which completes the public policy cycle. Simply defined, policy evaluation assesses the effectiveness of a public policy in terms of its perceived intentions and results.

The primary task of policy evaluation is to reduce problems in the face of policy delivery, and is generally used for one or more of the three purposes of assessing: policy efficiency, policy effectiveness and policy impact. Policy monitoring and evaluation is, therefore, the best opportunity for those interested in knowing whether a commitment has been called out in line with its design. It is also the last major opportunity to bring the policy back into the decision-making arena if it has been mismanaged or if it has led to undesirable impacts. With its emergence in the 'back-end' of the public-policy framework, monitoring and evaluation has become a predictor of further action to come.

Difference between Monitoring and Evaluation

Monitoring is the systematic and regular collection and occasional analysis of information to identify and possibly measure changes over a period of time. Evaluation is the analysis of the effectiveness and direction of an activity and involves making a judgment about impact and progress. The main differences between monitoring and evaluation are the timing and frequency of observations and the types of questions asked. However, when monitoring and evaluation are integrated as a project management tool, the line dividing the two is blurred. Participatory monitoring and evaluation (PM&E) is the joint effort or partnership of two or more stakeholders—such as researchers, farmers, government officials, extension workers—to systematically monitor and evaluate one or more research or development activities (Vernooy, Sun and Xu 2003). However, for the purposes of this chapter, we will look into various aspects of both these processes together.

Categories of Monitoring and Evaluation

The nature of the actors involved in initiating or implementing the policy, the amount of information available for analysis and what is intended to be done with the findings, dictate the type of PM&E employed. Wholey et al. identify three types of policy evaluation activities:

1. *Programme impact evaluation*: This is an assessment of overall programme impact and effectiveness. The emphasis is on determining the extent to which programmes are successful in achieving basic objectives and on the comparative evaluation of national programmes.
2. *Programme strategy evaluation*: This is an assessment of the relative effectiveness of the strategies and variables of the programme. The emphasis is on determining which programme strategies are most productive.
3. *Project monitoring*: This is an assessment of individual projects through site visits and other activities with the emphasis on managerial and operational efficiency. (Wholey et al. 1970: 62)

While some monitoring and evaluation techniques are likely to produce more credible estimates of policy outcomes than others, in practice it is difficult to adopt the best technique due to time and resource constraints. The policy evaluator should choose the best possible technique by taking into consideration the importance of the policy, the practicality of evaluation techniques, and the probability of producing useful and credible results. Systematic monitoring and evaluation directs attention to the effects a policy has on the problem it aims to address.

It permits at least some tentative responses to the question 'Is this policy accomplishing anything?' and gives policymakers and the general public some notion of the actual impact of policy and provides some grounding in reality for policy discussions to take place.

Methods of Policy Monitoring and Evaluation

Monitoring and evaluation is a challenging task that requires intricate knowledge and proper use of different techniques. In the past monitoring and evaluation had mostly been in terms of economic analyses of policies. Therefore, most tools of monitoring and evaluation have been taken from economics. They have been aimed at setting up of economic targets of productivity analysis, efficiency evaluation and the cost-benefit studies. In recent years, however, several standard techniques have emerged to assess the effectiveness of specific public policies. The three most commonly used tools of monitoring and evaluation are: cost-benefit analysis, programme-planning and budgeting system (PPBS) and the experimental method.

1. *Cost-benefit analysis*: This is the most commonly used approach in monitoring and evaluation studies. It employs the balancing of the costs and the benefits of policies in a manner so that the intervention could be assessed purely in economic terms. All benefits—those that are quantifiable and those that are difficult to measure—that will accrue if the project is adapted are enumerated. With this information in hand, the analyst should be able to subtract the total cost of each alternative from the total sum of its benefits and identify the net gain in each case. This was the most reliable and clear-cut system of analysis, but it was incapable of evaluating policies of the intangibles like the impact of the free meal policy for children, the loss of environment due to mining or the impact of oil refinery on coastal marine and human life.
2. *Planning, programming and budgeting systems (PPBS)*: PPBS is another widely accepted method of monitoring and evaluation by the government agencies. It is an attempt to rationalise decision-making in a bureaucracy. The focus of this system is the budgetary process, more specifically the expenditures. The aim of PPBS is to specify the output of a government programme, and then to minimise the cost of achieving this output and to learn whether benefits exceed the cost. The first step in PPBS is to define programme objectives. The next critical step is to develop measures of the level accomplishment under each programme—i.e. the 'output'. Then the cost of the programme can be calculated per unit of output—for example, how much it costs to teach one pupil per year, to keep one child in a day-care centre.
3. *Experimental method*: In this method the basis of monitoring and evaluation is an 'ideal' laboratory-like situation. In a population some units who have received some service under the policy measure and others who have not received it are randomly selected for comparative analysis. Relevant variables of the groups are then studied before and after, and even during, the programme period in order to find out the difference of impact. Subsequently, statistical methods are used for testing the data for significance levels.

Agencies involved in Policy Monitoring and Evaluation

Another significant area of study in the field of policy monitoring and evaluation is the role of various agencies involved in it. Within government, a few agencies of official policy monitoring and evaluation are the various legislative bodies and their committees, the audit office, commissions of enquiry and the departmental evaluation reports. A common practice in democratic countries is the involvement of legislative bodies in policy monitoring and evaluation. The legislative body exercises policy monitoring and evaluation through the technique of questions and debates—motions like call attention, no-confidence, committee hearings and investigations—and the budgetary process. Since the Legislative is a large body and overburdened with the routine matter, it is the smaller committees that take up detailed investigative and evaluative work. In India, for example, we have a number of such committees—public accounts committees, committee on the welfare of SC/ST, etc.

In India, the auditor's office has broad statutory authority to audit the operation and finance of the activities of government agencies, monitor and evaluate their programmes and report their findings to Parliament. Evaluation studies may be taken up *suo moto* by the office of the Comptroller and Auditor General (CAG) of India, or on the basis of directives in legislation, or at the request of financial committees, or sometimes at the request of individual members of Parliament. The office of the CAG, which is regarded as an arm of Parliament, has broad statutory authority to ensure the accountability of the Executive to Parliament. It assists the Legislative in the Executive exercise of its financial control. A number of administrative agencies are also involved in the evaluation process. All government departments prepare their internal evaluation reports, which provide an opportunity to appraise the working of the programmes and projects undertaken by the department. Similarly, every department while sending its own demand for grants to the Ministry of Finance valuates its annual plans, programmes and performance. The organisation and methods division in the various ministries also indirectly perform the task of policy evaluation.

Besides auditing and administrative agencies, from time to time the government appointments certain commissions—such as the planning commission, the administrative reform commission and various ad-hoc commissions—who play an important role in public policy evaluation by presenting their detailed research reports on the consequences and impact of particular government policies. Monitoring and evaluation is also carried on outside the government. Research scholars in universities, private research institutes, pressure groups and public interest organisations monitor and evaluate policies that have an impact on the public to some extent. They also provide the public at large with information, publicise policy action or inaction, advocate enactment or withdrawal of policies and often effectively voice the demands of the weaker sections of the public.

Challenges in Policy Monitoring and Evaluation

There is no doubt that monitoring and evaluation must be objective, systematic and empirical. But a number of challenges stand in the way of those who are engaged in evaluating policies.

The first problem is regarding uncertainty over policy goals. When the policy goals are unclear or diffused, policy monitoring and evaluation becomes a difficult task. In such a case, officials may define goals differently and act accordingly. Second, there is the difficulty of measuring the extent to which these goals have been achieved. Evaluators themselves may not be impartial individuals to take an objective view of a policy issue. The same condition can be interpreted differently by different evaluators. Third, a shortage of accurate and relevant data and statistics may hinder the work of a policy evaluator. Resistance by officials is another barrier in policy monitoring and evaluation, because agencies and programme officials see the possible political consequences of evaluation. If the results do not come out in their favour they may discourage or disparage evaluation studies, refuse access to data or keep incomplete records. Finally, it is a general observation that organisations tend to resist change, while evaluation implies change. Organisational inertia may thus be an obstacle to evaluation, along with more forms of resistance.

The above discussion makes it clear that public policy monitoring and evaluation is a very tedious and complex process. Many participants are involved and many factors influence the outcome in this process. Nevertheless, monitoring and evaluation has taken its place as a vital element of the public policy process. It is a powerful mechanism that compares promise with performance, and is the linkage between the present and the future. Thus, although monitoring and evaluation may seem to be an almost gratuitous 'back-door' of the policymaking cycle, it serves as a window for policymaking decisions yet to come. The quest for checking or assessing the outcomes of policies and looking for areas of improvements, therefore, is a key step in effective policymaking.

EMERGING DIMENSIONS IN POLICY SCIENCE

Policy science is relatively a new subfield in political science whose intellectual seeds were sown in the 1940s. It emerged out of the recognition that traditional analysis of government decisions were incomplete explanations of political realities. As the relationship between society and its different public institutions became more complex and interdependent, the need for more comprehensive assessments of what governments do, how and why they pursue some policy alternatives over others have developed (Gerston 1974: 3). The policy sciences as described by Lasswell (1951) were the culmination of efforts to define a discipline for producing and applying socially relevant knowledge.

During the initial periods, the policy sciences were explicitly problem-oriented and utilised broad contextual approaches. In the post-War period, there was a renewed interest in the policy aspects of administration because of the practical encounters and alliances formed during the War, creation of international organisations and emergence of developing countries. Governments also reinvented themselves from being a keeper of peace and provider of services to becoming a welfare state. Public expenditure in most parts of the world also expanded greatly as governments started taking more and more initiatives for the welfare of society. A lot of reforms were carried out in areas not just regarding the content of public policy but also the ways in which they were formulated. The complex problems of public policy in the 1950s were resolved by public authorities and whomever they chose to consult. In the 1960s due to the emergence of complex issues like urban disorders, environmental issues, weapons systems, poverty programmes and civil rights, specialists entered the policymaking arena.

In the 1970s much effort was devoted to expand the relevance of the policy sciences while simultaneously emphasis was laid on scientific rigour. The focus on 'sciences' as well as well as on 'democracy' by Lasswell led to the emergence of two separate approaches to the policy sciences: policy analyses and policy process. One emphasised knowledge of the policy process, and the other emphasised knowledge for use in the policy process. A new approach gained momentum in the policy domain by the end of the 1970s and especially, by the early 1980s, when a lot of analysis started happening around the way government policies affected the people: the Vietnam War and Watergate scandal in the US, the Administrative Reforms Commission in India in 1966, the initiative to reduce public expenditure in order to reduce direct taxation under Margaret Thatcher in 1979, the creation of the Malaysian Administrative and Management Planning Unit in 1977.

The 1990s brought great interest in the public management approach to public policies. Osborne and Gabbler's book *Reinventing Government* (1992) and its subsequent adoption by the Clinton administration pushed an agenda of management reform at all levels of government. One of the themes of the book was deceptively simple: it is not so much that the policies and intentions of government are bad, but it is the way government goes about governing that needs to be more market-like and less command- and control-oriented. It created a new perspective of what some would label the post-bureaucratic approach to organisations and government (Barzelay with Armajani 1992). Today new issues have provided ample grist for the policy sciences' mills. Environmental issues like global warming and climate change, terrorism, immigration, information technology and globalisation policies are the most recent in a long series of public policy issues that would benefit from the systematic lenses of policy sciences.

That the policy sciences are able to address most issues from a number of competing perspectives lends support to the idea that the policy sciences have become one voice in the chorus of social change. The present policy studies are shifting their focus on normative truths and improving its ability to serve knowledge needs of the administrative and political community. Normative values and public management are the core concerns of the policy sciences of today. Another significant concern of contemporary policy sciences is the role of post-positivism in general and participatory policy analysis in particular. As a result, there is now a greater concern for values and greater public participation in the policy process. There is a realisation that human behaviour is often beyond the capability of quantitative approaches to analyses.

Shifting Policy Dynamics

Public policy draws on both domestic socio-economic circumstances and global stimuli though their influence varies from one situation to another. In the wake of globalisation, newer issues and problems have emerged requiring a completely different kind of mechanism involving both national and global agencies. In other words, issues are such that they cannot be effectively addressed by an individual country; they require collective attention. Besides the context, the role of institutions, authority and prevalent ideological preferences do play an invaluable role in the making of public policies. Being dependent on the context which is in constant flux, public policy cannot be static. By reinventing their roles in light of growing democratisation and decentralisation, newer political and social institutions, have become critical in policymaking. Governance is no longer a statist exercise; it involves civil society articulating new demands and issues, the changing notions of citizenship, the growing democratisation of politics and the assessment of public policy impact. Governance and democracy are now inter-linked with the public sphere becoming crucial and public policy a critical field. So, policymaking is not the exclusive domain of the government but an area in which multiple agencies of governance cooperate to evolve appropriate policies on the basis of specific ideological preferences.

Public policy has international roots, more so in view of those global issues which need global attention. Environment and terrorism, among others, have transnational implications since they adversely affect the whole of mankind; so, the policies adopted by individual nation-states to address environment degradation and terrorism may not be adequate unless they are complemented by international efforts. These are supra-national issues with serious adverse implications for the globe. Only through meaningful global cooperation, can effective policies be designed for arresting environmental decadence and throttling the growth and consolidation of terrorism in any part of the world.

Challenges Ahead

Public policies play an important role in resolving societal problems. But at the same time we must also recognise the limitations of policies in affecting societal conditions. Dye (2002: 16–17) identifies a number of such limitations. First, some societal problems are incapable of solution because of the way they are defined. If the problems are defined in relative rather than absolute terms, they may never be resolved by public policy. For example, if the poverty line is defined as the line which places one-fifth of the population below it, then poverty will always be with us regardless of how well off the 'poor' may become. Thus, relative disparities in society may never be eliminated. Second, expectations may always outrace the capabilities of governments. Third, policies that resolve the problems of one group in society may create problems for other groups. For example, solving the problem of inequality in society may mean redistributive tax and spending policies which take from persons of above-average wealth to give to persons with below-average wealth. The latter may view this as a solution, but the former may view this as creating serious problems. Thus, there are no policies which can simultaneously attain mutually exclusive ends. Fourth, societal problems may have multiple causes, and a specific policy may not be able to eradicate the problem. For example, job training may not affect unemployment if their employability is also affected by chronic poor health. Finally, the political system is not structured for completely rational decision-making. The solution of societal problems generally implies a rational model, but the government may not be capable of formulating policy in a rational fashion. Instead, the political system may reflect group interests, elite preferences, environmental forces or incremental change more than rationalism. Presumably, a democratic system is structured to reflect mass influences, whether these are rational or not. Elected officials respond to the demands of their constituents, and this may inhibit completely rational approaches to public policy.

Public policy is a response to the societal problems, but it is conditioned by the environment in which it is framed. However, despite a number of limitations, the study of public policy enables us to understand the causes and consequences of policy decisions and improves our knowledge about the society. Public policy as an activity and area of study would continue to hold relevance as long as it caters to the societal needs.

CONCLUDING OBSERVATIONS

The development of policy sciences is characterised by multidisciplinary perspective, contextual and problem-oriented nature and explicitly normative character. It is evident that the policy sciences, perhaps more than any other intellectual pursuit, are intimately affected by exogenous events. As Rabin, Hildreth and Miller (2007) note:

> They are, by definition, problem oriented, so they cannot absent themselves from the political and social environments without abandoning an integral part of their raison d'être. It is evident that the policy sciences have been profoundly affected by their heritage of problem orientation. There is no ready solution for this situation, for the policy sciences have deliberately set themselves in the midst of the real-world circus and must therefore endure whatever political acts might come down the boardwalk. The discipline's professional challenge, then, is to be able to accommodate in the face of changing conditions. (Ibid.: 519)

Public policies are basically aimed at feeding oxygen to political life. Policymaking is therefore an art of developing responses to public problems. Policy sciences emerged as an aspiration for socially-relevant knowledge. They are the means by which the ends of a collective community are served. Public policymaking is a complex, dynamic and creative process. It decides major guidelines of action directed at the future, mainly by governmental institutions. These policies or guidelines aim at achieving what is in the public interest by the possible means (Dror 1968: 12). There are various models and approaches to get a better understanding of the public policy process. Each model provides a different focus on political life, and each helps us understand different things about public policy. Altogether, they enrich our understanding of public policy dynamics.

Though, policy science has emerged as a significant area of study in addressing public issues, its nature and character is primarily Western, and particularly American. Developing countries like India have different socio-economic and political environments. Their problems and issues are different from the West. And that is where the limitations of the applicability of policy models lie. These models can't be applied universally, more so in developing nations which require indigenous approaches to their problems. Thus, it can be concluded that policy science holds the promise of improving public policymaking process and serves as a significant mechanism to address public problems. However, we need to keep in mind the contextual nature of policy studies before applying to different socio-economic environments.

REFERENCES

Agarwal, O. P. and T. V. Somanathan. 2005. 'Public Policy Making in India: Issues and Remedies'. Occasional paper no. 20, Centre for Policy Research, New Delhi.

Anderson, James E. 1975. *Public Policymaking: An Introduction*. London: Thomas Nelson and Sons Ltd.

———. 1979. *Public Policymaking*, second edition. London: Thomas Nelson and Sons Ltd.

———. 2003. *Public Policymaking: An Introduction*, fifth edition. Boston: Houghton Mifflin Harcourt.

Barzelay, Michael with Babak J. Armajani. 1992. *Breaking through Bureaucracy: A New Vision for Managing in Government*. Berkeley: University of California Press.

Bhattacharya, Mohit. 2003. 'Public Choice Theory: Government in the New Right Perspective' in *Contemporary Debates in Public Administration*, edited by Alka Dhameja, 71–78. New Delhi: PHI Learning Private Ltd.

————. 2013. *New Horizons of Public Administration*. New Delhi: Jawahar Publisher and Distributors.

Birkland, Thomas A. 2011. *An Introduction to the Policy Process: Theories, Concepts and Models of Public Policy Making*. Third edition. New Delhi: PHI Learning.

Bogason, Peter. 2006. 'Networks and Bargaining in Policy Analysis' in *Handbook of Public Policy*, edited by B. Guy Peters and Jon Pierre, 97–114. London: Sage.

Cairney, Paul. 2013. 'Policy Concepts in 1000 Words: Multiple Streams Analysis'. Podcast transcript on *Paul Cairney: Politics & Public Policy*. Available at https://paulcairney.wordpress.com/2013/10/31/policy-concepts-in-1000-words-multiple-streams-analysis/ (accessed 1 June 2017).

Cohen, Michael D., James G. March and Johan P. Olsen. 1972. 'A Garbage Can Model of Organizational Choice'. *Administrative Science Quarterly* 17 (1): 1–25.

Daft, Richard L. 2010. *Organization Theory and Design*. Hampshire: South-Western.

Delican, Mustafa. 2000. 'Elite Theories of Pareto, Mosca and Michels'. *Sosyal Siyaset Konferansları Dergisi* 43–44 (1): 323–35.

Dey, Prabir Kumar, ed. 2012. *Public Policy and Systems*. Delhi: Pearson.

Dror, Yehezkel. 1968. *Public Policymaking Reexamined*. San Francisco: Chandler Publishing Co.

———. 1974. *Public Policymaking Reexamined*. Reprint. Bedfordshire, England: Leonard Hill Books.

Dye, Thomas R. 1975. *Understanding Public Policy*. New Jersey: Prentice Hall.

———. 1992. *Understanding Public Policy*, seventh edition. Englewood Cliffs, N.J.: Prentice-Hall.

———. 2002. *Understanding Public Policy*, tenth edition. New Delhi: Pearson Education.

———. 2004. *Understanding Public Policy*, eleventh edition. New Delhi: Pearson Education.

Easton, David. 1965a. *A Systems Analysis of Political Life*. New York: Wiley.

———. 1965b. *A Framework for Political Analysis*. New Jersey: Prentice Hall.

Egonmwan, J. A. 1991. *Public Policy Analysis: Concepts and Applications.* Benin City: S.M.O. Aka and Brothers Press.

Elmore, Richard. 1979. 'Backward Mapping: Implementation Research and Policy Decisions'. *Political Science Quarterly* 94 (4): 601–16.

Faculty of Law and Political Science. n.d. '"Garbage Can" Models: Multiple Stream Theory', University of Tehran. Available at http://www.geocities.ws/policy_making/en/publicpolicy/garbagecan.pdf (accessed 9 December 2016).

Gerston, Larry N. 1974. *Public Policy Making: Process and Principles*, second edition. New York: M.E. Sharpe.

———. 2008/2015. *Public Policymaking in a Democratic Society: A Guide to Civic Engagement.* New York: Routledge.

Henry, Nicholas. 2007. *Public Administration and Public Affairs*, tenth edition. New Delhi: PHI Learning Private Limited.

Hill, Michael and Frédéric Varone. 2014. *The Public Policy Process.* London: Routledge.

Jéquier, Nicolas. 1972. 'Science Policy in the Developing Countries: The Role of the Multinational Firm' in *The Gap Between Rich and Poor Nations*, edited by Gustove Ranis and Annette Förster, 336–64. London: Macmillan.

Lewis, Janet and Rob Flynn. 1979. 'The Implementation of Urban and Regional Planning Policies'. *Policy & Politics* 7 (2): 123–42.

Lasswell, H. 1951. 'The Policy Orientation' in *The Policy Sciences: Recent Developments in Scope and Method* by D. Lerner and H. Lasswell, 3–15. Stanford: Stanford University Press.

Lindblom, Charles E. 1959. 'The Science of "Muddling Through"'. *Public Administration Review* 19: 79–88.

Lowi, Theodore J. 1972. 'Four Systems of Policy, Politics, and Choice'. *Public Administration Review* 32 (4): 298–310.

Mandal, U. C. 1997. *Public Administration: Principles and Practice.* New Delhi: Sarup & Sons.

Matland, R. E. 1995. 'Synthesizing the Implementation Literature: The Ambiguity-Conflict Model of Policy Implementation'. *Journal of Public Administration Research and Theory* 5 (2): 145–74.

Osborne, David and Ted Gaebler. 1992. *Reinventing Government: How the Entrepreneurial Spirit is Transforming the Public Sector.* New Delhi: PHI Learning Private Limited.

Parsons, D. W. 1995. *Public Policy: An Introduction to the Theory and Practice of Policy Analysis.* Cheltenham: Edward Elgar.

Peters, B. Guy. 1996. *American Public Policy: Promise and Performance*, fourth edition. Chatham, NJ: Chatham House.

Popoola, Olufemi O. 2016. 'Actors in Decision Making and Policy Process'. *Global Journal of Interdisciplinary Social Sciences* 5 (1): 47–51.

Pressman, Jeffrey L. and Aaron B. Wildavsky. 1973. *Implementation: How Great Expectations in Washington are Dashed in Oakland.* Berkeley: University of California Press.

Quade, Edward S. 1970. 'Why Policy Sciences'? *Policy Sciences* 1 (Spring): 1–12.

Rabin, Jack, W. Bartley Hildreth and Gerald J. Miller. 2007. *Handbook of Public Administration*, third edition. New York: Taylor & Francis.

Regional School of Public Administration. 2015. 'Monitoring and Evaluation of Public Policies'. Draft Conference Concept Note and Programme, Danilovgrad (Montenegro) Regional School of Public Administration, 13–14 October.

Ripley, Randall B. and Grace A. Franklin. 1986. *Policy Implementation and the Bureaucracy*, second edition. Chicago: Dorsey Press.

Sapru, R. K. 2010. *Public Policy: Art and Craft of Policy Analysis*. New Delhi: PHI Learning Private Limited.

———. 2014. *Public Policy: Formulation, Implementation and Evaluation*. New Delhi: Sterling.

Shafritz, Jay M. and Albert C. Hyde. 2012. *Classics of Public Administration*. Boston: Wadsworth Cengage Learning.

Simon, Herbert. 1968. *Administrative Behavior: A Study of Decision-Making Processes in Administrative Organization*, second edition. New York: The Free Press.

Visvanathan, Shiv. 2015. 'A New Public Policy for a New India'. *Hindu*, 6 April.

Vernooy, Ronnie, Sun Qiu and Xu Jianchu, ed. 2003. *Voices For Change, Participatory Monitoring and Evaluation in China*. Singapore: Yunnan Science & Technology Press.

Wanna, J., J. Butcher and B. Freyens. 2010. *Policy in Action: The Challenge of Service Delivery*. Sydney: UNSW Press.

Wholey, J. S., J. W. Scanlon, H. G. Duffy, J. S. Fukumoto and L. M. Vogt. 1970. *Federal Evaluation Policy: Analysing the Effects of Public Programs*. Washington, DC: The Urban Institute.

Xun, Wu, M. Ramesh, Michael Howlett and Scott A. Fritzen. 2010. *The Public Policy Primer: Managing the Policy Process*. London: Routledge.

8

MAJOR PUBLIC POLICIES IN INDIA

HIGHLIGHTS

- Environment policy
- Education policy
- Health policy
- Employment policy

Over these many years since Independence, the Government of India has formulated a number of policies. This chapter will discuss four important policy domains—environment, education, health and employment. The first part of the chapter deals with the environmental issues in India, legal and constitutional provisions for environmental protection, and the response of Judiciary and civil society to environmental challenges in India. Following this we will discuss the important strides made in the other three policy domains.

ENVIRONMENT POLICY

India is passing through a phase of acute ecological crisis. Air and water pollution, deforestation, biodiversity loss, solid waste mismanagement, noise and vehicular pollution in big cities are major environmental challenges. Environmental protection presents one of the most fundamental challenges to achieving economic growth, high levels of industrialisation, and fulfilling the basic needs of the growing population. The dilemma for policymakers is how to strike a balance between environment and development.

Environmental Issues in India

Worsening air quality is a scary story unfolding in urban India. Clinching evidence of this has emerged from a recent study titled 'Global Burden of Disease' (WHO 2010), carried out by 450 experts of five international organisations, including the WHO; the study ranks outdoor air pollution as the fifth largest killer in India. The report says that the decade-long air quality management efforts have failed to contain the problem. The cocktail of toxic air is increasing the health risk and compromising the 'livability' of Indian cities (Roychowdhury, Banerjee, Samajdar and Madan 2013: 35). The health costs of dirty air in India is the highest among all damages—with a cost amounting to over Rs 1,10,000 crore. Every year, outdoor air pollution claims the lives of 1,09,000 adults and 7,513 children under five. The cost of particle-pollution-related health damage amounts to one per cent of India's GDP (CSE 2014: 149).

Water pollution is another major environmental issue in India. Municipal sewage and industrial waste are the major sources of water pollution in India. More than 80 per cent of the total pollution load comes from municipal sewage. This is due to unscientific disposal of garbage in most parts of India, ultimately leading to increase in the pollutant load on surface and groundwater courses (CPCB 2013: 5). WHO statistics indicate that half of India's morbidity is water related. Water pollution is responsible for a number of diseases like typhoid, dysentery, hookworm, jaundice, poliomyletis, pneumonia, influenza and whooping cough. In the year 2000, there were around 66,000 reported cases of gastroenteritis infections. In the same year, 955 people were reported to suffer from cholera. Also 1,106 people suffered from malaria (*Times of India* 2001: 4). Major reason for water-borne diseases was mixing of sewer lines with the drinking water lines.

Noise in major cities and towns in India is a growing menace. The WHO's 1999 guidelines states that noise above 80 decibels can cause hearing impairment, especially among children, and that noise above 30 decibel can cause sleeping disorders and impact spoken communication, cardiovascular activity and trigger negative social behaviour. The first ever real-time data on noise pollution in 35 locations around seven cities—released by CPCB on 23 March 2011, a decade after India notified noise standards—indicated that average day time noise levels in metros was much higher than the national standard of 65 decibel ampere. As Janardhan (2011) notes, 'CPCB data shows that noise levels in all the major Indian metros are far above permissible limits and may have reached dangerous levels. The levels could cause hypertension, psychological diseases and depression.'

India has a very rich biodiversity in the world. It is recognised as one of the 12 mega centres of biodiversity. However, under the pressure of an exploding population and the growing demands of industries, our natural living resources are fast dwindling and several species of wildlife are being rapidly lost. At least 10 per cent of India's recorded wild flora and possibly a large fraction of its wild fauna are on the threatened list. The forest cover in India is disappearing at a staggering rate of 1.3 million hectares each year. India has a forest cover of 21.05 per cent of the country's land surface as against the target of 33 per cent prescribed by the National Forest Policy of 1952. The major causes of deforestation in India are encroachment of forest lands for cultivation, shifting cultivation, diversion of forest land to non-forest use, grazing, unauthorised and commercial felling and industrial use. Deforestation is mainly responsible for global warming, low rainfall, air pollution and soil erosion.

Constitutional Provisions

India is one of the very few countries of the world which has enshrined a commitment to environmental protection in its Constitution. Although some provisions in the Constitution relating to improvement in the quality of life were made in 1950, a direct reference to environmental protection and improvement was introduced through the 42nd Constitution Amendment Act of 1976. It was perhaps the UN conference on Human Environment held in Stockholm in 1972, that impressed on the government the necessity of legal and organisational frameworks for the protection of environment. The Amendment interjected a new dimension to public responsibility by making it obligatory for the Centre, states and citizens to protect and improve the environment.

The 42nd Amendment Act added two-fold provisions in the Constitution. On the one hand, it directed the State for the protection of environment and, on the other, it cast a duty on every citizen to help in the preservation of the natural environment. Article 48-A of the Directive Principles of State Policy lays down that 'The State shall endeavour to protect and improve the environment and to safeguard forest, and wildlife of the country' (Basu 1998: 446). Article 51-A(g) specifically refers to the fundamental duty regarding the environment: 'It shall be the duty of every citizen of India to protect and improve the natural environment including forests, lakes, rivers and wildlife and to have compassion for living creatures' (ibid.: 447). Further the Directive Principles of State Policy in Article 47 clearly underlines the environmental duty of the State to improve public health. There is no direct provision for the protection of environment in the fundamental rights. But the high courts and the Supreme Court of India have read right to wholesome environment as part of the right to life. Therefore, the right to life guaranteed in Article 21 of the Constitution is now considered a fundamental right to environment and preservation of nature's gifts without which life cannot be enjoyed.

Enactment of Law and Policies

The legal sanction to protect different segments of environment in India has been provided by successive enactments and laws. It is a well-known fact that Jawaharlal Nehru had tremendous interest in wildlife, but the honour goes to Indira Gandhi for enacting the Wildlife (Protection) Act, 1972. It is clearly evident from the title of the Act that its main objective is to protect wild animals, particularly rare species such as the lion and the great-horned rhinoceros. The Wildlife (Protection) Act was followed by the Water (Prevention and Control of Pollution) Act, 1974 aimed at preventing and controlling water pollution, and maintaining and restoring the wholesomeness of water. Towards achieving these objectives, provisions were made for setting up central and state boards for prevention and control of water pollution. This was followed by the Forest (Conservation) Act, 1980 which was aimed at protecting forest resources and the Air (Prevention and Control of Pollution) Act, 1981 which was aimed at prevention, control and abatement of air pollution. The Bhopal Gas Tragedy of 1984 gave the impetus for stringent environmental protection legislation in the 1980s. The Environment (Protection) Act, 1986 was enacted to prevent a repeat of such an industrial disaster. The Act was passed with the following objectives: protections, regulation of discharge of environmental pollutants; handling of hazardous substances, speedy response in the event of accidents threatening environment; and awarding deterrent punishment to those who endanger human/environment safety and health.

The establishment of the National Green Tribunal (NGT) in 2011 by the Ministry of Environment and Forests under the National Green Tribunal Act, 2010 was a remarkable event in governmental efforts at environmental protection. The NGT was established for the effective and expeditious disposal of cases relating to environmental protection, conservation of forests and other natural resources, including enforcement of any legal right relating to environment, and giving relief and compensation for damages to persons and property and for matters connected therewith or incidental thereto. The NGT is a specialised body equipped with the necessary expertise to handle environmental disputes involving multi-disciplinary issues.

In pursuance to the international Convention on Biological Diversity (CBD), to which India is a signatory, the Biological Diversity Act, 2002 was enacted. The Act addresses access to biological resources and associated traditional knowledge to ensure equitable sharing of benefits arising out of their use. It is a major legislative intervention to empower the local communities by involving them in the protection of the biodiversity around them. The Recycled Plastic Manufacturing and Usage Rules, 1999 prohibit vendors of foodstuff from packing their wares in bags or containers made from recycled plastics. In 2000, the Noise Pollution (Regulation and Control) Rules came into effect. These rules prescribe ambient air quality standards in respect of noise for industrial, commercial and residential areas as well as identified 'silence zones'. India is a party to the Montreal Protocol on substances that deplete the ozone layer, such as the chlorofluorocarbons (CFCs) used in refrigerators. The production and consumption of these substances are to be phased out as per the Protocol. In this regard, the Government of India formulated the Ozone Depleting Substances (Regulations) Rules, 2000, which placed restriction on production levels of ozone depleting substances (ODS) and specified annual reductions (Rajagopalan 2008: 91).

Keeping in mind the emerging environmental scenario and the need to strengthen and make existing laws more comprehensive, the Ministry of Environment and Forests prepared a draft New Environment Policy of India in 2004. It finally became effective as the National Environment Policy, 2006. Its preamble states that it seeks to extend the coverage, and fill in gaps that still exist, in light of present knowledge and accumulated experience. It does not displace but rather builds on earlier policies. Later in 2006, the Scheduled Tribes and Other Traditional Forest Dwellers (Recognition of Forest Rights) Act, a key piece of forest legislation, was passed. Also called the 'Forest Rights Act' or the 'Tribal Rights Act', the law concerns the rights of forest-dwelling communities to land and other resources, denied to them over decades as a result of the continuance of colonial forest laws. The 2006 Act makes provision for ownership of land that is already being cultivated by forest dwellers; rights to minor forest produce, grazing areas and pastoralist routes; provision of rehabilitation in case of illegal eviction or forced displacement; and the right to protect the forest and wildlife.

India has evidently formulated and reformulated a number of policies to protect its environment. They cover a wide range of issues, such as noise, hazardous waste, hazardous micro-organisms, environment impact assessment, etc. and have spawned new enforcement agencies and strengthened the ones already in place. It is therefore clear that the environmental policy framework of India reflects three foundational aspirations: (*a*) human beings should be able to enjoy a decent quality of life; (*b*) humanity should become capable of respecting the finiteness of the biosphere; and (*c*) neither the aspiration for good life nor the recognition of biophysical limits should preclude the search for greater justice in the world.

However, in spite of these, environmental degradation and pollution have not been controlled to a great extent. A number of reasons can be cited for this. First, most provisions of the administrative and legislative laws remain only on paper, or are twisted out of shape during implementation. Second, lack of proper coordination and cooperation among the various administrative institutions is a loophole in the entire set-up. A further weakness of the present official programme for environmental protection is its lack of recognition of the crucial role that NGOs can play in complementing the government's own efforts.

Judicial Impetus to Consolidate Environmental Policies

In the background of Executive failure, the Indian Judiciary has emerged as a catalyst to secure environmental safety and protection. In the early 1980s the role of the higher Judiciary in India underwent a transformation. A new and radically different kind of case altered the litigation landscape—instead of being asked to resolve private disputes, the Supreme Court and High Court judges were asked to deal with public grievances over flagrant human rights violations by the State, or to vindicate the public policies embodied in statutes or constitutional provisions. This new type of judicial business is collectively called as Public Interest Litigation (PIL). Most environmental actions in India fall within this class and the Judiciary has exhibited enlightened creativity and foresight whenever it has had an opportunity to decide on issues relating to the environment. A survey of the numerous judgments of the various high courts and the Supreme Court shows that most of the technical hindrances have been brushed aside by devising new tools of legal interpretation and construction.

The landmark judgment of the Supreme Court in *Ratlam Municipality vs Vardhichand* (AIR 1980 SC 1622) is representative of the new outlook of the Judiciary towards environmental conservation. In this case, the Supreme Court laid down two founding principles: first, no municipality in India can put forth lack of money as a ground for not discharging its primary duty of looking after the health and safety of its residents; second, the absence of public conveniences and the use of industrial pollutants to the detriment of the health of citizens are violative of the human rights of decency and dignity which are non-negotiable. In *Rural Litigation and Entitlement Kendra Dehradun vs State of UP*, also known as the 'Dehradun Quarrying case' (AIR 1985 SC 652), the Supreme Court held for the first time that the fundamental right to a wholesome environment is a part of the fundamental right to life under Article 21 of the Constitution. The question of water pollution, especially that of the Ganges, came up before the Supreme Court in the case of *M. C. Mehta vs Union of India* (AIR 1987 SC 463). The river passes through the industrial belt of three states and most of these industries are tanneries and leather processing industries. The Supreme Court ordered the closure of thirty tanneries of Kanpur which were releasing untreated effluents into the Ganges. While recognising that the closure of the tanneries might cause unemployment, the Court held that 'life, health and ecology have greater importance to the people'.

The judgements of the Judiciary have come to be referred to as judicial activism as they have given new dimensions to the right to life and personal liberty guaranteed by Article 21 of the Constitution. Right to healthy environment has been made and construed as a fundamental right by the Supreme Court while deciding various PILs filed by the environmental-legal expert M. C. Mehta. Article 21 which assures every citizen the right to 'life', is interpreted as including all attributes necessary for the enjoyment of life. In *Munn vs. People of India* (AIR 1988 SC 236), it was pointed out that by the term 'life' something more is meant than mere animal existence. Pollution causes permanent disabilities leading to malfunctioning or non-functioning of the vital organs of the body, reducing a person to mere animal existence and thereby denying him the right to life. *M. C. Mehta vs Union of India* (AIR 1987 SC 463) is yet another milestone of judicial concern to environmental protection. The Supreme Court, inter alia, pointed out that (*a*) the government should evolve a national policy for the location of chemicals and other hazardous industries in areas where population is scarce and there is little risk to the community, and care should be taken to minimise pollution, and (*b*) a principle of absolute liability should be in place to compensate the harm caused to persons due to environmental pollution.

The Supreme Court has played a vital role in the case of the Bhopal Gas Tragedy. It showed its deepest concern for the life and liberty of people affected by the leakage of poisonous gas. In *Union Carbide Corporation vs Union of India* (AIR 1990 SC 273), the Court directed the government to immediately provide interim relief for the victims of the tragedy. The Court directed Union Carbide Corporation to pay a sum of $ 470 million to the Union of India in full settlement of all claims and liabilities related to and arising out of the gas leakage disaster. The Court considered it a compelling duty, both judicial and humane, to secure immediate relief to the victims. The Court also held that the right to live in a healthy environment is supreme.

Environmental pollution is also caused by other activities such as stone-crushing, which deprive the citizens of fresh air and the right to live in pollution-free environment. In *M. C. Mehta vs Union of India* (1992 SCC 256), the Supreme Court ordered the stopping of mechanical stone-crushing activities in and around Delhi, Faridabad and Ballabhgarh Complexes. Another historic judgment was delivered by the Supreme Court in *M. C. Mehta vs Union of India*, also known as the Delhi Gas Leak Case (Mathew 2000: 14). The petitioner had alleged the infringement of the right to life of several thousand people due to the hazardous activity of Shri Ram Food and Fertilizers, which manufactured oleium and chlorine and was situated in the heart of the city of Delhi. The Supreme Court ordered the management to pay compensation to the victims of oleium gas leak. Thus, the Court not only widened the scope of Article 21 by including in it protection of the environment but also included a liability for those harmed by pollution.

Unplanned and unregulated development in Delhi over the past few decades has turned it into the most polluted city in the world. The Supreme Court has played a significant role in protecting the environment of Delhi by taking the following policy measures:

- Introduction of cleaner fuel, CNG-based public transport system in 2001
- Ban on the plying of commercial vehicles which are 15 years old, by 2 October 1998
- Strict enforcement of the restriction on plying of vehicles carrying goods during the day from 15 August 1998
- Establishment of emission norms of vehicles, i.e. Bharat Stages (BS) II, III and IV (equivalent to Euro II, III and IV). Only vehicles complying with BS III emission norms were being registered from 1 April 2005 (Government of National Capital Territory of Delhi 2001: 1). And from 1 April 2017 onwards, vehicles complying with BS IV norms were only being registered
- Closure and relocation of polluting industries
- Setting the limits for noise and loud speakers
- The use of noiseless generators mandated by environmental laws
- Ban on the use of plastic less than 40 microns thick
- The law concerning public nuisance has been sharpened as a powerful weapon to promote public health and safety

These judgments make it clear that the Judiciary has exhibited dynamism in evolving a new dispensation to tackle the problem of pollution: establishing the PIL, replacing punitive sentencing policy with a policy based on affirmative action, judicial search for less harmful alternatives of economic development plans, the attempts to encourage social activists to enforce social rights through cost awarding techniques. These landmark judgments and orders of the Supreme Court have triggered a wave of environmental consciousness in the country. The striking features in all these cases was the Court's attempt at encouraging petitions to utilise the instrument of PIL to energise the Judiciary to play a more interventionist role in areas where the country's Executive had failed to act. Judicial revolution in the field of environmental litigation has swept away outmoded doctrines and has fashioned new remedies and strategies to fight the environmental onslaught.

Role of Civil Society in Evolving Environmental Policies

One of the most significant aspects of Indian environmentalism is the vital role played by civil society actors in evolving eco-friendly policies. They have attacked various anti-people policies of the government and awakened the masses about the destruction of the environment. We can see the role of the civil society in various movements such as the Chipko movement, Narmada Bachao Andolan and the Silent Valley Andolan. The main demand of movements like these has been to protect the rights of the local masses over their '*jal, jamin and jangal*', i.e. water, land

and forest. This section describes how civil society actors in India have played a significant role in evolving eco-friendly policies.

The origin of modern environmental movements in India can be ascribed to the Chipko (meaning 'to hug') movement of the early 1970s in the central Himalayan region. This movement was basically a people's movement that resisted the felling of trees. The movement began in early 1973 when the forest department refused to allot ash trees for making agricultural implements to a local cooperative named Dashauli Gram Swarajya Sangha (DGSS) in Chamoli district. However, at the same time, the department allotted the trees to a private firm called Simon Company. This incident provoked the collective to fight injustice. People lay down in front of timber trucks and burnt resin and timber depots. These methods failed to make a dent, and it was then that one of the leaders, Chandi Prasad Bhat, suggested embracing the trees in the locality en masse. This strategy worked and was instrumental in driving away that private company. As the success of the movement spread to other neighbouring areas, it came to be known internationally as the Chipko movement. As Guha (1989) states, the local people considered Chipko as a fight for the basic subsistence denied to them by institutions and policies of the State. With its wide following and success, the Chipko movement can be termed as a watershed in the landscape of Indian environmental movements. It kindled the environmental aspects of development and gave rise to numerous conflicts and protests over natural resources and ecological issues. It helped understand the close links between the livelihoods of the local people and the environment. It also signified the role of the locals, especially women, in protecting and conserving their environment.

The Silent Valley Movement is another civil society-led struggle to protect the environment in India. In 1978, an NGO called Kerala Sastra Sahitya Parishad (KSSP) raised a voice against a hydel project that was proposed in the Silent Valley, a tropical forest renowned for its biodiversity. Kerala was a power deficit state and the government felt that a hydroelectric project inside the deep tropical forest would be a good idea. Since this was the last-remaining tropical forest in the country, environmentalists protested and filed a case in the high court that they eventually lost. The movement gathered steam and got the support of the general public and the media. Finally, at the intervention of Indira Gandhi, the project was cancelled by the state government.

The pro-tribal Narmada Bachao Andolan (NBA), founded by Medha Patkar in 1989, is one of the most popular movements in India's eco-history. It began as a protest against the construction of dams on the River Narmada. The projects were aimed at generating hydroelectricity and developing irrigation facilities to drought-prone areas of Gujarat and Rajasthan. These two projects—Sardar Sarovar Project and Narmada Sagar Project—were projected to have enormous utility to the people as it ensured supply of electricity and irrigation water. However, the estimated environmental costs of the projects were too high to ignore. It was estimated that the construction of the two dams would incur environmental costs equivalent to Rs 30,923 crore and Rs 8190 crore respectively. Besides, the projects will submerge about 1,30,482 ha of land, of which 55,681 ha are prime agricultural land and 56,066 ha are forests. More than one lakh people from 248 villages would be displaced, of which 57 per cent were tribals. Though the protests against Sardar Sarovar Project started in the late 1970s, when the project received clearance, it received momentum only during the late 1980s. The NBA effectively exposed the ecological implications of the dam and the lacuna in the resettlement and rehabilitation policy of the government. During its earlier phase, the main demand of the NBA was complete stopping of the dam, but later it began focusing on reducing the height of the dam and ensuring a proper resettlement and rehabilitation policy for the displaced people. The movement gained wider public attention with mobilisation and organisation of the displaced, and the joining of eminent social workers like Baba Amte and Sunderlal Bahuguna. The movement succeeded in garnering international support and ultimately forced the World Bank (WB) to withdraw funding for the hydroelectric and irrigation projects. This may be termed as only a partial success of the movement as the ultimate success of NBA lies in convincing the government to stop the project with the support of the people, a situation highly unlikely given the present socio-economic conditions of the country.

Another important civil society movement which deserves special mention is the Appiko Movement started in 1983 by the people of the village of Balegadde in Uttar Kannada district of the state of Karnataka. The people protested the cutting of teak trees similar to the Chipko Movement, by embracing the trees. The activists spread the movement throughout the region through padayatras, meetings, folk dance, etc. The movement mainly focused on conserving and growing trees. This movement has played the most crucial role in preserving the environment and ecosystem of the Western Ghats.

We have a number of other environmental initiatives and movements led by the civil society in India. These include the Chilka Bachao Andolan for people's traditional rights over natural resources in Odisha; Beej Bachao Andolan (Save Seed Movement) for protecting bio-diversity; the Anti-Tehri Dam movement for protecting the ecology and preventing the displacement of people in the Garhwal region of Uttrakhand; the Rain Harvesting Movement by Tarun Bharat Sangh in Rajasthan; the Ganga Mukti Andolan for making the Ganges pollution-free in Bhagalpur district of Bihar; the Pani Panchayat in Maharastra for conserving soil and water; etc. A number of such successful grassroots environmental initiatives and movements force us to think of alternative ways of harnessing natural resources so as to ensure ecological sustainability and social equity in the society. These civil-society-led environmental movements have successfully linked the degradation of nature with the survival of the masses. These movements challenge the present model of development which has been responsible not only for environmental destruction but also displacing the common masses.

Governance of the natural environment in the world of today has emerged as one of the most complex challenges ever faced by humanity. The variety of environmental changes generated by human activities, from the local to the global levels, are not new. However, the magnitude of the diverse changes and the resulting impacts on the functioning of the natural eco-systemic processes have grown rapidly over the past two centuries, more so in the second half of the last century. The UN Conference on the Human Environment held at Stockholm in 1972 turned out to be a watershed event in the recognition of the challenges in environmental governance by the global community. Since then, the environment has only got increasingly internalised in the governance agenda at all spatial levels of governance.

There can be little doubt that the independent Indian State has passed a number of laws, rules and regulations to protect the environment. India was one of the participants of the Stockholm conference of 1972. India is one of the very few nations in the world that have enshrined the commitment to environmental protection and improvement in its Constitution. However, despite initiatives of the government and constitutional provisions, the problems of environmental pollution persist. The main reason for this is the non-implementation of these provisions. Over the past four decades, the Supreme Court has not only played a significant role in environmental protection, it has also secured a firm foothold in environmental governance. The judgments of the Court in many cases pertaining to the environment have had significant impact on the overall environmental governance process in India. Judicial activism, particularly in recent times, has given a new direction to the protection and improvement of the environment. Another significant feature of Indian environmental governance is the role of the civil society in making the people aware and involve in environmental protection which can be seen in various successful movements.

EDUCATION POLICY

Education is a joint responsibility of the Centre and the state governments in India. The state governments have the freedom to organise education within the national framework. The Union Ministry of Human Resource Development (MHRD), under which the Department of Elementary Education and Literacy and the Department of Secondary and Higher Education operate, is responsible for educational policy planning. The following discussion will focus on the major educational policies in independent India and examine the major issues and challenges facing the country today.

Constitutional Vision of Education

Since Independence, the central government has been paying utmost attention to education as a vital factor to the nation-building process. Three provisions in the Constitution directly address the issue of education. First, Article 39(f) of the Indian Constitution states that the State shall 'direct its policy towards securing … that children are given opportunity and facilities to develop in a healthy manner and in conditions of freedom and dignity and that childhood and youth are protected against exploitation and against moral and material abandonment'. Second, Article 45 directs the State to 'provide within a period of ten years from the commencement of the Constitution, free and compulsory education for all children until they complete the age of fourteen years'. As Sadgopal (2009: 2) notes, this Article has been interpreted to include (*a*) early childhood care, nutrition, health and pre-primary education (kindergarten, nursery) for children below six years of age; and (*b*) elementary (not primary) education of eight years (Class I–VIII) for children in the 6–14 age group. Third, Article 46 directs the State to 'promote with special care the educational and economic interests ... of the Scheduled Castes and the Scheduled Tribes. ...'

Educational Policies in India

The first effort made by the Indian government in the field of education was the setting up of the University Education Commission (1948–49). The sole purpose of the Commission was to analyse and make recommendations regarding the university education system. Chaired by Dr S. Radhakrishnan, the Commission laid down the philosophical, scientific, moral, cultural and vocational aims of education and presented an insight into the state of affairs in higher education. The Commission recommended that wisdom, knowledge and skills of the past were to guide the actions in the present and the present was to provide a roadmap for the future. The Secondary Education Commission (1952–1953) developed proposals to modernise India's secondary education system. Led by Dr A. L. Swami Mudaliar, the Commission stated the main objectives of education as development of democratic citizenship, vocational efficiency, personality development and qualities of leadership. It recommended institution of industrial education, vocational guidance and improvement in the system of examination. The next development in the arena of education was the adoption of the Scientific Policy Resolution by Jawaharlal Nehru-led central government in 1958. Under this policy, the government sponsored the development of high-quality scientific education institutions such as the Indian Institutes of Technology (IITs). In 1961, the Centre formed the National Council of Educational Research and Training (NCERT) as an autonomous organisation that advises both the central and state governments on formulation and implementation of educational policies. The following is a detailed discussion of the policies from the 1960s onwards.

National Education Commission (1964–66)

Also known as the Kothari Commission, the National Education Commission was appointed in 1964 to advise the Centre on the national pattern of education and on the general principles and policies for the improvement in the quality of education at all stages and in all aspects. The final report of the Commission reads in its introductory statement that '[t]he most important and urgent reform needed in education is to transform it, to endeavour, to relate it to the life, needs and aspirations of the people and thereby make it a powerful instrument of social, economic and cultural transformation necessary for the realisation of the national goals' (GoI 1964: 1). It stressed on the importance of early fulfilment of the Directive Principle that sought to provide free and compulsory education for all children up to the age of 14 under Article 45 of the Constitution. Stressing the importance of the teacher in determining the quality of education, the Commission focused on the need for employing qualified and responsible teachers and advocated better emoluments and other service conditions for them. The report is considered unique as it was the first that suggested a 'Common Schooling' in India. It is also significant as it was widely discussed and a national policy on education emerged in 1968 as a result.

National Education Policy, 1968

Drawing from the discussions around the Kothari Commission report, the government announced the first National Policy on Education in 1968. The policy stated that strenuous efforts should be made to equalise educational opportunity and called for a 'radical restructuring' and equalising of educational opportunities in order to achieve national integration and greater cultural and economic development. Regional imbalances in the provision of educational facilities were proposed to be corrected and good educational facilities were to be provided in rural and other backward areas.

A 'common school system' was to be adopted—i.e. a broadly uniform educational structure in all parts of the country with the ultimate objective being to adopt the 10+2+3 pattern, the higher secondary stage of two years being located in schools, colleges or both according to local conditions. Efforts were proposed to improve the standard of education in general schools. Government schools were required to admit students on the basis of merit and provide free studentships to prevent segregation of social classes. The schools were mandated to promote the education of girls. Intensive efforts to develop education among the backward classes and among the tribals were identified. At the secondary education stage, the state governments were to adopt and vigorously implement the three-language formula—i.e. the study of Hindi, English, and a modern Indian language, preferably one of the southern languages or the regional language. The policy had felt it necessary to identify and cultivate talent across fields at an early age as far as possible. The school and the community were to be brought closer through programmes of mutual service and support. National service, i.e. participation in meaningful and challenging programmes of community service and national reconstruction, were therefore made integral to education. These programmes were to lay emphasis on self-help, character formation and developing a sense of social commitment.

With a view to accelerating the growth of the national economy, science education and research were to receive high priority. Science and mathematics were to be an integral part of general education till the end of the school stage. Special emphasis was to be placed on the development of education for agriculture and industry—the government proposed establishing at least one agricultural university in each state. Practical training in industry was to form an integral part of technical education. And technical education and research, in turn, were to be related closely to industry. Moreover, in terms of the number of full-time students to be admitted to a college or university department, the policy stated that this decision should be determined considering the laboratory, library and other facilities available and the strength of the staff in the department. The policy also stressed that considerable care was needed while establishing new universities—their setting-up should be contingent on adequate provision of funds and only if proper standards could be met. The policy also stated that there was the need to give increased governmental support to research in the universities.

Thus, the National Education Policy of 1968 which recommended free and compulsory education; respectable status, emoluments and education of teachers; development of languages; equalisation of educational opportunities; identification of talents; and linking education with agriculture and industry was an important historical event for education in independent India. This was the first attempt to give direction to the country's educational system.

National Education Policy, 1986

The National Policy on Education (1968) envisaged a five-yearly review of the progress and implementation of educational policies and programmes. The National Education Policy of 1986 was the result of such a review of the extant policies and programmes. The aims and objectives of the 1986 Policy as per the policy documents are as follows:

- Education is essentially for all. This is fundamental to all-round development, material and spiritual.
- Education should further the goals of socialism, secularism and democracy enshrined in our Constitution.
- Education should develop manpower for different levels of economy. It should give further guarantee of national self-reliance.
- Education is a unique investment in the present and future. This cardinal principle is the main aim of the National Policy on Education. (GoI 1998: 6)

Set along the same lines as the earlier national policy, the National Policy on Education (1986) was an extensive document that covered all aspects of education from the elementary to university levels, and even adult education. The policy emphasises the importance of special programmes for marginalised groups. Towards this the policy called for expanding scholarships, adult education, recruiting more teachers from the SCs, incentives for poor families to send their children to school regularly, development of new institutions and providing housing and services. What was unique in this policy was the recognition of the impact of the early years in the development of a child. The policy, therefore, makes room for early childhood care and education through the Integrated Child Development Services programme. It makes three very important commitments: universal access and enrolment, universal retention of children up to age 14 and a much needed improvement in the quality of education that allows for children to achieve a certain level of learning. The highest priority was placed on solving the problem of dropouts, and ensuring retention at the school level. Towards this objective, the Policy suggested a child-centred approach, an approach that catered to the needs of the child on an individual level. Corporal punishment was to be excluded from the teaching system. The policy introduced a new programme called 'Operation Blackboard', wherein it was ensured that one teacher was made available per class, and all necessary equipment and teaching materials were provided for.

In order to enhance the quality of higher education, the policy proposed that boards of secondary education were to be granted autonomy. The policy introduced generic vocational courses in higher education to enhance individual employability and meet the manpower need of India's growing economy. Children who have special talents were given the opportunity to enhance their aptitude through Narvodaya Vidyalayas. Education was to be culturally applicable and inculcate values in the children. The need to develop the use of local languages in education was reiterated. The need for low-priced books and improvement in library management as well as setting-up additional libraries was emphasised. The policy provided for work experience as a part of education, using math as a tool to teach analytical thinking, strengthening science education, and supporting sports, physical education and yoga. The policy called for greater participation of educated youth and changes in the system of evaluation so that it does not encourage rote learning. It emphasised the importance of teacher training and continual teacher education. The policy spoke at length about overhauling the planning and management system surrounding education at the national, state, district and local levels. It expanded the Open University System with the setting up of the Indira Gandhi National Open University (IGNOU) in 1985. The policy also called for the creation of the 'rural university' model, based on Gandhian philosophy, to promote economic and social development at the grassroots level in rural India. Finally, it emphasised the need to raise government expenditure to six per cent of the GDP in the Eighth Five-Year Plan.

National Programme of Action, 1992

The National Policy on Education of 1986 had stipulated review every five years. Such a review took place in 1992 and the policy that stemmed out of it is known as the National Programme of Action (NPA). The revised programme accepted 10+2+3 educational structure as the national system. Education for women was considered a vital component of the overall strategy of securing equity and social justice. Also, the policy suggested ensuring universal access to education and adequate incentives for children, particularly girls. Reservation was to be made. Operation Blackboard was to cover all schools in tribal areas and Dalit bastis. Regarding higher education, the main recommendations were to impart dynamism by consolidation and expansion of institutions by granting autonomy to colleges and departments, redesigning courses, training teachers, strengthening research and improving the efficiency and coordination at the state and national levels.

The Yashpal Committee Report, 1992–93

The National Programme of Action of 1992 had observed that 'the tendency on the part of some schools, particularly in urban areas, to recommend a large numbers of books, had contributed to overburdening of students'. This statement was picked up by the mass media which heavily criticised the system; R. K. Narayan had raised pertinent questions in the Parliament about overburdening school children. A Committee under the leadership of Professor Yashpal was set up to examine the National Programme of Action of 1992 and advise on the ways and means of reducing the burden of the school-going child. After studying the problem of curriculum load in detail, the Committee observed that the majority of school-going children viewed learning at school as a boring, unpleasant and bitter experience. The limited purpose of preparing for the examination was identified as a very important factor for the unpleasantness of learning. The Committee concluded that the problem of curriculum load was not only an urban phenomenon but also in rural areas, where students do not carry heavy bags—it is the problem of non-comprehension that makes things extremely difficult for a majority of rural children. This was largely because though the authors of textbooks were experts in the subject, either they were isolated from the realities of the classroom as they were not familiar with the learning process of children or the textbooks they prepared were too difficult for the majority of the children. The main recommendations of the Committee, included in the broad framework suggested to the states and union territories in June 1994, are:

- Greater involvement of teachers in framing the curriculum and preparation of textbooks at the State/UT level.
- Amendment of School Education Acts or Rules of State/UTs for laying down norms for pre-school.
- Abolition of tests/interviews for admission in pre-schools and discontinuance of textbooks and homework at pre-school stage.
- Abolition of homework and project work at primary stage.
- Extensive use of audio-visual material and enforcing teacher–pupil ratio to be at 1:40.

Thus, the Yashpal Committee was a significant endeavour to look into the problem of overburdening of the students and suggest remedial measures. The Committee's findings were highly appreciated and a monitoring committee was set up in the MHRD to periodically review the pace of the implementation of the Committee's recommendations.

Right to Education, 2009

The implementation of the Right to free and compulsory Education (RTE) Act, 2009 marks a historic moment for the children of India. This act ensures that every child has a right to guaranteed quality elementary education. The State, with the help of families and communities, is now under a legal obligation to fulfil this duty. With specific provisions targeted towards disadvantaged groups, the Act provides an effective platform to reach the unreached. For instance, in view of reducing disparities, the Act has mandated that private schools must ensure that they set aside 25 per cent of the seats for children belonging to disadvantaged groups.

The Act strives for quality with equity by banning corporal punishment to ensure classrooms are free of fear and anxiety as well as providing education in the mother tongue to the extent possible. School management committee would be made up of parents, local authorities, teachers and the children themselves. The inclusion of 50 per cent women and parents of children from disadvantaged groups in these committees was envisioned to help overcome the widely-prevalent disparities. These management committees will support to form school development plans and monitor the entire environment of the school, including sanitation and hygiene practices and the management of mid-day meals.

New Education Policy (NEP), 2016

The NDA-led government set up a Committee under the chairmanship of T. S. R. Subramanian in October 2015 to frame a new education policy. On the basis of this Committee's report, the MHRD has come out with a draft of the National Education Policy in August 2016. The preamble of the draft reads as follows:

> since the formulation of the National Policy on Education 1992, significant changes have taken place in India and the world at large. India's political, social and economic development is passing through a phase which necessitates a robust and forward looking education system. The National Education Policy, 2016 which is designed to guide the renewal process in education in India represents an attempt in this direction.[1]

The draft policy envisions a credible education system capable of ensuring inclusive quality education and lifelong learning opportunities for everyone. The system must produce students equipped with the knowledge, skills, attitudes and values that are required to lead a productive life and participate in the country's development process; respond to the requirements of the fast-changing, ever-globalising, knowledge-based societies; and develop responsible citizens who respect the diversity of heritage, culture and history and promote social cohesion and religious amity. This vision recognises the central role of education in India's social, economic, political and cultural development. The Policy is aimed at meeting the current requirement in respect to quality education, innovation and research, to make India a knowledge superpower. The main highlights of the draft New Education Policy are:

- Priority to pre-school education for children in the age group of 4–5 years
- Importance to improve learning outcomes of school children to enhance the quality of elementary education
- Extending RTE up to an appropriate age so as to cover secondary level education as well
- Curricular reforms to meet the emerging aspirations and align to national goals of social cohesion, religious amity and national integration
- Reorienting skill development programmes not only for gainful employment but also to develop entrepreneurial skills

---

[1] Based on 'Some Inputs for Draft New Education Policy 2016'. Reproduced with permission. For details, see http://mhrd.gov.in/nep-new (accessed 14 December 2016).

- A concerted effort to make Information and Communication Technology (ICT) an integral part of education across all levels and domains of learning
- Formulating transparent and merit-based norms and guidelines for recruitment of teachers in consultation with the state governments
- Independent teacher recruitment commissions to be set up by state governments to facilitate transparent, merit-based selection and recruitment of teachers, principals and other academic cadres
- Teacher development programmes to have components that help teachers appreciate the importance of co-scholastic activities—especially life skills, ethical education, physical education and arts and crafts—and introduce these effectively into the teaching learning process in schools
- All states and UTs to provide education in schools up to Class V in the mother tongue, local or regional language as the medium of instruction, if they so desire. If the medium of instruction up to primary level is the mother tongue or local or regional language, the second language will be English and the choice of the third language (at the upper primary and secondary levels) will be with the individual states and local authorities, in keeping with the Constitutional provisions
- Physical education, yoga, games and sports, NCC, NSS, art education, Bal Sansad, covering local art, craft, literature and skills and other co-scholastic activities to be made an integral part of the curriculum and daily routine in schools for the holistic development of children
- More importance to be given to community participation and parental involvement in schools
- An Education Commission to be set up every five years to look into the governance reforms in higher education
- Separate education tribunals to be established at the Centre and in the states to deal with litigation and address public grievances against government as well as private schools/institutions
- An independent mechanism for administering the National Higher Education Fellowship Programme to be put in place
- More emphasis to be given to quality assurance in higher education through measures like getting NAAC or NBA accreditation
- Selected foreign universities from the top 200 in the world to be encouraged to establish their presence in India through collaboration with Indian universities
- Faculty development in higher education to be given priority through promotion of research, innovation and new knowledge
- To take steps to reach the long pending goal of raising the investment in education sector to at least 6 per cent of GDP as a priority

- The culture of accountability to guide the functioning of the education system.[2]

The draft of the new education policy also observes that there is sufficient evidence to show that past policy recommendations have remained unrealised due to lack of mechanisms in place for effective implementation. To avoid such a situation, the draft policy recommends that each state and UT formulate a Framework For Action (FFA) synchronous to its regional, social and cultural needs. This will entail making institutional arrangements and laying down administrative processes with clear performance indicators to achieve quantifiable targets and desired qualitative outcomes. Thus, the new policy believes that it is imperative that the Centre and the states work together in a spirit of cooperative federalism to translate the intended goals and actionable strategies into realities that can result in the transformation of the education landscape. The New Education Policy, therefore, is proposed to be framed through an inclusive, participatory and holistic approach.

Issues and Challenges Facing Indian Education

First, poverty. To be sure, a citizen can now go to court if a child is denied the Right to Education, but such is the condition of the poor, especially of the disadvantaged sections, that they want their children to work rather than go to school. So here is a dilemma. Development cannot take place without universalisation of education, but universalisation is not possible without improvement of economic conditions. Second, globalisation. Globalisation has changed the shape of classrooms. It has changed the role and functions of teachers and expanded their universe of activity and self-learning. Teachers are now required to regularly upgrade and enhance their competency and skills. Indian education is facing a number of such challenges: realising the goals of universal primary education, modernisation of education, necessity of value education, ensuring quality education, vocationalisation of education and accessibility of education to the poor. In fact, RTE poses a number of challenges. In terms of the challenge of finding trained manpower, for example. Mukul (2010) reports that over 5.23 lakh teaching posts are vacant across the country. Additionally, 5.1 lakh teachers are required to bring the teacher:pupil ratio to that prescribed by the RTE Act. Over and above recruitment, about 5.48 lakh untrained teachers at the primary level and 2.25 lakh at upper primary level have to acquire necessary qualifications (ibid.).

Third, quality of education. Educational institutions would find it difficult to meet the challenge of globalisation if one fails on this front. Emphasis on quality parameters becomes all the more necessary in light of the mushrooming of private institutions following liberalisation. The quality of education can improve through extensive use of audio-visual technologies and the internet. The courses could be so designed that teachers and students are able to make good use of these modern developments. While restructuring the syllabi and courses, efforts could be made

[2] Ibid.

to develop an optional combination of acquisition of theoretical and practical skills. The courses could be so designed that critical reading and interpretation of the classics, practical fieldwork where relevant, and application of readings and other skills are given importance.

Fourth, regulation. As mentioned above, private educational institutions are a reality now. There should be a proper scrutiny mechanism that will be able to identify those institutions where the commercial interest dominates over the interests and ethics of higher education. This is because higher education is a public good and it cannot be left to the market forces to control. Therefore, a strong regulatory mechanism is required immediately to monitor and control their activities with the objective of ensuring quality and social accountability.

Finally, overall development of the individual—both students and teachers. The traditions that Indian universities have built up since Independence have been able to provide graduates the capability of pursuing only a limited number of careers. In the new globally competitive environment, the Indian student is now required to develop a multifaceted personality to cope with rapid changes due to globalisation. This challenge requires the educational institution to invest in the development of the body, mind and spirit of each of their student as they pass through the system. Value education has today become a moral necessity as competence is of little value if ethics are forgotten (UGC 2003: 22; Sadgopal 2009: 2). The teachers should also be equipped to inspire the students with ideas and values. They have to be oriented towards educating students on the need to recognise the equality of men and women in our democracy, to discard all caste exclusiveness and pride, communal distinctions and antagonisms and to strengthen 'the dignity of individual and the unity of nation' as proclaimed in our Constitution. Towards this, teachers must be made acquainted with the noble humanistic sentiments of our Constitution and impressed with the passion to translate them into socio-political realities. Directing such efforts towards teachers would definitely ensure a bright future of education in India.

The above discussion makes it clear that, since Independence, a number of important Committees, Commissions and education policies have been framed by the Indian policymakers. A major concern of the Centre and the states has been to give increasing attention to education as a vital factor in national progress and security. All of the Committees, Commissions and policies have reviewed the educational system and recommended measures to improve the quality, accessibility and utility of our educational system. All of them have made a mark in one way or the other in trying to reform the system and make it capable of facing the challenges of a modern society. Reforms are desirable and necessary in order to bring about quality changes in education, but reforms should be brought by consensus, dialogue and taking the concerned parties into confidence. The sad reality is that serious effort is not forthcoming on this front. Moreover, politics is taking a heavy toll on academic life in higher education. There is a lack of professionalism in universities. Materialistic motives are uppermost in the minds of the managements. Teachers' apathy and resistance to educational reforms have formed a vicious circle. Teachers and students are more eloquent and militant in matters of payscale and power but care little about making the university a place of creativity. In this matter an urgent need of introspection is required.

HEALTH POLICY[3]

The public healthcare system in India is a saga of continuous experimentations, innovations and negotiations. Emerging out of centuries of colonial subjugation, India embarked on a comprehensive providential nature of public health policy with a country-wide network of primary health centres (PHCs) and sub-centres. However, it is not a post-Independence development altogether; it is rather a byproduct of the colonial rule in India. Public health is among the many positive externalities that the colonial empire had to face in India. Born out of the sheer exigency of salvaging the army cantonments and civilian enclaves from the repeated scourge of tropical diseases, public health eventually came about to encompass the native habitations. Moreover, it was found that the vectors can hardly be confined to colonial diktats. The health sector did not experience much transformation after Independence. In fact, the Indian State did not have a separate health policy document until as late as 1983, and that too only in the wake of the 1978 Declaration of the WHO. Until the adoption of the National health Policy 1983, public healthcare relied heavily on the policies of the erstwhile colonial state. After 1983, several health Committees and Commissions were constituted to streamline the sector. However, the major problem with these committees was the lack of integration and coordination. With Liberalisation there has been a fundamental change in the sector: the providential nature of universal primary healthcare has given way to chargeable services on user-pay basis. And this change has reflected in the policies since then. The following section would briefly discuss the origin of public health policy in India in the post-Independence period, the radical changes that took place post-liberalisation and the challenges currently facing us.

Bhore Commission Report, 1946

The need for a national health policy was mooted as early as the 1930s by a group of modernisers within and outside the Indian National Congress. However, the first major event in public health policy came with the Bhore Committee Report that was submitted in 1946. Set up under the chairmanship of Sir Joseph Bhore, the Committee was to take a stock of the state of health in colonial India. Though it was commissioned by the colonial administration in 1943, it had very little of the colonial perspective. In fact, the final report had an overall welfare motive. This was because the freedom movement was in its final and most decisive phase and the decline of the Empire was almost in sight. The final report of the Bhore Commission is still considered as the template of public health policy and administration in India. It is perhaps one of the most researched and minutely documented plans that the Indian health sector has ever had. The Committee had proposed universal providential health services for independent India. However, the Committee did not confine itself merely to pre-Independence promises. In fact, it laid out a detailed three-tier referral system of healthcare infrastructure across the country: preventive

[3] This section draws on Roy (2016: 219–29). Originally published in *Public Policy: Concepts, Theory and Practice*, Copyright 2016 © Bidyut Chakrabarty and Prakash Chand. All rights reserved. Reproduced with the permission of the copyright holders and the publishers, Sage Publications India Pvt. Ltd, New Delhi.

healthcare in the PHCs at the village level; curative services in the secondary healthcare centres at the district level; and medical teaching and research institutions associated with the tertiary healthcare services at the urban centre.

Post-Independence Initiatives

Ever since the Bhore Committee report, the relevance of good health has been considered as a major precondition to nation-building and overall national development. Subsequent governmental policies on healthcare have taken the Bhore Committee report as an important benchmark. A number of committees have been formed over the years to guide the future course of healthcare policies in India: Mudaliar Committee (1961), Chadha Committee (1963), Mukherjee Committee (1965), Jungalwalla Committee (1967), Katar Singh Committee (1973), Srivastava Committee (1975) and the Rural Health Scheme (1977). However, none of these committees deviate from the core policy blueprint chalked out by the Bhore Committee.

During the 1950s and 1960s, the primary focus of the Indian health sector was to contain the periodic bout of epidemics. Massive campaigns were launched to eradicate various diseases like malaria, smallpox, tuberculosis, leprosy, filariasis, trachoma and cholera with the help of several international funding agencies like the UNICEF, WHO and the Rockefeller foundation. A huge army of personnel was commissioned to implement those programmes. The National Malaria Eradication Programme (NMEP), which alone appointed 1,50,000 workers in 400 units, was a case in point. Similarly, the tuberculosis eradication programme, which involved vaccination with BCG, TB clinics, domiciliary services and after-care, had also engaged several workers. However, given the size of the country and the population, containment of diseases and epidemics required a much more extensive network of health infrastructure. As Rao argues,

> [They often administered medication] without an understanding of the nature of diseases, their distribution, their underlying causes and inter-linkages, their behaviour over time, and indeed often even their quantum. Their launch had been guided not so much by epidemiological priorities as by the technological determinism, often inspired by Western aid agencies and experts. (1999: 18)

The health policies during the first two Five-Year Plans remained unchanged with a seemingly urban bias. Rural health was put under the fold of Community Development Programme (CDP). The Mudaliar Committee was set up in 1959 to take stock of the healthcare services of the first two Five-Year Plans. The committee acknowledged substantial achievements of the disease control programmes and highlighted the apparent lacuna in the basic healthcare infrastructure, especially the appalling conditions of the district hospitals in terms of acute shortage of doctors, paramedical staff, infrastructure, beds, etc. The Committee recommended upgrading existing PHCs and district hospitals, setting up mobile clinics in non-PHC areas, and improvement of service conditions of doctors to attract them to work in rural areas.

From the Third Five-Year Plan in 1961 there has been a change in the doctor-centric approach of healthcare—a lot of emphasis has been put on the need for auxiliary personnel. In the face of rising birth rate and falling death rate, the third plan also asked for population stabilisation.

The 'camp approach' was introduced during this phase. The Chadha Committee report of 1963 recommended the integration of health and family planning services and its delivery through one male and one female multipurpose worker per ten thousand of the population. At the end the third plan period, there was high emphasis on population control. The government also commissioned a Special Committee to Review the Staffing Pattern and Financial Provision under Family Planning. This Committee, popularly known as Mukherjee Committee, identified the vacuity of the camp approach and recommended target-based approach in family planning and motivation and incentives for the receivers. The Fourth Five-Year Plan (1966–1969) reiterated the centrality of PHCs in the overall health topography of the country. It lamented the poor state of PHCs across the country and asked for their immediate streamlining. For the first time a separate fund was allocated for the smooth functioning of the PHCs under this plan. The family planning measures which got a real impetus during the third plan continued to enjoy the same predominance in the fourth plan period too.

By the Fifth Five-Year Plan, sanity seemed to have been restored among the policymakers as they identified lopsided development of the health sector—a lion's share of the funding was directed towards the urban centres. Again, this plan recommended strengthening of rural health infrastructure. As a result of this realisation, the fifth plan envisaged increasing the accessibility of health services to rural areas through the Minimum Needs Programme, improvement of qualities in education and training of health personnel, and development of referral services. The Katar Singh Committee which came out with its report in 1973 identified that the scheme of a uni-purpose worker in several vertical health programmes had resulted in a huge waste of public money. The Committee recommended a multipurpose worker scheme. The Srivastava Committee which was primarily concerned with medical education and addressing manpower shortage, recommended more trained manpower for the rural hinterlands in its report of 1975. In the middle of the Fifth Five-Year plan a state of national emergency was proclaimed. This led to a huge spurt in population control activities with the largest-ever plan outlay since Independence. The family planning measures took an authoritarian overtone with compulsory and forced sterilisation. With the end of emergency, the policy priority shifted to sanitation and safe drinking water.

From the 1980s onward, a deliberate attempt was being made to 'de-colonise' the public healthcare system by inducting indigenous systems of medicine and health practices. Following the 1978 WHO International Conference, official healthcare policies were formulated to achieve 'Health for All' by 2000 through a comprehensive healthcare approach that later culminated in the first-ever National Health Policy in 1983. The health policies in India experienced a paradigm shift after 1983. Until then, health policies were considered as a part of the Five Year Plans and other programmes. A series of events forced the Centre to chalk out its maiden nation-wide policy document on public health, which include among others, the appalling conditions of health manifested in terms of communicable and non-communicable diseases, poor health infrastructure, especially the lack of a country-wide network of PHCs and overreliance on curative health. This piecemeal approach to health was replaced by a systematic blueprint for the future with the introduction of the National Health Policy.

National Health Policy of 1983

The National Health Policy of 1983 is the first comprehensive official policy on public healthcare in India. It not only integrated the varied initiatives undertaken in the health sector since Independence, but also acted as a precursor to the future course of Indian health policy. The salient features of the national health policy are:

1. It was critical of the curative-oriented Western model of healthcare
2. It emphasised a preventive, promotive and rehabilitative primary healthcare approach
3. It recommended a decentralised system of healthcare, the key features of which were low cost, de-professionalisation (use of volunteers and paramedics) and community participation
4. It called for an expansion of the private curative sector which would help reduce the government's burden
5. It recommended the establishment of a nation-wide network of epidemiological stations that would facilitate the integration of various health interventions
6. It set up targets for achievement that were primarily demographic in nature (GoI 1983).

The 1983 Policy has also underscored the importance of community participation in providing healthcare to the people. As the report read:

> the various health programmes have by and large, failed to involve individuals and families in establishing a self- reliant community. … Also over the years the planning process has become largely oblivious of the fact that ultimate goal of achieving a satisfactory health status for all our people cannot be secured without involving the community in the identification of their health needs and priorities as well as in the implementation and management of the various health and related programmes. (Ibid.: 3)

There is no denying that the 1983 National Health Policy led to a massive expansion of PHCs across the country. But if there was any lasting impact of the Policy in the history of public health in India, it was obviously its tacit support for private sector intervention in health sector under the garb of comprehensive primary healthcare. It paved the way for a smooth transition from the totally providential nature of public health to a partial privatisation of health sector. Any serious reading of the 1983 Policy document would give one a clue as to how privatisation of healthcare has been discreetly allowed in India. For example, the apparent innocuous pledge of ensuring healthcare services' at an affordable price, in the policy document carries an implicit message that healthcare service henceforth would not come for free. Similarly, under the pretext of 'constraint of resources', the policy document advocates partial entry of private sector in the provision of curative services. Moreover, the policy overlooked the criticality of women's health.

Post-Liberalisation Initiatives

The healthcare sector has received further blow with the onset of globalisation and the built-in conditionality of the withdrawal of State from the social sector. Consequently, the concept of free medical care was revoked in the Eighth Five-Year Plan (1992–1997) which recommended user-fee. The overall expenditure in public health in India reduced from a moderate 1.3 per cent of GDP in 1990 to a miserable 0.9 per cent by the end of 1999. Moreover, a substantial amount of the said expenditure was taken up by revenue expenditure—particularly, the payment of salaries—rather than capital expenditure, viz. buying of essential drugs, creation of much coveted physical infrastructure. Despite, the UPA's electoral promises of raising health expenditure to 3 per cent of GDP in 2004, it raised it over a mere 1.3 per cent. The global average of expenditure to healthcare is 5.5 per cent of GDP (Raman and Bjorkman 2009).

The model of healthcare adopted in this phase curtailed 'the comprehensive primary healthcare to selective primary healthcare' by downsizing its ambit to reproductive and child health, immunisation, control of selective diseases and emergency services. It was argued that for any other health problems, the patients had to avail the services of private health providers. Consequently, an exponential growth of private healthcare institutions was registered in curative services. In this phase public hospitals did not cease to exist. In fact, they exist and are open to receive anybody who likes to avail the grand old institutions of public health. But as a part of Structural Adjustment Programme (SAP) conditionalities, there has been a sharp decline of public investment in public health institutions, leading to a sorry state of affairs with poor infrastructure, neglected maintenance, and perennial shortage of funding and personnel.

The above discussion reveals that the State has lost the autonomy to design its own healthcare policies and assertiveness to implement equity-oriented measures. In this macroeconomic-political ambience, the State has lost its leveraging power. In addition to that, equity and access to healthcare continue to be a major cause of concern and the disparity in allocating resources between primary and the tertiary healthcare sectors has seriously impaired the primary healthcare sector, thereby leading to unnecessary reliance of the poor on the private healthcare sector.

National Health Policy, 2002

If the National Health Policy of 1983 marked the entry of private capital in the health sector, National Health Policy of 2002 firmly endorsed it as the dominant pattern of health policy in India. The major objectives of the 2002 Policy can be enumerated as follows: achieving an acceptable standard of good health of Indian population; decentralising the public health system by upgrading the infrastructure in existing institutions; ensuring a more equitable access to health service across the social and geographical expanse of India; enhancing the contribution of the private sector in providing health service for people who can afford to pay; giving primacy for prevention and first-line curative initiatives; laying emphasis on the rational use of drugs; and, increasing access to tried systems of traditional medicine.

The National Health Policy of 2002 has categorically deleted the concept of comprehensive and universal healthcare. Broadly speaking, it focuses on the need for enhanced funding and an organisational restructuring of the national public health initiative in order to facilitate more equitable access to health facilities. Also, the policy has identified those diseases which are principally contributing to the disease burden, such as tuberculosis, malaria, blindness, and 'newly emerging diseases' like HIV/AIDS. The 1983 Policy also proposed a robust disaster management plan to cope with any sort exigency, either natural or man-made calamities.

National Rural Health Mission, 2005

With a view to improving the health status of the rural population throughout the country and to make 'necessary architectural correction in the basic healthcare delivery system' (Bijli 2012: *vii*), the Centre has adopted a flagship health project in 2005 called the National Rural Health Mission (NRHM). The primary objective of NRHM is

> increasing public expenditure on health, reducing regional imbalance in health infrastructure, pooling resources, integration of organizational structures, optimization of health manpower, decentralization and district management of health programmes, community participation and ownership of assets, induction of management and financial personnel into district health system, and operational zing community health centres into functional hospitals meeting Indian public health standards in each block of the country.

The major components of the NRHM have been: increasing the number of Accredited Social Health Activists, strengthening of sub-centres, strengthening of PHCs, strengthening of Community Health Centres as the First Referral Care centres, formulating district health plans, converging sanitation and hygiene under NRHM, strengthening disease control programme, public private partnership for public health goals (including regulation of private sector), setting up a new health financing mechanism and reorienting medical or health education to support rural health issues. The NRHM has brought about a total shift in the health sector by adopting a holistic approach to health—it has integrated virtually all the stakeholders (viz. state government, panchyats, NGOs) within its fold with the underlying objective of the well-being of rural people. It is a landmark programme because it sought to correct the urban centricity of the public health programme in India by exclusively concentrating on rural health.

National Health Policy, 2015

The draft document of the National Health Policy of 2015 has categorically underlined the imperatives behind formulating another national health policy:

> The primary aim of the National Health Policy, 2015, is to inform, clarify, strengthen and prioritize the role of the Government in shaping health systems in all its dimensions – investment in health, organization and financing of healthcare services, prevention of diseases and promotion of good health through cross-sectoral action, access to technologies, developing human resources, encouraging

medical pluralism, building the knowledge base required for better health, financial protection strategies and regulation and legislation for health.[4]

Major objectives of the draft NHP 2015 can be enumerated as follows:

1. Public health sector should incorporate all the services one would expect from a public health sector, i.e. preventive, promotive, palliative and rehabilitative services
2. Reduction of out-of-pocket expenditure for availing healthcare services so that households would not fall into the vicious cycle of poverty and resultant impoverishment
3. Assurance of universal availability of free and comprehensive primary health services as an entitlement for all aspects of reproductive, maternal, child and adolescent health, and for most prevalent communicable and non-communicable diseases
4. Enabling universal access to free essential drugs, diagnostics, emergency ambulance services, and emergency medical and surgical care services in public health facilities for all sections of the population
5. Ensuring improved access and affordability of secondary and tertiary care services through a combination of public hospitals and strategic purchasing of services from public health sector
6. Influencing the growth of the private healthcare industry and medical technologies to ensure alignment with public health goals.[5]

The draft document of NHP 2015 is significant on a number of counts. First, it has made a realistic correction of the target of public health expenditure from 4–5 per cent of the GDP to 2.5 per cent of the GDP. Second, the document has underlined the importance of preventive and promotive health. Third, the document has underscored the legacy of medical pluralism in the country as it lays emphasis on good propagation of the potential of AYUSH (Ayurveda, Unani, Siddha, Homeopathy) remedies. Fourth, another hallmark is an attempt to close the persistent infrastructure and human resource gaps. Fifth, it brings into consideration the National Urban Health Mission for strengthening the primary healthcare needs of the urban population. Sixth, it has brought in the pertinent issue of gender—it has sought to go beyond maternal health while addressing the issue of women's health and also brings in the often neglected issues like health responses to victims of gender violence, ranging from sexual assault to acid attacks. Seventh, it calls for an integrated nation-wide disease surveillance programme down to the district level and well-equipped laboratories backed by tertiary care centres to preempt any sudden outbreak of epidemics. Eighth, it has also underlined the 'expansion of the pool of professional and technical human resources for health'. Ninth, it has proposed a sharing of financial burden of healthcare:

[4] Drawn from the draft of the National Health Policy of 2015 available at http://www.thehinducentre.com/multimedia/archive/02263/Draft_National_Hea_2263179a.pdf (accessed 8 July 2017).

[5] Ibid.

'Free primary care provision by the public sector supplemented by strategic purchase of secondary care hospitalisation and tertiary care services from both public and private sector would be the main financing strategy of assuring healthcare services.'[6]

Challenges before the Healthcare System in India

Despite a number of policies and programmes, public healthcare in India is in a very poor state of affairs. Several factors can be held responsible for this condition. On the basis of an assessment of the successive health initiatives crafted in the Five-Year Plans, expert committees and health policies, the following observations may be made. First, almost all the committees relied on the model of service delivery[7] with bureaucracy at the helm of affairs. The model envisaged an impartial and efficient administration, informed by five distinctive features—bureaucratic structure, professional domination, accountability to the public, equity of treatment, and self-sufficiency (Butcher 1995). But, the model does not take into account the innumerable socio-cultural diversity which seemed to have determined the health-seeking behaviour of the people on the pretext of universal common good. In consequence, service delivery in general and delivery of health services in particular has encountered problems. Second, the pivotal role of the State in provisioning the social services in general and health services in particular has impinged on several bottlenecks such as the lack of proper infrastructure, inadequate funding, poor level of health consciousness among the stakeholders and the absence of proper access. The criticality of the gender perspective in health has never been properly considered while formulating public health policies in India, barring a few passing references. Third, the myopic view that has not taken into account the built-in medical pluralism of the Indian society is another challenge to balanced public health policy in India. Public health initiatives in India have repudiated the inherent pluralism of medical practices in favour of a straightjacket approach based on the positivist model of biomedicine. Consequently, indigenous pharmacopeia have been relegated to the margins as any reference to it would have defeated the nation-building project. Fourth, the financing of public health is another very critical area of public health policy in India. With the onset of globalisation and health sector reform, the nature of financing public health initiatives has undergone a sea change as the State has been forced to part with its ability to formulate, regulate and finance the health initiatives. Fifth, one of the most important challenges of public health governance is the overlapping allocation of responsibility and accountability between the Centre and the states.[8] Finally, the poor mobilisation of the community as critical stakeholders in the health sector, including local bodies, civil society actors and private partners are responsible for the poor performance of public health in India.

On the basis of the forgoing analysis, the following observations may be made. The appalling conditions of public health in India cannot be properly understood if we de-contextualise the

[6] Ibid., p. 41.

[7] By 'public administration model of service delivery' we generally mean bureaucratically managed model of service delivery. For details, see Butcher (1995).

[8] Drawn from the draft of the National Health Policy of 2015, p. 53.

present scenario from its colonial antecedents. In fact, a majority of public health institutions are a colonial inheritance. However, health policy in independent India has been couched in a welfare approach where medical service has assumed a providential nature. This commitment of the Indian State has impelled it to adopt public health policies with a holistic approach. The entire package of this approach has been supply-oriented, clientele approach through which the State has drawn legitimacy. But the dependence on alien sources for funds and technical knowhow has crippled the State's ability to make any major breakthrough in the health sector. In rural areas, therefore, we have a thin presence of qualified doctors, nurses, modern amenities and infrastructure. These factors have also contributed to the perpetuation of pre-modern belief systems and health behaviour of the people.

The post-liberalisation reforms have made a sort of a U-turn. Health services are no longer providential in nature. The advent of the market economy has made the service demand-oriented, and demand management has come to occupy a dominant space. This has reduced the welfare bent of the Indian State and has made it surrogate to the global market economy to a large extent. Improvement of the healthcare system is an urgent requirement, only then can the health issues of the people, especially the rural poor who cannot afford the market services, be addressed.

EMPLOYMENT POLICY[9]

Addressing the challenge of unemployment in the rural areas of the country is central to rural development. The Mahatma Gandhi National Rural Employment Guarantee Act (MGNREGA) was legislated to tackle the problem of unemployment in rural India. Passed in the Lok Sabha in August 2005 as the Employment Guarantee Act, it was renamed as MGNREGA on 2 October 2009 as a tribute to Mahatma Gandhi who felt strongly that India needed mass production and not production by the masses. His concern was to make the poorest of the poor happy by associating them with nation-building. MGNREGA is considered a milestone in the history of rural development in India. Unlike the previous employment generation schemes, for the first time, MGNREGA legally guarantees employment to India's poor. This discussion will provide a brief description of employment-related policies of the past and delve into an analysis of the MGNREGA with reference to its main provisions and the consequences. It will also dwell on how this specific legislation has radically altered the rural socio-economic texture by making the right to employment a justiciable entitlement.

Contextual Response to Socio-economic Circumstances

The MGNREGA was conceptualised as part of the drive to contribute to the well-being of the underprivileged, especially those who are at the margins of development. This was a significant

[9] This section is drawn from Singh (2016: 241–48). Originally published in *Public Policy: Concepts, Theory and Practice*, Copyright 2016 © Bidyut Chakrabarty and Prakash Chand. All rights reserved. Reproduced with the permission of the copyright holders and the publishers, Sage Publications India Pvt. Ltd, New Delhi.

component of the social welfare legislations that have been brought about by the Indian State. MGNREGA was introduced at a crucial time when the rural economy was on the verge of stagnation. Many studies on rural economy ascertain the erosion of livelihoods as the main cause of rural unemployment. Numerous poverty alleviation schemes have not helped in solving the problem. Seasonal migration of labourers to urban areas due to poverty and unemployment has been very high in rural India during the slack season. As Drèze observes, the predicament of casual labours did not seem fundamentally different from that of slaves, except that they were driven by economic necessity than physical coercion (2011: 3). MGNREGA was introduced to address this issue. The Act is essentially a rights-based policy design that would undoubtedly empower the rural masses who have been deprived of the benefits of development in the wake of globalisation. It is aimed at removing poverty from amongst rural poor who have faced a history of exclusion, particularly identity-based groups, backward castes, tribes, and women who face subjugation at the hand of local elites. It is therefore fair to argue that this rural employment scheme was a contextual response to the prevalent socio-economic circumstances which have simultaneously favoured empowering policy decisions along with the consolidation of globalising political forces.

Employment Policy in India

The need for work programmes were recognised early during development planning in India. These wage employment programmes were self-targeting and the objective was to provide enhanced livelihood security, especially for those in casual labour work. Some of the programmes implemented by the government that offered wage employment on public works on minimum wages are Rural Man Power (1960–61), Pilot Intensive Rural Employment Programme (1972), Small Farmers Development Agency, Marginal Farmers and Agriculture Labour Scheme, Food For Work Programme (1977), National Rural Employment Programme (1980), Rural Landless Employment Guarantee Programme (1983), Jawahar Rojgar Yojana (1993–94), Jawahar Gram Samriddi Yojana (1999–2000), Sampoorn Grameen Rojgar Yojana (2001–02) and National Food For Work Programme (2005).

MGNREGA is a paradigm shift in generating employment in India as all the previous wage employment programmes were schemes, whereas MGNREGA is an Act which places an enforceable obligation on the State. An Act creates accountability whereas a scheme places the labourers at the mercy of the government. Unlike the previous schemes, MGNREGA provides a statutory guarantee of wage employment. The Act came into force in February 2006 in 200 districts and was extended (in two phases) to the entire country by 1 April 2008.

Main Provisions of MGNREGA

The new Act aims at enhancing livelihood security in rural areas by creating needs-based productive assets at the village level, empowering rural women, reducing rural-urban distress migration and fostering social equity. It promises 100 days' work per year to all rural households whose adults are willing to do unskilled manual labour at the statutory minimum wage notified in the programme. Work is made available to anyone who demands it by applying to work through the job card.

Employment will be given within fifteen days of the receipt of application, if not then the daily unemployment allowance as per the Act has to be paid. The minimum days of employment has to be 15 and the maximum days has to be 100. Wages are to be paid according to the Minimum Wages Act of 1948 for agricultural labourers in the respective state, unless the Centre notifies a wage rate. Equal wages will be provided to both men and women. At least one-third of the beneficiaries who have registered and requested work under the scheme should be women.

Implementation

MGNREGA was launched at Anantapur in Andhra Pradesh and initially covered 200 'poorest' districts of the country. The Act identifies Panchayati Raj Institutions (PRIs) as the key implementing body. MGNREGA is also a step towards making this Act a participatory process and empowering the people at the grassroots level. The Act authorises the gram sabha to recommend works to be taken up under the scheme, to monitor and supervise these works, and to conduct social audit of the implementation. The gram panchayat is responsible for the planning of works, registering households, issuing job cards and monitoring of the scheme at the village level. The Act advises appointment of Gram Rojgar Sewak in each panchayat for this purpose. The panchayat samiti is responsible for planning, monitoring and supervision at the block level. The zilla parishad is responsible for finalising the district plans for MGNREGA which is a comprehensive plan of action for the scheme of the district. The state government formulates regulations based on the guidelines of the Act to facilitate overall implementation. It sets up the State Employment Guarantee Council to advise the government on the implementation of the scheme, and to evaluate and monitor it. The central government's rural development ministry is the nodal ministry for implementation and fund disbursal. It also monitors and evaluates the scheme. Besides, it sets up the Central Employment Guarantee Council for advising it on various issues related to MGNREGA.

Schedule I of the Act enumerates eight categories of work that are supposed to be the 'Focus of the Scheme':

- Water conservation and water harvesting; drought proofing (including afforestation and tree plantation); irrigation canals (including micro and minor irrigation work)
- Provision of irrigation facility to land owned by households belonging to SCs and STs or to lands of beneficiaries of land reforms or that of the beneficiaries under the Indira Awas Yojana of the Government of India
- Renovation of traditional water bodies (including desilting of tanks)
- Land development
- Flood control and protection works (including drainage in water-logged areas)
- Rural connectivity to provide all-weather access
- In addition, there is a residual category, i.e. any other work, which may be notified by the central government in consultation with the state government.

Under the Act each state is supposed to formulate a Rural Employment Guarantee scheme within six months of its enactment. Broadly speaking, the village- and block-level panchayats are entrusted with the task of implementation activities, while coordination activities are left for the district-level panchayat institution. Planning, supervision and monitoring take place at all levels. The Act was implemented in a phased manner—130 districts were added in 2007–08. With its spread to over 625 districts across the country, the flagship programme of the erstwhile UPA-led central government has the potential to increase the purchasing power of rural poor, reduce distress migration and to create useful assets in rural India. Also, it can foster social and gender equality as 23 per cent workers under the scheme are SCs, 17 per cent are STs and 50 per cent are women. According to the rural development ministry's figures, initially more than 1.36 crore people—above one per cent of India's total population—were given jobs under the Act. In 2008–09, it provided employment opportunities to more than 4.47 crore households. The National Sample Survey shows an eightfold increase in employment in public works after MGNREGA. There is also an increase in the share spent on rural employment schemes out of the total Plan expenditures at the Centre. It has increased from an average of 11.8 per cent in the three years before MGNREGA (2002–03 to 2004–05) to 13.3 per cent in the three years from 2009–10 to 2011–12 (GoI 2013: 42).

Achievements

In a country with rampant rural poverty and unemployment, the scheme has been able to achieve two objectives—rural development and employment. Focusing entirely on the rural areas, the Act has been able to involve local people in activities that help them directly: water conservation and harvesting, forestation, rural connectivity, flood control, construction and repair of embankments, etc. MGNREGA has benefitted the most depressed sections of the society, to whom social programmes still rarely reach.

India has a history of employment generation schemes but these were largely left to the discretion of the administrative machinery. It is clear from past experiences that most of the schemes have failed due to the lack of right planning, focus on local needs and dominantly bureaucratic rules. Wage employment programmes of the past were allocation-based, MGNREGA is rights-based. MGNREGA is not supply-driven but demand-driven. MGNREGA provides a statutory guarantee of wage employment—i.e. work becomes a right. And, this guarantee will act as a shield for the rural poor and the landless by saving them from the exploitative agricultural class.

One of the greatest merits of this social welfare policy is that it has been able to reduce poverty to a great extent. Hundred days of employment may not appear to be attractive, but for a section of population that is at the brink of starvation it is a great relief. Because of its bottom-up, demand-driven approach, this policy aims to empower the rural poor. In many rural areas, poor people have benefitted from rising wage rates, particularly unskilled labour, and this rise is partly due to MGNREGA. Drèze points out that, 'The policy is a means of strengthening the bargaining power of the unorganised workers—it gives them the opportunity to mobilise and organise themselves' (2011: 3). As a result of MGNREGA, the workers get an opportunity to organise and break the 'dictatorship of the private employer'.

If not completely, MGNREGA has also helped in reducing distress migration to urban areas. In the minds of rural migrant labourers migration is associated with hardship and they resort to it only when there is no alternative. There is enough evidence to suggest that the government-guaranteed job closer to home have kept the rural people rooted in the village instead of running to the cities during the slack season. MGNREGA is also making an impact on the earning capacities of women, and will positively affect gender equations in the community (Pankaj and Tankha 2010: 45). There are instances where women have been able to buy books for their children, medicine for ailing family members, rice to feed their family and celebrate festivals. It has enabled women to get the same wage as men. The provisions that are conducive for women are: equal wages, crèches for children of women workers, work within a radius of 5 km from their house, and absence of contractors (Lakshman 2006). These provisions are encouraging and meant to ensure that rural women come out to work and benefit from the scheme as much as possible. As a result of MGNREGA, women have been able to play a more powerful role in decision-making in the family, their dependence on male members for meeting expenditure related to personal needs has reduced, etc., all of which have led to subtle changes in their confidence and bridging gender relations.

Shortcomings

Despite the achievements mentioned earlier, MGNREGA is criticised on a number of grounds. There are many reports which speak of the corruption and misuse of funds provided for the scheme. Corruption has cropped up as one of the major stumbling blocks in the implementation of MGNREGA. This holds true in all those villages where contractors are playing a prominent role despite the fact that contractors or middlemen are completely banned by the Act. These contractors are involved in fudging of muster-rolls, adjustment in work/measurement records, embezzlement and cheating on the material component. The unpleasant nexus among local political leaders, contractors and bureaucrats is responsible for the perpetuation and promotion of corruption. Corruption has thrived through the percentage system whereby all the functionaries receive a fixed percentage of amount released.

In most of the states transparency safeguards have been neglected leading to further corruption. For instance, dual attendance records are maintained—one is the informal notebooks (*kaccha*) at the worksite and official (*pucca*) records maintained elsewhere, making fudging easy. Mandatory website boards consisting of relevant details like wage rate, list of sanctioned workers, implementing agency are not followed. Thus, instead of warning users against the possible inconsistencies in record-keeping, the information system often covers them up.

A common feature in all the states is delayed payment of wages. Payments are made on the basis of the measurement of work done rather than attendance alone. The common practice in most of the states is the maintenance of temporary attendance and measurement records which are formalised later on official muster rolls subject to the approval of junior engineers or the Block Development Officer or the *sarpanch* (head of the gram sabha). The process is quite lengthy and cumbersome leading to delay in payment of wages. Another source of delay is in the release of funds by the state governments. For example, in Bihar, Jharkhand and Karnataka release of funds has been delayed in the past due to poor planning or withholding of funds by the Centre due to Centre–state politics. In the transition from cash to payment of wages through bank accounts, banks and post offices have been overburdened and have therefore contributed to delay in crediting the wages.

MGNREGA also includes provisions for setting up grievance redressal mechanisms which have been sidelined by most state governments. Therefore, in case of violations of entitlements relating to minimum wages, unemployment allowance, etc. there is no mechanism to deal with the complaint of any aggrieved person. The absence of transparency safeguards and lack of a grievance redressal mechanism has raised serious questions about accountability. In the case of violation of MGNREGA provisions, it becomes difficult to ascertain who should be held accountable. Another important criticism is that the completed products of the public works scheme are vulnerable to being taken over by wealthier sections of society. A monitoring study of MGNREGA in Madhya Pradesh showed that the types of activities undertaken there were more or less standardised across villages, suggesting little local consultation. Further, concerns included the fact that corruption in the local government lead to the exclusion of specific sections of society. Local governments have also been found to embezzle funds by claiming job cards for more people than the actual number who work, thereby generating more funds than needed. Bribes as high Rs 50 are paid in order to receive the job cards. There is criticism from construction companies that MGNREGA has affected the availability of labour as labourers prefer working under MGNREGA than working under construction projects. It is also widely criticised that the policy has contributed to farm labour shortage. In July 2011, the government had to advise the states to suspend the MNREGA programme during peak farming periods.

To sum up, MGNREGA is a unique initiative in the history of social security in India. It is not just an employment scheme but also a tool of economic and social change in rural areas. It is definitely a 'silver lining' in the gloom of rural poverty. It is a good beginning to revamping rural economy and thereby leading to reducing the huge rural–urban divide in India. Despite a number of shortcomings, MGNREGA has played a significant role in empowering rural women and curbing gender discrimination. The Act has far reaching economic, social and political significance. Although, MGNREGA is unlikely to succeed without sustained political commitment and public pressure, its enactment is a victory of Indian democracy. It shows that the underprivileged majority is not completely marginalised in the elitist political system. As Drèze shows, with adequate political organisation, the demands of the underprivileged sometimes prevail over privileged interests (2011: 5). If adequate energy with strong political commitment and sustained public pressure is invested in this process, the battle for employment guarantee would definitely be won.

CONCLUDING OBSERVATIONS

Public policies are contextual responses to public anxieties under the prevalent socio-economic circumstances. The policies discussed in this chapter reflect the same spirit. Emerging environmental crises, the poor state of educational and health services and growing poverty and unemployment have forced policymakers across the decades to come out with pragmatic solutions. Public policy, therefore, is not made in a vacuum. It is governed by socio-economic conditions, the political values and public mood, the structure of government, and national and local cultural norms. Public policy can therefore never be conceptualised without reference to these criteria that are critical so far as the actual shape of the policy concerned.

Public policy is an exciting area of human activity. It can never be static because it is dependent on the public sphere, which is always contested. Similarly, newer issues are being articulated to make society a better living space, and while addressing them public policy is constantly expanding its domain. This is supplemented by the proactive role of citizens as custodians of democracy which is no more a passive exercise of citizenship reduced merely to casting votes in periodic elections. Public policy is thus not merely governmental in nature, but social, political and ideological in character.

India is a nation of paradoxes. For example, in the recent past, India has experienced rapid economic growth, but people continue to even meet their basic needs. Economic inequalities have grown and the struggle for survival for those at the grassroots remains grim. Small farmers, artisans, self-employed people and workers have increasingly faced difficult conditions in protecting their livelihoods. In the face of these bitter experiences the question that comes to our mind is: where did we gone wrong? It is with this spirit that major policy issues need to be clearly discussed: what has gone wrong, what are the risks ahead and what correctives ought to be made. Bharat Dogra says:

> The policy-framework for our country should be in conformity with the pressing needs of the entire world for protecting the environment, checking climate change, eliminating weapons of mass destruction, disarmament, peace and ensuring the basic needs for all people. These wider considerations of the entire world should be carefully kept in mind while deciding various policy-options for our country. (2014: 17)

Overall, policymaking is an invitation to construct a desirable future As Shiv Visvanathan (2015) writes:

> The contested nature of public sphere makes it exciting, protean and potentially inventive. It is weaved in a diversity of perspectives which challenges the dominance of one disciplinary approach. For example, economics, which was almost a canonical discipline, now realizes that it confronts a new commons of social sciences which sees its sense of measure as inadequate to understand freedom or suffering. The new developments in feminism, cultural studies, future studies and science studies have added an increasing plurality to the fields of knowledge. Today, the relation between

the "expert" and the "citizen" has changed and new forms of knowledge have to be considered. One sees this particularly in the development of ecological policy. Nature which was once taken for granted or seen as passive in the realm of knowledge is now becoming a part of the social contract. The problems of climate change and the energy crisis have revealed that science and economics are inadequate to answer questions related to ecology.

Today, disciplines like ethics and morality can provide answers to the puzzles of environmental decay, corruption, urban decay and human frustration, which are beyond the reach of science and technology. Thus, policymakers need to address public issues through the lens of interdisciplinarity.

REFERENCES

Basu, D. D. 1998. *Introduction to the Constitution of India*. New Delhi: Prentice-Hall India.

Bijli, Heena K. 2012. *Women and Health: Intersectional Issues and Social Constraints*. New Delhi: Authors Press.

Butcher, Tony. 1995. *Delivering Welfare: The Governance of the Social Services in the 1990s*. Philadelphia: Open University Press.

Central Pollution Control Board (CPCB). 2013. 'Status of Water Quality in India 2011'. Report submitted to the Ministry of Environment and Forests, New Delhi.

Centre for Science and Environment (CSE). 2014. *A Down to Earth Annual State of India's Environment 2014*. New Delhi: CSE.

Dogra, Bharat. 2014. 'Development Path of India: Some Major Policy Issues'. *Mainstream* 52 (9): 13–22.

Drèze, Jean. 2011. 'Employment Guarantee and the Right to Work' in *The Battle for Employment Guarantee*, edited by Reetika Khera. New Delhi: Oxford University Press.

Government of India (GoI). 1964. 'Report of the Education Commission, 1964'. Ministry of Education, New Delhi.

———. 1983. *National Health Policy*. New Delhi: Ministry of Health and Family Welfare. Available at https://www.nhp.gov.in/sites/default/files/pdf/nhp_1983.pdf (accessed 30 June 2016).

———. 1998. 'National Policy on Education'. Department of Education, Ministry of Human Resource Development, New Delhi.

———. 2006. 'National Environment Policy 2006'. Ministry of Environment and Forest, New Delhi.

———. 2013. *Twelfth Five Year Plan (2012–17): Faster, More Inclusive and Sustainable Growth*, vol. 1. New Delhi: Sage, for the Planning Commission.

Government of National Capital Territory of Delhi. 2001. *Eco-club Teachers' Manual*. New Delhi: Department of Environment, Forest and Wildlife.

Guha, Ramchandra. 1989. *The Unquiet Woods: Ecological Change and Peasant Resistance in the Himalaya*. New Delhi: Oxford University Press.

Jain, Ashok K. 2005. *Law and Environment*. Delhi: Ascent Publications.

Janardhanan, Arun. 2011. 'Noise Pollution: Chennai Lives with a Bang'. *Times of India*, 27 April.

Khera, Reetika, ed. 2011. *The Battle for Employment Guarantee*. New Delhi: Oxford University Press.

Lakshman, Nirmala. 2006. 'Employment Guarantee Signs of Transformation'. Opinion, *The Hindu*, 11 May.

Mathew, P. D. 2000. *For Ensuring a Safe Environment Law against Pollution*. New Delhi: Indian Social Institute.

Mukul, Akshaya. 2010. 'Right to Education Comes into Force Today'. *The Times of India*, New Delhi edition, 1 April.

Pankaj, Ashok and Rukmini Tankha. 2010. 'Empowerment Effects of the NREGS on Women Workers: A Study in Four States'. *Economic and Political Weekly* 45 (30): 45–55.

Rajagopalan, R. 2008. *Environmental Education*. New Delhi: Oxford University Press.

Raman, A. Venkat and James Warner Bjorkman. 2009. *Public-Private Partnerships in Health Care in India: Lessons for Developing Countries*. London and New York: Routledge.

Rao, Mohan, ed. 1999. *Disinvesting in Health: The World Bank's Prescriptions for Health*. New Delhi: Sage.

Roy, Arindam. 2016. 'Public Health Policy in India: A Critical Note' in *Public Policy: Concepts, Theory and Practice*, edited by Bidyut Chakrabarty and Prakash Chand, 219–29. New Delhi: Sage Publishing.

Roychowdhury, Anumita, Souparno Banerjee, Papia Samajdar and Sheeba Madan. 2013. *Good News & Bad News: Clearing the Air in Indian Cities*. New Delhi: Centre for Science and Environment.

Sadgopal, Anil. 2009. 'India's Education Policy: A Historical Overview'.*COMBAT Law* 8 (3 and 4): 14–31.

Singh, Shivani. 2016. 'Rights-based Social Policy: Mahatma Gandhi National Rural Employment Guarantee Act (MNREGA), 2005' in *Public Policy: Concepts, Theory and Practice*, edited by Bidyut Chakrabarty and Prakash Chand, 241–48. New Delhi: Sage.

Tata Energy Research Institute (TERI). 2001. *State of Environment Report for Delhi*. New Delhi: TERI.

Times of India. 2001. 'The Birds have Flown the Banks of the River'. New Delhi edition, 7 June.

University Grant Commission (UGC). 2003. *Higher Education in India: Issues, Concerns and New Directions*. New Delhi: UGC.

Visvanathan, Shiv. 2015. 'A New Public Policy for a New India'. *The Hindu*, 6 April.

World Health Organization (WHO). 2010. *The Global Burden of Disease 2010*. Geneva: WHO Press.

Legal Cases

M. C. Mehta vs Union of India (AIR [All India Reporter] 1987 SC 463)

M. C. Mehta vs Union of India (1992 SCC [Supreme Court Cases] 123)

M. C. Mehta vs Union of India (1992 SCC 256)

Munn vs People of India (AIR 1988 SC 236)

Ratlam Municipality vs Vardhichand (AIR 1980 SC 1622)

Rural Litigation and Entitlement Kendra Dehradun vs State of UP (AIR 1985 SC 652)

Union Carbide Corporation vs Union of India (AIR 1990 SC 273)

9

ETHICS IN GOVERNANCE*

HIGHLIGHTS

- Attempting a definition of ethics in governance
- Recommendations of the ARC
- Ethics committees
  - Rajya Sabha ethics committee
  - Lok Sabha ethics committee

Governance is less efficient if there is a decline of ethics in public life. This obvious statement has serious implications in conceptualising public administration as an area of human activity. Two ideas are implicit here: governance is conceptualised as a phenomenon that is contingent on the nature of public life; the other aspect is the link between efficiency and the decline of ethics in public life. Norms, values and principles are supportive of stress-free public life and vital to the creation and consolidation of a space in which a system of behaviour is sought to be built. A norms-driven society is both a shield against delinquent public behaviour and a facilitator of processes that are conducive to the creation of a powerful opinion that is opposed to the derailment of the established values and principles. It is also believed that once ethics is organically linked to the prevalent socio-economic and political circumstances, it is no longer foreign, but becomes part and parcel of those being raised and nurtured in that milieu. As an argument, it is easy to understand because the dwindling of ethics and the nature of governance are dialectically interconnected. Difficulty arises as soon as one engages in trying to arrest the decline of ethics in public life. Challenging the Weberian conceptualisation of public administration as a technical design, the argument reinforces the point that the exact nature of governance, by virtue of being located in specific socio-economic and political contexts, cannot be independent of the stresses and tensions which vary from one milieu to another. One has to, therefore, understand ethics in governance in the wider context of public life which is subject to various influences

* Some sections of this chapter have been developed from Chakrabarty, *Ethics in Governance in India*, pp. 1–40, 140–57. With permission from Taylor & Francis.

that emanate from the society. In simple terms, what is critical here is the importance of those distinctive inputs and influences, not always explicit, that sway the mind of the public official either in favour of strengthening the norms, values and principles or undermining them. The principal concern here is to create circumstances to both boost and weaken these inputs and influences, as required.

Ethics is an important area of enquiry in public administration that cannot be addressed in a monochromatic way given the critical role that the wider public life plays in shaping, if not determining, the way in which governance manifests as an activity in a particular context. This chapter begins with an in-depth analysis of the phenomenon with reference to the available theoretical literature and draws to a close by drawing on the specific experiments that India has undertaken to sustain ethics in public governance. The aim here is to acquaint readers with the processes whereby the concern for ethics in governance is articulated and conceptualised in a historical context.

ATTEMPTING A DEFINITION OF ETHICS IN GOVERNANCE

Governance and ethics are intertwined. A government functions within certain broad moral and ethical parameters that are integrally linked with the sociological foundation of the polity in which it is articulated. The importance of ethics has acquired a significant place in contemporary theoretical discussion around governance, more so because of the growing decadence in governmental practices largely owing to a decline of values in public administration which is perhaps singularly responsible for the rise of 'corruption' in a virulent form. The possible reason is located in the overgrowth of the State in which bureaucracy has become 'rent-seeker' and is no longer performing its Benthamite role of being 'a benevolent guardian'. The World Bank (WB)-sponsored solution is to downsize the State and allow free play of the market and civil society—consolidating the ideology of neo-liberalism. As we have already noted, the question of whether this is an appropriate strategy for developing and underdeveloped nations needs to be addressed underlining the importance of 'public' in public administration. This is a challenge that involves a thorough analysis of the circumstances and the outcome in a historical context because dwindling of ethics in governance is not an overnight phenomenon but an offshoot of a long-term process.

It is difficult to conclusively define the term ethics because it is usually a context-driven conceptualisation. Nevertheless, on the basis of the literature on administrative ethics, one can derive a meaningful definition of what ethics is all about. F. M. Marx (1949) conceptualises the idea by linking it to the prevalent political ideology that the machinery of government is expected to translate into social reality. Public administration is thus an instrument in attaining the purpose of the political order. 'The core of administrative ethics lies', argues Marx, 'in the ideas that nourish the political system' implying thereby that the administrators are not free to follow their own personal values in the course of their professional activities but are obligated to be 'conscious agents of a democratic community' and to direct their action 'toward promoting the healthy growth of a free society dedicated to the common good' (ibid.: 1127–28). Ethics is therefore a set of standards that society places on itself to articulate its responses to societal needs. Mere adoption of rules cannot inject ethics in human behaviour. What is required is a set of mechanisms to execute rules and regulations by putting in place competent disciplinary agencies to investigate violations and deviations, and to impose sanctions quickly and firmly, and thereby promote a culture of integrity.

Corruption is an important manifestation of the failure of ethics. The word 'corrupt' is derived from the Latin word *corruptus* which means 'to break or destroy'. The word 'ethics' is from the Greek word *ethikos* which means 'arising from habit'. Although corruption represents 'deviation' from established norms, there is hardly any universal definition because of its contextual roots. Nonetheless, a definition provided by Friedrich (1989) seems to have captured its complex texture:

> [Corruption is] a kind of behaviour which deviates from the norm actually prevalent or believed to prevail in a given context. … It is a deviant behaviour associated with a particular motivation, namely that of private gain at public expense. … Such private gain may be monetary one, and in the minds of the general public it usually is, but it may take other forms. (Ibid.: 15)

Friedrich's suggestion is corroborated by another recently-articulated definition that states that corruption 'involves the distortion or subversion of the exercise of public office so that it meets public, partisan or sectional rather than public interests, so that some people gain who should not and some lose (or fail to benefit) who should not' (Philip 2015: 22). Key to the rise of corruption, as evident in this conceptualisation, is the decline of ethics in public life which encourages distortion of values. Public office becomes a space to gratify one's corrupt design and the system loses its vitality to combat tendencies striking at its foundation.

ARRESTING DERAILMENT IN GOVERNANCE: RECOMMENDATIONS OF THE ARC[1]

It is unfortunate that in India corruption has, for many, become a matter of habit—ranging from grand corruption involving highly-placed people to retail corruption touching the everyday life of common people. Anti-corruption effots by the government made thus far have been to be ineffectual and there is widespread public cynicism about governmental interventions at tackling corruption. The interventions are seen as mere posturing, without any real intention to bring the corrupt to book. They are also seen as handy political weapons to harass opponents. Corruption is so deeply entrenched in the system that most people regard it as inevitable and any effort to fight it as futile. The cynicism is spreading so fast that it bodes ill for our democratic

[1] This section draws extensively from the fourth and twelfth reports of the ARC (GoI 2007, 2009).

system itself. It is in this background that the Second Administrative Reforms Commission (ARC) was set up by the Indian government to prepare a blueprint to revamp the administrative system and to suggest measures to achieve a pro-active, responsive, accountable, sustainable and efficient administration for the country at all levels of government. The ARC met and heard from the various sections of the public during its visits across the country, and presented a series of reports.

According to the ARC, governance has to be ethics-conscious and so long as public servants are not accountable, steps towards creating an ethics-driven administration shall never be effective. What is thus required most is the empowerment of citizens in order to hold those in authority accountable and make them sensitive to their duties and responsibilities. Empowerment of citizens is easier said than done. Hence the ARC referred to certain powerful instruments which are useful in making citizens integral to governance: generating opportunities and incentives to promote the participation of proactive citizens, involvement of stakeholders in delivery of public services, public consultation in decision-making, social auditing, Right to Information and Citizens' Charters. Known as designs for external accountability, these instruments involve citizens while governance is articulated and also executed. These devices of accountability not only catapult the citizens to the centre-stage of governance but also promote integrity and prejudice-free decision-making in administration. With their integral role in rule-setting and execution, citizens become, in the new dispensation, critical to public authority. It has thus been argued that 'by involving citizens in monitoring government performance, demanding and enhancing transparency and exposing government failures and misdeeds … [these] accountability mechanisms are potentially powerful tools against … corruption and tendencies derailing governance' (Bhattacharya 2013: 273). This is the core of social accountability that relies on 'civic engagement, i.e. in which it is ordinary citizens and/or civil society organizations who participate directly or indirectly in exacting accountability' (Malena, Forster and Singh 2004: 3). Complementary to the internal mechanisms of accountability, social accountability mechanisms 'allow ordinary citizens to access information, voice their needs and demand accountability between elections … [and also] enhance the ability of citizens to move beyond mere protest toward engaging with bureaucrats and politicians in a more informed, organized, constructive and systematic manner, thus increasing the chances of effecting positive change' (ibid.: 5). These ideas are reflected in ARC's suggestion of instruments to arrest debasement of governance. The administrative and ideological steps that the ARC has proposed show that serious attempts have been made by the government to re-conceptualise governance in the globalising world where governance is no longer a captive of bureaucracy but is also drawn on what citizens feel most appropriate for their well-being.

What is striking here is the fact that unlike the Weberian notion of accountability which seeks to bring about a compatibility of interests between top-down policy and bottom-line implementation, the ARC insists on instruments which are driven by external agencies. Hierarchical governance is detrimental to public participation in decision-making since hierarchy 'creates more ethical problems than it solves, by fostering inequality, an inappropriate level of instrumentalism on the basis of technical rationality, and agency inattention to the needs of the community' (Stivers 1994: 444). Hence the argument for participatory governance gains far more credibility insisting on creating a situation 'for encouraging participation of the citizenry in the process of planning and providing public goods and services' (Cooper 1991: 141).

Nolan Principles

A report of the ARC (GoI 2007) has also tackled the subject of ethical values in politics. The ARC identifies that politics and those engaged in it are vital to governance as they form the Legislative and Executive branches of the State. The acts of commission and omission of these branches, while working the Constitution and the rule of law, become the point of intervention for the Judiciary. Aware of the fact that 'it is unrealistic and simplistic to expect perfection in politics in an ethically imperfect environment', the ARC states that 'there is no denying … that the standards set in politics profoundly influence those in other aspects of governance' (ibid.: 8). At this juncture, it mentions the Nolan principles as foundational ideas for a discussion on ethics in politics. These principles were identified by the 1994 Committee on Standards in Public Life in the United Kingdom as necessary for governance, and they are:

1. *Selflessness*: Holders of public office take decisions solely in terms of public interest. They should not do so in order to gain financial or other material benefits for themselves, their family or their friends.
2. *Integrity*: Holders of public office should not place themselves under any financial or other obligation to outside individuals or organisations that might influence them in the performance of their official duties.
3. *Objectivity*: In carrying out public business, including making public appointments, awarding contracts or recommending individuals for rewards or benefits, holders of public office should make choices on the basis of merit.
4. *Accountability*: Holders of public office are accountable for their decisions and actions to the public and must submit themselves to whatever scrutiny is appropriate to their office.
5. *Openness*: Holders of public office should be as open as possible about all the decisions and actions they take. They should give reasons for their decisions and restrict information only in the wider public interest.
6. *Honesty*: Holders of public office have a duty to declare any private interest relating to their public duties and to take steps to resolve any conflict arising in a way that protects the public interest.
7. *Leadership*: Holders of public office should promote and support these principles by leadership and example. (GoI 2007: 19–20)

Drawing on these Nolan principles, the ARC stipulates the following steps to ensure ethical behaviour in public life:

1. Codifying ethical norms and practices
2. Disclosing personal interest to avoid conflict between public interests and personal gain
3. Creating a mechanism for enforcing the relevant rules
4. Providing norms for qualifying and disqualifying a public functionary from office (ibid.: 19)

Code of Ethics

On the basis of the above directions, the ARC felt that there should be a Code of Ethics, especially for the ministers who are primarily public servants in a democratic form of governance. This is besides the already-existing Code of Conduct which ensures accountability. The Commission provides a long checklist of activities while articulating the Code of Conduct for ministers:

1. Ministers must uphold the highest ethical standards
2. Ministers must uphold the principle of collective responsibility
3. Ministers should have a duty to Parliament to account, and be held to account, for the policies, decisions and actions of their department and agencies
4. Ministers must ensure that no conflict arises or appears to arise, between their public duties and their private interests
5. Ministers in the Lok Sabha must keep separate their roles as minister and constituency member
6. Ministers must not use government resources for party or political purposes; they must accept responsibility for decisions taken by them and not merely blame it on wrong advice
7. Ministers must uphold the political impartiality of the Civil Services and not ask civil servants to act in any way that would be in conflict with their duties and responsibilities
8. Ministers must comply with the requirements that the two Houses of Parliament lay down from time to time
9. Ministers must recognise that misuse of official position or information is violation of the trust reposed in them as public functionaries
10. Ministers must ensure that public money is used with utmost economy and care
11. Minsters must function in such a manner as to serve as instruments of good governance and to provide services for the betterment of the public at large and foster socio-economic development
12. Ministers must act objectively, impartially, honestly, equitably, diligently and in a fair and just manner (GoI 2007: 26–27)

A checklist notwithstanding, the Code of Ethics also represents efforts towards creating an environment in which public functionaries are made to abide by certain basic rules while discharging their role. These are not new ideas, but what is distinctive about them is the force with which they have been articulated—these are State-sponsored ideas which were upheld to redesign governance by setting a specific Code of Ethics for those involved in governance. Nonetheless, not only are these steps well-directed, they are also context-driven since the decadence in governance in India was also the result of the abdication of ethics by those holding public office. In that respect, the ARC has set in motion processes where the Code of Ethics have become integral to the Code of Conduct. While it is true that 'the enunciation of ethical values and code of conduct puts moral pressure on public functionaries' (GoI 2007), they require effective monitoring and need to be backed by an enforcement agency within the Legislative; otherwise, they lose their meaning, especially between elections.

Article 311

The other serious recommendation relates to Article 311 of the Constitution which accords special constitutional guarantee to those in the Civil Services—even if they are implicated in charges of corruption, they cannot be dismissed by an authority subordinate to that by which s/he was appointed. The immunity granted by this provision, introduced by the Government of India Act of 1919, seems to have been utilised to placate the misdeeds of civil servants. The founders of our nation did not have to confront a situation where a constitutional guarantee is being misconstrued as an instrument to consolidate one's fiefdom in governance. In fact, the 1964 Santhanam Committee had expressed concern that the undue protection this provision accorded to civil servants was a source of corruption (GoI 1964: 39–40). Persuaded by the fact that corrupt officials need to be weeded out to generate public faith in public authority, the ARC was reluctant to extend the favour of the constitutional provision to civil servants. The ARC thus believes that

> The rights of a civil servant under the Constitution should be subordinate to the overall requirement of public interests and contractual rights of the State. It cannot be an argument that a corrupt civil servant's rights are more important than the need to ensure an honest, efficient and corruption-free administration. Ultimately, the public servant, an agent of the State, cannot be superior to the State and it is his fundamental duty to serve the State with integrity, devotion, honesty, impartiality, objectivity, transparency and accountability. (GoI 2007: 97)

In the words of the ARC, there exists 'a fairly common perception that explicit articulation of protection in the Constitution itself gives an impression of inordinate protection'. This led the ARC to suggest that 'on balance, Article 311 need not continue to be a part of the Constitution' (ibid.). In order to withdraw undue protection to the civil service, the ARC made the unequivocal recommendation to repeal Article 311 and enact appropriate legislations to provide protection to public servants against arbitrary action as guaranteed under Article 309. This is a very useful recommendation with far-reaching impact on public governance. In a democratic system where power emanates from the ballot box, extraordinary protection to civil servants amounts to contributing to a prejudiced system of governance. By instinct, bureaucracy has the urge for unwarranted power and it happens so often, especially when politicians lack the required technical ability to translate their ideological commitments to action. By way of helping them, bureaucrats become policymakers and tend to bend or distort rules to please their political bosses; this becomes a habit. In view of their constitutional protection (à la Article 311) and India's cumbersome judicial processes, civil servants seem to have been encouraged to resort to such malpractices of manipulating rules and regulations. Honest members of the Civil Services remain marginalised, while their colleagues, owing to their help to the political masters, hog the limelight. In such a gloomy scenario, the de-constitutionalising of Article 311 will have serious implications in the drive towards creating and consolidating an ethics-driven public governance.

Election-related Expenses

Indiscriminate and illegal funding of elections by businesses and corporate houses create an environment of *quid pro quo* arrangement. In return for the electoral funding, the winning candidate grants a favour when in power. It is striking that this issue was a cause of alarm to the Santhanam Committee in 1964 and continues to remain five decades later too. According to the ARC, '[e]xcesses in elections (in campaign-funding, use of illegitimate money, quantum of expenditure, imperfect electoral rolls, impersonation, booth-capturing, violence, inducements and intimidation), floor-crossing after elections to get into power and abuse of power in public office [have] became major afflictions of the political process' (GoI 2007: 8). What seems to have aggravated the situation is large, illegal and illegitimate expenditure during elections which is, the ARC underlines, 'another root cause of corruption' (ibid.: 9). Hence '[c]leansing elections is the most important route to improve ethical standards in politics, to curb corruption and rectify maladministration' (ibid.). And the ARC makes the following suggestions in the context of election funding:

- A system for partial state funding should be introduced in order to reduce the scope of illegitimate and unnecessary funding of expenditure for elections.
- The issue of disqualification of members on grounds of defection should be decided by the President/Governor on the advice of the Election Commission.
- Section 8 of the Representation of the People Act, 1951 needs to be amended to disqualify all persons facing charges related to grave and heinous offences and corruption, with the modification suggested by the Election Commission.
- The Constitution should be amended to ensure that if one or more parties in a coalition with a common programme mandated by the electorate either explicitly before the elections or implicitly while forming the government realign midstream with one or more parties outside the coalition, then members of that party or parties shall have to seek a fresh mandate from the electorate. (Ibid.: 13–15)

Decadent Moral Fabric

Similar to the Santhanam Committee report that attributed the decline of ethics in governance to 'the lack of moral alertness ... [hampering] the growth of strong traditions of integrity and efficiency' (GoI 1964: 139), the ARC also insisted on 'the inculcation of values facilitating the subordination of the self to a larger societal good' (GoI 2007: 41). This cannot be achieved overnight. But a conducive environment can be created by adopting complementary rules and regulations in which these values are well-appreciated. The ARC is thus of the view that there should be a set of public service values which should be stipulated by law. As in the case of Australia, there should be a mechanism to ensure that civil servants constantly aspire towards these values. The commission appreciates the values prescribed in the draft Public Services Bill, 2006 which was later made into an Act. The salient 'values' informing the Act are:

- Allegiance to the various ideals enshrined in the preamble to the Constitution
- Apolitical functioning
- Good governance for betterment of the people to be the primary goal of civil service
- Duty to act objectively and impartially
- Accountability and transparency in decision-making
- Maintenance of highest ethical standards
- Merit to be the criteria in selection of civil servants consistent, however, with the cultural, ethnic and other diversities of the nation
- Ensuring economy and avoidance of wastage in expenditure
- Provision of healthy and congenial work environment
- Communication, consultation and cooperation in performance of functions, i.e. participation of all levels of personnel in management (ibid.: 43)

As it envisages a public code of conduct and a public service management code, insisting on specific duties and responsibilities, the Act is a major intervention as far as public service is concerned. Keeping in view the importance of the public in public services, the Act lays out its basic goal by suggesting that (*a*) good governance is an inalienable right of the citizens in a democracy, (*b*) good governance should be participatory, accountable, governed by the rule of law, informed by equity and inclusiveness, effective and efficient, and (*c*) a politically neutral, professional, accountable and efficient public service is an essential instrument for promotion of good governance.[2] In order to fulfil its aim, the ARC recommends for a Public Service Authority to ensure that the Code of Conduct is sincerely followed. If stringent punitive measures are

[2] 'Draft Public Services Bill, 2006', available at PRS http://www.prsindia.org/uploads/media/vikas_doc/docs/1241499740~~DraftPublicServicesBill2006.pdf (accessed 14 August 2015).

applied to punish those deviating from the Code of Conduct, the ARC emphatically believes that corruption in public services will be significantly reduced.

Role of Civil Society

As the section above adumbrates, the arrangement that the ARC proposes is perhaps the best in putting the Civil Services in India back on track. It also confirms that institutional back-up is an adequate shield against the debasement of public services. Implicit here is also the argument that institutional support can never be effective unless there is adequate social back-up, i.e. social values supportive of corruption-free Civil Services need to be streamlined and strengthened wherever necessary. It has thus been argued:

> A strong and vigilant civil society can be a check on corruption and form the basis for countervailing action. ... Even the most comprehensive set of formal democratic institutions may not be in a position to produce the needed accountability in the absence of a strong and vigilant civil society to energize them.[3]

Civil society in India does not seem to be too organised to create a powerful voice. Nonetheless, there have been instances where civil society activism has been very effective in forcing the State to consider and deliberate on the demands that had roots in civil society. These are, however, stray instances because the civil-society-driven participatory governance is still in its infancy in India. Social disapproval is hardly a deterrent here unlike in Japan where social shaming of civil servants of questionable integrity is an effective form of reining in deviant public officials. In Japan, political embarrassment also acts as an effective deterrent to the truant public authority. The Indian situation, however, is different and the deviation from the established Code of Conduct causes embarrassment and may also evoke punishment, if caught, though it cannot be a permanently effective deterrent to those who resort to corruption for personal gains.

Protection to Whistleblowers

According to the ARC, the role of whistleblowers is critical in exposing the corrupt public servants. This is possible if there exists an alert citizenry which is also sensitive to its moral commitment and responsibility. Since theirs is clearly a social cause, citizens should feel empowered when they are involved in such a feat. There is every possibility that the whistleblowers restrain themselves fearing adverse consequences. This can be addressed meaningfully by establishing a complementary social environment in which the efforts of whistleblowers are always appreciated and respected. This is one way of encouraging those who appear to be less fearful of the consequences. There is another that the ARC strongly suggests: whistleblowers need to be protected with adequate

---

[3] Speech by M. Veerappa Moily, Chairman, Second Administrative Reforms Commission, on the occasion of the National Colloquium on Ethics in Governance, 'Moving from Rhetoric to Results', held on 1 September 2006; reproduced in GoI (2007: 223).

legal protection in case they suffer due to their role in unearthing the roots of corruption. In its recommendations, the ARC reiterates the views of the Law Commission of India and forcefully argues for the following steps to protect whistleblowers:

1. Whistleblowers exposing false claims, fraud or corruption should be protected by ensuring confidentiality and anonymity, protection from victimisation in career, and other administrative measures to prevent bodily harm and harassment.
2. The legislation should cover corporate whistleblowers unearthing fraud or serious damage to public interest by wilful acts of omission or commission.
3. Acts of harassment or victimisation of or retaliation against a whistleblower should be treated as criminal offence with substantial penalty and sentence. (GoI 2007: 78–79)

These are very useful suggestions that the ARC makes while seeking to provide legal protection which may not however be meaningful unless there is adequate social back-up. Being aware of this interconnection between what society transmits and the role of whistleblowers, the ARC points out that what is critical in arresting the governance debasement is

> the citizens' voice which can be effectively used to expose, denounce and restrain corruption. This calls for the engagement of civil society … in educating citizens about the evils of corruption, raising their awareness levels and securing their participation by giving them a voice. This also introduces a new dimension of accountability [which is contrary to] to the traditional horizontal mechanisms of legislative and legal accountability of the Executive and internal vertical accountability. (Ibid.: 125)

Increasing Civic Engagement

There are two fundamental points that the ARC has raised here: (*a*) besides external accountability, constant civic engagement also serves as a deterrent to practices thriving on corruption; (*b*) out of civic engagement emerges a powerful citizens' voice, which also acts as an effective hurdle to those preferring corrupt means for self-aggrandisement. The ARC notes that civic engagement is generally a spontaneous endeavour that has 'emerged out of an urge to serve the needs of the common man … [although] the state can create an environment whereby citizens' groups can effectively participate in its efforts to root out corruption' (ibid.: 127). Insisting that citizens should be made integral to governance to combat tendencies towards appropriating administration for private interests, the ARC recommends that

1. Citizens' charter should be made effective by stipulating the service levels and also the remedy if these services are not met
2. Citizens may be involved in the assessment and maintenance of ethics in important government institutions and offices
3. Reward schemes should be introduced to incentivise citizens' initiatives

4. School awareness programmes should be introduced, highlighting the importance of ethics and how corruption can be combated (ibid.: 129–30)

The Commission is also aware that an adequate social backing of these measures is assures their effective articulation. Governance is a collaborative act which succeeds not because of the institutions, but because of the support it receives from the citizenry. The more ethically-sensitive the government is the more support it generates among those endorsing its spirit.

Social Audit

One of the powerful instruments to ascertain ethics in governance happens to be social audit, as per the ARC:

> Social audit through client or beneficiary groups or civil society is a check on the wrong doing in procurement of products and services for government, in the distribution of welfare payments, in the checking of attendance of teachers, students in schools and hostels, staff in the hospitals and a host of other similar citizen service-oriented activities of government. (GoI 2007: 133)

The ARC report further elaborates that social audit is an interface between the State and citizens, where the latter play a critical role in fulfilling what the former is expected to do as a service provider. The idea that citizens are integral to governance is further reconfirmed. Social audit is fundamental in conceptualising governance as a philosophy of collective action and the ARC, by reiterating the idea, has reconfirmed once again how important it is in fulfilling the primary ideological goal that a government represents.

Ombudsman

This discussion on ethics in governance, though selective, shall remain incomplete without a brief note on the Commission's recommendation on the importance of the Lok Pal as an ombudsman to effectively address the issue of corruption in India. In line with the suggestion of the Santhanam Committee, the Central Vigilance Commission (CVC) came into being in 1964. Although the CVC was effective in raising a voice against corruption, it did not appear to be adequate in rooting out corruption. The other agency which is also critical in corruption-related cases and responsible for domestic security is the Central Bureau of Investigation (CBI), established in 1941 as the Special Police Establishment and re-christened as CBI in 1963. Deriving its authority from the 1946 Delhi Special Police Establishment Act, the CBI is responsible to investigate certain specified offences or classes of offences pertaining to corruption and other kinds of malpractices involving public servants. Although there are institutions for addressing cases of corruption in public life, 'the working of many of these anti-corruption bodies', the ARC laments, 'leaves much to be desired' (ibid.: 108). In light of rather disappointing performances of the available instruments, the ARC felt the need to create a national ombudsman or Lok Pal, which was also recommended by the First Administrative

Reforms Commission in 1964. However, the Lok Pal Bill was not made into a law due to various politico-ideological reasons though it was believed that Lok Pal could have become an effective instrument to weed out corruption from public life. In 2011, the demand for a Lok Pal provoked a Delhi-based campaign that had national implications. Similar to the institution of the ombudsman of Scandinavian countries which acts as a bulwark of democratic government against the tyranny of officialdom, the Lok Pal was conceptualised as a watchdog responsible for ascertaining the values of integrity among ministers and members of Parliament. In order to discharge its role most effectively, it was authorised to punish the truant members for violating the Code of Ethics. A serious endeavour notwithstanding, the Bill has so far been shelved since policy-makers have failed to arrive at a consensus presumably because of the obvious attack on their impunity. The expression Lok Pal has now been replaced by Lokayukta, which is the ARC's preferred vocabulary.

As suggestions, these recommendations are fine and probably reflective of the public concern for effective anti-corruption measures. In terms of substance, these suggestions are not new, but are repeated in a different language. Corruption continues to remain a menace in public life presumably because of the clear absence of a complementary social climate in which corruption can hardly flourish. This has two serious policy implications: on the one hand, the creation of multiple institutions for containment of corruption seems to be vacuous unless they have organic roots in the polity. On the other hand, while the Lok Pal or Lokayukta seems to have institutional sheen, it is unlikely to receive the nod of policy-makers simply because of the threat that they would lose their political immunity once these institutions are put to place. So it is politico-ideological constraints that are impediments to even constitutionally recognising these agencies. This also directs our attention to the fact that partisan aims prevails over the public concern for corruption-free governance in India. This is a reality though there have been constant endeavours to make various instruments part of the constitutional set-up to root out corruption by giving exemplary punishment to those indulging in corruption and malpractices.

ETHICS COMMITTEES

The two chambers of the Indian Parliament, Lok Sabha and Rajya Sabha, have also expressed concern over the decline of ethics in governance. Inspired by the functioning of the ethics committees in both houses of the US Congress, the Rajya Sabha took the lead and formed an Ethics Committee in 1997. The Lok Sabha quickly followed suit and the Lok Sabha Ethics Committee came into being in 2000. Based on their desire to revive public faith in institutions of governance, these committees made useful recommendations, partly drawing on some of the available codes of conduct and partly derived from practices followed elsewhere. Since the Rajya Sabha Ethics Committee was formed earlier, we will deal with that first and then follow it up with a discussion of its Lok Sabha counterpart.

The Rajya Sabha Ethics Committee

In response to the findings of the 1994 Vohra Committee report that highlighted the nexus between criminal gangs, police, bureaucracy and politicians, an all-party meeting convened in 1995 felt the need to set up a 'Parliamentary Committee on Ethics as distinct from the Committee of Privileges which would act as a guardian on the activities of members of Parliament'. It was also decided that Rajya Sabha needed to have 'an internal mechanism' which would act as 'a self-regulatory body' for the members of that chamber. The idea was justified by stating that 'a well-functioning Ethics Committee and well laid out procedures were the best guarantee for a correct perception in the public about an in-house mechanism for ensuring the ethical conduct of members'.[4] In his welcome address, S. B. Chavan, the chairman of the all-party meeting, justified the formation of the committee by saying:

> By and large, the ideological base and the spirit of service which activates most of the politicians is getting eroded and the kind of elements who are trying to influence the political parties and political system at large, make everybody think as to how we can possibly bring about probity in the entire system. The formation of the Ethics Committee as one of the instruments to ensure value-based politics has become imperative in the present situation. ... The Committee will persuade the members not to do such things which, perhaps, were beyond the accepted norms of behaviour.[5]

Sikander Bakht, then leader of the opposition in the Rajya Sabha, was far more categorical in his condemnation of politicians who were held responsible for the decline of ethics in public life:

> Our character is viewed with suspicion. Our tribe lost the faith of the people. Corruption has permeated not only the tribe of politicians but also society at large ... [and] I believe the constitution of Ethics Committee is the need of the hour. The politicians are on the receiving end of people's criticism and complaint. There is a great need to improve this image of politicians. The Ethics Committee may perhaps be of some help.[6]

The Rajya Sabha Ethics Committee remains a milestone in India's parliamentary politics for two reasons: on the one hand, it articulated the concern of the parliamentarians who were alarmed at the rapid decline of ethics in governance; on the other hand, it also reinforced the public outcry against the abuse of the government machinery for personal gains. In its first report of 1999, the Committee attributed the decline of moral values among those in public life to the lackadaisical attitude of political parties in selecting candidates to fight elections. The Committee observed that it was mainly the responsibility of political parties to prevent persons with criminal antecedents from entering political processes. It urged political parties to be selective while

---

[4] These extracts have been reproduced from the Rajya Sabha Debates with the permission of the Hon'ble Chairman, Rajya Sabha. See www.rajyasabha.nic.in/rsnew/publication_election/ethics_committee.pdf (accessed 12 August 2015), 6.

[5] Ibid., 26.

[6] Ibid., 28.

recruiting candidates for membership in Rajya Sabha or other institutions/organisations where they will engage in public work.

Similar to the Vohra Committee, the Rajya Sabha Ethics Committee took serious note of criminalisation of politics. While criminalisation of politics cannot be weeded out so easily, given its deep roots in socio-political processes, it will be easier to undertake meaningful electoral reforms. The Committee thus felt that 'the laws and rules … have not had the desired effect … and the problem of criminalization of politics and its causes and effects cannot be tackled by legislation alone'.[7] Instead of taking a legalistic view, the Committee decided to interact with the political parties to evolve a Code of Conduct for the members. Insisting that political parties should avoid nominating those with criminal records, the Committee echoed the suggestion made by the Santhanam Committee. The most serious problem that attracted maximum attention of the Committee was the role of money power in elections. It admitted that 'large sums of money and other monetary benefits encourage the electorate for [parliamentary elections] leading sometime to the defeat of the official candidate belonging to their own political party'.[8] The committee endorsed the need for electoral reforms, including 'the revision of ceiling on election expenses, corporate or State funding of political parties, foreign donations to them, among others'.[9] It identified the need 'to incorporate suitable provisions in the existing electoral laws with a view to breaking the nexus between the money power and elections'.[10] In line with the Nolan Committee Standards, it felt that once the loopholes in the procedures were sealed, most of the complaints of public grievance could satisfactorily be addressed. This is easier said than done since the vested interests are too powerful to give away the advantages of being financially supported during election campaigns, and the nexus between money power and election cannot be wished away so easily.

The concern for ethics for members of the Rajya Sabha figured prominently in the recommendations of the Committee which believed that

> the Members of Rajya Sabha should acknowledge their responsibility to maintain the public trust reposed in them and should work diligently to discharge their mandate for the common good of the people. They must hold in high esteem the Constitution, the Law, Parliamentary Institutions and, above all, the general public. They should commonly strive to translate the ideals laid down in the Preamble to the Constitution into a reality. (Quoted in GoI 2007: 30)

The Committee set a specific Code of Conduct which drew on the desire for establishing high moral standards. This is an elaborate checklist of dos and don'ts, applicable for the members of the Rajya Sabha who are elected to serve the public. Comprising fifteen items, the Code of Conduct was primarily a set of authoritative directions that members have to follow to morally

[7] Ibid., 9.

[8] Ibid., 12.

[9] Ibid., 9.

[10] Ibid.

justify their role as part of public policymaking. Three major instructive items are reproduced here to highlight the thrust of the recommendations:

1. In their dealings, if Members find that there is conflict between their personal interests and the public trust, which they hold, they should resolve such a conflict in a manner that their private interests are subordinated to the duty of their public office
2. Members should always see that their private financial interests and those of the members of their immediate family do not come in conflict with the public interest and if any such conflict ever arises, they should try to resolve such a conflict in a manner that the public interest is not jeopardised
3. Members should never expect or accept any fee, remuneration or benefit for a vote given or not given by them on the floor of the House, for introducing a Bill, for moving a resolution, putting a question or abstaining from asking a question or participating in the deliberations of the House or a Parliamentary Committee. (GoI 2007: 30–31)

Therefore, continuous efforts have been made to create an environment appreciative of the importance of ethics in public life. The Rajya Sabha Ethics Commitee stated that 'the meaningful electoral reforms be carried out … [so that] political life and processes be free of the adverse impact on governance of undesirable extraneous factors including criminalization'.[11] What is being emphasised here is institutional reforms are capable of reforming one's habit when one becomes a member of the house. Undoubtedly, institutional reforms are an effective means, provided they are backed by equally effective mechanisms which are not guided by partisan political priorities. Unless this is appreciated by those involved in policymaking, institutional reforms shall hardly be meaningful.

The decline of ethics in governance cannot be completely done away merely with institutional reforms. Appropriate steps to create processes for change in the wider social environment are also required to be undertaken. The efforts of the Ethics Committee will be futile if the values of ethics are not sincerely upheld by the wider public. Hence it is apprehended that the exercise will completely be wasted if it not complemented by parallel endeavours in evolving practices appreciative of ethics in public life. While identifying the Ethics Committee as certainly a definite step towards strengthening the campaign for ethics in public life, it was argued that

> The Ethics Committee is not intended as an essay in idealism, but as an exercise in pragmatic politics. It does not seek to usher in a moralistic regime in Parliament, but common ethical standards and decency in the conduct of its members, including, of course, ministers. … It will help in dissipating the widely held belief that "politics is a dirty game" repeated often by politicians and

[11] Ibid., 24.

> the public with some sort of acceptance of the inevitability of unethical behaviour in the practice of the political game.[12]

As mentioned earlier, the appointment of an Ethics Committee is is not enough if public life is vitiated to a significant extent. Only through 'continuous and proactive efforts ... greater transparency, probity and accountability in public life [are] ensured'.[13] These are values which are critical in evolving conditions appreciative of ethics-driven governance. Key to such a system of governance are citizens who hold the substance of participatory democracy. Therefore, the arguments in support of ethics in public life endorse the view that 'citizens are equal partners in all spheres of national endeavours, and not simply the beneficiaries of governmental initiatives'.[14] What it reinforces is the fundamental argument that institutional initiatives do not seem to be effective unless they receive adequate backing from the wider social environment. This is however not to argue that the former is absolutely futile; on the contrary, they remain critical in raising issues of ethics in the public domain which may further expedite effective campaigns in its favour. So it will not be an exaggeration to suggest that the dialectical interconnection between internal initiatives and the wider social milieu helps build the momentum for ethics in public life.

The Lok Sabha Ethics Committee

Unlike the Rajya Sabha Ethics Committee, the Lok Sabha Ethics Committee took a rather narrow view while suggesting remedies for decadence in governance. In its first report of 2001, this Ethics Committee reiterated that 'norms of ethical behaviour for members of the legislature had been "adequately provided for" in the rules and procedure, directions by the Speaker and in the convention which has evolved over the years on the basis of the recommendations made by various Parliamentary Committees' (quoted in GoI 2007: 205). So, steps towards containing decadence were very simple: the remedy with regard to unethical behaviour on the part of the legislators lay 'in the strict enforcement of the existing norms' (ibid.). Apart from the prevalent norms, members should abide by the following general ethical principles:

1. Members must utilise their position to advance the well-being of the people
2. In case of conflict between their personal interest and public interest, they must resolve the conflict so that personal interests are subordinate to the duty of public office
3. Conflict between private financial/family interest should be resolved in a manner that public interest is not jeopardised
4. Members holding public office should use public resources in such a manner as may lead to public good

---

[12] Ibid., 35.

[13] 'Resolution adopted by the Rajya Sabha on the occasion of the Golden Jubilee of Independence, 26 August–1 September 1997'. Reproduced in www.rajyasabha.nic.in/rsnew/publication_election/ethics_committee.pdf (accessed 12 August 2015), 24.

[14] Ibid.

5. Members must keep uppermost in their mind the fundamental duties listed in Article 51A, Part IVA of the Constitution
6. Members should maintain high standards of morality, dignity, decency and values in public life (ibid.: 31)

The approach that the Rajya Sabha Ethics Committee adopted was all-inclusive because along with creating and consolidating institutional back-ups it also suggested changes in the wider social environment, presumably because of its complementary role in creating a propitious environment for reform. Its Lok Sabha counterpart held the contrary view that internal institutional mechanisms were adequate to guide members in accordance with the best of ethical values. That is, the rules are in place—the system suffers because the rules are not properly implemented. This is a difficult proposition with a very limited appeal, though it is true that tendencies towards encouraging deviation in governance are likely to be curbed to a significant extent if the rules are stringently applied regardless of class, caste and idealogy—tendencies which seem to have been continuously boosted, instead of being discouraged, due to very specific socio-economic and ideological circumstances. Despite being politically free, India is perhaps one of those countries in the developing world that suffers due to the elite capture of political authority which impedes, to a great extent, the processes towards democratising governance and has resulted in the marginalisation of a large segment of the populace. This is probably key to understanding the decline of ethics in public life because, if governance is democratised, it will create space for the peripheral sections who, despite being franchised, continue to remain mere pawns in the chess of politics. Since ethics is a socio-psychological phenomenon, endeavours towards enforcing it through institutional means can never be successful. What is thus needed is a substantial overhauling of the social environment in which individuals are psychologically inclined to uphold those ethical values. Although there is a consensus that social environment is critical, the role of institutional changes cannot be undermined. By meting out exemplary punishment to those abusing public authority, the available institutional mechanisms help build a momentum in the wider social milieu which, if guided properly, is likely to trigger a bigger campaign for reform in governance. Hence, it is always argued that they are dialectically interconnected: institutional steps are useful inputs for social awareness and impulses from society do not allow the institutions to remain indifferent when they are strong enough to involve large segments of population. As history has shown, this is how the concern for ethics has become an integral component of democratic governance in which citizens, by virtue of being its core, always remain an important source of input for public authority.

CONCLUDING OBSERVATIONS

Ideally speaking, public administration is an ethics-driven exercise which means that it is articulated keeping in view those normative values which are tuned to impersonal goals and objectives. An analysis of how public administration functions in specific socio-economic contexts, however, reveals that the situation is otherwise: public administration is being continuously utilised for gratifying partisan/personal needs. The inevitable outcome is endemic corruption in governance. It has thus been argued that regardless of various control-mechanisms, corruption is 'a particularly viral form of bureaupathology', which is 'debilitating' and also 'contagious' (Caiden 1994: 320). This needs to be treated before it causes devastation. One can possibly think of specific administrative steps that evolve internally, but may not be adequate to conclusively root-out the sources of corruption in administration, presumably because of the prevalence of a well-entrenched mindset supporting deviation from established norms of public morality. Administrative reform is transitional, if not futile, unless it is backed by meaningful efforts at changing the overall political environment in which administration is grounded.

So, the basic question that needs to be asked is why this is so. The reasons are to be located in the maze of things in which public administration unfolds. Generally, the decline of ethics is attributed to morality-deficit in public life, which implies that the roots of decadence are spread out in the wider socio-economic milieu. The argument hinges on the decline of public morality to explain the visible ethics-deficit in public administration. What is public morality then? Waldo provides a list of twelve obligations which, if respected, will create a solid foundation for public morality and halt the dwindling of ethics in public administration:

> [1] obligation to the constitution, [2] obligation to law, [3] obligation to nation or country, [4] obligation to democracy, [5] obligation to organizational-bureaucratic norms, [6] obligation to profession and professionalism [7] obligation to family and friends, [8] obligation to self, [9] obligation to middle-range collectivities, [10] obligation to public interests or general welfare, [11] obligation to the humanity or the world, [12] obligation to religion or God. (Waldo 1996: 463–65)

This is a checklist of items which one has to respect to meaningfully realise public morality in its substantial sense. However, the conceptually pervasive checklist will be futile unless there are parallel efforts to consolidate a social ambience in which these obligations are universally respected. This is undoubtedly a hard task that cannot be accomplished overnight. Nonetheless, by articulating the various obligations that are necessary for public morality, Waldo has set the stage for a discussion over this issue.

The concern for public morality reverberated when Ambedkar introduced the idea of constitutional morality which, according to him, held the key to making public administration truly public. In his conceptualisation of constitutional morality, ethics is understood as critical moral values a specific that shape mindset, and is appreciative of responsibility and accountability. Given the fact that public functionaries are 'trustees of the people' in a democracy (GoI 2007: 19), the former is dialectically connected with the latter. The authority exercised by those in governance is thus not arbitrarily exercised, but conceptually drawn on public interests. For a morally-sensitive political order, appropriate laws and rules need to be made, and the public functionaries are to be imbued with the required moral values allowing the system to remain viable. The concern for public well-being is a key to perfect governance, which is conceivable if those responsible for governance are made aware of their constitutional obligations when in power. It is true that punitive measures, justified by laws, are restraining devices; they also create an environment in which civic virtues for upholding the constitutional values are nurtured. But this is short-lived unless a conducive environment is created in which the values of constitutional morality are ingrained. In the absence of constitutional morality, the operation of the Constitution, no matter how carefully written, 'tends to become arbitrary, erratic and capricious' (Béteille 2008: 36). So, what is required is to generate an impulse for constitutional morality as perhaps the most reliable shield against ethics-deficit in governance. This was a belief that Ambedkar held so dear when he presented the Constitution to the nation.

There are reasons to believe that the abuse of authority for personal benefit can never go unchallenged, especially in a democracy which thrives in intense civic engagement. As custodian of democratic values, an alert citizenry always puts hurdles, if not checks, as soon as efforts towards misappropriating public authority are made. Whenever attempts to thwart public institutions were made, as history shows, there have been serious public protests. Examples from India—the 1974 JP movement and the 2011 Anna Hazare's drive for a strong Lokpal—have proved the point beyond doubt. In recent years, there may not have been nation-wide campaigns against corruption, as was seen in 2011, though one can refer to other innumerable campaigns, showing that the abuse of authority usually provokes immediate opposition presumably because citizens are increasingly becoming vigilant.

In the Indian context, there have been changes in the conceptualisation of ethics in public administration. Administrative accountability is being reinvented in light of the changing texture of governance in which the role of citizens is as significant as those running the machine in accordance with well-defined rules and regulations governing its functioning. Citizens no longer remain mere recipients, they are active partners in framing policies for their well-being. For them, participatory democracy is not merely a descriptive category, but an empowering idea of connecting them with the actual articulation of public administration. Ethics has gained a wider connotation: an administrative action shall cease to be ethical if it violates citizens' constitutionally-guaranteed rights. What is ethical is now determined by criteria which may not have been devised internally, but by the those who are affected by specific administrative act.

Public administration is now a changed entity. In order to ascertain ethics in governance, the pyramidal structure of administration that is clearly top-down in character has undergone sea change, presumably because citizens have become active partners—it has become citizen-centric. There are two specific ways in which public administration is now less Weberian. On the one hand, changes in governance are attributed to civil society activism, which is essentially an outside influence. This is not new since politico-ideological movements have always remained an important source of change in Indian administration. The British administration was forced to change some of its unethical and draconian laws in response to the campaign that the nationalists had launched. The trend has continued in independent India. One of the most important interventions is the adoption of the Right to Information Act in 2005, following the decades-long ideological campaign for transparency in administration. The change is also visible within the administration. For instance, government offices have adopted the Citizens' Charter that identifies administrative obligations to the citizens; the charter is a powerful internal mechanism to translate ethics in governance as an achievable goal. Likewise, e-governance is another powerful aid that complements the endeavour to make public governance transparent, ethical and public in substance and spirit.

Citizens' involvement in governance is, therefore, a powerful aid for administrative transparency. This is being encouraged both globally and nationally. With the consolidation of a proactive citizenry in India, reflecting perhaps concern for transparency in administration, the rigid and hierarchical Weberian conceptualisation of bureaucracy does not seem to be a useful analytical tool to comprehend the changed texture of public authority. The impact is too commanding to be ignored easily. Change is visible and Weberian rigidity does not seem to be useful and it is, in fact, being described as an impediment towards making public administration a citizen-centric endeavour. In that respect, the idea that citizens are immensely significant in conceptualising public administration remains most critical in reformulating fundamental theoretical premises in the discipline. The next chapter will illustrate the changes in the texture of administration in this regard—contemporary administration will be understood in a theoretical backdrop where citizens remain the core of public administration. It will show how citizens have become integral to the decision-making processes by being proactive, and that administration cannot be hijacked so easily anymore presumably because of the prevalence of a transparent and ethically-tuned administration.

REFERENCES

Béteille, André. 2008. 'Constitutional Morality'. *Economic and Political Weekly* 43 (40): 35–42.

Bhattacharya, Mohit. 2008. *New Horizons of Public Administration*. New Delhi: Jawahar Publishers and Distributors.

———. 2013. *New Horizons of Public Administration*. New Delhi: Jawahar Publishers and Distributors.

Caiden, Gerald E. 1994. 'Dealing with Administrative Corruption' in *Handbook of Administrative Ethics*, edited by Terry L. Cooper, 429–56. New York: Marcel Dekker.

Cooper, Terry L. 1991. *An Ethic of Citizenship for Public Administration*. New Jersey: Prentice Hall.

Friedrich, Carl J. 1989. 'Corruption Concepts in Historical Perspective' in *Political Corruption: A Handbook* edited by Arnold J. Heidenheimer, Michael Johnston and Victor T LeVine, 15–24. New Brunswick, NJ: Transaction Publishers.

Government of India (GoI). 1964. 'Report of the Committee on Prevention of Corruption', submitted to the Ministry of Home Affairs, Government of India, New Delhi.

———. 2007. *Ethics in Governance*, fourth report of the Second Administrative Reforms Commission, Government of India, New Delhi.

———. 2009. *Citizen Centric Administration: The Heart of Governance*, twelfth report of the Second Administrative Reforms Commission, Government of India, New Delhi.

Malena, Carmen, Reiner Forster and Janmejay Singh. 2004. 'Social Accountability: An Introduction to the Concept and Emerging Practice'. Social Development Papers no. 76, The WB, Washington, DC.

Marx, Fritz Morstein. 1949. 'Administrative Ethics and the Rule of Law'. *The American Political Science Review* 43 (6): 1119–44.

Philip, Mark. 2015. 'The Definition of Political Corruption' in *Routledge Handbook of Political Corruption*, edited by Paul Heywood, 21–52. Oxford: Routledge.

Rouband, Luc, ed. 1999. *Citizens and the New Governance: Beyond New Public Management.* Amsterdam: IOS Press.

Stivers, Camilla. 1994. 'Citizenship Ethics in Public Administration' in *Handbook of Administrative Ethics*, edited by Cooper, 435–55.

Waldo, Dwight. 1996. 'Public administration and Ethics: A Prologue to a Preface' in *Public Administration: Concepts and Cases*, edited by Richard J. Stillman II, 472–81. Boston: Houghton Mifflin Company.

10

CITIZEN-CENTRIC ADMINISTRATION

The Heart of Good Governance*

HIGHLIGHTS

- Situating citizens in governance
- Reforms within the system
  - Administrative accountability
  - Decentralisation
  - Redressal of public grievances
  - Right to information
  - Citizens' charters
  - E-governance
- The role of civil society

Being a citizen is more than a status; it is about the entitlement of rights and privileges of a person and ensures a quality life. In fact, citizenship is more than a set of rights and obligations, it is intrinsic to the well-being of State and society. In fact, the participation of citizens in the governance of their society is the bedrock of democracy. The ancient Greeks realised this and the polity of Athens institutionalised citizenship through its diverse associations, councils and authorities within the urban framework. In that environment, citizenship meant participation in the co-production of policies, in principle. However, in modern times the status aspects of citizenship are stressed heavily and the qualitative aspects of citizenship appear to be grossly underestimated. In their wake, public administration as a discipline has become more focused on the improvement of state apparatuses than on the development of citizenship and the involvement of citizens in the making of governmental policies (Rouban 1999/2006: *v*). This dominant trend is responsible for the alienation of citizens and the corresponding increase in citizens' grievances against administration. These circumstances demand the exigency of a citizen-centric administration. There is also the realisation within governments that they need more direct participation by citizens in order to govern well—to ensure stability, to facilitate people's

* Some sections of this chapter have been developed from Chakrabarty, *Ethics in Governance in India*, pp. 1–30. With permission from Taylor & Francis.

well-being and to manage environmental, health, security and energy issues in a collaborative manner. Governments now realise that they must harness the ideas, knowledge, wisdom and skills of the various stakeholders and that failure to engage citizens will result in wastage of resources and opportunities.

Therefore, the theory and practice of public administration is increasingly concerned with placing the citizen at the centre of policymakers' considerations, not just as the target but as the agent. To that end, public servants are being urged to collaborate, not merely consult; to reach out, not merely respond to citizens. The German theorist Jürgen Habermas proved a seminal influence on the debate when he argued for what he termed 'communicative rationality', whereby competent and knowledgeable citizens engage with one another in good faith and, through the giving (or assuming) of reasons, arrive at a shared understanding about a situation (1984: 86). He contended that citizens will regard democratic governments—and thus the laws, policies and interventions which issue from them—as legitimate only 'insofar as the democratic process, as it is institutionally organized and conducted, warrants the presumption that outcomes are reasonable products of a sufficiently inclusive deliberative process' (Bohman and Rehg 2009). The recent efforts to secure a more robust place for citizens' involvement in democratic governance represent a renewed concern with the authenticity and legitimacy of democracy. Citizen-centric administration helps in establishing greater trust in the government and higher level of democracy.

Citizen-centricity, with the aim of ensuring citizens' welfare and citizens' satisfaction, is critical for any government that aims to facilitate good governance. Today, governments are trying to reinvent public administration by strengthening its capacities and making it more efficient and accountable to the citizens. Different methods and techniques are undertaken to ensure that citizens' demands are add ressed, and thereby reduce the gap between government and the people and enhance public trust. Citizen-centric administration has thus become the heart of good governance. It is in this background that this chapter attempts to trace Indian efforts at citizen-centric administration by discussing its significant dimensions—situating citizens in governance (citizens' perception about administration, pre-conditions for citizens-centric administration, people's participation in administration), forms of public accountability (right to information, citizens' charters, e-governance, civil society) and the role of public grievance redressal machinery.

SITUATING CITIZENS IN GOVERNANCE

In conventional public administration, citizens remain recipients and hence hardly have a role to play in governance. Endorsed by the Weberian notion of hierarchical bureaucracy, public administration did not seem to pay adequate attention to the role that citizens are expected to play in public governance. Public administration was hardly public in sum and substance though this was challenged on and off. Then there were changes in the texture and functioning of public administration. One of the fundamental changes brought about as a result of politico-ideological campaigns in various phases of history had to do with the nature of public governance—the role of citizens began to be recognised as integral to its functioning. It was made possible in a changed environment where top-down administrative values no longer remained as attractive as before. Instead, the idea of 'the bottom-up' administration, entailing the critical importance of the public in decision-making, seemed to have become theoretically far more acceptable. The idea that citizens are important in governance is not new; what is new, however, is the effort towards articulating this idea in practice: citizens need to be taken into account seriously while formulating policy decisions; they are not merely a cog in the machine, but actively involved in running the machine in accordance with their ideological priorities.

In efforts to make administration transparent, the role of stakeholders can never be undermined, because it is they who face the reality and know what is better for their well-being. Only if citizens are involved in the process can administrative decisions be based on an understanding of the reality, else as in the case of the top-down strategy they tend to miss the ground reality. The aim is to create and sustain an administration which is responsive enough to arrive at effective decisions for public well-being. What is basic here is to evolve mechanisms whereby the views of citizens are respected while making decisions that are pertinent to their well-being both individually and as a collective. This is an important aspect of governance in India, in its new avatar that has attracted immense attention. By concentrating on these instruments of citizens' empowerment in the changed socio-ideological circumstances, this section also located their contextual roots in India's volatile political milieu. The fundamental argument relates to the consolidation of newer devices for citizens' empowerment which are being meaningfully utilised to make public governance sensitive to the demands and requirements of stakeholders. These instruments seem to have become effective because of a favourable socio-political environment supporting proactive citizens as integral to democratic political processes.

Interactions between Citizens and Administration

In a democracy, administration–citizen relations are significant because the support and consent of the governed is a prerequisite for the sustenance of a representative government. Citizens are important because of the legitimacy they provide to government institutions. Without citizen support, the functioning and existence of public organisations are threatened (Easton 1975; Vigoda 2002). The State, and in actual terms the administration, has the responsibility of providing major amenities of life, such as education, health, employment opportunities, and improved means of transport and infrastructure. All these affect the individual and collective life of the population. In public administration two noticeable trends have emerged in recent times. First, there has been a large growth in the size of government administration as well as a vast expansion in its powers and activities. Second, in the wake of the spread of general education, and political and social awakening, there has been a rise in the expectations of people from the administration. The relationship between lawmakers and citizens in a democracy has been discussed by A. V. Dicey (1948). The importance of the subject grew sharply after World War II, thanks to the growth of welfare and socialist ideologies in the new states. People in affluent societies became less concerned about the old concept of liberty than with the love of material comfort and pleasure. The focus of the relationship between State and society shifted from political liberty to economic prosperity and social justice. The State expanded its political base through universal adult franchise. Administration had, therefore, of necessity penetrated into every aspect of civic life. The bulk of the citizens who are voters and beneficiaries of State services were more concerned with getting the services supplied than with the subtle aspect of how they get them (Agarwal 2004: 270). But the situation has changed today. The position of the citizens from being mere recipients of the administrative help and services has now shifted to their being the prime mover in the affairs of governance.

It is evident that citizens interact with administration every day in numerous ways. The purposes of contact may be varied: it may be for getting basic services like water, electricity and health services, or it may be for getting driving license or filing income tax returns with the IT department. There are different ways in which citizens interact with the administrative agencies in their day-to-day life. Bhattacharya (2008) illustrates six forms of such interactions.

1. *Clients*: In this form, citizens seek to obtain benefits or services from governmental agencies. For example, a patient visits a governmental hospital for medical check or treatment.
2. *Regulatees*: As regulatee, the public interacts with many regulating government agencies, such as the police, income tax authorities, and licensing authorities.
3. *Litigants*: As litigants, the public moves the court against 'unjust' actions of public agencies. For example, people seek redressal from the court when the motor vehicles authority delays issuance of car licence.
4. *Participants*: In this form people become direct participants in decision-making in public policy at different levels. For example, parents become members of a school's guardians' committee, an irrigation project associates farmers in the command area with the different decision-making processes of the project.
5. *Cutting-edge encounters*: In this form, people approach agencies which are responsible for the day-to-day primary services and facilities to the public. For example, people approach the municipal corporation for water, electricity and sanitation facilities.
6. *Protesters*: People often interact with government agencies as protesters, opposing injustice in government policy and action. For example, people oppose the construction of a dam in their locality. (Ibid.: 248–49)

Sometimes, therefore, people get an opportunity to directly participate in policymaking and implementation of a project. When people do not get services in time or are harassed by public authorities, they seek redressal of their grievances from the court and when they do not see justice coming from any side they resort to criticism and protests against the unjust policy and action of the government. Through these happy or unhappy interactions citizens form an opinion about public administration. Ideally speaking, the interaction between citizens and administration is supposed to be trustworthy and purposeful, However, in reality, it is always plagued by conflicts, stresses and strains.

Citizen's Perception about Administration

Discontent among citizens, due to the wide disparity between the performance of administration and popular expectation, has become a normal feature. The general feeling that persists among people is not that policies are cumbersome or that processes of administration unjust, but that the standards of honesty and integrity in both politics and administration have deteriorated. Rigid observance of rules and regulations, non-acknowledgement of complaints, inordinate delay in disposal of various matters, etc. account for the lack of faith of the public in the administration. A number of studies have examined the relationship between citizens and administration in India, such as on police administration by Davis H. Bayley (1969), on rural development by Rakesh Hooja (1987) and on urban government by V. Jagannadham (1978). The findings of these studies reveal interesting information on citizens' perceptions about public administration in India. According to Bhattacharya (2008), the general perception emerging out of these studies include:

- Unhelpful attitude of officials, especially lower-level functionaries
- Inordinate delay and waiting period
- Favouritism
- Need for middlemen (brokers) to get things done
- Citizens' ignorance about procedures involved in getting things done
- Rich-poor discrimination—the rich have access to administration and officials tend to avoid the poor and underplay their needs and interests (ibid.: 257)

In this regard, Sharma and Surapaneni (2006) note:

> A recent Centre for Media Studies study shows that a majority of citizens are not satisfied with the delivery of public services. In seven out of the 11 departments covered in the study, less than one-third of the citizens are satisfied with the services delivered.
>
> In fact, in most need-based services such as the police, judiciary and municipalities, (which enjoy a greater discretion and power), not even 20 per cent of the households are satisfied with their services. Even in essential services such as the PDS, hospitals, and electricity and water supplies, a mere 30-40 per cent of the households are happy with the services [GoI 2009: 12].

Thus, administration in India is generally perceived as unresponsive, insensitive and corrupt. Robson (1964) observes

> The maladies from which bureaucracy most frequently suffers are an excessive sense of self-importance on the part of officials or an undue idea of the importance of their office; an indifference towards the feeling or the convenience of individual citizens; an obsession with the binding and inflexible authority of departmental decisions, precedents, arrangements or forms, regardless of how badly or with what injustice they may work in individual cases; a mania for regulations and formal procedure; a pre-occupation with the activities of particular units of administration and an inability to consider the Government as a whole; a failure to recognize the relations between the governors and the governed as an essential part of democratic process. (Ibid.: 18)

In the case of India, the comments of the Sixth Central Pay Commission's report (GoI 2008a) are worth noting:

> For the common man, bureaucracy denotes routine and repetitive procedures, paperwork and delays. This, despite the fact that the government and bureaucracy exist to facilitate the citizens in the rightful pursuit of their legal activities. Rigidities of the system over centralization of powers, highly hierarchical and top-down method of functioning with a large number of intermediary levels delaying finalization of any decision, divorce of authority from accountability and the tendency towards micromanagement have led to a structure in which form is more important than substance and procedures are valued over end results and outcomes. Non-performance of the administrative structures, poor service quality and lack of responsiveness, and the subjective and negative abuse of authority have eroded trust in governance systems which needs to be restored urgently. (Ibid.: 365)

In its twelfth report on citizen-centric administration, the Second Administrative Reforms Commission (ARC) reports that most of the observations by citizens were about the poor quality of services provided by the government, the indifferent attitude of government servants, corruption and abuse of authority, red-tapism and lack of accountability (GoI 2009). It goes on to identify the following five barriers to citizen-centric administration:

1. Wooden, inflexible, self-perpetuation and inward looking attitude of the civil servants
2. Lack of accountability of civil servants
3. Red-tapism
4. Ineffective implementation of laws and rules
5. Low levels of awareness of the rights and duties of citizens (ibid.: 14–16)

Thus, it may be said that the attitude and work of some government servants, deficiencies in existing institutional structures and the lack of awareness about rights and duties on the part of the citizens have led to widespread public dissatisfaction with administration.

Pre-conditions for Citizen-centric Administration

The poor image of the government in the minds of large sections of the public points to inefficient and ineffective administration. This highlights the need for substantially reforming our governance system. Former Prime Minister Manmohan Singh observed the following in his Civil Services Day speech of 2007:

> It is in this context that "reform of government" becomes relevant. "Administrative Reforms" is a phrase that has been used widely to mean many things. It is used by some to mean change of any kind to deal with government problems of any description. Some regard "administrative reform" merely as a means of "making the government work" better. Others in fact see "reform" as "less government". I view the reform of government as a means of making citizens central to all government activities and concerns and reorganizing government to effectively address the concerns of the common people. (GoI 2009: 17)

An analysis of the barriers to citizen-centric administration reveals that there are several pre-conditions that must be fulfilled. Some of these are:

- *Accountability*: Accountability is defined as the state of being accountable, liable or answerable. To be accountable means to be obliged to report, explain or justify something. By insisting that public servants must be accountable to the public, they are not only accountable to the questions asked by the people but they also have to respond to demands and provide services to the people. Since accountability ensures that something is carried out as expected, it is a key requirement of good administration.
- *Accessibility*: A good administration has to be accessible to the people. If people have any problem, administrative officials should be ready to listen to them and respond accordingly. There has to be no fear in the mind of the people regarding the status and rigidity of the bureaucracy. There should be no discrimination and the oppressed and poor sections of the society must have an easy access to the administration.
- *Transparency*: Transparency is an essential pre-condition for good administration. It is the antonym of secrecy, the traditional hallmark of public administration. Transparency implies that the governmental policies and functioning be known to the larger society by making information directly available to people who will be affected in an easily understandable form. Transparency enables citizens to keep themselves informed of the policies of the government, the rights they have and what they should expect as service from the government. Right to information and the citizens' charter are means of ensuring transparency in administration.
- *Participatory*: Promoting citizen-centric administration also implies giving a voice to citizens in the governance process. It means involvement of people in administrative activities, particularly the participation of beneficiaries of developmental activities both at the formulation and implementation stages. People's participation is also an important

safeguard against the abuse of administrative authority. It is a method of tapping human and material resources for development. Meaningful participation by citizens in governance can be promoted through *panchayati raj* institutions, *bhagidari* (partnership) programmes and by involving citizens groups in certain aspects of governance.

- *Responsiveness*: Responsive administration is an apparently moral concept in public administration in as much as it calls for public functionaries' accountability directly to the people. It is a micro-level concept deriving credibility and validity from the delivery system of a country's public administration. By being responsive, governmental institutions gain 'legitimacy' in the public realm, which will automatically ensure their wider acceptance and result in effectiveness in governance. A responsive administration entails the mechanism of grievance redressal also.

In addition to these necessary pre-conditions of citizen-centric administration, decentralisation and delegation of policies, adoption of modern technology, process simplification and integrity of the civil services are other features and norms of successful administration. In this connection, the words of Dr S. Radhakrishnan, former Vice-President of India, are worth noting. Agarwal (2004: *iii–iv*) discusses his speech on the occasion of the First Annual Day of the Indian Institute of Public Administration (IIPA) on 20 November 1959. According to Radhakrishnan, the administration has to be fair to all sections of the population. Administrators must not feel that they are there to lord over the public but that 'they are essentially servants of the people'. Also 'administrators are not to regard them themselves as a privileged class. They are not to grow into bureaucracy'. The higher civil servants 'must understand the needs and aspirations of the common man and woman and try to protect them from the petty officials who are inclined to harass them and show their authority'. Above all, Radhakrishnan was particular that 'we should have administrative integrity first, efficiency next, economy third – with these conditions we will be able to build a happier Indian Society' (ibid.). Evidently, he placed integrity in administration above all other requirements for better governance.

One of the significant reports of the ARC relates to citizen-centric administration (GoI 2009). According to this report, there are several requirements to ensure citizen-centric governance. Some of the requirements are: sound legal framework, robust institutional mechanism for proper implementation of laws and their effective functioning, competent personnel staffing these institutions; and right policies for decentralisation, delegation and accountability. The ARC has also tried to examine the finer details of how strategies and processes, tools and mechanisms can be usefully employed to make the administration citizen-centric. These are: (*a*) re-engineering processes to make governance 'citizen-centric', (*b*) adoption of appropriate modern technology, (*c*) right to information, (*d*) citizens' charters, (*e*) independent evaluation of services, (*f*) grievance redressal mechanisms and (*g*) active citizens' participation through public-private partnerships (GoI 2009: 17). In addition, process simplification, integrity of the civil services and making the bureaucracy accessible, responsive and accountable are other important norms necessary for building a citizen-centric administration.

People's Participation in Administration

As mentioned earlier, people's participation in the administrative process—i.e. the direct involvement of citizens in the process of administrative decision-making, policy formulation and implementation—is an effective tool to establish citizen-centric administration. Peoples' participation also means collective and continuous efforts by the people themselves in setting goals, pooling in resources and taking actions that aim at improving their living conditions. As Morrow (1980) defines, the term citizen participation means the direct participation of ordinary men and women—in contrast to public and private elites—in policymaking. Furthermore, the term can also be employed to focus on the direct participation of the underprivileged and enfranchised in decisions that affect their lives (ibid.: 190). Thus, people's participation is a mechanism of involvement and participation of the people in the decision-making process of the nation. Citizens' participation in governance embodies a shift in the development paradigm from citizens as the recipients of development to one that views them as active participants in the development process. Equally, it involves a shift from a 'top-down' to a 'bottom-up' approach to development involving increasing decentralisation of power away from the Centre and closer to the grassroots.

The concept of citizens' participation in governance is based on the premise that citizens have a legitimate role in influencing decision-making that affects their lives, their businesses and their communities. At the ideological level, direct participation of the citizens in governance is seen as contributing to a healthy democracy because it enhances and improves upon the traditional form of representative democracy to transform it into a more responsive and participative grassroots democracy. It is now widely accepted that active citizens' participation can contribute to good governance in various ways:

- It helps promote healthy grassroots democracy
- It enables citizens to make government accountable, more responsive, efficient and effective
- It helps make government programmes and services more effective and sustainable
- It enables the poor and marginalised to influence public policy and service delivery to improve their lives
- It enables the individual develop a sense of civic maturity—they become more educated, tolerant and compassionate, which finally helps in improving the quality of policy
- It helps in recognising that citizens have vital contributions to make towards the betterment of public policy
- It develops a better understanding between the government and the people

People's participation in administration is thus a means to ensure a transparent, accountable, participatory, responsive, effective and efficient government. However, peoples' participation is not free from barriers. One of them is the existence of widespread inertia in the larger society, resulting in apathy and passivity. In addition, under the name of people's participation, what may happen is a situation which Morrow (1980) calls 'abdication', 'pacification', 'co-operation' and 'client-building'. Citizens' participation does not necessarily lead to the leaders representing their constituencies. Rather, they may strike a tie-up with the local bureaucracy, which may silence them. When interfacing with the bureaucrats, the representatives may represent their individual interest and not their constituencies' cause. In such cases, participation becomes a kind of formality and paperwork, not the empowerment of the common people in its true sense.

The fact that participatory efforts are occasionally perverted does not mean that the perversions make the participatory movement meaningless. Avasthi and Maheswari (2010) mention a few pre-conditions that are required to make citizens' participation in administration more effective: enlightened political leader; citizens should be knowledgeable and competent; conscientious civil servants; informed and co-operative public; ensuring that information required for taking decisions are clear and precise; well-organised communication network; both authority and citizens must demonstrate willingness to take responsibility; to make practical survey of the environment for which it is intended; and participation at all levels, both rural and urban (ibid.: 643). According to them, these conditions and actions are necessary, both on the part of officials as well as the common people, for a true representative and participatory democracy.

Administration in the Service of Citizens

The Indian Constitution underpins an elaborate legal and institutional framework that articulates the vision of a welfare State and, by implication, provides for creation of a citizen-centric governance structure. However, the popular perception as well as the reality belies that spirit. The increase of citizens' expectations for administrative performance can be achieved through the use of a variety of political, legal and administrative mechanisms that are designed to ensure that public officials remain answerable and accessible to the people they serve (Batalli 2011: 65). In 2009, the Organization for Economic Cooperation and Development (OECD) released the following guiding principles for an open, inclusive and citizen-centric policymaking:

- Commitment from politicians and senior managers to open and inclusive policymaking
- Citizens' rights to information and participation firmly grounded in law, with independent oversight mechanisms to enforce these rights
- Clarity about the roles, responsibilities, limits and expectations of all participants
- Early engagement in the policy process and adequate time for participation
- Inclusiveness to ensure a wide variety of people are engaged, and through multiple channels

- Adequate financial, technical and human resources made available; and public officials with the required skills; and organisational culture that supports both traditional and online engagement
- Co-ordination across levels of government to ensure coherence of effort and leverage the knowledge networks and communities of practice within and beyond government
- Government accountability to participants about how their inputs are received and acted upon
- Proper evaluation of the performance of government in effecting public participation.
- Active support from government in building the problem-solving capacity of, and encouraging citizens' participation in, civil society organisations (OECD 2009: 14–15)[1]

REFORMS WITHIN THE SYSTEM

As mentioned earlier, the negative image of the bureaucracy in the minds of large sections of the society points to an inefficient and ineffective administration. This highlights the need for substantially reforming the governance system. The main focus of such reform has to be on making citizens central to all government activities and reorganising administration to effectively address the concerns of the common people. This section will discuss the theory and practice of some of the preconditions listed in the previous section, such as accountability, transparency and responsiveness of bureaucracy, decentralisation of authority, simplification of rules, efficient grievance redressal machinery, citizens' charter, right to information and e-governance.

Administrative Accountability: Making Bureaucracy Answerable to Citizens

Accountability is an essential feature of all forms of democratic governments. The concept refers to the liability of government servants to give a satisfactory account of the use of official power or discretionary authority to the people. This is considered as an effective safeguard against the misuse of power and abuse of public authority. The substance of accountability, according to Bhattacharya (2008), places at least four requirements on public administrators: make laws work as intended with a minimum of waste and delay; exercise lawful and sensible administrative discretion; recommend new policies and propose changes in existing policies and programmes as needed; and enhance confidence of citizens in the administrative institutions. The notion of accountability carries two basic connotations: answerability, which stands for the obligation of public officials to inform about and explain what they are doing; and enforcement, i.e. the capacity of accounting agencies to impose sanctions on people who hold power and have violated their public duties.

In India, administrative accountability is enforced by means of various controls. The purpose of control is to ensure that public servants exercise their powers and discretion in accordance with laws and regulations. Broadly speaking, there are two types of administrative control: internal and external. The internal control operates from within the administrative machinery. The techniques of internal control are: budgetary system, hierarchical order, enquiries and investigations, pressure groups, press reports and confidential internal reports. The external accountability over administration in India is maintained through legislative, executive and judicial control. The administration is made responsible to the elected representatives because people are supreme in a democracy. Thus the Legislative has been given certain powers to keep an effective check on malpractice and abuse of authority through the Constitution and by convention. The Legislative applies a number of methods for controlling administration—some of which are asking questions during question hour, parliamentary discussions, parliamentary audit, non confidence motion and complaints to ombudsman. Executive control over administration is another potent instrument in a responsible government. It is exercised through a number of means and techniques, such as the power of appointment and removal, rule-making power, ordinances, the civil service code, delegated legislation, budgetary system and making an appeal to public opinion. Another important instrument through which administrative accountability is ensured is judicial control which may take the shape of judicial review or statutory appeal to the suits and writs against the government. The primary objective of judicial control over administration is the protection of the rights and liberties of citizens by ensuring the legality of administrative acts (Singh 2002: 216–17).

Decentralisation: Giving Autonomy to Local People

Decentralisation is a prime mechanism through which democracy becomes truly representative, responsive and citizen-centric. Conceptually speaking, at the heart of any decentralisation scheme is the conscious effort to de-centre power (administrative, political or fiscal) with a view to improving the status of the people. It is also the most valued antidote of authoritarianism and bureaucratisation. Cheema and Rondenilli have defined decentralisation as 'transfer of planning, decision-making or administrative authority from the central government to its field organizations, local administration units, semi-autonomous and para-statal organizations, local governments or NGOs' (1983: 56–57). In this sense, a decentralised local authority would have a separate legal existence, its own budget and the authority to allocate substantial resources to a range of different functions, and decisions would be made by the representatives of the local people who constitute the body.

The concept of decentralisation has the following characteristics: first, it is both a philosophy and institutional mechanism that seeks to de-centre power from traditional centres to far-flung areas with a view to empowering local communities. Second, autonomy forms the heart of decentralisation. Third, the recent spate of enthusiasm for decentralisation can be attributed to globalisation. Fourth, decentralisation facilitates people's participation by creating a new institutional space beyond the Centre and thereby ensures further deepening of democracy. Fifth, decentralisation instils confidence among the local community to govern their own affairs. Decentralisation thus creates a sense of responsibility in local decision-making agencies with more or less independent existence and powers. In other words, decentralisation is sharing the decision-making authority with the lower levels, thereby improving their efficiency, effectiveness and responsiveness.

India embarked on the ambitious decentralisation initiative in the 1990s via a couple of landmark amendments to the Constitution—the 73rd and the 74th Constitution Amendment Acts—to reinforce local democracy by empowering rural and urban self-governing institutions. The 73rd Constitutional Amendment Act, 1992 is considered landmark in the history of local government in India. It has proved fruitful in establishing citizen-centric governance in rural India. Some of the provisions of the 73rd Amendment Act are radical. These range from granting constitutional status to Panchayati Raj Institutions (PRIs); empowering the socially and economically disadvantaged groups such as Dalits, Adivasis and women; ensuring free, fair and regular elections; fixing the terms of local councils; empowering PRIs to formulate and implement policies; and addressing financial issues of local bodies. Overall, the Act provided for a significant degree of fiscal, administrative and political decentralisation from the State to local levels. We will discuss local governance in detail in the next chapter.

Redressal of Public Grievances

A 'grievance' is a 'complaint, or a condition felt to be oppressive', and may arise out of the non-fulfilment of certain demands and expectations. These demands may be related to policies of the government or to the performance of the administration in the implementation of policies framed by the government. A grievance is thus any sort of dissatisfaction, which needs to be redressed. Some of the common grievances faced by the people against the administration may be classified in the following categories:

- *Red-tapism*: delay in administrative functioning
- *Corruption*: demand and acceptance of money for doing things
- *Favouritism*: obliging powerful and influential people
- *Nepotism*: helping the people of one's own kith or kin
- *Discourtesy*: use of abusive language or misbehaviour in public dealing
- *Neglect of duty*: Not doing things as per law
- *Discrimination*: ignoring the poor and weak and favouring the rich
- *Mal-administration*: inefficiency in achieving the goals
- *Lack of redressal machinery*: absence of machinery to attend public complaints against officials

The ARC defines the basic principle of a grievance redressal system as follows: if the promised level of service delivery is not achieved, then it is the right of a citizen to be able to take recourse to a mechanism that attends to her/his complaint. This mechanism should be well publicised, easy to use, prompt, and, above all, citizens must have faith that they will get justice from it.

Grievance Redressal in India

Today, with increased awareness, the aspirations of the Indian citizen have gone up as also the demand for prompt and effective resolution of their grievances. The central and state governments, as well as various organisations under them have set up grievance redressal mechanisms to look into the complaints of citizens. At the Centre, there are two designated nodal agencies handling these grievances: Department of Administrative Reforms and Public Grievances, within the Ministry of Personnel, Public Grievances and Pension; and Directorate of Public Grievances, within the Cabinet Secretariat. Besides these nodal agencies there are other institutional mechanisms like the Central Vigilance Commission and Lokpal and Lokayuktas which have the mandate to look into complaints of corruption and abuse of office by public servants. Many organisations, for example, the Reserve Bank of India (RBI), have set up ombudsman in their respective organisations to look into grievances. Institutions such as the National Human Rights Commission and various state human rights commissions; National Commission for Women and various state women's commissions; National Commission for Scheduled Castes and the National Commission for Schedules Tribes also look into complaints from the public in their prescribed areas. The roles of some of the important institutions and other initiatives for redressal of public grievance in India are discussed below:

1. *Central Vigilance Commission*: On the basis of recommendations made by the Committee on Prevention of Corruption, popularly known as the Santhanam Committee, the Central Vigilance Commission (CVC) was set up by the Government of India in 1964. The CVC advises the Centre on all matters pertaining to the maintenance of integrity in administration. As per the Central Vigilance Commission Act, 2003, the CVC consists of a Central Vigilance Commissioner who is the Chairperson of the Commission and at most two vigilance commissioners who are members. The CVC exercises superintendence over the functioning of the Delhi Special Police Establishment (i.e. the CBI) in so far as it relates to the investigation of offences under the Prevention of Corruption Act, 1988; inquires or investigates into cases referred by the Centre; inquires or investigates into any complaint received against any official under its jurisdiction; and exercises superintendence over the vigilance administrations of the various ministries, departments and organisations under the central government. The CVC has been conceived as the apex vigilance institution, free of control from any executive authority, monitoring all vigilance activity under the Centre and advising various authorities in planning, executing, reviewing and reforming their vigilance work. The Government of India has made the CVC the 'Designated Agency' to receive disclosure of any allegation of corruption or misuse of office from whistleblowers and recommend appropriate action.

2. *Lokpal and Lokayukta*: Lokpal is an independent body to inquire into cases of corruption against public functionaries. The First Administrative Reforms Commission headed by Morarji Desai submitted an interim report on 'Problems of Redressal of Citizen's Grievances' in 1966. Here the Commission recommended the creation of two special authorities, designated as 'lokpal' and 'lokayukta', for redressal of citizens' grievances. After the recommendations of this Commission in its report in 1968, many states constituted lokayuktas to investigate into allegations or grievances arising out of the conduct of public servants, including political executives, legislators, officers of state governments, local bodies, public enterprises and other government establishments. Maharashtra was the first state to introduce the lokayukta through the Maharashtra Lokayukta and Upa-Lokayuktas Act in 1971. Under this Act, a member of the public can file specific allegations with the lokayukta against any public servant for enquiry. The lokayukta can also initiate suo moto inquiry into the conduct of public servants. At presently, more than 17 states in India have set up lokayuktas.
3. *The Lokpal and Lokayuktas Act, 2013*: Following the recommendation of the First Administrative Reforms Commission, a Lokpal Bill was first introduced in the Lok Sabha in 1968. Since then the bill has been introduced nine times in the Parliament, but due to various reasons it was not passed. However, following a huge public protest led by the anti-corruption crusader Anna Hazare, the bill was introduced in the Parliament once more in 2013. The bill was passed on 18 December 2013 and came into force from 16 January 2014, and was officially called as the Lokpal and Lokayuktas Act, 2013. The Act sought to provide for the establishment of the lokpal, an institution that would inquire into allegations of corruption against certain public functionaries and matters related to them. The lokpal would be at the Centre and various lokayuktas would be set up at the level of the states. As per the composition, the lokpal will consist of a Chairperson and a maximum of eight members, of which 50 per cent will be judicial members. The remaining 50 per cent would be from SC/ST/OBCs, minorities and women. The selection of Chairperson and members of lokpal will be carried out through a selection committee comprising the prime minister, speaker of the Lok Sabha, leader of the opposition in the Lok Sabha, Chief Justice of India (CJI) or a sitting Supreme Court judge nominated by the CJI. The prime minister, ministers, current and former legislators, government employees, employees of firms funded by the Centre, societies and trusts that collect public money, or those that receive funds from foreign sources come under the purview of this anti-corruption law.

The new Act provides that all anti-corruption inquiry should be completed within 60 days and investigation has to be completed within six months. The lokpal shall order a probe only after hearing the public servant. An enquiry against the prime minister has to be held in-camera and will have to be approved by two-thirds of the full bench of the lokpal. The lokpal can initiate prosecution through its Prosecution Wing before a special court and the trial has to be completed within two years. The Act also incorporates provisions for attachment and confiscation of property acquired by corrupt means, even while prosecution is pending. The Act is significant in the sense that it includes even the prime minister under its purview. It is more inclusive, effective and time-bound. Adequate provisions are provided to protect whistleblowers and honest and committed officers. The provision of penalty and punishment is a deterrent for the corrupt and dishonest public servant.

Right to Information: Public Accessibility to Information

Right to Information (RTI) is one of the most effective and accessible tools to redress public grievances. It implies that the citizens should have free access to all files and documents pertaining to the governments, working. RTI empowers citizens to demand and get information about public policies and actions, and thereby lead to their welfare. Moreover, transparency ensures that government organisations function more objectively and predictably. In recognition of the need for transparency, Parliament enacted the Right to Information Act in 2005 and provided for the setting up of a practical regime to enable and empower citizens to secure information that is under the control of public authorities (Sharma and Devasher 2007: 356). Also, the Act lays down thirty days as the time limit for normal applications and forty days where a third party submission is to be called for. In a novel approach, these time limits have been reduced to a mere 48 hours where information sought 'concerns the life and liberty of a person'. The application fee is Rs 10 per request and no fee is charged from people living below the poverty line. The Act provides for the appointment of Public Information Officers (PIOs) in all administrative units/ offices as may be necessary to provide information to persons requesting it. Assistant IPOs are also to be appointed at each sub-divisional or sub-district level. These provisions are designed to bring access closer to the people by ensuring that applicants can submit requests in their local areas. Every PIO can be penalised Rs 250 per day up to a maximum of Rs 25,000 for not accepting an application, delaying information without reasonable cause and providing incomplete or incorrect and misleading information. Information must be provided in writing, including by e-mails. Where no response is received, it will be deemed as refusal. If an application has been rejected, the appropriate reason should be communicated in writing.

The Act aims at keeping the Civil Services active through feedback. Information asked by the people can also help civil servants in ascertaining the overall satisfaction. However, it is also to be kept in mind that mere conferment of the Right to Information without changing the prevalent style of governance would make the entire exercise futile. In the present scenario, that is characterised by the lack of political will and the reluctant attitude of bureaucracy to recognise the people's Right to Information, the role of civil society organisations is crucial. Their sustained and significant involvement in RTI can help usher in a new era of open, transparent and accountable governance. The more these organisations come forward to enlighten and mobilise people at the grassroots, the more would be the realisation of the immense potential of RTI.

Citizens' Charters: Ensuring Standards of Service

The Citizens' Charter is an instrument that seeks to make an organisation transparent, accountable and citizen-friendly. The aim was to ensure that public services are made responsive to the citizens they serve. A Citizens' Charter is basically a set of commitments made by an organisation regarding the standards of service it delivers. It is a public statement that defines the entitlements of citizens to a specific service, the standards of the service, the conditions to be met by users and the remedies available in case of non-compliance of standards. The concept empowers citizens to demand the standards of service committed by the organisation.

The basic thrust of Citizens' Charter is to make public services citizen-centric by ensuring that these services are demand-driven rather than supply-driven. The ARC lays down six principles that characterise the Citizens' Charter: quality (improving the quality of services), choice (for the users wherever possible), standards (specifying what to expect within a time frame), value (for taxpayers' money), accountability (of the service provider) and transparency (in rules, procedures, schemes and grievance redressal) (GoI 2009: 34). When introduced for the first time in the UK in the early 1990s, the Charter represented a landmark shift in the delivery of public services. In India, 111 central ministries/departments/organisations have thus far formulated Citizens' Charters.

E-governance: Harnessing Technology to Deliver Public Services

E-governance is short for 'electronic governance'. This is another mechanism to redress public grievances and thereby bring people closer to administration. E-governance is the delivery of services through the use of Information and Communication Technology (ICT). E-governance directly implies a reform in the way the government works, shares information and delivers services to internal and external clients. Increasingly, e-governance has come to refer to the performance of governmental functions through the application of ICT, the most well-known component of which is the internet. Specifically, e-government harnesses ICTs such as the internet, the web and mobile phone to deliver information and services to citizens and businesses. As a first step, information about the services is published on a website and citizens can interact with the site to download application forms for a variety of services. The next stage involves the use of ICT in the actual delivery of services, such as filing a tax return or renewing a driver's license. More sophisticated applications can process online payments (Bhatnagar 2008: 247). E-governance has emerged as a device of cutting administrative burden on citizens.

E-governance thus provides citizens the ability to obtain government services through electronic means, enabling access to government information and completion of government transactions on an 'anywhere, anytime' basis. In this way it is a tool for bringing people closer to the government and administration. The idea is simply to create the capability for providing citizens' access to government departments through electronic networks. The ultimate goal is to bring about better governance which has been termed as simple, moral, accountable, responsive and transparent (SMART) (GoI 2008b: *i*), the aim of which is to create a space for regular involvement of citizens who, as customers of public services, now have direct access to governmental activities through the ICT. Thus, through e-governance, the goal of SMART governance is achieved.

In India, digital governance has been legalised by the Information Technology Act of 2000. This Act is a watershed in conceptualising administrative reforms in India. More importantly e-governance is certainly an attack on red-tapism. It is a tool for achieving 'good governance especially with regard to improving efficiency, transparency and making interface with government user friendly' (Chakrabarty and Bhattacharya 2008: 52). The citizens can not only view online the governmental actions, they can also provide significant inputs through electronic devices (ibid.). ICT is thus an important tool that connects citizens and the government.

ICT-based e-governance has ushered in a new era in government innovations with capacities to reduce the cost of government, increase citizens' input into government, improve public decision-making and increase the transparency of government transactions. The object of e-governance is to arm the citizens to act as a watchdog to the government. In view of these well-defined functional characteristics, e-governance is also a meaningful step towards combating corruption. By reducing discretionary powers, it curbs opportunities for arbitrary action. E-governance also empowers the citizens by making their intervention in the transactions of governmental business regular through the ICT. The project E-Sewa that began in West Godavari district of Andhra Pradesh is a good example in this regard. As Chakrabarty and Bhattacharya (2008) document, the E-Sewa project is a tool 'to bridge the digital divide in the rural areas' through extensive use of information technology 'for providing access to various citizen to citizen (C2C) and citizen to government (C2G) services to the people in rural areas'. Managed by a women's self-help group, the project is a class by itself as it enables 'the local women-participants' to emerge as 'information leaders', who remain critical in realising the goal of E-Sewa (ibid.: 52). Thus, e-governance articulates public administration in a refreshing new way. It seeks to forge a link between citizens and government in terms of electronic public service. By doing so it creates conditions for strong citizens' participation in government decision-making process.

THE ROLE OF CIVIL SOCIETY

The shortcomings of the State-led development paradigm have given rise to an approach involving local people and local resources in a decentralised, people-centric, self-development mode. What is critical in this conceptualisation of development is the presence of a civil society that has emerged as the third sector alongside the State and the market. A significant departure from the conventional conceptualisation of public administration, civil-society-centred governance creates spaces for voluntary action in areas from where the State has already retreated. Civil society gains salience in developing countries presumably because the State-led development paradigm has failed to eradicate poverty to a large extent and to contain the emergence of an 'insensitive' and mechanical bureaucracy. Civil society contributes to the consolidation of the decentralised bottom-up, people-centric grassroots governance where the citizen has more freedom and autonomy. Also, civil society effectively articulates citizens' interests in a market economy.

Public administration, in its new avatar of governance, articulates a trilogy of State, market and civil society. Governance is not merely governmental, but a design which is both market-driven and civil-society-induced. While the market has redefined citizens as clients or consumers, civil society has expanded the public sphere by including a whole range of civic actions that hardly figured in the bureaucratic model of public administration. Civil society is therefore most effective in governance by mediating between the citizen and the State, by articulating citizens' interests to the government, by inculcating participatory norms and by restricting government through citizens' involvement in its day-to-day functioning. Drawing from the shared accountability of stakeholders, i.e. civil society, the new governance paradigm secures accountability by reducing discretion or delegation in public bureaucracy through collaborative governance. This also makes public participation meaningful and effective in the sense that the involvement of the stakeholders in decision-making brings about changes in the organisational structure from one that is hierarchical and centralised to a more decentralised and flexible form for enhancing self-management. Thus, civil society makes participation in governance people-centric and development-oriented.

Voluntary Agencies: New Players of Grievance Redressal

As an important component of civil society, the Non-Governmental Organisations (NGOs) play an important role in supplementing government efforts in redressing citizens' grievances. The Seventh Five-Year Plan laid emphasis on the involvement of voluntary agencies, NGOs and other interest groups in making the bureaucracy more responsive to legitimate demands of citizens. They create an awareness of their rights among the public, and interact with administrative departments/ministries in the formulation of policies and action programmes. They also provide counselling and spokesperson services. Standing Committees of Voluntary Agencies (SCOVA) have already been set up in various departments, such as Youth Affairs, Sports, Pension and Pensioners, Welfare and Health and Family Welfare. Seva Mandir (Udaipur), Saheli (Jaipur), Aastha (Udaipur) and Sulabh International are some NGOs working on the field (Ahuja and Ojha 2008: 186).

The role of voluntary agencies is increasingly being recognised not only to design better programmes but also to monitor them effectively, because they have the special advantage of the knowledge of local conditions. Even their contribution to making people aware of various developmental schemes of the State is now highly appreciated. In view of the gradual withdrawal of the State from the social sector, voluntary organisations have grown in importance not only as an alternative to what is being pursued in the name of development but also as a relatively new experiment in which the role of the conventional agencies is largely being eclipsed. They play the role of activists who execute programmes and deliver services, and as mobilisers of opinion who spread awareness and consolidate support of the people concerned.

CONCLUDING OBSERVATIONS

This chapter noted that citizenship is a key component of public administration. As observed earlier, the governance discourse which is a neo-liberal response to public administration is radically changing the role of citizens. While it has provided diverse channels for articulating and aggregating citizens' interests, it has also enabled them to act in various capacities, as citizens, voters, consumers, clients or members of interest groups. Today, governance speaks for the empowerment of customers, not citizens, and an empowered government that provides a range of choices that meet the needs of the customer. In this paradigm, the significance accorded to the consumer represents an economic view of human behaviour. There is a stark distinction between a citizen and a client/customer. A citizen is an individual in a constitutional State, a repository of rights and duties endowed upon her/him by law, rules and regulations. A customer or client, on the other hand, functions in a market space, holding certain rights and responsibilities, and is willing to pay for the services received (Medury 2010: 159). The governance approach gives primacy to consumers instead of citizens, or to their rights and participation in public services. Most contemporary movements in public administration advocate increased citizen participation or involvement in administrative governance, yet have significantly different definitions of citizens' participation. New Public Management (NPM), for instance, views participation from a managerial perspective, building citizen participation into managerial techniques often drawn from 'Total Quality Management' and similar management movements in the private sector (Osborne and Hutchinson 2004: 15). In these models, citizens are the consumers or customers of government services and their input is important in order to deliver high-performance products and services. Citizen participation is encouraged in the form of citizen satisfaction panels or surveys and in performance measurement.

It is increasingly becoming clear that the 'public' aspect of administration is losing significance and making way for private service providers. This chapter reiterated that 'public interest' is the central concern of public administration. To remain robust, resilient and relevant it must continually evaluate its own performance and test its worth in the court of citizens. In order to be citizen-centric, public administration should be participative and transparent. It should be effective, efficient and responsive to the citizens. The ethos of serving the citizens should permeate all government organisations. Government organisations should be accountable to the people. An evaluation of the functioning of the institutions of governance should necessarily be based on the satisfaction they provide to the common person. In this regard, the voice of the citizens should attain prominence (GoI 2009).

Citizens and administration interact with each other constantly. There are different ways in which the citizen interfaces with administrative agencies in everyday life. As the discussion in this chapter shows, through these interactions people have felt that the Indian bureaucracy is generally unresponsive, insensitive and corrupt. Citizens' grievances against administration are on the rise, at the same time concerted efforts are being made by the government to reduce the growing discontent among citizens by providing various channels for redressal of their grievances.

RTI, Citizens' Charter and e-governance have emerged as effective and accessible tools to redress citizens' grievances. In the changing scenario, the position of the citizens from being mere recipients of administrative support and services has now shifted to their being the prime movers in the affairs of governance. It is a change from local, beneficiary status, to active 'participant status'. In a democracy, the main purpose of public administration is to serve the people. An accountable, accessible, transparent, participative and responsive administration is inevitable to address the problems of the people.

REFERENCES

Agarwal, U. C., ed. 2004. *Public Administration: Vision and Reality*. New Delhi: Indian Institute of Public Administration.

Ahuja, Kanta and A. K. Ojha. 2008. *Governance and Reforms*. Jaipur: Aalekh Publication.

Avasthi, A. and S. Maheswari. 2010. *Public Administration*. Agra: Lakshmi Narain Agarwal.

Batalli, Mirlinda. 2011. 'Impact of Public Administration Innovations on Enhancing the Citizens' Expectations'. *International Journal of e-Education, e-Business, e-Management and e-Learning* 1 (2): 156–62.

Bayley, D. H. 1969. *The Police and Political Development in India*. Princeton: Princeton University Press.

Bhatnagar, Subhash C. 2008. 'E-Government: Building a SMART Administration for India's States', in *The Governance Discourse: A Reader*, edited by Bidyut Chakrabarty and Mohit Bhattacharya. New Delhi: Oxford.

Bhattacharya, Mohit. 2008. *New Horizons of Public Administration*. New Delhi: Jawahar Publishers.

Bohman, J. and W. Rehg. 2009. 'Jürgen Habermas' in *The Stanford Encyclopedia of Philosophy* (Summer 2009 Edition). Available at http://plato.stanford.edu/archives/sum2009/entries/habermas/ (accessed 10 December 2016).

Chakrabarty, Bidyut and Mohit Bhattacharya, eds. 2008. *The Governance Discourse: A Reader*. New Delhi: Oxford University Press.

Cheema, G. S. and D. A. Rondinelli, eds. 1983. *Decentralization and Development: Policy Implementation in Developing Countries*. Beverly Hills, CA: Sage.

Dicey, A. V. 1948. *Lectures on Relation between Law and Public Opinion in England During the Nineteenth Century*, second edition. London: Macmillan.

Easton, D. 1975. 'A Re-assessment of the Concept of Political Support'. *British Journal of Political Science* 5 (4): 435–57.

Government of India (GoI). 2008a. 'Report of the Sixth Central Pay Commission'. Submitted to the Ministry of Finance, Government of India, New Delhi.

———. 2008b. 'Promoting e-Governance: The SMART Way Forward'. Eleventh Report of the Second Administrative Reforms Commission, December.

———. 2009. *Citizen Centric Administration: The Heart of Governance*. Twelfth report of the Second Administrative Reforms Commission (ARC), submitted to the Department of Administrative Reforms and Public Grievances, Ministry of Personnel, Public Grievances and Pensions, Government of India, New Delhi.

Habermas, Jürgen. 1984. *The Theory of Communicative Action*, translated by T. McCarthy. Boston: Beacon Press.

Hooja, Rakesh. 1987. *Administrative Interventions in Rural Development.* Jaipur: Rawat.

Jagannadham, V. 1978. 'Public Administration and the Citizen: How Far Public Administration can be Public'. *Indian Journal of Public Administration* 24 (2): 355–73.

Medury, Uma. 2010. *Public Administration in the Globalisation Era: The New Public Management Perspective.* New Delhi: Orient BlackSwan.

Morrow, William L. 1980. *Public Administration: Politics and the Political System.* New York: Random House.

Organization for Economic Cooperation and Development (OECD). 2009. *Focus on Citizens: Public Engagement for Better Policy and Services.* Available at http://www.oecd.org/dataoecd/20/3/42658029.pdf (accessed 21 November 2016).

Osborne, David and Peter Hutchinson. 2004. *The Price of Government: Getting the Results We Need in an Age of Permanent Fiscal Crisis.* New York: Basic Books.

Robson, W. A. 1964. *The Governors and the Governed.* London: George Allen and Unwin.

Rouban, Luc, ed. 1999/2006. *Citizens and the New Governance: Beyond New Public Management.* Reprint. Amsterdam: IOS Press.

Sharma, Manu Vatsal and Naveen Surapaneni. 2006. 'What's ailing public services?'. *Rediff.com*, 25 March. Available at http://www.rediff.com/money/2006/mar/25guest1.htm (accessed 11 July 2017).

Sharma, Pradeep K. and Mandakini Devasher. 2007. 'Right to Information in India: Legislation and Beyond' in *Decentralisation: Institutions and Politics in Rural India*, edited by Satyajit Singh and Pradeep K. Sharma, 348–79. New Delhi: Oxford University Press.

Singh, Amita. 2002. *Public Administration: Roots and Wings.* New Delhi: Galgotia Publishing.

Vigoda, E. 2002. 'From Responsiveness to Collaboration: Governance, Citizens, and the Next Generation of Public Administration'. *Public Administration Review* 62 (5): 527–40.

11

LOCAL GOVERNANCE*

Empowering People at the Grassroots

HIGHLIGHTS

- History of decentralisation in India
- Rural local governance
  - 73rd Constitutional Amendment Act, 1992
  - Weaknesses of the system
- Urban local governance
  - 74th Constitutional Amendment Act, 1992
  - Major challenges before the system
- Implications of the 73rd and 74th Constitutional Amendment Acts

Participatory democracy and devolution of power are dialectically connected. In fact, it will not be an exaggeration to argue that the very spirit of democracy shall always remain elusive unless power is meaningfully devolved to the *demos*. History is a witness to many political movements which were organised to establish the invincible rights of the demos in governance; they always remain deprived as the better-off sections never cede their privileges so easily. It is true that the age-old social imbalances cannot be fixed overnight, however campaigns opposed to social and economic vested interests create a space for change. The idea of democratic decentralisation of power, supportive of localising governance, is an outcome of such an effort in which an ideological urge was formally institutionalised in the form of a design. This is a significant change in our conceptualisation of governance from the Weberian hierarchal form of organisation. Nonetheless, the idea has gained ground in recent years for the sustained campaign for democratising governance and the governance-deficit at the grassroots due to the gradual withdrawal of the State from areas of its traditional concern. So, democratic decentralisation is a

* Some sections of this chapter have been developed from Chakrabarty, *Localizing Governance in India*, pp. 213–38. With permission from Taylor & Francis. The discussion on the 73rd and 74th Amendment Acts of 1992 is drawn on Chakraborty and Chand (2016: ch. 6).

contextual conceptual construct which radically altered the texture of governance in recent years. In practice, the idea creates a space for self-governing local institutions to play a pivotal role in the provisioning of public services and the formulation and implementation of developmental goals. This is a path-breaking event as it has not only laid and consolidated the foundation of a completely new kind of thinking in governance, but has also created a momentum for change that cannot be halted so easily. This chapter is devoted to an extensive probing of the processes which culminated in formally establishing the structures of democratic decentralisation, and thereby help understand the revolutionary impact of localising governance in India, or public administration in general. This chapter will show that the changed texture of governance at the grassroots is not a matter of chance, but an outcome of intensive politico-ideological drive over a period of time.

HISTORY OF DECENTRALISATION IN INDIA

The campaign for decentralisation of authority has a long past. As history shows, sustained attempts were made to decentralise authority in India since the 1880s with the acceptance of the famous Rippon Resolution of 1882. The efforts continued in independent India because it was strongly felt that a centralised administration would hardly be adequate to manage such a diverse country. Despite appreciating the need to decentralise power, the makers of our Constitution did not seem to have been persuaded to refer to villages as the basic unit of self-governance in the face of strong opposition, spearheaded by the chairperson of the drafting committee, Dr B. R. Ambedkar. Notwithstanding their support for participatory democracy, a majority of the Assembly's members were not favourably disposed to Gandhi's insistence on village-based governance. As the debates in the Constituent Assembly (1946–49) show, there were two contrasting points of view: there were Gandhians who held the view that the panchayati raj that Gandhi had elaborated was the appropriate form of governance in India; their detractors claimed that the Gandhian model was not only archaic but also ineffective in the changed socio-economic and ideological environment, they therefore argued for individual-centric governance which had contributed significantly to the success of Western democracies. Ambedkar was opposed to the very idea of the village being a focal point of governance as he strongly felt that it was a source of oppression; to remain in the village meant 'remaining tied to the same humiliating occupations that had so far been their fate' (Viswanathan 1998: 238). For Gandhi, the village was the basis for building 'a republican society, uncontaminated by colonialist ideology'; for Ambedkar, 'it was the black hole of Indian civilization' (ibid.). Persuaded by Ambedkar's argument, Nehru too came out openly in his support by stating that 'a village, normally speaking, is backward intellectually and culturally and no progress can made from a backward environment. Narrow-minded people are much more likely to be untruthful and violent' (Nehru 1945/1988: 508). With the support of Nehru, Patel and other leaders of the Congress, it was easier for Ambedkar to persuade other members. In contrast to Ambedkar's arguments in favour of an individual-driven Constitution, there were leading Gandhians who built their arguments in favour of a State constituted of self-sufficient village republics. Although they did not succeed in the Assembly, they set the process rolling towards democratic decentralisation. The idea subsequently received adequate attention, as is evident in the constitution of several committees across the years to suggest ways to galvanise institutions of local governance. All these committees supported revitalisation of PRIs as perhaps the only way to revamp the institutions of local governance. One of the most clearly-stated justifications for PRIs was given by the report of the Ashok Mehta Committee, *Panchayati Raj: Review and Evaluation* in 1978:

> Politically speaking, [Panchayati Raj] became a process of democratic seed-building in the Indian soil, making average citizens more conscious of his rights than before. Administratively speaking, it bridged the gulf between the bureaucratic elite and the people. Socio-culturally speaking, it generated a new leadership which was not merely relatively young in age but also modernistic and pro-social-change in outlook. Finally, looked at from the developmental angle, it helped rural people cultivate a developmental psyche. (Quoted in Satyanarayana 1990: 168)

The Committee unambiguously held that one of the serious limitations of PRIs was the absence of constitutional guarantee since they were placed in the non-enforceable section of the Constitution. So long as local self-government remained in Part IV of the Constitution, it had no future, the Committee warned. Another categorical statement articulating the same concern was made by the report of the 1986 L. M. Singhvi Committee, *Revitalization of PRIs for Democracy and Development*, which went to the extent of suggesting an amendment to the Constitution to make this happen: 'the Committee envisages and recommends that local self-government should be constitutionally recognized, protected and preserved by the inclusion of a new chapter in the Constitution' (quoted in Satyanarayana 1990: 222). For democracy to take root at the grassroots level, the Committee felt, local self-government and more particularly PRIs 'should be constitutionally proclaimed as the third tier of Government' (ibid.). What was strongly argued became a reality with the adoption of the 73rd Amendment Act in 1992, which not only constitutionalised local self-government in India but also gave the long overdue constitutional recognition to PRIs. These were momentous policy designs that radically altered the texture of governance in India in two complementary ways: on the one hand, they made governance far more widespread than before by constitutionally guaranteeing the role of the mass of villagers who had thus far remained peripheral; on the other hand, this caused sea change in the nature of governance as it became more receptive to inputs from the grassroots, which was not always accessible given the obvious systemic constraints of the Weberian hierarchical and centralised administration that India had adopted following decolonisation in 1947.

Given its critical importance, this chapter is directed to comprehend the nature and consequences of the 1992 Amendments along with the context in which they became more or less *fait accompli* in light of growing democratisation across the length and breadth of India. The chapter makes two major arguments and one supplementary argument: first, reflective of significant socio-economic churning, leading to perceptive changes in policy decisions, the 73rd Amendment Act was the culmination of long-drawn processes that had begun at the dawn of India's Independence with the insistence on reorganising governance around Gandhi's notion of oceanic circle. The second argument is linked to the analysis of the context that had undergone change following the urge for democratisation of governance, especially at the grassroots. What is sought to be shown is the idea that changes at the grassroots get manifested at the level of policymaking, i.e. those responsible for policy design cannot remain aloof from socio-political churnings. Seeking to capture the dialectical interconnection between policymaking and the prevalent socio-economic context, this chapter reiterates the point that a radical policy-prescription like the 73rd Amendment Act cannot be conceptualised without reference to the milieu in which it was thought-about, devised and finally implemented. The supplementary argument is about the changing nature of India's political leadership that was receptive to the grassroots initiatives and responded favourably to chart out a new ideological path of action.

The Context

The legislative origins of the 73rd Constitutional Amendment Act can be traced back to the Constitution (64th Amendment) Bill, which was introduced in the Parliament in 1989 by the government of the then prime minister, Rajiv Gandhi. The introduction of the bill was perhaps the first attempt to confer constitutional status on rural local governments. Though the bill failed to clear the test of the Rajya Sabha, its broader objective of reviving the country's centuries-old institution of rural local self-government was highly appreciated. The major reservation against the said bill was that it provided very little space for state governments regarding local governance. However, after much deliberation, the issue of conferring constitutional status on rural local governments came into being with the passage of the 73rd Constitution (Amendment) Act, 1992.

Though the manifest reason behind the Act 1992 was to bring about an efficient delivery mechanism for development, there were serious political compulsions before the political leadership to bring up the issue of local democracy. The 1970s and 1980s had witnessed several anti-establishment movements on ethnic, religious and linguistic lines across the country. The militant secessionist movements of the North-East, Punjab and the northern hilly tract of West Bengal, and the demand for separate statehood in Bihar and Uttar Pradesh had challenged the credibility of the Indian State to govern. Under the circumstances, sharing power with communities at the grassroots was conceived as a desperate attempt to release the mounting pressure on the Indian State. Moreover, this policy of decentralisation was hailed because it would substantially downsize the powers of the recalcitrant and demanding opposition-ruled state governments, and establish a direct linkage between district collectors and the panchayati raj bodies.

There are evidences to suggest that an amendment with far-reaching consequences could not have been possible without favourable circumstances in which arguments were marshalled in its support. In other words, the 73rd Amendment Act was clearly a contextual response. With the disillusionment with centralised planning, it was felt that decentralised democracy would perhaps be an appropriate mechanism to bring about inclusive growth. As the Act underlines:

> Though the Panchayati Raj Institutions have been in existence for a long time, it has been observed that these institutions have not been able to acquire the status and dignity of viable and responsive people's bodies due to a number of reasons, including absence of regular elections, prolonged supersessions, insufficient representation of weaker sections like Scheduled Castes, Scheduled Tribes and women, inadequate devolution of power and lack of financial resources.[1]

Because of its non-enforceability, Article 40 of Part IV (Directive Principles of State Policy) of the Constitution, which insists that the State shall take steps to organise panchayats, never became an effective constitutional direction. Hence, the Act reiterated:

> in light of the experience in the last forty years and in view of the short-comings which have been observed, it is considered that there is an imperative need to enshrine in the Constitution certain basic and essential features of Panchayati Raj Institutions to impart certainty, continuity and strength to them.[2]

It appears that the PRIs did not seem to be adequate to accomplish the constitutional goal of democratic decentralisation. The developmental State, it was highlighted, had completely failed to pursue the goal that the founding fathers had set. As Ronald deSouza points out, because of 'the insensitivity, casualness, lack of accountability and also inertia of the delivery processes' the State became 'a captive' of the vested interests in rural areas where the benefits meant for rural uplift were usually appropriated by the rural elite given their control over the government structures at the grassroots (2003: 103). The 73rd Amendment Act with its recommendations for decentralisation of planning and powers and functions, and also mandatory elections to the PRIs, was seen 'as a solution to this continued asymmetry of power' (ibid.). A study of the past reveals that the policymakers seem to have been disillusioned with India's development trajectory. While seeking to identify the roots of malice in local governance, in a series of speeches at workshops for district magistrates and collectors that spanned almost two years between 1987 and 1989, Rajiv Gandhi condemned the administration for being

> paternalistic … which is not suitable for a society where the main thrust of administration is on development. It was agreed that the regulatory functions of administration should be seen as an end in themselves, as they tended to be in colonial times, but as a means of reinforcing and sustaining the processes of broad-based development. [A] more representative and more responsive administration would be better placed to relate the purposes of administration to the larger goals of our national life – democracy, socialism, secularism and non-alignment. (Gandhi 1988)

According to him, PRIs should not merely be construed as instruments of devolution of power but also as avenues of democracy and representation. He believed that the Amendment Acts would provide a well-designed arrangement for meaningful representation of people at the

[1] Text of the 73rd Amendment Act, 1992, reproduced from the government notification available at http://indiacode.nic.in/coiweb/amend/amend73.htm (accessed 8 June 2016).

[2] Ibid.

grassroots in governance for the first time in India's administrative history. In Rajiv Gandhi's own words, 'with the passage of [the legislation for democratic decentralisation], the panchayats would emerge as a firm building block of administration and development ... as an instrument in the consolidation of democracy at the grassroots [which will surely] purge the administration of the power brokers, the middlemen and vested interests' (Gandhi 1989: 10). He was critical of the 'dependency syndrome', where people in general waited for the government to do 'the simplest things which they can do themselves'. The system had become 'so top-heavy and top-oriented' that at every level, people looked to the level above for a solution. What was required was 'to push the administration down, not just in the administration but also sometimes out of the administration to the community'. By involving people in both planning and executing developmental programmes at the grassroots, the administration would surely become 'responsive and representative' in character, Rajiv Gandhi felt (ibid.: 13).

In its analysis of India's development trajectory, the Planning Commission attributed the failure of the PRIs to take off to: (*a*) top-down and target-oriented rather than a bottom-up approach, (*b*) lack of accountability of the implementing agencies to both the government and the people, (*c*) social sector programmes formulated without addressing the question of sustainability of benefits, and (*d*) failure to ensure timely and adequate flow of funds to the implementing agencies (GoI 2002b). The aim was to create people-centric governance where people, as the main stakeholders, would uphold its democratic concern by making administration accountable and attentive to what was needed to make the PRIs effective instruments of democratic decentralisation of power and authority. Conceptually, the entire exercise was directed to redesign governance by insisting simultaneously on localisation, externalisation and de-bureaucratisation. With the devolution of power to the grassroots, PRIs would automatically become de facto authorities with adequate constitutional protection for their functions. The instant outcome of this process was the flow of power from the top to the bottom where actual decisions were executed. It was an attempt to establish an intimate relationship between the administrators and the recipients who had thus far remained peripheral in decision-making. This is a reiteration of the Gandhian notion of participatory democracy articulated through the concepts of *swaraj* (self-government) and *swadeshi* (community's control over resources), and invoking the imagery of the village republic (*gram swaraj*) as representing India's democratic tradition (Seth 2004). Localisation was therefore a significant process with far-reaching consequences at the grassroots, transforming both the existent power structure and the processes in which power was exercised. Implicit in these processes was also the roots of externalisation which, in contemporary management vocabulary, means 'contracting-out' to non-public agencies. This also entails, besides government-sponsored public authorities, numerous other agencies which have a stake in governance. By being important to grassroots decision-making, the local populace thus not only become recipients but also instigators of change. So power is externalised to make participatory democracy real in its manifestation and execution. Localisation and externalisation hardly make sense without governance being substantially de-bureaucratised.

As argued above, one of the principal factors for the decline of PRIs was the hegemonic control of public bureaucracy that flourished with the connivance of the local vested interests. The aim of the 73rd Amendment Act was to destroy this evil and the well-entrenched nexus that appeared to have crippled participatory democracy and prevented it from taking root in rural areas. With governance being democratically-decentralised, following the creation of institutional spaces for participation, a parallel process began whereby the peripheral sections were drawn to decision-making by being sensitive to their roles and responsibilities as members of the localities. As a result, governance which thus far remained distant has now become closer to the people and reduced the so-called dependency syndrome, making governance a people-centric and largely de-bureaucratised exercise.

RURAL LOCAL GOVERNANCE

PRIs are the institutionalised pan-Indian form of rural local governance that came into existence with the passage of 73rd Constitutional Amendment Act in 1992. This legislation heralded a three-tier structure of rural local governance—*gram panchayat*s at the lowest level, *panchayat samiti* at the intermediate level and *zilla parishad* at the highest level. This section will provide a detailed discussion on the 73rd Amendment Act of 1992.

73rd Constitutional Amendment Act, 1992

The 73rd Constitutional Amendment Act of 1992 is a watershed event in the history of local government in India. It virtually salvaged the centuries-old tradition and institution of local governance from a dependent status to one of self-reliance by conferring the much-coveted constitutional status on it. Until the passage of the 73rd Constitutional Amendment Act, states were the only sub-national units officially recognised by the Indian Constitution. The provision for local government remained under the state list and hence there was no uniform pattern across the country. The functional domain of rural local bodies was limited largely to the provision of some core services such as water supply, sanitation, local roads, etc. The 'developmental' activities were limited to the role of implementing developmental schemes sponsored by either central or state governments. The passage of the Act has now empowered local bodies to formulate and implement development plans of their own.

Main Features of the Act

Whatever the motive behind the constitutionalisation of panchayats, the Act has changed the very contours of local governance at the rural level. Some of the main features of the Act are as follows:

- The Act has clearly devolved power, authority and responsibilities to rural local bodies to enable them to function as institutions of self-government (Article 243G).

- The Act has made it mandatory for all levels of PRIs to conduct periodic elections every five years. In the case of early or premature dismissal of PRIs, elections are to be held within a period of six months, with the newly elected members would serve out the remainder of the five-year term (Article 243E).
- The Act has also made provisions for the reservation of seats for SC and ST members in all panchayats at all levels in proportion to their respective share in the panchayat concerned. In addition, the Act has also made mandatory reservation of one-third of all seats in all panchayats at all levels for women, of which one-third is to be reserved for women belonging to the SC and ST communities. The constitutional provision for the reservation of seats for SCs and STs also extends to the position of panchayat chairperson at all three tiers of PRIs and one-third mandatory reservation is earmarked for them.
- The Act has stipulated the constitution of a state-level Election Commission for a period of five years to ensure free and fair elections to local bodies.
- The Act has also empowered the state government to constitute another independent state-level Finance Commission for a period of five years to review the overall financial position of local bodies and recommend the principle that should govern the allocation of funds and taxation to local bodies. The governor of the state is entrusted with the power of constituting the Finance Commission, which will make recommendations to her/him.
- The Act has also made provision for the constitution of *gram sabha*, a body of the electorate of gram panchayats, and has established a more direct channel of people's participation. The underlying rationale was that gram sabha would function as a fulcrum of the developmental process, where the community would participate both at the formulation and implementation of developmental plans. Moreover, this body will function as the organ of local accountability and oversight.
- The XI Schedule (Article 243G) has been added which gives the list of 29 functions to be performed by PRIs.

According to Article 243G of the Act, 'Panchayats shall be given powers and authority to function as institutions of self-government'. This would be done by delegating powers and responsibilities to panchayats at the appropriate level, such as preparation of plan for economic development and social justice, and implementation of scheme for economic development. Article 243H authorises the panchayat to levy, collect and appropriate taxes, tolls and fees. These two Articles clearly lay out the powers, authority and responsibilities of panchayats vis-à-vis state governments. They empower rural local bodies to play a pivotal role in the provision of public services, creation and maintenance of local public goods and planning, and implementation of developmental activities and programmes to alleviate poverty and promote distributive equality. Unlike in the past, PRIs are now constitutionally authorised to act in those areas which are earmarked as their domain in the XI Schedule. The Ninth Five-Year Plan (1997–2002) clubbed these areas under five broad categories (GoI 2002b: 191, Appendix I) as follows:

1. Agriculture and allied activities
    - Land improvement, implementation of land reforms, land consolidation and soil conservation
    - Minor irrigation, water management and watershed development
    - Animal husbandry, dairying and poultry, fisheries
    - Social forestry and farm forestry
    - Minor forest produce, and fuel and fodder
2. Rural industrialisation
    - Small-scale industries, including food processing industries
    - Khadi, village and cottage industries
3. Infrastructure development
    - Rural housing, drinking water
    - Roads, culverts, bridges, ferries, waterways and other means of communication
    - Rural electrification, including distribution of electricity, non-conventional energy sources
    - Markets and fairs, maintenance of community assets
4. Human development
    - Technical training and vocational education, adult and non-farm education, primary and secondary education, cultural activities
    - Health and sanitation, including hospitals, PHCs and dispensaries
    - Family welfare
    - Poverty alleviation programme
5. Social welfare and gender development
    - Women and child development
    - Social welfare, including welfare of the physically and mentally challenged
    - Welfare of weaker sections and in particular of SCs and STs
    - Public distribution system

The above list contains all those critical activities which need to be meaningfully attended to bring about inclusive rural development. What is striking here is the idea that rural development does not necessarily mean economic prosperity but also human development for which one is required to devise effective policies. Hence, the goal that has been constantly emphasised, both by stakeholders in villages and policymakers, is to localise governance whereby governance emerges as an instinctive design for the villagers to fulfil their aspired goal by dint of their own endeavour.

It is evident from the above discussion that there are some radical provisions in the 73rd Amendment Act. They seek to address some of the problems encountered by PRIs in previous years, such as: (*a*) granting PRIs constitutional status, (*b*) empowering socially and economically disadvantaged groups, i.e. Dalits, Adivasis and women, (*c*) ensuring free, fair and regular elections (*d*) keeping terms fixed, (*e*) identifying a list of items which would fall under the jurisdiction of PRIs, and (*f*) addressing the issue of PRI finances (Ronald deSouza 2005: 379). Thus, the Act has provided for a significant degree of fiscal, administrative and political decentralisation from the State to the local level, and has come to be known as a 'silent revolution'.

Weaknesses of the System

Now that the democratic decentralisation experiment has been with us for more than twenty-five years, it is necessary to evaluate the experiment. In this sub-section we will interrogate the democratic decentralisation experiment by asking a few important questions: Are we really ready for decentralisation? Is democratic decentralisation an end in itself? Does democratic decentralisation truly empower local community? These questions require a lot of introspection. In this section we will critically appraise the role of democratic decentralisation in delivering development and social justice.

Despite much accolade and fanfare, PRIs have indeed failed to bring about the much needed transformation in Indian society and polity. In fact, several shortcomings surfaced within a decade of its functioning. First, panchayat as the institution of local self-government suffers from an identity crisis as the meaning of self-government has not been clearly articulated. Second, PRIs have inherited a culture of subservience, deliberately inculcated by the colonial era. This has gone against the fullest realisation of decentralisation in post-Independence India. Third, though PRIs have an avowed stand on gender empowerment, panchayats are actually witnessing the typical phenomenon of proxy participation, where male members of the women candidate wield power on her behalf—the infamous *pradhan-pati* syndrome being a case in point. Fourth, another major weakness of this system is the over-politicisation of the panchayats. In a parliamentary democracy, thanks to being in power for many years, panchayat administration and party administration have often become identical and inseparable, thereby leading to an overlap of responsibilities. Consequently, panchayat administration has become the extended branch of party administration, as the same set of persons discharge both the duties simultaneously, leading to a lot of confusion. However, politicisation is nothing unique, as the panchayati raj system has allowed political mobilisation. In a democratic system, competitive political mobilisation could have enhanced the status of the community if political parties were allowed to mobilise freely. For, in this system political parties always want to outpace their contenders by improving the quality of services. Distortions occur only when any political party or combination of parties hold power unilaterally for a long time. Fifth, over-reliance on PRIs as institutions of local governance often leads to 'system overload' as too many developmental projects are vying for attention in panchayats at the same time. Finally, a strong centralising tendency with the centrality of the development State has been implicit in the decentralisation initiatives in independent India. Starting from the Balwantrai Mehta Committee to the 73rd constitution Amendment Act, there has been a distinct tradition of centrality, nonetheless.

The functioning of the new panchayati raj system reveals the fact that though the legislative and electoral formalities have been completed in almost all the states, there are large variations among them at the operational level. The 29 subjects mentioned in the XI Schedule do not give power of legislating to the local bodies, they are given the power only to take decisions. The recommendations of the State Finance Commissions are not mandatory in nature. It is completely up to the state government to devolve or not devolve functions, functionaries and resources to the local bodies. As of 2007, only three of India's 28 states had passed executive orders devolving all 29 functions to the local level, as required by the Amendment. The high-handedness of bureaucracy, with a few exceptions, over the autonomy of the PRIs still prevails. As Mishra (2016: 242) documents, 'The experience gained so far is that, at the district level, various departments and agencies still implement programmes and function under the overall supervision and control of the District Collectors. The PRIs, therefore, have to be content with backseat driving.'

The experience of democratic decentralisation makes it clear that it cannot be a solution to one and all the ills of governance. The rigid patriarchal structure inhibits the participation of the oppressed castes and women in village governance. The 73rd Amendment stipulates that one-third of all panchayat seats should be reserved for women and provides a similar provision for SCs and STs. In North India, where caste and gender inequalities are particularly resilient, the local elites have tended to adapt to this requirement by putting up 'proxy' candidates from the required group, and continuing to wield power through them. The submissive female chairperson or *sarpanch* sitting quietly in a corner while her husband (often initially mistaken for the sarpanch) answers the questions is a familiar figure in the critical literature on panchayati raj in North India. Moreover, a majority of the elected representatives are first timers with little or no prior knowledge of the functioning of PRIs. It is not easy for the rural weaker sections to actively participate in the development process. The literacy level among SCs/STs and women is quite low. The distribution of rural assets and powers is heavily skewed in India—the bottom 39 per cent of rural households belong to oppressed castes and own only five per cent of all assets, while the top five per cent own 46 per cent of all assets. This makes the opportunities and social choices shrink for the deprived villagers at the grassroots.

Inadequate financial resources are another crucial constraint in effective functioning of decentralised governance. The panchayats have to depend on devolution and the grants-in-aid from the state governments and they have not developed any independent sources to raise revenues. Besides, most of the states have not transferred funds for the subjects transferred to these local bodies. A study of 12 states has shown that in nine of these the tax revenue of the local bodies (both panchayats and urban local bodies) was less than five per cent of the total tax revenue of the state government (GoI 2002a: 29). The limited fiscal autonomy of panchayats renders them excessively dependent on the central and state governments.

The constraints and problems that mark democratic decentralisation initiatives, though numerous, should not create a panic. This is because we are passing through a transitory phase and any kind of transition takes time to show positive results. It is a fact that a 'silent revolution' is indeed taking place in rural India where people are becoming conscious of their rights. One of the most heartening aspects of the panchayati raj experiment has been the inclusion and participation of various disadvantaged groups such as Dalits, Adivasis and women. It is unarguable that the provision of quotas has generated widespread awareness. Studies have shown that the developmental outcomes in panchayats headed by women are impressive, even if empowerment impacts have been rather slow in materialising what is expected (Jayal, Prakash and Sharma 2006: 13). The renewed movement towards democratic decentralisation has eroded the bureaucratic monopoly over the development processes and has shifted the locus of power to those who matter at the grassroots level.

The panchayati raj system represents an institutional watershed which has bought 'the people' back into the political process. People have been given a voice. This voice, even in a situation of pervasive asymmetric power, will result in a flattening of the asymmetry, a process that can have only emancipative consequences. To paraphrase B. S. Baviskar 'the Seventy-Third Amendment Act can rightly be termed as "a silent revolution", which in many respects salvaged the institution of self-government from a mere "agent" of provincial government to one of "self-reliant" one' (Baviskar and Mathew 2009: 10–11). In spite of all these positive developments, the panchayat members belonging to SCs and STs have, warns Baviskar, 'miles to go before achieving full and meaningful inclusion' and, in some case, he further adds, 'the power enjoyed by them is often symbolic' (ibid.). This is however not a mean achievement, given the fact that they were completely ostracised even for social communication in the past. In that respect, the amended constitutional provision can easily be identified as a harbinger of significant socio-economic transformation at the grassroots.

URBAN LOCAL GOVERNANCE

74th Constitutional Amendment Act, 1992

Unlike rural governance, urban governance is not hierarchical. Article 243Q of the 74th Amendment Act, 1992 stipulates that there shall be three types of urban local bodies in India, viz. nagar panchayat for the transitional areas, municipal councils or municipalities for smaller urban areas and municipal corporations for larger urban areas. State governments are allowed to design their own municipal Acts in accordance with the broad parameters outlined in the Act.

Functions

Article 243W of the Constitution deals with the power, authority and responsibilities of municipalities, which clearly lays out the functions of the municipality including the list of functions enumerated in the XII Schedule. The details of those functions can be organised around the following major concerns:

1. *Urban well-being*: Planning for social and economic development; regulation of land use and construction of buildings; planning for urban poverty alleviation, slum improvement and upgradation
2. *Infrastructure development*: Building of roads and bridges; water supply for domestic, industrial and commercial purpose; public amenities, including street lighting, parking lots, bus stops and public conveniences
3. *Human development*: Public health, sanitation conservation and solid waste management; urban forestry, protection of the environment and promotion of ecological aspects; safeguarding the interests of weaker sections of society, including the physically and mentally challenged; provision of urban amenities and facilities such as parks, gardens and playgrounds; promotion of cultural, educational and aesthetic aspects; burial and burial grounds; cremations, cremation grounds and electric crematoriums
4. *Concomitant requirements*: Cattle ponds; prevention of cruelty to animals; vital statistics including registration births and deaths; regulation of slaughter houses and tanneries

Similar to the XI Schedule, the XII Schedule is also a checklist of items that are necessary aids for inclusive urban development. Here too, the idea is to encourage participation of the local populace in activities which they deem appropriate for their own benefit. As the list shows, an attempt is made to bring about all-round urban development by addressing those major concerns that make urban life better and humane. By encouraging participation of the stakeholders in urban affairs and creating a supportive institutionalised system of governance, the 74th Amendment Act radically changed the texture of urban governance by making it responsible, accountable and sensitive to the constituents. In that respect, this legislative design can be said to have ushered in a new era of the State–citizen interface in the context of growing democratisation in India.

Main Provisions of the Act

The 74th Amendment Act is incorporated in Article 243 Part IXA of the Indian Constitution. Major provisions of the Act are as follows:

- Urban local bodies (ULBs)—to be known as municipal corporation, municipal council and nagar panchayat, depending on the population—shall be constituted through universal adult franchise in each notified urban area of the country
- These shall be constituted for a period of five years
- Not less than one-third of the total number of seats in each ULB shall be reserved for women

- These bodies shall be endowed with the power and authority to formulate and implement schemes for economic development and social justice on 18 subjects
- In order that the ULBs can perform the functions assigned to them, the legislature of the state concerned shall assign them specific taxes, duties, tolls and levies, and authorise them to impose, collect and appropriate the same
- Each state shall also constitute a Finance Commission which shall review the financial position of the ULBs and recommend the principles which should govern the devolution of resources including grants-in-aid from the Consolidated Fund of the respective state
- The superintendence, direction and control of the preparation of electoral rolls for, and the conduct of, all elections to the ULBs shall vest in the State Election Commission
- The Act has made provisions for the constitution of a wards committee in all municipalities with a population of three lakh and more
- District Planning Committee and Metropolitan Planning Committee shall be constituted to prepare a development plan

The 74th Amendment Act provides ULBs with legitimacy through regular elections and devolution of functional and financial powers. In order to make these ULBs a forum for inclusive governance, the Act earmarks specific domains for them. The Act also suggests the creation of wards committees in ULBs. Ghosh and Mitra observe that the wards committee is 'the most promising institution in which citizens from all sections of society can take part in local governance' (2008: 85). Being an important mechanism to achieve this goal, the wards committee is hailed as an instrument with 'the potential to introduce participation, partnership, proximity, transparency and accountability in urban governance' (ibid.: 86).

By guaranteeing constitutional status to the municipalities, the Act seeks to redefine their role, power, function and finances. This has ushered in a new era of urban governance and urban management in India. The Act is significant because apart from the traditional functions, it has also allocated to municipal bodies the function of economic development and social justice, suggesting their elevation from mere instrumentalities for 'agency functions' to responsible bodies for development planning. The provision of a State Finance Commission is a landmark step in providing financial autonomy to the ULBs. Reservation of seats ensures the participation of socially-deprived sections of society. The new Act has become an instrument of political education. In the context of urban politics, people are learning to organise, to question established patterns of authority, to demand their rights, to resist corruption, and so on. This learning process enhances their preparedness not only for local democracy but also for political participation in general.

Major Challenges before the System

The 74th Amendment has surely revived the ULBs in India, but they still face a number of problems. The first and most serious problem facing the ULBs is the acute scarcity of finance. In the absence of proper funds, power becomes meaningless because it cannot be translated into real efforts and outcomes. The new Act provides for the constitution of a State Finance Commission to look into the financial sources of local bodies, but the recommendations of the Commission are not binding on the respective states. People's participation in ULBs is still negligible. A major reason for this is that people look at the municipal bodies with suspicion and assume that their problems and grievances will not be taken care of. Moreover, just as it is in the XI Schedule, there is no clear demarcation of functions the XII Schedule does not clearly demarcate the functions of different local units of the urban local government. This has given the states the liberty to impose their own choices, which have at times created more confusion than order, regarding what function is to be delegated and what not.

In the changing scenario, ULBs need to exclusively devote themselves to the task of development, and should therefore enjoy a large measure of autonomy. But the ground reality depicts a contrary picture. Criticising the 74th Amendment Act, Nirmal Mukarji argues that 'it is almost a carbon copy of the Seventy-Third Amendment Act' and 'a hasty afterthought' (1993: 860). Comparing it with the 73rd Amendment Act, Mukarji further notes that 'it looks as if some independent thinking went into the panchayat law and then, one day, the *municipality wallahs* suddenly woke up and said "we too, please" and were simply served the panchayat dish with municipal sauce' (ibid.). Second, it thoughtlessly 'constitutionalizes an artificial dichotomy between rural and urban when all previous thinking has stressed a continuum between the two' (ibid.). Another limitation of the Act is the 'panchayats for rural areas' bias it generates, i.e. the locking of panchayats into a 'rural only' bind. Urban governance is also facing new challenges as a result of the process of liberalisation, privatisation, globalisation and urbanisation. Besides certain obvious limitations for structural and socio-political reasons, the ULBs present two contrasting patterns. On the one hand, there is the conventional model which seeks to organise ULBs in accordance with constitutional guidelines; on the other hand, there is another model which allows the state government to draw on informal networks among urban dwellers to evolve their own forums. The Kerala model of urban governance is, for instance, a State-induced participatory exercise in which the State formulated the policies of participation of the local population and facilitated this process through official channels. In contrast, there is the unique design of urban governance that Delhi has crafted, by drawing upon informal networks across various segments of Delhi's population, the state built an institutional forum for people's participation in civic governance by creating Residents' Welfare Associations (RWAs), which are democratic grassroots-level agencies dealing with planning and implementation of projects as per the aspirations of the people concerned. This system is neither constitutionally-supported nor has it emerged as a legislative design. It has just been formed out of an executive decision to create an alternative administrative set-up for urban well-being.

IMPLICATIONS OF 73RD AND 74TH AMENDMENT ACTS

As already argued, the Acts are phenomenal in many respects. Besides setting a three-tier system of governance, the establishment of a district planning committee (Article 243ZD) to consolidate the plans prepared by both panchayats and municipalities for the district as a whole is a distinctive feature of the Acts. It is true that the district authority is responsible for finalising the plan, however the inputs it receives from the panchayats and municipalities remain its core. As a result, the district plan is expected to be inclusive in its goal and objective. In this section we will specifically highlight some of the other such implications of these two Acts.

Constitutional Status

The first and foremost implication of the 73rd and 74th Amendments is the conferment of constitutional status on local government. Initially, the Constitution did not confer any special status on local government, except as an entry in the state list of the VII Schedule and as a specific article in the Directive Principles of State Policy The Constitution expected state governments to take the initiative in organising panchayats. Until recently, there was no uniform pattern of local self-government across the country. Formation and nurturing of local government was entirely dependent on the goodwill of state governments. With the passage of these Acts, it has become mandatory for state governments to establish rural and urban local governments. Hence, the constitutionalisation of local governments has engendered an exclusive legislative domain for what is known as the 'third stratum' of government, paving the way for a direct linkage between the governance process and the community per se.

Administrative Powers

The Acts have provided much-needed administrative autonomy in terms of functional devolution to both the urban and rural local bodies. So long as local bodies were considered as the mere 'agents' of the state governments they did not have the authority of taking administrative decisions independent of state control. But the new Acts have enabled local governments to manage their own affairs. For instance, the authority of local bodies to superintend overall development of the area concerned may mentioned. This authority includes, among others, the preparation of plans for economic development and social justice, and implementation of various developmental schemes or any other developmental initiative as the local bodies deem necessary.

Financial Autonomy

Another important implication of these Acts is the aspect of financial autonomy. Financial autonomy is the *sine qua non* of any organisation. Local bodies in India were known for their perennial financial stringency. The Acts have virtually salvaged the cash-strapped local bodies (both the urban and rural institutions) with substantial financial authority. The Acts have allowed panchayats and municipalities to mobilise their own resources, apart from the normal sources of finance, i.e. the grants-in-aids, which they usually receive from the government. The Acts provide for the mandatory constitution of a State Finance Commission by the state governments once every five years to review the comparative financial positions of local bodies and to make recommendations to the state government on the following issues: (*a*) the distribution between the state and the local bodies (panchayat and municipalities) of the net proceeds of the taxes, duties, tolls and fees leviable by the state, and the allocation between the local bodies (panchayats and municipalities) at all levels of their respective shares of such proceeds; (*b*) the determination of the taxes, duties, tolls and fees which may be assigned to or appropriated by the local bodies (panchayats and municipalities); (*c*) the grants-in-aids to the local bodies (panchayats and municipalities) from the Consolidated Fund of the state.

Transparency in Governance

Nowadays transparency has become a buzzword. It is considered a necessary precondition to ensure integrity in local government and an inseparable element of good governance. By making open deliberation on the issues of governance, decision-making at the grassroots has become really transparent, which was simply inconceivable in the past when it was bureaucracy-centric. Moreover, Article 243J of the 73rd Amendment Act and Article 243Z of 74th Amendment Act mention provisions for the mandatory audit of accounts of panchayats and municipalities respectively.

Accountability in Governance

Being elected by adult suffrage, the panchayats are also held accountable to the voters. Gone are the days when panchayats were controlled by dominant sections at the cost of the majority who always remained peripheral in so far as decision-making was concerned. Now, with regular elections, the situation has undergone sea change. Those who hold power need to be sensitive to the needs of the people if they want to be re-elected. Regular elections are thus not merely a mechanism for translating democracy in practice; they also provide voters with the opportunity to assert by casting votes in favour of candidates who, they think, are capable of being impartial administrators. Besides regular elections, the electorate is also informed and always keeps those involved in grassroots governance on tenterhooks.

Deepening of Democracy

It is often said that the secret formula behind the success of the Indian democracy lies in the embeddedness of the democratic spirit of Indian society. This has not happened overnight. There were a series of political movements that consolidated the urge for democratisation which was, inter alia, formalised by recognising the centrality of the demos in governance. The 73rd and 74th Amendment Acts are distinct examples. By setting up an all-inclusive popular body—i.e. the gram sabha at the lowest level (and *gram sansad* below the gram sabha in West Bengal) in the case of panchayats and the wards committee in the case of municipalities—the Acts have paved way for greater penetration of democracy into the interstices of Indian society. Mathur comments that 'a virtual democratic revolution has been brought about with the promulgation of these Amendment Acts' (Mathur 2013: 37). In fact, prior to the Acts, elections in these local bodies were more or less voluntary. Barring a few instances, it was, in most cases, occasional and sporadic. By legally endorsing the importance of regular elections to these bodies, these Acts have contributed to the consolidation of democracy at the grassroots.

Gender Empowerment

Another redeeming feature of the Acts is the institutionalisation of the participation of women via reservation of seats. Womenfolk, especially in rural India, have been subject to systematic and systemic exploitation by patriarchy. The Acts have substantially elevated the status of Indian women from a subjugated status to a self-reliant one. The Acts have stipulated in categorical terms that 'not less than one-third of the total number of seats to be filled by direct election in every panchayats shall be reserved for women'. As the 'Report of the Task Force on Panchayati Raj Institutions (PRIs)' set up under the Planning Commission in 2001 observed:

> One of the significant achievements of the provisions of the 73rd Amendment Act concerning reservation of seats and political offices in favour of women and the disadvantaged sections of the rural community is that it had improved their awareness and perception levels and has created an urge in them to assert their rightful share in the decision making process at the local level. (Quoted in Pal 2004: 142)

The 73rd Amendment was a threat to the prevalent socio-economic dispensation since it challenged the male-chauvinistic mindset that remains a threat to realising gender equality. The policy of reservation was a powerful legislative design that sought to replace the mindset supportive of gender prejudices. Most earlier efforts towards making local governance inclusive were scuttled since the vested interests played a critical role in panchayat affairs, which allowed neither women nor the oppressed communities to participate as equal partners. There are instances that show that seat reservations have 'provided underprivileged groups with increased visibility and an opportunity to influence local affairs' (Robinson 2005: 20). In many panchayats, women have managed to direct local affairs in accordance with their priorities, by marshalling adequate financial resources and lobbying bureaucrats and politicians at higher levels. However, while it is true that the situation has undergone sea change after granting reservation for women, SCs and STs in the PRIs in proportion to their share in India's demography, the effectiveness of these provisions is uneven. We also have reasons to be alarmed because there are panchayats where elite dominance continues to prevail and traditional caste leaders and the landed elite 'dominate decision-making by proxy or manipulations' (ibid.). A recent study shows that female pradhans usually act as proxies for husbands, sons or powerful neighbours. In effect, the 'functions of the gram Pradhan are performed by husbands, brothers-in-law, fathers-in-law [and their] role is … limited to household chores' (Buch 2005: 351). In his study of panchayats in Western Uttar Pradesh, Lieten has shown how the typical patriarchal mindset stood in the way of realising gender parity in local governance. He says:

> Most male members [insist] that girls should go to school, but only to learn and write, and there is no need for them to go for higher education, for in that case they "go and sit on the head" of the males. Their freedom should be limited and they should not indulge too much in public activities. They are regarded as not knowing anything, and of not being of much use in panchayats: "she should take proper care of the house only" is an often heard proposition. (Lieten 1996: 2704)

Hence the hope that PRIs are effective challenges to well-entrenched gender biases seems an overstretch. The argument goes because 'the pious hopes of some members [of panchayats], including female members, of furthering human, social and economic development through the panchayats have proven to be out of touch with reality' (ibid.: 2705). However, the scene does not seem to be as disappointing as it is made out. Studies of women panchayats in Madhya Pradesh, Rajasthan and some parts of Uttar Pradesh provided inputs challenging 'the myths about rural women's lack of interest in politics, their passivity and nonparticipation in local political institutions, proxyism by male relatives, women's universal political connectivity and women's entry into panchayats from only well-off sections' (Buch 1999). Limitations notwithstanding, these amendments have initiated processes of significant socio-political changes at the grassroots by making PRIs 'a democratic forum to grapple with social and political issues in the open [and] churning process will continue' (Lieten 1996: 2705). These amendments are thus the beginning of an era of empowerment of women and the underprivileged when the social, economic and political hegemony of the privileged is being questioned justifiably to fulfil the aspired goal of making India an equitable society, free from prejudices of any kind. There is no denying that in an unequal patriarchal society like ours, reservation of seats for women has invariably uplifted the status of women. However, it should not be taken as *the* way of empowering women. It is only a step towards empowerment, not the empowerment in itself, as it is often mistakenly equated. The issue of reservation boils down to an irreducible duality between differences versus equality. The feminist epistemology seems to have been caught in this perennial dilemma. Putting it bluntly, the debate centres around whether women should struggle for equal rights or valorise their differences from menfolk and thereby ask for preferential treatment.

Empowerment of the Disadvantaged

It is quite fashionable these days to talk about 'inclusive development', which calls for an all-embracing formula and framework of development so that the disadvantaged sections are not left out at the margins. Modern political philosophers like Ronald Dworkin, John Rawls, et al. have justified, at least in essence, the necessity of inclusive development in their argument for equity and social justice. The Constitution of India has devoted considerable portion for the uplift of the SCs, STs and Other Backward Classes (OBCs). In addition to that, the 73rd and 74th Amendment Acts have enabled the least advantaged sections (i.e. the SCs and STs) to have a greater chance of representation at the local bodies by reserving one-third of the seats for them in both the urban and rural local bodies. It has thus been rightly observed that 'the political space given to marginalized sections has, to some extent, dealt a blow to the asymmetrical social structure at the local level and given greater space for their participation and involvement in decision making' (Pal 2004: 142).

A new, perhaps powerful, voice was articulated with the acceptance of the 73rd Amendment Act—a voice which was, thus far, suppressed under age-old social prejudices that always privileged one's ascribed identity over any other considerations. These constitutional amendments can thus be said to have introduced newer ways of conceptualising human relations. However, that is not enough, because constitutional amendments alone cannot bring about the expected transformation unless the demand for 'de facto decentralization does not arise from the grassroots' (ibid.). Nonetheless, the 73rd Amendment Act stands out as one of these radical pieces of legislations that has not only created newer parameters of conceptualising interpersonal relationships but also initiated movements for inclusive growth of communities in the midst of well-entrenched divisions along caste, class and ethnic axes.

Popular Participation

The Acts have institutionalised popular participation in local governance. The introduction of 'participatory development' as an alternative paradigm of development in the 73rd and 74th Amendment Acts is a case in point. The Acts have also formalised popular participation through the mandatory construction of gram sabha or wards committee at the lowest level.

Decentralised Planning

Another important hallmark of the two Acts is the introduction of the decentralised planning process. For long, planning was couched as a highly technical job to be done by a group of seasoned mandarins. But, of late, the notion of planning has undergone sea change as we are now favouring the 'bottom-up' approach. Governmental efforts of decentralising planning are evident in both rural and urban local bodies. In the case of rural local bodies, for instance, the state-initiated rural development through scheme-based activities—where people at the grassroots were involved in implementing the activities—has been replaced by people-initiated rural development programmes in which the government participates. People are now recognised as the stakeholders of development. Article 243G, for example, has identified the panchayats as 'institutions of self-government' and entrusted to them the responsibilities of preparing plans for promoting economic development and social justice.

The State Panchayat Act has, at least formally, given necessary powers and functions to the panchayats to formulate plans. However, barring a few states like Kerala, Karnataka and Tamil Nadu, the track record of grassroots planning in the rest of the country is anything but inspiring. In fact, Kerala has taken giant strides in this direction. Kerala's much-hyped 'people's campaign for the Ninth Plan' may be mentioned in this context. Under this programme panchayats were entrusted to prepare and prioritise projects in an integrated and scientific manner. The programme also ensured maximum participation of local people at every stage of the planning process. The decentralised planning model is not confined to panchayats alone. The 74th Amendment Act endorses decentralised planning which is articulated by institutionalising, for instance, Metropolitan Planning Committee and District Planning Committee.

CONCLUDING OBSERVATIONS

The 1992 Amendments created a new set of political opportunities for deepening of democracy by creating a space for the participation of the majority of the population, especially the underprivileged, in governance. There are problems and occasional hiccups; nonetheless, these Amendments have set in motion processes whereby citizens are empowered to understand their rights and duties to make the country a viable democracy.

As the fundamental impulse of policymaking moves away from centralised state institutions towards the market, these Amendments, in principle, should facilitate the creation of structures that devolve power to the local bodies. As per the 73rd Amendment Act, the underlying principle of panchayati raj is the use of local knowledge, popular experience and participation in the making of decisions that affect local people. There is no doubt that the reformed PRIs are supposed to reconstitute the decision processes on the basis of local participation on a continuous basis and thus, in principle, represent an institutionalised shift in power towards disempowered sections of rural population. The only flaw in this argument is that the village-based institutions continue

> to reflect unequal social and economic structures … and higher castes and economically powerful groups within the village continue to be the de facto leaders in panchayats; while the women, despite the reservation, remain "proxies" to male counterparts who participate in panchayat affairs and decisions. (Roychowdhury 2002)

Notwithstanding the obvious structural constraints, the PRIs provide a form of governance that is based on community resources. At the grassroots, community is the organic unit of cultural, social, economic and political organisation. In view of the growing popularity of the panchayat institutions, there is no doubt that a better administration can easily be achieved by building on the community resources rather than trying to import 'managerialisation' of public services. Similarly, by empowering the wards committees as the locus of decision-making in the wards, the 74th Amendment Act has created space of participatory democracy which is complementary to localising governance. As a constitutional structure, and acting as nurseries of civic virtues, the wards committees have become proactive in urban affairs by being involved both in planning and implementation. With reservation for women and the socially underprivileged, the wards committee, like the PRI, is also a stepping stone towards building inclusive urban governance.

REFERENCES

Baviskar, B. S. and George Mathew. 2009. 'Introduction' in *Inclusion and Exclusion in Local Governance: Field Studies from Rural India*, 1–18. New Delhi: Sage.

Buch, Nirmala. 1999. 'From Oppression to Assertion: A Study of Panchayats and Women in Madhya Pradesh, Rajasthan and Uttar Pradesh'. Mimeo, Centre for Women's Development Studies, New Delhi.

Buch, Nirmala. 2005. 'Women and Panchayats: Opportunities, Challenges and Support' in *Decentralisation and Local Governance*, edited by L. C. Jain, 343–65. Hyderabad: Orient Longman.

Chakrabarty, Bidyut and Prakash Chand. 2016. *Indian Administration: Evolution and Practice*. New Delhi: Sage.

Gandhi, Rajiv. 1988. 'Responsive Administration'. Speech delivered on 18 June at Coimbatore. Reproduced in *The Times of India*, New Delhi edition, 19 June.

Gandhi, Rajiv. 1989. Speech delivered on 13 February 1988 at Hyderabad. Reproduced in *Responsive Administration*, New Delhi: Government of India Press.

Ghosh, A. and M. Mitra. 2008. 'Institutionalizing People's Participation in Urban Governance: An Inter-city Perspective of Wards Committees in West Bengal' in *New Forms of Urban Governance in India: Shifts, Models, Networks and Contestations*, edited by I. S. A. Baud and J. de Wit, 84–114. New Delhi: Sage.

Government of India (GoI). 2002a. 'Report of the National Commission to Review the Working of the Constitution of India'. Submitted to the Department of Legal Affairs, Ministry of Law, Justice and Company Affairs, New Delhi.

———. 2002b. 'Rural Development' in *Ninth Five Year Plan (1997–2002)*, Planning Commission. New Delhi: Government of India. Available at http://planningcommission.nic.in/plans/stateplan/sdr_punjab/sdrpun_ch5.pdf (accessed 12 October 2016).

Jayal, Niraja Gopal, Amit Prakash and Pradeep K. Sharma. 2006. *Local Governance in India: Decentralization and Beyond*. New Delhi: Oxford University Press.

Lieten, G. K. 1996. 'Panchayats in Western Uttar Pradesh: Namesake Members'. *Economic and Political Weekly* 31 (39): 2700–05.

Mathur, Kuldeep. 2013. *Panchayati Raj*. New Delhi: Oxford University Press.

Mishra, Sweta. 2016. 'Decentralization and Local Governance' in *Public Administration: Approaches and Applications*, edited by Alka Dhameja and Sweta Mishra, 230–48. Delhi: Pearson.

Mukarji, Nirmal. 1993. 'The Third Stratum'. *Economic and Political Weekly* 28 (18): 859–72.

Nehru, Jawaharlal. 1945/1988. Letter to Gandhi, 9 October, 1945. Compiled in *A Bunch of Old Letters*, Delhi: Oxford University Press.

Pal, Mahi. 2004. 'Panchayati Raj and Rural Governance: Experiences of a Decade'. *Economic and Political Weekly* 39 (2): 137–43.

Robinson, Mark. 2005. 'A Decade of Panchayati Raj Reforms: The Challenge of Democratic Decentralisation in India' in *Decentralization and Local Governance*, edited by L. C. Jain, 10–30. Hyderabad: Orient Longman.

Ronald deSouza, Peter. 2003. 'The Struggle for Local Government: Indian Democracy's New Phase'. *Publius* 33 (4): 99–118.

———. 2005. 'Decentralization and Local Government: The "Second Wind" of Democracy in India' in *India's Living Constitution: Ideas, Practices, Controversies*, edited by Zoya Hasan, E. Sridharan and R. Sudarshan, 370–404. New Delhi: Permanent Black.

Roychowdhury, Supriya. 2002. 'Globalization and Decentralization'. *The Hindu*, 5 January.

Satyanarayana, P. 1990. *Towards New Panchayati Raj: Critical Perspectives on the Reorganisation of Rural Local Government*. New Delhi: Uppal Publishing House.

Seth, D. L. 2004. 'Globalisation and New Politics of Micro-movements'. *Economic and Political Weekly* 39 (1): 45–58.

Viswanathan, Gauri. 1998. *Outside the Fold: Conversion, Modernity and Belief*. Delhi: Oxford University Press.

CONCLUSION*

I

Public administration is first and foremost a practice, and only then an idea. That is, the former is critical to the latter. Being an activity, public administration can never be conclusively conceptualised as it constantly undergoes change depending on its context. Two ideas are implicit here: on the one hand, since it is about an endeavour which is context-dependent, it cannot be captured in a universal theoretical design; on the other hand, however, this does not completely negate the importance of some of the critical ideas which are part and parcel of our conceptualisation of governance. The point needs elaboration. As already argued, public administration is situation-specific though there are certain general features that governance represents in any socio-economic location. For instance, regardless of the socio-economic roots, bureaucracy—an important instrument for executing public administration—tends to be centralised and hierarchical, and generally seeks to expand its influence beyond what is given by definition. Hence, besides taking into account the importance of the context, an analysis of governance should also draw on these factors to arrive at a fairly reasonable understanding. In other words, public administration is, as an effort, contingent on the prevalent socio-economic circumstances though its distinctive nature hardly varies from one place to another because it is instinctively hierarchical, centralising and politically-engendered. It is, therefore, fundamental to remember is that since public governance epistemologically derives its fundamental features from the Western tradition--specifically the Weberian tradition, that is supportive of the pyramidal structure of public administration--there has been no definitional deficit.

The thinkers dominating the Western discourse on public administration at the dawn of Capitalism—Hegel, Weber and Wilson, among others—argued for a strong State. They preferred to build a system of governance which was efficient, but impersonal and aloof while discharging its assigned responsibility, primarily to uphold the rule of law. They also endorsed the conceptualisation that public administration is a historically-textured and ideology-driven endeavour, and generally projected it as a design for public well-being. In contrast, the non-Western

* Some sections of this chapter have been developed from Bidyut Chakrabarty, *Indian Politics and Society since Independence: Events, Processes and Ideology* (London: Routledge, 2008), pp. 171–79. With permission from Taylor & Francis.

thinkers—Gandhi, Nyerere and Mao—were critical of centralised administration. According to them, only through the involvement of the demos in governance, could public administration be both public and democratic in character. As they were nurtured in circumstances completely different from those of the West, they drew on ideas which had hardly any takers in the Western tradition.

This brief discussion underlines two important conceptual points: first, since public administration defies a pattern, it would be conceptually restraining to argue for a universal design. Implicit here is the critical importance of the context in which public administration unfolds by inculcating the fundamental ideological impulses and values of the existent socio-economic circumstances. The second point relates to the argument that decision-making follows a specific technically construed pattern. There are, therefore, certain specific technical characteristics that public administration will invariably articulate while fulfilling its objective of being an impersonal instrument for public welfare. To justify that public administration is required to be endowed with these features to achieve the goal, Western thinkers prepare a fool-proof logical defence of their argument in favour of the one-size-fits-all formula. There is substance in this conceptual argument since it has been historically substantiated by drawing on how public administration evolves across different socio-economic circumstances.

The argument that bureaucracy is universal in character is attributed to Weber, who, it appears, did not pay adequate attention to the socio-economic compulsions while designing his model of the ideal form of organisation. *Max Weber and the Theory of Modern Politics*, a classic by David Beetham (1985) on social and political thought, suggests that according to Weber bureaucracy was only a technical instrument that was adopted to realise social obligations that the polity desired. Weber was also persuaded to believe that bureaucracy had the inherent tendency to exceed its instrumental functions and become a separate force within society, capable of steering in accordance with its ideological priorities:

> [Bureaucracy is] a social force with interests and values of its own, and as such has social consequences over and above its instrumental achievements. As a power group it has the capacity to influence the goals of the political system; as a status stratum, it has a more unconscious effect upon the values of at large. At the same time, it is not independent of other social forces. (Ibid.: 67)

Beetham reiterates that despite having typical instrumental functions, bureaucracy is, in every respect, a social force that tends to usurp power and authority if the situation so evolves. That it is not insulated from other social forces also reinforces the argument that public administration evolves both in conjunction and contradiction with a plethora of forces that are operative in a specific milieu. As a technically adept instrument, bureaucracy has certain universal characteristics though, as a social force, its nature varies from one context to another, and which further questions the tendency for universalising bureaucracy in a deterministic ideological format. There is hardly any room for confusion: for Weber, bureaucracy is socially-governed and politically adept at crossing the earmarked boundary of its functioning, presumably because it also generates selfish interests, supportive of its distinct ideological predilections. Nonetheless, he favoured bureaucracy for being impersonal in contrast to patriarchal and patrimonial authorities. So, in Weber's perception, bureaucracy was preferred in the place of instruments of partisan governance, being executed by individuals by virtue of their privileged socio-economic location and political importance at a particular juncture of history.

II

As an activity, public administration requires guidelines which are determined by the nature of polity in which it evolves. In other words, the concern of public administration for the rule of law is inevitable. Implicit here are two important ideas which are mutually inclusive: on the one hand, since public administration is always couched in ideological terms, it acquires distinctive characteristics from the wider political environment shaping its nature; on the other hand, the political environment is not static because political priorities change in response to the stimuli that are rooted in the processes of social churning. Nonetheless, the rule of law, as enunciated in the Constitution or any rulebook, provides certain well-defined guidelines and directions to steer public administration in conformity with the established ideological fabric of the system. The rule of law is therefore both directional and deterministic: directional because it directs administrative action in a specific way; deterministic since it restricts public administration within the ideological domain, justified within the ideological contour of governance.

In contemporary parlance, the Constitution represents a major space housing the rule of law. It is therefore not surprising that the expressions—'the Constitution' and 'rule of law'—are interchangeably used in the academic discourse to mean the same thing. The juxtaposition may not be entirely wrong though 'rule of law' has a much wider scope since, in principle, it contains all those rules and regulations that are justiciable. Be that as it may, the crucial point here is the importance of the Constitution as a principal agency for the rule of law which governs public administration. As a value-setting device, the Constitution also guides the administration in a specific direction. In this sense, the administration articulates the constitutional design in the form of decisions. Being ideology-driven, the Constitution is not just a pack of rules and regulations, but comprises those value preferences which are rooted in a particular socio-economic and political milieu. In other words, the Constitution is an ideologically-charged document with a definite purpose to fulfil. This is fundamental in any study of the interface between the Constitution and administration. The interface needs to be studied dialectically because a deterministic understanding of the interrelationship that privileges one over the other will be self-defeating. Even a cursory look at the interface reveals that the Constitution and administration are dialectically connected; the nature of this connection, however, differs according to the socio-economic and political circumstances. This reinforces the fact that without grasping the dialectical connection between the Constitution and administration, neither the Constitution nor the administration can retain its vitality as a powerful ideological instrument for setting in motion a specific path of political governance.

There is another point of massive theoretical significance: the interaction between the Constitution and administration is constant and not a one-time shot, further confirming that they are organically-linked. One can thus think of the interrelationship in the form of a diagram showing the interaction between the Constitution and administration within a specific milieu fulfilling an ideological goal. One should also be aware of the fact that the interrelationship is not always friction-free, because administrations change the changing of its personnel, and they may not continually be tuned to the fundamental constitutional values. Likewise, the Constitution cannot remain static in view of its organic linkages with the socio-economic and political reality. This is likely to create uncertainty which is usually circumvented if there is an ideology that cements the Constitution–administration bond for a common socio-political and economic goal.

While conceptualising the interrelationship, one cannot avoid referring to the role of history. In India, neither the Constitution nor administration is absolutely new, they are a continuity of the past. Structurally, and also in terms of its nature, Indian administration has hardly showed any break with the past since Independence; similarly, the Constitution of India replicates much of the British constitutional provisions and practices, of course, within the changed ideological circumstances. In the early years of India's Independence cases of administration overruling the Constitution, given what was identified as 'exigencies', were not uncommon. The scenario however has changed—as is the case with other stable political systems—once the values of democracy, socialism and republicanism were accepted as sacrosanct for governance. With the consolidation of these fundamental values, the Constitution is no longer merely an instrument of authority but a path-finder for administrators who cannot afford to ignore constitutional directions in view of systemic requirements. The Constitution has also created circumstances where political differences are usually sorted amicably through dialogue and negotiation, except perhaps during some stray instances where it did not happen. Nonetheless, the fact remains that the Constitution has created circumstances where values espoused by the founders of our nation have flourished. So, the administration–Constitution interface is nothing but a complementary network in which governance is structured and executed. This is conceptually fundamental because (*a*) it enables us to capture the complex interrelationship between the Constitution and administration and (*b*) it also shows the importance of an ideology in sustaining an atmosphere in which the Constitution and administration remain complementary to each other.

The deep-rooted ethos and functional vibrancy of democratic life in India is, arguably, the direct result of the endeavour of the makers of our Constitution. Not only did they envision India as a modern, secular and democratic nation that maintains the primacy of fundamental rights over other state imperatives and is governed by the rule of law; they also ensured comprehensive and precise provisions in the Constitution to facilitate the progress of the nation in that desired direction. Given the immense importance of the Constitution in shaping administration, it is thus obvious that no discussion of administration shall remain complete without a thorough understanding of the value-preferences that the Constitution seeks to pursue. Besides the peculiar socio-economic and political circumstances in which public administration is located, one also needs to be sensitive to exogenous factors, particularly in the context of the growing consolidation of what is characterised as 'the LPG Regime' (i.e. the liberalised, privatised and globalised regime). Transformed because of the increasing grip of globalisation, especially in developing countries, public administration cannot thus be conceptualised in a typical Weberian formulation of boundary-conscious bureaucracy of a rather simple society in which domestic circumstances are critical. This was perhaps the reason why Weber conceived bureaucracy as 'an instrument of functioning', the nature of which is contingent on the prevalent socio-economic circumstances, as Beetham (1985) has shown. Critical of the argument that Weber did not show any concern of the existent socio-economic circumstances, Beetham argues that '[f]ar from embodying the universal and disinterested outlook ascribed to it by conservative mythology, in practice, it was unable to free itself from the outlook of the social classes from which it was recruited and to which it was allied' (ibid.: 66). By seeking to understand governance as a situation-specific exercise, Beetham reinforces a fundamental argument in favour of contextual public administration which, despite being bound by the rule of law, is receptive to the changing socio-economic circumstances. Conceptualising public administration, therefore, is an ongoing process in which the role of the Constitution is as significant as the context in which the former gets crystallised. Since neither the Constitution nor the context remains static, it is a matter of common sense to suggest that public administration cannot but be flexible. The basic point is that, being tuned to the public, public administration is clearly a well-informed response, drawn on the dialectical interconnection between the text (the Constitution) and the context. And, here lies the challenge because both the text and the context, despite being located in analytically separate domains, provide useful and critical inputs in the shaping/reshaping of public administration as an area of activity.

III

Public administration is also institution-driven. In a democratic polity, the Legislative, the Executive and the Judiciary are endowed with specific powers which they exercise while discharging their respective roles in governance. They are separate and complementary to one another at the same time: separate because their domain of functioning is clearly demarcated by constitutional provisions, and accepted conventions and norms; complementary because they pursue the same ideological goal for the polity and work in tandem. An analytical exploration of their role in policymaking which is the core of public administration will illustrate how institutions of governance shape its responses in accordance with the constitutional mandate.

Legislative bodies are concerned with the central political tasks of policy formation and law-making. In the process, the Legislative performs other important functions like deliberating, scrutinising, criticising and publicising government policies and their consequences for the public on the floor of the house. Usually, it lays down the broad objectives that the administration is to pursue and, in more important cases, the machinery and the procedure through which they are to be pursued. From the public policy perspective, the Legislative is an important centre of policymaking, the institution we most often study when trying to assess what issues are gaining and losing prominence and which alternative policies are being weighed. In India, for example, the Parliament, the state legislative assemblies and the local bodies provide an ideal political platform for raising the issues that are of importance to the people. While the Parliament is the highest law-making body in the country, the state legislatures are empowered to make laws for the states and the local bodies have the authority to make laws for areas that fall under their jurisdiction.

Modern governments everywhere depend upon Executive leadership both for policy formulation and execution. In the parliamentary form of government, all policies must have the approval of the cabinet and the ministers of the government introduce the bill in the house. The Executive probably has more influence in policymaking in developing countries than in developed countries. In India, the immediate policy-makers are members of the cabinet, which is a relatively small body consisting only of the cabinet ministers and the prime minister (Banerjee 2006: 3838). Practically, it is the cabinet which shapes public policies in India. However, administrators are also involved in the policy formulation process in more than one way. The classical doctrine of politics–administration dichotomy does not appear to be tenable anymore because administration cannot be meaningfully conceptualised independent of politics. In complex industrial societies, the technicality and complexity of many policy matters, the need for continuing control, the lack of time and information, etc. have led to the delegation of much discretionary authority to administrative agencies, in what is formally recognised as 'the rule making power'. Public officials are associated with policy formulation in three important ways. First, they supply facts, data and analysis (regarding the workability of a policy) to the ministers or to the Legislative and impart content to a policy. Second, they are constantly in touch with the public, so they have a better understanding of their problems and the solution required in the form of policies. Third, on account of lack of time and knowledge, the Legislative passes 'skeletal' acts and leaves the 'body' to be filled by the administration. It is here that administrators have maximum scope for 'policymaking'.

The Judiciary also plays an important role in public administration. In countries where courts have the power of judicial review, they have played an important role in policy formation. They have the power to determine the constitutionality of actions of the Legislative and the Executive branches and to declare them null and void if such actions are found to be in conflict with constitutional provisions. They play an important role in giving direction to social, economic and political policies of national importance. In India, the Judiciary has been an instrument of socio-economic change. It has been instrumental in delivering a number of judgments on important issues like land reforms, child labour, environmental pollution and women's empowerment, all of which have immensely contributed to the articulation of radical policy designs.

The nature of public administration is intimately linked to institutions of governance; the more efficient these institutions are the more efficient public administration will be in its response. A scan of the role of the Indian Parliament, for instance, reveals its gradual decline in the sphere of policymaking. Not only has the quality of the debate on policy issues gone down, parliamentarians also tend to lose their dignity on the floor of Parliament once they are challenged by their colleagues. While attributing the steady decline of Parliament in India to the general moral decadence and growing importance of extra-constitutional factors in elections, Banerjee also underlines (*a*) the lack of common adherence to the basic norms of parliamentary democracy and (*b*) the lack of a sense of awareness of the line between the responsible exercise of the right to freedom of speech and unrestricted license of speech within the walls of the Parliament (2006: 3838).

Parliamentary decline seems to be matched by the ascendancy of other political institutions of Indian democracy. For instance, the President, the Supreme Court and the Election Commission have shown remarkable resilience while upholding some of the intrinsic liberal values. In declining to approve the 2006 Office of Profit Bill which was sent to him after it was passed by both the houses of Parliament, the President redefined the role of the institution in the changed socio-political environment. Three important principles were consolidated in this controversial episode: first, the underlying principle debarring the holder of an office of profit under the government from being a member of Parliament is drawn on the doctrine of separation of powers, namely, there should be a demarcation of authority and power between the Executive and the Legislative to avoid 'misappropriation of authority and power' by these two wings of the government. The famous 1973 Kesavananda Bharati case judgment of the Supreme Court endorses this principle as part of the Basic Structure of the Constitution of India. Second, the President's decision to not approve the bill is also suggestive of the fact that there should be uniformity in interpreting the law. In fact, given the Supreme Court ruling, there is no scope of a different interpretation, and as an apex judicial institution in the country, the Supreme Court is constitutionally authorised to enforce uniformity in this regard. Finally, by sending the bill back to Parliament for reconsideration, the President also upheld the judicial sanctity of the criteria that the Supreme Court had devised to settle the controversy. These criteria are: (*a*) it must be a post created by and under the control of the government, (*b*) the appointee of the post should also be under governmental control, (*c*) the holder of the post must be entitled to some profit or benefit other than compensatory allowance, whether s/he takes it or not, and (*d*) the power/authority attached to that position that can be exercised by the holder.[1]

[1] While elaborating the office of profit controversy, we have drawn on an unpublished article by J. S. Verma, former Chief Justice of India. We are thankful to Justice Verma for sharing this unpublished article, a part of which was printed in *The Times of India*, 4 September 2006.

The controversy was finally resolved not by following judicial wisdom but by political considerations. Though the President had to give his assent when the bill was approved by the Parliament for the second time, the episode is reflective of the growing independence of India's highest constitutional authority. This episode, therefore, has established beyond doubt a healthy trend, which is constitutionally creative and politically challenging in so far as the institutions of governance are concerned. The bill was a significant intervention in redefining the political which is located in the institutions that had also creatively responded to the issues which were perhaps linked to the deepening of democracy by meaningful participation of 'the people' in the political processes.

Similarly, in the famous Bommai judgment of 1994 (*S. R. Bommai vs Union of India*; AIR 1994 SC 1918), the Supreme Court also radically altered the progress of the debate on the Basic Structure of the Constitution. The Supreme Court came out heavily against the union government for the indiscriminate application of Article 356 to dismiss duly-elected state governments. Dr B. R. Ambedkar was confident, as his statements in the Constituent Assembly attest, that Emergency provisions in the Constitution of India would rarely be invoked and as Indian democracy matured, the need to do so would be less compelling, thereby reducing Article 356 to 'a dead letter'. However, by 1994, this provision was applied more than ninety times, the Supreme Court noted, making this Article instead 'a death letter'. The judgment put to rest all speculations regarding the 'delicate balance of powers in a federal polity' by saying that 'federalism envisaged in the Constitution is a basic structure. … The state *qua* the Constitution is federal and independent in its exercise of legislative and executive power'. It is true that the Constitution prefers an arrangement which is tilted in favour of the Centre. But that does not mean that 'the States are mere appendages of the Centre. Within the sphere allotted to them, States are supreme. The Centre cannot temper with their powers'. Simultaneously, by clarifying the constitutional status of the states, the judgment also redefined the role of the President by underlining that

> the provision requires that the material before the President must be sufficient to indicate that unless a proclamation (under article 356) is issued, it is not possible to carry on the affairs of the state as per the provisions of the Constitution. It is not every situation arising in the State but a situation which shows that constitutional government has become an impossibility, which alone will entitle the President to issue the proclamation. (*Bommai vs Union of India*)

Dr Ambedkar was right when he suggested that growing democratisation will make the Emergency provision redundant. The Supreme Court is certainly an important component in this process. By creatively interpreting the constitutional provisions, the apex court contributed to the redrawing of the basic contours of Indian federalism that has evolved organically out of an engagement with the constantly changing social, economic and cultural milieu. The Bommai judgment is a watershed, perhaps the most significant, in the evolution of an organic federalism in India.

The revival of the Election Commission as a political watchdog is a remarkable development supporting growing democratisation of Indian politics. The Election Commission was set up in 1950 as a constitutional agency and entrusted with the task of superintendence, direction and control of all national and state-level elections. The Commission holds substantial power as far as the procedural aspects of the elections are concerned. In fact, it derives its strength from the code of conduct, which is formulated by consensus by all political parties participating in the election. There is no doubt that by its sincere involvement in the processes of elections, starting from the preparation of voters' roll to the declaration of the poll results, the Commission has played a critical role in redefining the political in India. The role of the Commission in the 2006 state elections in West Bengal is illustrative here. With the announcement of the dates of elections, the Commission took control of the state election machinery in an unprecedented manner. It took ample care to revise the voter's roll since the incumbent Left Front government had been charged with manipulating the list. During the clean-up operation, the observer found an astonishingly high percentage of false voters and struck them off the list. Hence the charge seemed authentic and the media attributed the sustained electoral victory of the Left Front to 'bogus voters'. Following its success in Bihar in holding a free and fair election under strict surveillance, the Commission decided to conduct the polls in five phases stretching across two months. The Commission requisitioned police and paramilitary forces from outside the state simply because the state police did not appear to be reliable. Because the dates were dispersed, it was possible to get an adequate number of the forces to supervise voting. It was a remarkable election in West Bengal, being held under the strict control of the Election Commission that implemented its authority in accordance with its constitutional obligation. Although the election brought back the incumbent Left Front government to power—unlike in Bihar where a new government replaced the government that had held power for more than fifteen years—the Commission provided critical inputs to the processes of democratisation by empowering ordinary voters who now became 'the movers and shakers' of Indian democracy. In other words, voters are not merely seasonal participants, they have also been made to feel their importance in the political processes that hardly mattered thus far in their everyday life.

The Indian experience is significant in re-conceptualising public administration as an activity which is also dependent on how the institutions of governance behave. As is shown, the Indian Parliament seems to have failed to discharge its role in policymaking to the extent it is expected, though the lack is being more than matched by the growing importance of other institutions of governance. This cannot be understood without reference to the processes of democratisation that has radically altered the texture of administration which is no longer the exclusive domain of politicians and administrators. This is a trend that India has witnessed since Independence. With the involvement of these institutions, public administration has also become a platform in which the idea of the public seems to have gained critical importance in governance. This is an important aspect which needs to be taken into account while seeking to understand public administration in the context of the increasing importance of the market-centric neoliberal ethos.

IV

Feminism has acquired immense significance in public administration in recent years. A political movement on the belief in equality of men and women and committed to the elimination of gender-based injustice, feminism is a powerful input in reconceptualising public administration in its contemporary manifestation. The primary aim is to evolve a system of administration which is free from gender bias; this does not seem to be an easy task presumably because of the well-entrenched prejudices in the policy designs. The social imbalance due to gender-discrimination is institutionalised by public law and public policy which are not tenable in a democratic world where the argument supportive of gender-distinction loses validity. In public administration, the gender concern has not received adequate scholarly attention so far largely due to the fact that the patriarchy appears to have swayed inquisitive minds away from this sphere of enquiry. It was not therefore odd when Nausbaum argued that

> the relationship between gender and governance has too often been neglected in both theoretical and empirical work. Until very recently, most influential political thought has been built around a conceptual distinction between the "public" realm of politics, military affairs and administration and the "private" realm of family and domestic life. Women's role, in a wide range of traditions and in theoretical work influenced by them, has typically been associated with the "private" realm, and men's role in the "public" realm. The public/private distinction has been thoroughly criticized as being in many ways misleading and untenable. Nonetheless, it continues to influence both theoretical and empirical work, with the result that women's efforts to gain a voice in governance have often been ignored. (2003: 4)[2]

According to Nausbaum, the gender prejudices in governance need to be conceptualised in the public–private distinction which does not seem to be tenable unless one appreciates the arguments appreciative of patriarchy and the so-called natural division between man and woman. In pursuit of what Nausbaum argued, Stivers (2002) persuades us to believe that arguments denying a legitimate space to women in administration are drawn on archaic values that force them to accept the a 'second role' in society. While defending her point of view, Stivers argues that the prevailing conceptualisation seeking to defend gender prejudices is linked to a masculine understanding of power and achievement. So long as this exists, no efforts towards reconceptualising the role of women in public administration would succeed. Attacking the stereotypical societal expectations from women, Stivers argues that women who pursue public administration as a career are faced with the fundamental dissonance between what is 'expected of them as women and what is expected of them as professional experts' (ibid.: 53). She argues that professional characteristics 'give masculinity an advantage over femininity and depend on structural arrangements that make it difficult for women to meet professional expectations'. According to her, it is 'fraudulent' to provide women with the equal opportunity to be public servants and rise through the ranks of

---

[2] Reproduced by permission of UNDP.

the bureaucracy, while the requirements and qualities required for that career remain 'inconsistent with what is expected of them as women' (ibid).

The argument that Stivers puts forward is directed at the structural inequality embedded in public institutions and values. What is thus required is to evolve a mindset that is sensitive to women's issues, which are also part and parcel of public administration. There are two major arguments that feminists, including Stivers, pursue to articulate a feminist perspective in governance: (*a*) since public administration has instrumental in systematically excluding women from the public space because they are biologically different from men, it cannot be gender-neutral, and (*b*) in such a context, public institutions are clearly structures of subordination as they instinctively uphold patriarchal prejudices. So, the main effort should be directed, as the argument goes, to get rid of the mindset endorsing prejudices against biological difference!

Besides arguing strongly for a sustained political campaign against gender-driven bias, Stivers defends her ideological mission by developing a persuasive conceptual design in favour of gender equality in public administration. Her main thesis underlines the argument that professional expertise, management, leadership and public virtue, all of which are critical to administrative power, are conceptualised in such a way as to project women as 'incapable' in so far as public administration is concerned. Since these qualities are associated with masculinity, they are always upheld to deny women their legitimate space in governance. This masculine challenge cannot be combated so easily because it is supported by a well-entrenched mindset nurtured by the prevalent power relations that sustain the imbalance in support of privileges at the cost of women.

As is shown, there are two major arguments that seem to have informed the feminist approach to public administration. First, feminists base their arguments on the much-hyped public–private distinction which is, according to them, neither fair nor tenable since it is ideologically tilted against women. Being critical of the distinction, Catharine MacKinon argues that

> for women the measure of intimacy has been the measure of the oppression. This is why feminism has had to explode the private. This is why feminism has seen the personal as the political. The private is public for those for whom the personal is political. In this sense, for women there is no private, either normatively or empirically. (MacKinon 1989: 191)

The feminist challenge allows us to understand 'the cost of coerced privatisation' and 'the importance of public culture in the personal lives of individuals'. It also provides 'a strong reminder that "out of sight is out of mind", that low visibility and suppression distort public perception of what is important' (Gavison 1992: 43). That women continue to remain marginalised in public administration stems from multiple sources of disadvantages besides those which are obvious by virtue of being biologically different from their male counterparts. This, second major argument in the feminist approach, is conceptualised as 'intersectional perspective or intersectionality' in contemporary literature. The argument is that since one's being is based on an intersection of identities drawn on one's race, class and gender, it needs to be grasped not in isolation of one factor as against another, but by appreciating a dialectical interconnection involving them. Explaining the perspective, Stivers argues:

> Examining gender dilemmas in public administration does not imply the view that other factors such as race and class are less important. Gender is tied to race and class; gender's importance is not as the solo source of domination but as a lens that enables one to see things that other lenses miss. (2002: 5)

Highlighting the importance of intersectionality as a persuasive theoretical tool, Stivers has shown that the denial of women's legitimate place in public administration cannot be attributed merely to gender prejudices, since they are nurtured and strengthened by other devices of oppression around class, race and other discriminatory social systems. Conceptually defined as 'multiple jeopardy', the argument affirms that by being a woman, she is 'subject to multiple, simultaneous forms of discrimination' (Bearfield 2009: 385). The idea is simple: gender-perspective in public administration will help us understand the theme better not in isolation but in conjunction with other axes of politico-ideological powers that seek to define human existence in a particular fashion.

V

The articulation of public administration as governance has ushered in a new era. The structure-centric conceptualisation of public administration is being replaced by a process-driven design of governance. As public bureaucracy is reduced to a rent-seeking agent of those holding substantial power, arguments against the strictly Weberian pyramidal structure of governance receive immediate attention. At a time when the rigid bureaucratic form of administration is subjected to severe criticism, efforts towards debureaucratising governance is hailed as a boon, especially in developing countries. So there is a context in which the idea of governance was conceptualised and also gained credibility. What is also striking about governance is the fact that it was the practitioners' contribution to public administration in the sense that the Bretton Woods institutions, the World Bank (WB) and International Monetary Fund (IMF), conceptualised the idea which was later utilised to recover monetary loan from the sub-Saharan African countries. First articulated in the World Development Report of 1989, governance insisted on more governance and less government which, by highlighting the effective delivery of services, is actually a powerful critique of the expansion of governance merely by adding to its prevalent structure. The idea was first articulated by Harlan Cleveland when he devised a system of governance by stating that it comprises 'systems—interlaced webs of tension in which control is loose, power diffused and centres of decisions plural' (1972: 13). Appreciative of the spirit in which Cleveland articulated his feelings, the WB argued strongly for the creation of 'a public service that is efficient, a judicial system that is reliable, and an administration that is accountable to its public' (1989: *xii*). The aim was to develop a system that is functionally efficient and attentive to its responsibilities to the public. Hence, the WB suggested, in another report, that governance is 'the manner in which power is exercised in the management of a country's economic and social resources for development' (1992: 18). Later, the WB reviewed the concept and called for 'good governance' which was:

> epitomized by predictable, open and enlightened policymaking (that is, transparent processes); a bureaucracy imbued with a professional ethos; an executive arm of government accountable for its actions; and a strong civil society participating in public affairs; and all behaving under the rule of law. (1994: *vii*)[3]

This is a four-dimensional conceptualisation emphasising (*a*) transparency in administration, (*b*) bureaucratic accountability, (*c*) the role of civil society as a critical actor and (*d*) the importance of the rule of law. In a nutshell, governance is now envisaged as an activity in which multiple actors act, and is therefore no longer State-centric. It points to networks in society that are involved in policymaking and 'moves away from the well-established notions of authoritative single agencies at work' (Mathur 2008: 9). As a result, the State loses its centrality in public administration: it is but one of the actors (though important) in governance. This creates difficulty in conceptualising public administration in the governance mould since it insists on a laboratory mode of governance which will remain relevant regardless of socio-economic circumstances. In other words, by insisting on the one-size-fits-all formula, the governance paradigm takes out the dynamism inherent in public administration the socio-economic context. Furthermore, there is no guarantee that the externally-devised mode of governance will be readily accepted since reform in administration is also a matter of political contestation. So, the idea has its inherent limitation. As discussed in this book, public administration that is not organically linked with the prevalent socio-economic reality is a structure without a foundation. Upheld in the conceptual framework of text–context duality, this truth has universal validity, as Braibanti confirms by saying that 'decision making is enmeshed so intricately and so deeply in the surrounding culture that it cannot be extricated as an autonomous behaviour and transplanted' (1966: 165). There is, therefore, hardly any room for confusion that public administration cannot be insulated from the context if it is to evolve as a system of governance.

If the WB-sponsored model of governance cannot be fool-proof, as argued above, does it mean that the effort is without substance? A brief perusal of the history of the idea demonstrates that the WB conceptualisation gave a jolt to the prevalent mindset in support of the Weberian hierarchical form of public governance. It was a conceptualisation that was articulated at the

---

[3] All verbatim extracts from WB (1994) in this chapter: © World Bank. License: Creative Commons Attribution CC by 3.0 IGO.

same time as the consolidation of neoliberal ideological priorities. As the WB noted, governance is a journey from

> a highly interventionist paradigm of government to one in which the role of the public sector is to create an enabling environment for the private sector, to regulate where necessary, and to ensure efficient delivery of key public services. … In addition to decentralisation … [governance entails] a sharper distinction between the core functions of government and those that can be contracted out or otherwise left to the private sector. In this way, governance is strengthened by shifting the boundary between the public and private sectors, thereby enlarging the latter, with the government's role changing from direct provision to regulation. (1994: 2)

The ideological aim notwithstanding, governance has ushered in a new era in the conceptualisation of public administration by recognising the importance of multiple actors in decision-making. Contrary to the fundamental guiding principle of traditional public administration, that draws on the Weberian notion of authority, this neoliberal mode of conceptualising government also creates space for private actors and considers them integral to decision-making. What is suggested here is a model which, by not being State-centric, contributes to the processes leading to the expansion of the base of public administration. With the legitimate involvement of multiple actors, governance ceases to be a mere technical act, but a platform for contestation over policy design. In other words, this also means that governance, in order to be an agency for development, epitomises continuous negotiations among the actors to formulate appropriate policies. If one takes into account the multifaceted character of governance as a practice, and not in that the sense the WB conceptualised it, one is persuaded to accept that bereft of politics (in the sense of receiving specific politico-ideological inputs, articulated in a way that conforms to the prevalent socio-economic context) it may be an intellectually defensible conceptual category which will hardly be empirically viable. And, in that sense, governance will just reinforce neo-Taylorism and be remembered as an endeavour, which, despite having provoked debate, would likely lose steam because of its inherent weaknesses.

VI

In conceptualising public administration as a context-driven exercise, the growing politicisation of communities and individuals as a means for democratisation cannot be ignored. Politicisation refers to processes whereby stakeholders are drawn to decision-making and contribute to the democratisation of public administration. In a typical Western liberal context, deepening of democracy invariably leads to consolidation of 'liberal values'. In the Indian context, democratisation is translated to greater involvement of people not as 'individuals', which is a staple to liberal discourse, but as communities or groups. Individuals are being drawn to the public sphere not as 'atomised' individuals but as 'members of primordial communities' drawn on religious, caste or *jati* (sect within a caste) identity. Similarly, a large section of women is being drawn to the political processes not as 'women' or individuals, but as members of a community and holding a sectoral identity. It is not therefore surprising that the so-called peripheral groups continue to maintain their identities with reference to the social groups (caste, religion or sect) to which they belong while getting involved in the political processes, despite the fact that their political goals remain more or less identical. Nonetheless, the processes of steady democratisation have contributed to the articulation of a political voice, hitherto unheard of, which is reflective of radical changes in the texture of the political. The expanding circle of democratic participation since Independence has thus transformed 'the character of politics as previously subordinate groups have gained a voice' (Adeney and Wyatt 2004: 1). By helping to articulate the political voice of the marginalised, democracy in India has led to 'a loosing of social strictures' and empowered the peripherals to be confident of their ability to improve the socio-economic conditions in which they are placed (Alam 2004: 22). This is a significant political process that has led to what Christophe Jaffrelot (2005) describes as 'a silent revolution' through a meaningful transfer of power from the upper caste elites to various subaltern groups within the democratic framework of public governance.

Public administration is being democratised in the sense that it is no longer the exclusive domain of the State which is just one of so many actors involved in decision-making. Core to the conceptualisation of governance is the role of the stakeholders who hardly had a role in the past when public administration was largely guided by the Weberian insistence on hierarchical and centralised form of organisation. As argued above, the change in our perception about public administration is attributed to the consolidation of neoliberal values, especially in the aftermath of the disintegration of the former Soviet Union. The reinvention of public governance, which appeared to have lost its vitality in view of the consolidation of a rent-seeking bureaucracy, was inevitable. The idea of governance that the WB sponsored was a way out. However, this conception is riddled with weaknesses given its implicit support to the one-size-fits-all formula. Born out of an ideological concern, governance fails to emerge as an acceptable mode though it has provoked fierce debate among practitioners and thinkers alike regarding the viability of rigid bureaucratic governance in an era of democratisation that results in de-centering power and authority. This is where the journey towards governance is intellectually useful because, besides having exposed the limitations of the Weberian conceptualisation of pyramidal bureaucracy, it has also led to a concerted search for an appropriate model of administration which will take care of citizens' needs and aspirations. Since government deficit cannot be conclusively tackled, an argument in favour the idea of 'good enough governance' has gained credibility. According to Grindle who is credited with its conceptualisation,

> good enough governance means that interventions thought to contribute to the ends of economic and political development need to be questioned, prioritized and made relevant to the conditions of individual countries. They need to be assessed in light of historical evidence, sequence and timing, and they should be selected carefully in terms of their contribution to particular ends such as

poverty reduction and democracy. Good enough governance also directs attention to considerations of the minimal conditions of governance necessary to allow political and economic development to occur. (2004: 526)

By drawing attention to the historical context of individual countries as critical to efficient administration, good enough governance seems to be a realistic conceptual category seeking to address some of the major limitations of the WB's design of governance. Being largely process-centric, the idea of governance has certain obvious deficits, as mentioned above. Nonetheless, it has toppled the applecart by raising uncomfortable questions relating to the existing system of administration in most developing countries. Here lies the reason as to why governance continues to remain one of the most widely-discussed approaches to public administration.

REFERENCES

Adeney, Katharine and Andrew Wyatt. 2004. 'Democracy in South Asia: Getting Beyond the Structure-Agency Dichotomy'. *Political Studies* 52: 1–18.

Alam, Javeed. 2004. *Who Wants Democracy?* New Delhi: Orient Longman.

Banerjee, Sumanta. 2006. 'Salvaging an Endangered Institution'. *Economic and Political Weekly* 41 (36): 3837–41.

Bearfield, Domonic A. 2009. 'Equity at the Interaction: Public Administration and the Study of Gender'. *Public Administration Review* 69 (3): 383–86.

Beetham, David. 1985. *Max Weber and the Theory of Modern Politics.* Cambridge: Polity Press.

Braibanti, Ralph. 1966. 'Transnational Inducement of Administrative Reform: A Survey of Scope and Critique of Issues' in *Approaches to Development: Politics, Administration and Change*, edited by John D. Montgomery and William J. Siffin, 133–83. New York: McGraw Hill.

Cleveland, Harlan. 1972. *The Future Executive: A Guide for Tomorrow's Managers.* New York: Harper & Row.

Gavison, Ruth. 1992. 'Feminism and the Public–Private Distinction'. *Stanford Law Review* 45 (1): 1–45.

Grindle, Merilee S. 2004. 'Good Enough Governance: Poverty Reduction and Reform in Developing Countries'. *Governance: An International Journal of Policy, Administration, and Institutions* 17 (4): 525–48.

Jaffrelot, Christophe. 2005. *India's Silent Revolution: The Rise of the Low Castes in North Indian Politics.* New Delhi: Permanent Black.

MacKinon, Catharine. 1989. *Toward a Feminist Theory of the State.* Cambridge, MA: Harvard University Press.

Mathur, Kuldeep. 2008. *From Government to Governance: A Brief Survey of the Indian Experience.* New Delhi: National Book Trust.

Nausbaum, Martha. 2003. 'Gender and Governance: An Introduction' in *Essays on Gender and Governance*, edited by Martha Nausbaum, Amrita Basu, Yasmin Tambiah and Nirja Gopal Jayal, 1–19. New Delhi: Human Development Resource Centre, UNDP.

S. R. Bommai vs Union of India (AIR 1994 SC 1918)

Stivers, Camilla. 2002. *Gender Images in Public Administration: Legitimacy and the Administrative State*. Thousand Oaks: Sage.

World Bank (WB). 1989. *From Crisis to Sustainable Growth, Sub-Saharan Africa: A Long-term Perspective Study*. Washington, DC: The WB.

———. 1992. *Governance and Development*. Washington, DC: The WB.

———. 1994. *Governance: The World Bank Experience, Development in Practice*. Washington, DC: The WB.

SELECT BIBLIOGRAPHY

This is a very short bibliography, the aim of which is to acquaint the readers with the basic texts in the field of public administration. As the literature is vast, it is not an easy task. Nonetheless, we have eased our task by selecting those titles which we consider useful to understand the complex processes of governance. The primary concern here is to locate those texts which are conceptually well-endowed and provocative. Contrary to the conventional understanding of the discipline, the objective here is also to familiarise readers with the text–context dialectic which is critically important since public administration is clearly context-driven. We feel that a bibliography is not merely a list of books but also identifies a specific way in which the discipline needs to be understood. Critical of the neo-Taylorist mode of conceptualising public administration, the book provides an argument which is substantiated by drawing on the texts supportive of this claim. This is not an uncommon claim because the literature is in abundance. What is distinctive about this book is its focus on the fundamental theoretical premises and assumptions with reference primarily to the Indian milieu, for obvious reasons. Hence we have also included some of the basic texts on Indian administration.

Although the bibliography is not demarcated neatly there are two complementary parts focusing on administrative theories and the practice of public administration. Given the fact that it is a select bibliography, we have generally picked up only books though there are some articles which have been significant in our effort towards conceptualising public administration as a process.

Ahn, Byung-Joon. 1975. 'The Political Economy of the People's Commune in China: Changes and Continuities'. *Journal of Asian Studies* 34 (3): 631–58.

Anderson, James E. 1994. *Public Policymaking: An Introduction.* Boston: Houghton Mifflin.

Beetham, David. 1985. *Max Weber and the Theory of Modern Politics.* Cambridge: Polity Press.

Bhattacharya, Mohit. 2013. *New Horizons of Public Administration.* New Delhi: Jawahar Publishers.

———. 1999. *Restructuring Public Administration: Essays in Rehabilitation.* New Delhi: Jawahar Publishers.

Buchanan, James M. and Gordon Tullock. 1965. *The Calculus of Consent: Logical Foundations of Constitutional Democracy.* Ann Arbour: The University of Michigan Press.

Castells, Manuel. 1978. *City, Class and Power.* London: Macmillan.

Chakrabarty, Bidyut. 2007. *Reinventing Public Administration: The Indian Experience.* New Delhi: Orient Longman.

———. 2016. *Ethics in Governance in India.* London and New York: Routledge.

Chakrabarty, Bidyut and Mohit Bhattacharya, ed. 2003. *Public Administration: A Reader.* New Delhi: Oxford University Press.

———. 2008. *The Governance Discourse: A Reader.* New Delhi: Oxford University Press.

Chakrabarty, Bidyut and Prakash Chand. 2012. *Public Administration in a Globalizing World*. New Delhi: Sage.

———. 2016. *Indian Administration: Evolution and Practice*. New Delhi: Sage.

———. 2016. *Public Policy: Concept, Theory and Practice*. New Delhi: Sage.

Chi, Wen-shun. 1967. 'The Ideological Source of the People's Communes in Communist China'. *Pacific Coast Philology* 2 (April): 62–78.

Cochrane, Allan. 1993. *Whatever Happened to Local Government*? Buckingham: Open University Press.

Cockburn, Cynthia. 1977. *The Local State: Management of Cities and People*. London: Pluto Press.

Dahl, Robert A. 1947. 'The Science of Public Administration: Three Problems'. *Public Administration Review* 7 (1): 1–11.

Dror, Yehezkel. 1968. *Public Policymaking Reexamined*. Pennsylvania: Chamber Publishers.

———. 1971. *Design for Policy Sciences*. New York: Elsevier.

Dunleavy, Patrick. 1986. 'Explaining the Privatization Boom: Public Choice versus Radical Approaches'. *Public Administration* 64 (1): 13–34.

———. 1991. *Democracy, Bureaucracy and Public Choice: Economic Explanation in Political Science*. Hemel Hempstead, UK: Harvester Wheatsheaf.

Dunn, William N. 1981. *Public Policy Analysis*. New York: Prentice-Hall.

———. 2016. *Public Policy Analysis*, fifth edition. London and New York: Routledge.

Dye, Thomas. 2003. *Understanding Public Policy*. Indian reprint. New Delhi: Pearson Education.

Esman, Milton J. 2000. 'The State, Government Bureaucracies and Their Alternatives' in *Handbook of Comparative and Development Public Administration*, 751–58. New York: Marcel Dekker.

Farazmand, Ali. 1994. 'The New World Order and Global Public Administration' in *Public Administration in the Global Village*, edited by Jean-Claude Garcia-Zamor and Renu Khator, 61–82. Westport, CT: Praeger.

Farmer, David John. 1995. *The Language of Public Administration: Bureaucracy, Modernity and Post-modernity*. Tuscaloosa and London: The University of Alabama Press.

Fouéré, Marie-Aude. 2014. 'Julius Nyerere, Ujamaa and Political Morality in Contemporary Tanzania'. *African Studies Review* 57 (1): 1–24.

Frederickson, George H. 2008. 'Whatever Happened to Public Administration? Governance, Governance Everywhere' in *The Governance Discourse: A Reader*, edited by Bidyut Chakrabarty and Mohit Bhattacharya, 132–59. New Delhi: Oxford University Press.

Gandhi, M. K. 2006. *The Hind Swaraj or Indian Home Rule*. Reprint. Ahmedabad: Navajivan Publishing House.

Gay, Paul du. 2000. *In Praise of Bureaucracy: Weber, Organization and Ethics*. London: Sage.

Goodin, Robert E. 1982. *Political Theory and Public Policy*. Chicago: The University of Chicago Press.

Henry, Nicholas. 2009. *Public Administration and Public Affairs*. New Delhi: PHI Learning Private Limited.

Huang, Lucy Jen. 1976. 'Communes in People's Republic China: Retrospect and Prospect'. *International Review of Modern Sociology* 6 (1): 189–204.

Hydén, Göran. 1997. 'Democratization and Administration' in *Democracy's Victory and Crisis*, edited by Axel Hadenius, 242–60. Cambridge: Cambridge University Press.

Ibhawoh, Bonny and J. I. Dibua. 2003. 'Deconstructing Ujamaa: The Legacy of Julius Nyerere in the Quest for Social and Economic Development'. *African Journal of Political Science* 8 (1): 59–83.

Kooiman, Jan. 1993. *Modern Governance: New Government-Society Interactions*. New Delhi: Sage.

Lane, J. E., ed. 1987. *Bureaucracy and Public Choice*. London: Sage.

Lerner, D. and H. Lasswell, eds. 1951. *The Policy Sciences: Recent Developments in Scope and Method*. Stanford: Stanford University Press.

Maheshwari, S. R. 1968. *Indian Administration*. New Delhi: Orient Longmans.

Marini, Frank, ed. 1971. *Toward a New Public Administration: The Minnowbrook Perspective*. New York: Chandler.

Mason, Philip. 1985. *The Men who Ruled India*. Reprint. New Delhi: Rupa & Co.

Mathur, Kuldeep. 2013. *Panchayati Raj*. New Delhi: Oxford University Press.

Minogue, Martin. 1998. 'Changing the State: Concepts and Practice in the Reform of the Public Sector' in *Beyond the New Public Management: Changing Ideas and Practices in Governance*, edited by Martin Minogue, Charles Polidano and David Hulme, 17–37. Cheltenham: Edward Elgar.

Niskanen, William A. 1971. *Bureaucracy and Representative Government*. Chicago: Aldine-Atherton, Inc.

O'Malley, L. S. S. 1931. *The Indian Civil Service, 1600–1930*. London: John Murray.

Osborne, David and Ted Gaebler. 1992. *Reinventing Government: How the Entrepreneurial Spirit is Transforming the Public Sector*. Reading, MA: Addison-Wesley.

Peters, B. Guy. 1995. *The Politics of Bureaucracy: An Introduction to Comparative Public Administration*. London and New York: Routledge.

———. 1996. 'Models of Governance for the 1990s' in *The State of Public Management*, edited by Donald F. Kettl and H. Brinton Milward, 15–44. Baltimore: Johns Hopkins University Press.

Pierre, Jon and B. Guy Peters. 2000. *Governance, Politics and the State*. New York: Macmillan.

Rosenau, James N. 1992. 'Governance, Order and Change in World Politics' in *Governance without Government: Order and Change in World Politics*, edited by James N. Rosenau and Ernst-Otto Czempiel, 1–29. Cambridge: Cambridge University Press.

Salamon, L. M. 1989. *Beyond Privatization: The Tools of Government Action*. Washington, DC: Urban Institute Press.

Smith, B. C. 1985. *Decentralization: The Territorial Dimension of the State*. London: Allen and Unwin.

Stillman II, Richard J., ed. 1996. *Public Administration: Concepts and Cases*. Boston: Houghton Mifflin Co.

Waldo, Dwight, ed. 1971. *Public Administration in a Time of Turbulence*. New York: Chandler.

Welch, Eric and Wilson Wong. 1998. 'Public Administration in a Global Context: Bridging the Gaps of Theory and Practice between Western and non-Western Nations'. *Public Administration Review* 58 (1): 40–49.

White, Leonard D. 1955. *Introduction to the Study of Public Administration*. New York: Macmillan.

Wilson, Woodrow. 1887. 'The Study of Public Administration'. *Political Science Quarterly* 2 (2): 197–222.

INDEX